ARTICULATING THE GLOBAL AND THE LOCAL

D1448530

POLITICS AND CULTURE
Avery Gordon and Michael Ryan, *editors*

Politics and Culture is a serial publication that publishes material from a diverse number of disciplinary perspectives, from literature to law, from anthropology to political science, from cultural studies to sociology. The serial is concerned with the political significance of cultural forms and practices as well as with the cultural character of social institutions and political formations.

5

POLITICS AND CULTURE

ARTICULATING THE GLOBAL AND THE LOCAL

Globalization and Cultural Studies

edited by

ANN CVETKOVICH
DOUGLAS KELLNER

WestviewPress
A Division of HarperCollins*Publishers*

Politics and Culture

Chapter 10 is reprinted from: Lora Romero, "Nationalism and Internationalism: Domestic Differences in a Postcolonial World," *American Literature,* 67:4 (December 1995), pp. 795–800. Copyright © Duke University Press, 1995. Reprinted with permission.

Published in 1997 in the United States of America by Westview Press, 5500 Central Avenue, Boulder, Colorado 80301-2877, and in the United Kingdom by Westview Press, 12 Hid's Copse Road, Cumnor Hill, Oxford OX2 9JJ

Library of Congress Cataloging-in-Publication Data
Articulating the global and the local/edited by Ann Cvetkovich and
    Douglas Kellner.
        p. cm.—(Politics and culture)
    Includes bibliographical references and index.
    ISBN 0-8133-3219-2 — ISBN 0-8133-3220-6 (pbk.)
    1. Politics and culture. 2. Internationalism. 3. Nationalism.
4. International business enterprises. I. Cvetkovich, Ann, 1957–
II. Kellner, Douglas, 1943–   III. Series
JA75.7.A77 1997
306.2—dc20   96-9473
                                                                              CIP

The paper used in this publication meets the requirements of the American National Standard for Permanence of Paper for Printed Library Materials Z39.48-1984.

10   9   8   7   6   5   4   3   2   1

Contents

PART THREE
TRANSLOCAL CONNECTIONS

ARTICULATING THE GLOBAL AND THE LOCAL

Introduction: Thinking Global and Local

ANN CVETKOVICH & DOUGLAS KELLNER

As globalization confronts local traditions throughout the world, influencing all levels of social life, arguments concerning tensions and conflicts between global and local forces traverse contemporary theory. Both modern and postmodern theorists argue that the world today is organized by increasing globalization, which is strengthening the dominance of a world capitalist economic system, supplanting the primacy of the nation-state by transnational corporations and organizations, and eroding local cultures and traditions through a global culture.[1] Marxists, advocates of worlds-systems theory, functionalists, Weberians, and many other contemporary theorists are converging on the position that globalization is a distinguishing trend of the present moment. Even some advocates of a postmodern break in history argue that developments in transnational capitalism are producing a new global historical configuration of post-Fordism, or postmodernism as a new cultural logic of capitalism (Harvey 1989; Soja 1989; Jameson 1991; Gottdiener 1995). In significant modern and postmodern social theories, globalization is thus taken as a salient feature of our times.

Yet an equally wide range of theorists have argued that the proliferation of difference and the shift to more local discourses and practices define the contemporary scene and that theory and politics should shift from the level of globalization and its often totalizing and reductive macrotheories to focus on the local, the specific, the particular, the heterogeneous, and the microlevel of everyday experience. Indeed, a wide range of theories associated with poststructuralism, postmodernism, feminism, and multiculturalism focuses on difference, otherness, marginality, the personal, the particular, and the concrete over more general theory and politics that aim at more global or universal conditions.[2]

Dichotomies, such as those between the global and the local, express contradictions and tensions between crucial constitutive forces of the present moment; consequently, it is a mistake to overlook focus on one side in favor of exclusive concern with the other (rejecting the local and particularity, for instance, in favor of exclusive concern with the global, or rejecting the global and all macrostructures for exclusive concern with the local). Our challenge is to think through the relationship between the global and the local by observing how global forces in-

1

fluence and even structure ever more local situations and ever more strikingly. One should also see how local forces and situations mediate the global, inflecting global forces to diverse ends and conditions and producing unique configurations for thought and action in the contemporary world.

Indeed, in many diverse fields and disciplines, theorists are beginning to consider how global, systemic, and macrostructures and forces interact with local, particular, and micro-conditions and -structures. Such dialectical optics attempt to theorize the intersection of the global and the local, how they interact and mediate each other, and the new constellations being produced by their current interactions. In this way, one overcomes the partiality and one-sidedness of undialectical theories that fail to perceive the ways that the global and the local interact so as to produce new social and cultural constellations.

Analogous to the question of conceptualizing the interactions of the global and the local on the level of theory, debates have emerged over the proper locus and focus of politics today. Some theorists argue that global and national problems require macrostructural solutions; others argue that the proper sphere of the political is the local and the personal, not the global or national. Postmodern theories of power, for instance, have stressed how power inhabits local, specific, and micro realms, ignored by modern theories that located powers in centers such as the economy, the state, or patriarchy. Postmodern politics urges local and specific actions to intervene in discursive sites of power ranging from the bedroom to the classroom, from prisons to mental institutions.[3]

Here too the old modern and new postmodern politics seem one-sided. Power resides in both macro *and* micro institutions; it is indeed proliferating with new configurations of global, national, regional, and more properly local forces and relations of power generating new conflicts and sites of struggle ranging from debates over "the new world order"—or disorder as it may appear to many—to struggles over local control of schools or the environment. Rethinking politics with these conditions in mind thus requires thinking through the complex interconnection of the global and the local. Theorizing the configurations of the global and the local also requires developing new multidimensional strategies ranging from the macro to the micro, the national to the local, to intervene in a wide range of contemporary and emerging problems and struggles. The following paragraphs will attempt to contextualize the need to think together the global and the local, and the studies collected in this book will exemplify this project.

Globalization: Economy/State/Culture

The term *globalization* is often used as a code word that stands for a tremendous diversity of issues and problems and that serves as a front for a variety of theoretical and political positions. It might serve as a substitute term for modernization and thus continue as a legitimating ideology for the westernization of the world, obscuring cultural differences and struggles. Globalization might replace concepts such as imperialism, therefore displacing focus on the domination of developing countries by the overdeveloped ones or on national and local economies by transnational corporations. Yet a critical globalization theory can inflect the discourse to point precisely to these phenomena and can elucidate a series of contemporary problems and conflicts.

In view of the different concepts and functions of globalization discourse, it is important to note that the concept is a theoretical construct that varies according to the assumptions and commitments of the theory in question. We use the term to describe the ways global economic, political, and cultural forces are rapidly penetrating the earth in the creation of a new world market, new transnational political organizations, and a new global culture. The expansion of the capitalist world market into areas previously closed to it (i.e., in the communist sphere or developing countries that attempted to pursue their own independent line of development) is accompanied by the decline of the nation-state and its power to regulate and control the flow of goods, people, information, and various cultural forms. Globalization involves systematically overcoming distances of space and time and the emergence of new international institutions and forces.

Globalization is not, however, an entirely new phenomenon. There have, of course, been global networks of power and imperialist empires for centuries, accompanied by often fierce local resistance by the colonized entities. National liberation movements disrupted colonial empires of power and created a "third way" between the capitalist and communist blocs, especially in the period after World War II, marked by the success of a large number of anti-imperialist revolutions. But as we approach the end of the twentieth century, it would seem that neither decolonization nor the end of the cold war has loosened the hold of transnational systems of domination.

Globalization also involves the dissemination of new technologies that have tremendous impact on the economy, polity, society, culture, and everyday life. Time-space compression produced by new media and communications technologies are overcoming previous boundaries of space and time, creating a global cultural village and dramatic penetration of global forces into every realm of life in every region of the world. New technologies in the labor process displace living labor, make possible more flexible production, and create new labor markets, with some areas undergoing deindustrialization (e.g., the rust belt of the Midwest in the United States), while production itself becomes increasingly transnational (Harvey 1989). The new technologies also create new industries, such as the computer and information industry, and allow transnational media and information instantaneously to traverse the globe (Morley and Robins 1995). This process has led some to celebrate a new global information superhighway and others to attack the new wave of media and cultural imperialism.

Yet the very concept of globalization has long been a contested terrain described in conflicting normative discourses that provide the concept with positive, negative, or ambivalent connotations. It is perhaps the early theorists and critics of capitalism who first engaged the phenomenon of the globalization of the capitalist system. Not surprisingly, the defenders of capitalism, such as Adam Smith, saw the process positively, whereas Karl Marx and Friedrich Engels had more critical perceptions. Producing one of the first major discourses of globalization, Smith saw the European "discoveries" of the Americas and the passage to the East Indies as creating a new world market with highly significant consequences. Smith wrote:

> Their consequences have already been great; but, in the short period of between two and three centuries which has elapsed since these discoveries were made, it is impossible that the whole extent of their consequences can have been seen. What benefits, or what misfortunes to mankind may hereafter result from these events, no human wisdom can foresee. By uniting, in some measure, the most distant parts of the world, by enabling them to relieve one another's wants, to increase one another's enjoyments, and to encourage one another's industry, their general tendency would seem to be beneficial. To the natives, however, both of the East and West Indies, all the commercial benefits which can have resulted from these events have been sunk and lost in the dreadful misfortunes which they have occasioned. These misfortunes, however, seem to have arisen rather from accident than from any thing in the nature of those events themselves. At the particular time when these discoveries were made, the *superiority of force* happened to be so great on the side of the Europeans, that they were enabled to commit with impunity every sort of injustice in those remote countries. Hereafter, perhaps, the natives of those countries may grow stronger, or those of Europe may grow weaker, and the inhabitants of all the different quarters of the world may arrive at that equality of courage and force which, by inspiring mutual fear, can alone overawe the injustice of independent nations into some sort of respect for the rights of one another. But nothing seems more likely to establish this equality of force than that mutual communication of knowledge and of all sorts of improvements which an extensive commerce from all countries to all countries naturally, or rather necessarily, carries along with it (Smith 1962, Vol. 2, 141).

Smith thus envisaged the emergence of a world market system as one of the most important features of modernity that would eventually benefit the entire world. Although perceiving the injustices of unequal relations of power and force, Smith generally appraised the globalization of the world market as "beneficial." With characteristic honesty, he cited the "misfortunes" of the process of colonization but optimistically believed the injustices of the process might be overcome. In "The Communist Manifesto," Marx and Engels followed Smith in seeing the importance of the globalization of the capitalist market, although, of course, they differed in their evaluation of it. Following the optic of Smith, they claimed:

> Modern industry has established the world market, for which the discovery of America paved the way. . . . [The] need of a constantly expanding market for its products chases the bourgeoisie over the whole surface of the globe. It must nestle everywhere, settle everywhere, establish connections everywhere. . . . The bour-

geoisie, by the rapid improvement of all instruments of production, by the immensely facilitated means of communication, draws all, even the most barbarian nations into civilization. . . . In a word, it creates a world after its own image (Marx and Engels 1976, 486ff).

Both the classical liberalism of Smith and classical Marxism see capitalism as a global economic system characterized by a world market and the imposition of similar relations of production, commodities, and culture on areas throughout the world, creating a new modern world system as the capitalist market penetrates the four corners of the earth. For both classical liberalism and Marxism, the bourgeoisie constantly revolutionized the instruments of production and the world market generated immense forces of commerce, navigation and discovery, communications, and industry, creating a new world of abundance, diversity, and prosperity:

> In place of the old wants, satisfied by the production of the country, we find new wants, requiring for their satisfaction the products of distant lands and climes. In place of the old local and national seclusion and self-sufficiency, we have intercourse in every direction, universal interdependence of nations. And as in material, so also in intellectual production. The intellectual creations of individual nations become common property. National one-sidedness and narrow-mindedness become more and more impossible, and from the numerous national and local literatures there arises a world literature (Marx and Engels 1976, 488).

The preceding passage points to the resources and positive results of the world market that provide the basis for a higher stage of social organization. But in the Marxian vision, the globalization process is appraised more ambiguously. For Marx and Engels, the world market produced a new class of industrial proletariat that was reduced to abstract labor power, rendered propertyless, and had "nothing to lose but its chains" and a world to win. Marx and Engels believed that the industrial proletariat would organize as a revolutionary class to overthrow capitalism and produce a new socialist society that would abolish poverty, inequality, exploitation, and alienated labor, making possible the full development of the individual and a more equitable division of social wealth. They also envisaged the possibility of a world global crisis that would generate world revolution, enveloping the earth in a titanic struggle between capital and its opponents. Working class revolutionaries would be resolutely internationalist and cosmopolitan in the Marxian vision, seeing themselves as citizens of the world rather than members of specific nations.

Curiously, the Marxian theory shared the illusions of many market liberals that the development of a world system of free trade would eliminate nationalism and the nation-state, with both downplaying their importance, in a new world economic system—be it capitalist or communist.[4] Both Smith and Marx present colonization and the globalization of the market society as inevitable and as the basis of material progress. Both recognize the injustices of the process for the victims of colonization and the use of violence and superior force to subjugate non-Western culture, but both are sanguine about the process and draw distinctions between "barbarian nations" and civilizations that ultimately present globalization as a "civilizing process"—this would indeed emerge as one of the dominant ideologies of imperialism (which the Marxian tradition otherwise opposes).

Indeed, globalization has also had important political implications. As Giovanni Arrighi documents, colonization benefited successively the Italian city-states, Holland, and England, which accrued political power and, in the case of England, world empire through their role in trade, the establishment of colonies, and finance and industry. In the aftermath of World War II, the United States emerged as a dominant global power and at this time world-systems theory described "the creation of a system of national states and the formation of a worldwide capitalist system" as "the two interdependent master processes of the [modern] era" (Tilly 1984, 147). Both Marxism and world-systems theory stress the importance of the rise to global dominance of a capitalist market economy that is penetrating the entire globe, while world-systems theory stresses the equal importance of a system of national states.

With the collapse of the Soviet Union and its satellite nations—which provided the bulwark of a global alternative to a capitalist market system—the capitalist market is now largely unopposed by any system of nation-states, including those that emerged out of opposition to colonial domination, with few corners of the world able to resist the global flow of capital and its products. Indeed, a world market economy disseminates throughout the planet fantasies of happiness through consumption and the products that allow entry into the phantasmagoria of consumer capitalism. A world financial market circulates capital in international circuits that bind together the world in a global market dominated by the forces and institutions of finance capital. Capitalist modernization circles the globe, producing new products and fashions while eroding tradition and national economies and identities.

Global economic change often has tremendous local impact. Whole regions are devastated with the shutting down of industrial production, moved to regions with lower wages and less government regulation. Such deindustrialization has created vast rust belts of previously prosperous industrial regions, as in the case of Flint, Michigan, which suffered major economic decline with the closing of General Motors automobile plants, documented in Michael Moore's film *Roger and Me*.[5] Automation, computers, and new technologies have eliminated entire categories of labor; corporate reorganization has abolished segments of management, producing vast unemployment. More than ever, the world economy is bound together so that hurricanes in Japan or financial irregularities in Britain influence the entire world.

Consequently, globalization involves "the intensification of world-wide social relations which link distant localities in such a way that local happenings are shaped by events occurring many miles away and vice versa" (Giddens 1990, 64).

Especially during the period of the cold war arising after World War II, the system of modern nation-states divided into two camps—capitalist and socialist—producing a shifting series of alliances and conflicts influencing countries from Vietnam to Nicaragua. During this period, nations either pursued the capitalist or socialist model of development or in the case of some so-called Third World nations, attempted to forge their own paths of development. As the term suggests, the so-called Third World nations created by decolonization were often considered less important to global affairs than the conflict between the world superpowers. Moreover, the dominant binaristic cold war model provided a convenient rubric for economic, political, and cultural intervention into Third World affairs, dividing the world into a global field of conflict between the two superpowers with much of the planet caught in the middle.

But with the collapse of the communist system, this period of history came to an end and during the 1990s the capitalist market model of globalization has become dominant and practically uncontested.[6] The analogue of such economic globalization is said to be the triumph of democracy throughout the world with its discourse and institutions of a pluralistic system of checks and balances with parties, elections, and human rights (Fukuyama 1992). For some decades, indeed, democracy has been interpreted as the necessary accompaniment and/or condition of capitalism (Walt Rostow, Milton Friedman, Francis Fukuyama), while a tradition of critical theory documents the tensions and conflicts between democracy and capitalism.[7]

And yet the decline of the power of the nation-state produces a new geopolitical matrix in which transnational organizations, corporations, and forces challenge national and local sites of power and influence. In the wake of political developments such as decolonization, the end of the cold war, the formation of new trade agreements and political unions, and the rise of global transnational capitalism, national borders have shifted, resulting in the increased power of transnational institutions. Accompanying such momentous political changes are the increasing prominence of world trade, financial speculations and investment, and global cultural forces that operate outside the confines of the nation-state as a discrete entity (Held 1995).

In addition to the development of a new global market economy and shifting system of nation-states, we consider the rise of global culture especially salient during the present moment. Accompanying the dramatic expansion of capitalism and new transnational political organizations is a new global culture, emerging as a result of computer and communications technology; a consumer society with its panorama of goods and services; transnational forms of architecture and design; and a wide range of products and social forms that are traversing national boundaries and becoming part of a new world culture. Global culture includes the proliferation of media technologies that veritably create Marshall McLuhan's dream of a global village in which people all over the world watch political spectacles like the Gulf War, major sports events, entertainment programs, and advertisements that relentlessly promote capitalist modernization (Wark 1994). At the same time, more and more people are entering into global computer networks that instantaneously circulate ideas, information, and images throughout the world, overcoming boundaries of space and time.

Global culture involves promoting lifestyle, consumption, products, and identities. Transnational corporations deploy advertising to penetrate local markets, to sell global products, and to overcome local resistance; moreover, expansion of private cable and satellite systems have aggressively promoted a commercial culture throughout the world. In a sense, culture itself is being redefined, for previously local and national cultures have been forces of resistance to global forces, protecting the traditions, identities, and modes of life of specific groups and peoples. Culture has been precisely the particularizing, localizing force that distinguished societies and people from each other. Culture provided forms of local identities, practices, and modes of everyday life that could serve as a bulwark against the invasion of ideas, identities, and forms of life extraneous to the specific local region in question. We argue that culture is an especially complex and contested terrain today as global cultures permeate local ones and new configurations emerge that synthesize both poles, providing contradictory forces of neocolonization *and* resistance, global homogenization and new local hybrid forms and identities.

The problematic of culture had been excluded from many previous forms of globalization and modernization theory that tended toward economic, technological, or political determinism. Our studies will highlight the importance of culture and in turn will call on cultural studies to focus on globalization and the dialectic of the global and the local that provides the matrix for the studies collected in this book. It is curious indeed how classical liberalism, Marxism, and modernization theory neglected culture and local forms of social association, positing the inexorable advance of the modern economy, technology, and politics, which would supposedly level out and homogenize all societies and cultures, producing a world global culture. Capitalism with its world market and communism with its international socioeconomic system and political culture were supposed to erode cultural differences, regional particularities, nationalism, and traditionalism. Thus, both classical liberalism and Marxism promoted or predicted globalization as the fate of the world: For capitalist ideologues, the market was going to produce a global world culture, whereas for Marxism the proletariat was going to produce communism that would eliminate nationalism and create a communist international without exploitation or war. Both saw the significance of national borders being eliminated and both seriously underestimated the endurance of nationalism and the nation-state.

Missing from both Marxist and liberal models has been an understanding of how race, ethnicity, and nationalist sentiment might intersect with class to produce local, political struggles with complex causes. Indeed, since the late 1980s there has been a resurgence of nationalism, traditionalism, and religious fundamentalism alongside trends toward growing globalization. The explosion of regional, cultural, and religious differences in the former Soviet Union and Yugoslavia—as well as explosive tribal conflicts in Africa and elsewhere—suggests that globalization and homogenization were not as deep as its proponents hoped and critics feared. Culture has thus become a new source of conflict and an important dimension of struggle between the global and the local. National cultures have produced confrontations between Serbs, Muslims, and Croats; Armenians and Azerbaijanis; Mohawk First Nation peoples and Quebecois; and in South Africa struggles between the Umkatha tribe and the African National Congress (ANC). Thus, both culture and nationalism turned out to be more enduring, deeper, and more fundamental than expected, and clashes between conflicting national and regional cultures continue in a supposedly globalized world.

It is also in the realm of culture that globalization is most visible and apparent. Global media and information systems and a world capitalist consumer culture circulate products, images, and ideas throughout the world. Events such as the Gulf War; social trends and fashions; and cultural phenomena such as Madonna, rap music, and popular Hollywood films are distributed through global cultural distribution networks and constitute global forms of popular culture. This global culture, however, operates precisely through the multiplication of different products, services, and spectacles targeted at specific audiences. Consumer and media industries are becoming more differentiated and are segmenting their customers and audiences into more categories. In many cases, this involves the simulation of minor differences of fashion and style as significant, but it also involves a proliferation of a more highly differentiated culture and society in terms of an ever-expanding variety and diversity of cultural artifacts, products, and services.

However, there has also been a significant eruption of subcultures of resistance that have attempted to preserve specific forms of culture and society against globalization and homogenization. Indeed, subcultures have been a major focus of cultural studies since the 1970s when new subjects of political resistance were found in youth subcultures and the subcultures of women, gays and lesbians, blacks and ethnic minorities, and other groups that have resisted incorporation into the hegemonic mainstream culture. Cultural studies has explored both mainstream hegemonic cultures and oppositional subcultures. It has focused on articulations of class, race, gender, sexual preference, ethnicity, region, and nation in its explorations of concrete cultural configurations and phenomena.[8] And as our research indicates, cultural studies has also taken on a global focus, analyzing how transnational forces intervene in concrete situations and how cultural mediations can inflect the sway of such global configurations.

Culture, Identity, and Hybridization

The problem of identity has come to the forefront of attention in recent times. On one hand, as a form of resistance, emphasis on national and individual identity has emerged as a response to homogenizing global forces. On the other hand, ever-proliferating globalization produces new configurations of identity—national, local, and personal. The flow of products, culture, capital, and information is accompanied by flows of people and emigration (see Hall 1991; Lash and Urry 1994, 171ff.). A transnational diaspora from every continent involving vast migrations of peoples and individuals produces the conditions for new transnational hybridized cultures and identities. Salman Rushdie's collection of stories *East, West* (1994) describes the new hybridization of cultures and identities and the conflicts and choices globalization forces on individuals in search of identity and values. After receiving a British passport, one of Rushdie's Indian characters tells how the document allows him to make more choices and have more freedom than previously.

> But I, too, have ropes around my neck, I have them to this day, pulling me this way and that, East and West, the nooses tightening, commanding, *choose, choose.*
> I buck, I snort, I whinny, I rear, I kick. Ropes, I do not choose between you. Lassoes, lariats, I choose neither of you, and both. Do you hear? I refuse to choose.[9]

As the preceding passage indicates, even individual identity is more and more a question of articulating often conflicting cultural elements into new types of hybridized identity that combine national cultures with global ideas and images. Gurinder Chadha's 1994 British Film Institute documentary *I'm British, but . . .* depicts the various hybridizations between immigrant Asian youth and various regions of Great Britain with some of the young people interviewed describing themselves as Scottish-Asian, or Welsh-Pakistani, or English-Indian—always with one or another form of hybrid identity. In many countries, there is a struggle over cultural identity. In the 1980s in the United States for example, the term African-American increasingly came to replace black, although as Michael Hanchard points out (1990), the term African-American is a transnational term that should encompass many identities created by the African diaspora, not just U.S. citizens. Rap artists even appropriated the tabooed term "nigger" as a badge of in-group identification and to signify the denigration of people of color in a white-dominant culture.

The confluence of global culture with local and national culture is appraised quite differently. For some, a global media culture provides new sources for pleasures and identities that redefine gender, new role models and fantasies, and new cultural experiences. These lead to the fragmentation of old identities and subjectivities, and the constructions of new identities out of the multifarious and sometimes conflicting configurations of traditional, local, national, and now global forces of the present time. From this perspective, the intersection of the global and the local is producing new matrixes to legitimize the production of hybrid identities, thus expanding the realm of self-definition. And so although global forces can be oppressive and erode cultural traditions and identities they can also provide new material to rework one's identity and can empower people to revolt against traditional forms and styles to create new, more emancipatory ones.

For some theorists, this allegedly postmodern heterogeneity is positive, but for others it makes it easier to manipulate fragmented selves into consumer identities, synthetic models produced by the culture industries. From this perspective, the fragmentation and even dissolution of traditional identities result in superficial changes of fashion and style that reconceive identity in terms of looks and attitudes as opposed to fundamental commitments, choices, and action.[10] New postmodern selves who go from moment to moment without making fundamental choices or commitments live on the surface, lost in the funhouse of hyperreal media images and the play of floating signifiers, themselves becoming mere images and signifiers in the postmodern carnival.

Most of the new global populars that produce resources for identity come from North American media industries, thus from this perspective globalization becomes a form of Americanization. Figures of the global popular such as Rambo, Madonna, Beavis and Butt-Head, gangsta rappers, and other figures from U.S. culture produce seductive models for new identities that find their adherents all over the world. But precisely such global figures can be appropriated locally to provide new hybridized models of identity. Global culture is indeed disseminating throughout the world; new fashion, style, sexuality, and images are appropriated in many ways by individuals in specific local situations. But global models are confronted by national, regional, and traditional models in many parts of the world.

In Asian countries, such as Japan, Korea, Taiwan, Hong Kong, and Singapore, there are intense clashes among traditional, national, and global models of identity. Traditional culture and religion continue to play an important role in everyday life, and compromises and syntheses are often constructed between traditional and modernizing global forces. Likewise, on the level of culture, young musicians often combine traditional musical forms with contemporary transnational ones or produce specific forms like Chinese rap or Japanese heavy metal. And on the level of sports, countries like Japan play baseball but in ways that reinforce traditional Japanese values and structures. Such a synthesis and hybridization is highly uneven, however. Singapore uses authoritarian state measures to protect traditional culture; Japan uses more paternalistic measures to privilege national culture; and Hong Kong and Taiwan are more open and laissez-faire.

In Europe, Asia, and Latin America, for example, MTV is adapted to local conditions and produces new hybrid forms. Indeed, the defining characteristics of global media culture are the contradictory forces of identity and difference, homogeneity and heterogeneity, the global and the local impinging on each other, clashing, or simply peacefully coexisting—or producing new symbioses as in the motto of MTV Latino that combines English and Spanish: *Chequenos!*—meaning "Check us out!" Yet globalization by and large means the hegemony of transnational cultural industries, largely American. In Canada, for instance, about 95 percent of films in movie theaters are American; U.S. television dominates Canadian television; seven American firms control distribution of sound recordings in Canada; and 80 percent of the magazines on newsstands are non-Canadian.[11] In

Latin America and Europe the situation is similar: American media culture, commodities, fast food, and malls are creating a new global culture that is remarkably similar on all continents.[12]

Today, under the pressure of the dialectics of the global and the local, identity has global, national, regional, and local components, as well as the specificities of gender, race, class, and sexuality. Identity construction is thus heavily overdetermined, and the dialectics of the global and the local are producing new conflicts in which choices must be made concerning what features will define national and individual identity. This situation is highly contradictory with reassertions of traditional modes of identity in response to globalization and a contradictory melange of hybrid identities—and no doubt significant identity crises—all over the world. From this perspective, celebrations of or attacks against allegedly postmodern selves miss the dynamics of the conflicts between the global and the local, which problematize self-hood, create the need for new choices and commitments, and produce new possibilities for the creation of identities that could be empowering.

Indeed, seeing identity as a construct rather than as a given, as something to be made and created rather than as an essential bedrock of personality, can empower people to increase their range of choices and can challenge individuals to choose to create their own unique selves and communities. The problematic of the global and the local can thus produce new insights into the construction of identity and show how identity today is more complex. Not only is there a proliferation of postmodern reconstructions of identity through image, but once again, tradition, religion, and nationalism must be confronted as forces that remain fundamental to the contemporary world and that continue to play important roles in national and personal life. Expanded modernization and globalization also create, as Anthony Giddens and others argue, increased capacities for reflexivity that put in question both traditional and novel forms, sorting out positive or negative features—terms that will obviously be different for different individuals.

Rethinking identity requires openness to new forms of global identity or citizenship. If democracy is to play a genuinely progressive role globally, nationally, and locally, new ways must be created for citizens to participate in the different levels and dimensions that constitute their lives. In response to proliferating globalization, societies and individuals must rethink the problematics of democratization and the site and scope of democracy. Modern societies were predicated on the basis of a nation-state that would govern the area within its boundaries. Modern democratic theory gave citizens rights within their polis and, in theory at least, sovereignty over their common affairs—although there have been centuries of struggles over those rights and citizenship. But the space of both the nation-state and the power of its citizens are potentially undermined or are at least redefined in a new era of transnational corporations; a global information and media economy; supranational political and financial institutions; and the rapid penetration of national and regional boundaries by a cornucopia of products, services, and images from a global culture. Consequently, new modes of rethinking politics and democracy are necessary to respond to the new configurations of the global and the local.

Theorizing the Global and the Local

Configurations of the global and the local constitute the economic, political, social, cultural, and even personal matrixes within which individuals increasingly live and die, define themselves, and experience the world today. The contributions collected in this book explore how discourses of the local, the particular, the everyday, and the situated are being transformed by new discourses of globalization and transnationalism, as used both by government and business and in critical academic discourse. The essays contribute to current discussions of globalization and local cultural transformations that describe the economics, politics, and culture of what appear to be dramatically new geopolitical maps of the present age. They explore the impact of the new forces of globalization on local and specific conditions and how local cultures and forces adapt to, appropriate, inflect, and rework global phenomena.

In particular, most of the contributors focus on the importance of culture, both in terms of articulations of global culture and its impact on specific situations, as well as on the ways local subcultures of resistance can preserve their specificities and uniqueness against global forces, or appropriate global forces and culture for their own ends. Contextualizing these essays, however, requires further reflection on the discourse of the global and the local and the complex problematics in which they are emerging as central in contemporary theoretical and political debates.

In attempting to conceptualize the terms of the global and the local it is first important to divest them of normative baggage, especially conceptualizations that would positively valorize one side of the equation and denigrate the other. For instance, it would be a mistake to theorize the global as merely homogenizing, universalizing, and abstract in some pejorative and leveling sense in opposition to a more heterogeneous, particularizing, and concrete local sphere. Such a discourse labels the global in advance as a purely negative and oppressive force while assuming that the local is more positive and commendable. Globalizing forces such as human rights can be progressive in some local contexts, and indeed the local has often been the site of the most oppressive, patriarchal, and backward forms of domination against which more global and universalizing forces have progressive effects in eroding domination and oppression.

One should be equally suspicious of purely positive and uncritical normative discourses of the global. In many mainstream social theories, the discourse of the global is bound up with ideological discourses of modernization and modernity, and from Saint-Simon and Marx through Habermas and Parsons, globalization and modernization are interpreted in terms of progress, novelty and innovation, and a generally beneficial negation of the old, the traditional, and the obsolete. In this discourse of modernization, the global is presented as a progressive modernizing force; the local stands for backwardness, superstition, underdevelopment, and the oppressiveness of tradition.

With such highly charged terms, one needs to be very careful of their use and connotations. With these considerations in mind, we propose theorizing the global as that matrix of transnational economic, political, and cultural forces that are circulating throughout the globe and producing universal, global conditions, often transversing and even erasing previously formed national and regional boundaries. But the concept of the global also includes those constituents of class, gender, and race that cut across local differences and that provide fundamental axes of power and subordination, constituting the structures around which contemporary societies are organized. In particular, we oppose seeing categories such as gender as merely local, for such categorizations reproduce the dichotomies that, for instance, divide society into the private and the public and that often equate the feminine with the private, or local, as opposed to the public and global domain implicitly gendered as masculine. Discourses of the local or the specific can thus consign women to the margins, cut off from public culture, while forcing men to define themselves in terms of their roles within the public domain alone.

The personal and affective dimensions of cultural experience, the focus of many of the articles in this collection, have often been neglected because of the gendering of these domains as feminine, with the result that analyses of the global remain invisibly masculinist. Although the local and global might be understood as two different directions from which to challenge the viability of nationalism as a category of political, economic, and cultural analysis, they should not necessarily be understood on the quantitative or spatial model of a continuum between smaller (local) and bigger (global) spaces or places. Other grids of power and space, such as race and gender, can require a different way of conceiving the relations between the local and the global. For example, a gendered analysis of the relation between public and private spheres might question the mechanisms by which certain locations, such as the boardroom or the legislature, are considered more global in their impact than other sites, such as the bedroom or the kitchen.

One of the most eloquent analysts of this danger is Cynthia Enloe, who has discussed, for example, the role of marital and sexual relations in international politics in *Bananas, Beaches, and Bases* (1989). For Enloe, the local is an aspect of the global rather than a discrete or separate space. Global or international analysis must consider phenomena such as the marriages of national leaders, the birth control methods of women soldiers, and the culture of prostitution that flourishes around international military bases. In *The Morning After* (1993), Enloe demonstrates that militarism is crucially founded on ideologies of masculinity and hence grounded in questions of gender and sexuality. Those who proclaim a new global culture following the end of the cold war might consider the implications of her claim that the demilitarization of culture cannot take place merely through the dissolution of national borders; a reconfiguration of the gendered and sexualized relations that sustain military culture, including intimate and personal relations, is also required.

Without attention to categories such as the personal, the feminine, and the sexual, any discussion of politics—whether national, international, or transnational—will be lacking. It would be unfortunate if discourses of globalization and transnationalism continued to perpetuate the problems of discourses of nationalism given the challenges they offer to the debate about nationalism. In their introduction to *Scattered Hegemonies,* Inderpal Grewal and Caren Kaplan (1994) evaluate the absence of feminist analysis in many global theories of postmodernity and postcoloniality and propose the use of the term "transnational" to "problematize a purely locational politics of global-local or counter-periphery in favor of what Mattelart sees as the lines cutting across them. As feminists who note the absence of gender issues in all of these world-system theories, we have no choice but to challenge what we see as inadequate and inaccurate binary divisions" (13). Without refusing the use of the terms "global" and "local," we also seek to challenge binaristic understandings of this dichotomy, especially as it is transformed by categories of gender and sexuality.

Many of the essays in this collection conceive of the local in ways that intervene against the tendency to map the local/global onto the dichotomy between the national and the transnational. Central to this effort is their concern with gender and sexuality and hence with the complexity of locations where those categories of identity and experience have been most immediately visible, such as the family. The local then, in contrast to the global, describes in our usage those constellations of conditions that are particular and specific according to country, region, tradition, and other determinants, such as the creation and preservation of local subcultures. Yet we would problematize absolute dichotomies and distinctions among these terms, as if they referred to discrete and separate domains of experience. Given that there have been centuries of colonization, there is no pure or "authentic" local that is untouched by global developments (Sreberney-Mohammadi 1993, 106ff.), so that the concept of the local itself is a discursive concept defined against its ideal type opposite.

Indeed, it is important to note that both the global and the local are cultural constructs and thus subject to discussion, debate, and development. Such terms are ideal types that delineate constellations of phenomena and in this case indicate opposing domains that are articulated into various configurations and constellations that include the features described in both dimensions. As noted, the local itself is a hybrid construct that is often formed out of regional, national, and even global forces. This is especially true today when there are few corners of the world immune from the viral forces of a global consumer and media culture and when global forces offer resources for local constellations.

Yet the concept of the global is also a theoretical construct, and there are serious debates concerning how to theorize it. Structuralists stress the importance of fundamental and enduring economic, political, and cultural structures and institutions that organize contemporary life. Poststructuralists such as Arjun Appardurai (1990), by contrast, characterize global culture as a series of "flows" of people, technology, goods, money, and ideas, which exist in an often "disjunctive" relation to one another. His model questions constructs of the global that ascribe fundamental significance to the economy, even those models, such as Fredric Jameson's, that focus on the "cultural logic" of late capitalism (1991).

Discourses of transnationalism and globalization emerge from a tradition of describing capitalism, but certain forms of poststructuralism reject macrotheory and attack previous discourses, arguing that new economic, cultural, and political processes require new analytic models to describe them. In particular, among critical and oppositional groups, interest in globalization has been generated not only by the urgency of describing new developments in the history of capitalism, of charting the economic underpinnings of the current geopolitical map, but by the sense that in addition to the decline of the power of the nation-state, nationalism for many is no longer a political ideal.[13] Discourses of globalization and transnationalism have helped to explain the fate of Third World nationalisms, which initially provided the rubric for independence from colonial rule but subsequently failed to galvanize economic or cultural prosperity. Masao Miyoshi (1993), for example, argues that the spread of transnational corporations, increasingly less tied to a single national identity, becomes colonialism under another guise, thus challenging the implication of the term "postcolonialism" that colonialism is over.

The concept we are proposing for mediating the global and the local is thus *articulation*. Articulation describes how various societal components are organized into an event such as the Gulf War or a phenomenon like Madonna. Madonna has been able to market and publicize a set of images that appeal to diverse audiences all over the world, producing a global popular. Analysis of figures such as Madonna is important not only because she reveals the global reach of media culture, but because she exemplifies how issues such as race and sexuality are increasingly articulated through culture rather than politics in the narrow sense.[14]

The figure of Madonna is distributed through global media conglomerates and received in specific contexts in which she is appropriated according to local concerns, thus articulating in her reception an interconnection of the global and the local. A global phenomenon like Madonna, however, can be articulated in highly contradictory ways. Madonna wanna-bes all over the world imitate her style and fashion moves and perhaps make her their role model. But this might serve to integrate young fans into the dominant system of style and fashion in the consumer society or to rebel against dominant models to create their own style and look. It may make her audience conform to dominant roles of beauty and sexuality or legitimate revolt against middle-class norms that empower young women to define themselves and choose their own pleasures, sexualities, and identities. "Madonna" will therefore be articulated very differently according to the class, ethnicity, sexuality, and region of her audiences, which may have very different effects in different local cultures.

The Madonna phenomenon is also a product of intense marketing and public relations campaigns, thus the relationships between the production of Madonna's texts and their reception by world audiences must be articulated. Madonna has targeted teenage girl audiences, as well as various ethnic audiences with performers of color and distinct ethnic markers appearing in her music videos and concerts. She also attracted gay and lesbian audiences, incorporating gay subcultures and subtexts in music videos such as "Vogue," and she pushed the boundaries of the acceptable in music videos, leading MTV to ban a 1990 video "Justify My Love" because of what was deemed excessively extreme sexuality. In addition, Madonna appealed to academic audiences through her use of postmodernist aesthetic strategies and her deft manipulation of image. She has thus been able to market and publicize a set of images that attract diverse audiences all over the world, producing a global popular that articulates a diverse range of issues concerning gender, sexuality, ethnicity, and class.

Cultural studies has also utilized the concept of articulation to describe political phenomena such as Thatcherism and Reaganism (see Hall and Jacques 1983; Hall 1991; Grossberg 1992). These conservative discourses articulated discourses of nationalism, the free market, tradition, individualism, and other elements into a new hegemonic common sense, a new political wisdom and consensus that has circulated throughout the world producing the discourses through which even neoliberals and social democrats now operate. These national political conservative discourses have thus taken on global form through local appropriations and articulations all over the world.

The studies collected in this book show how the discourses of the global and the local transverse the fields of social theory, cultural studies, and politics, and we hope that the optics generated here will open up new perspectives within and between these domains. Our essays begin in the field of social theory and proceed to elucidate how global political, economic, and cultural forces impact on local situations. The studies collected here indicate that social and political issues of the present age appear in a variety of sites and are producing new configurations for the enduring problems of class, gender, and race.

Globalization, Social Theory, and Politics

The studies collected in Part One illuminate some of the features of the problematic of the global and the local from economic, political, social, and cultural perspectives. In Chapter 1, Roland Axtmann argues that globalization is primarily a function of the ever-expanding global economy and a multifaceted process that has tremendous implications for contemporary culture, politics, and everyday life. Indeed, Axtmann holds out the possibility of new concepts of global citizenship that will make us responsible and participatory in the problems and challenges of the coming global village. To the slogan, "Think globally, act locally," we may thus add, "Think locally, act globally." From this perspective, problems concerning global environmental problems, the development of a global information superhighway, and the need for new global forums for discussing and resolving the seemingly intransigent problems of war and peace, poverty and inequality, and overcoming divisions between the haves and the have nots may produce new conceptions of global citizenship and new challenges for global intellectuals and activists.

Axtmann also suggests that global citizenship and thus the effects of globalization per se could promote a greater acceptance of diversity, heterogeneity, and otherness rather than globalization just promoting homogeneity and sameness. Yet globalization could produce as well new forms of imperialist domination under the guises of universality and globality. Indeed, there remains the danger that globalization functions as a cloak disguising a relentless westernization, or even Americanization, of the world, much as did the old modernization theory that to some extent globalization theory inherits and continues. But the resurrection of tradition, ethnonationalism, religious fundamentalisms, and other forms of resistance to globalization are motivated to at least some extent by a rejection of the homogenization and perhaps westernization associated with some forms of globalization.

Globalization is thus necessarily complex and challenging to both our theories and politics. Michael Peter Smith shows that phenomena celebrated by some as an expression of globalization—in his case, Los Angeles as a global city—are really best interpreted as a concrete conjuncture of global and local forces. In Smith's trenchant formulation, Los Angeles is characterized as a "basket case," a receptacle for all the waste, refuse, and victims of U.S. global economic and political policies of the post-1960s era. Although Los Angeles provides a perfect example of a concrete instance of the complex intersection of global and local forces, it provides a useful warning against the uncritical celebration of globalization as progressive per se—as many of the development and globalization theories of the past decades would have it.

David Andrews discusses the globalization of American basketball as an effect of the rapid proliferation of American global culture. He suggests that basketball's fast-paced action fits well into the format of television, which lends itself to action spectacles, quick editing, and the drama of sports. American basketball also fits into the formats of European, Asian, and other global cable and satellite systems that devote an inordinate amount of channel space to sports events. Indeed, it is precisely the penetration of national cultures by transnational cable and satellite television systems that has triggered intense debate throughout the world. Andrews's study illuminates some of the ways that a global culture, in this case produced in the United States, is increasingly becoming part of a new world culture.

One of the functions of the globalization discourse has been to show the limits of both national and local politics and the need for new types of theory and political strategies to deal with what are now at once global, national, and local problems. Andrew Light and Eric Higgs focus on the national and transnational dimensions of ecological problems and the need for commensurable solutions. They argue that the problematic of ecological restoration can take either technocratic or more democratic and participatory forms and that issues of political choices are of key importance in developing proper responses to problems such as destruction of the environment and the need for its restoration. In a comparative study of the reception of ecological restoration in the United States and Canada, they indicate some of the political dimensions of acting locally and globally in a transnational world.

Cultural Studies and the Locations of Culture

The articles in Part Two of this volume consider the significance of local artifacts, producers, and practices in an increasingly global mass culture. Although the work of individual writers such as Sara Suleri and Audre Lorde, or more regional cultures, such as those of Cajuns and Chicana/os in the United States, might seem too idiosyncratic or specific to provide insights about globalization, the essays in this section suggest otherwise, arguing for the local and cultural complexity of global processes. In their attention to specific national and regional identities and to cultural forms that do not necessarily have mass distribution, these essays reveal the ongoing persistence of "local" cultures even in the context of globalization and transnationalism. Rather than constituting the last vestiges of a heterogeneity being displaced by global culture, local cultures represent instances of what Stuart Hall has called a "counter-politics of the local" (41).[15]

Through specific case studies, these essays perform strategic interventions into debates about the local and global and make theoretical contributions. The concrete cases they consider should not be understood merely as local instances of global processes or examples that substantiate abstract theories. Instead, this collection seeks to establish the central role of local analysis in explanations of global processes, which cannot be accounted for by abstract or totalizing narratives. In addition, the detailed case histories chronicled in this section of the collection are by no means an exhaustive survey of the many locations relevant to analysis of the intersections of global and local cultures. Indeed, it would be a mistake to assume that the notion of a universal culture, which narratives of globalization run the risk of constructing, can be dismantled through a proliferation of investigations of specific local cultures. This strategy has too often produced problematic versions of multiculturalism that have no way of explaining the relations of power that connect different cultural contexts.

The essays in Part Two do not relinquish the global in their attention to the local. Instead they make the ambitious claim that the category of the local transforms the debate about globalization by redefining what counts as global culture. Revisionist histories of colonialism and imperialism, especially those that con-

sider race and ethnicity, provide important examples of this strategy. Theorists of
the global such as Stuart Hall, Arjun Appadurai, Masao Miyoshi, and Paul Gilroy
transform discourses of globalization and transnationalism by insisting on the
role of colonialism and slavery in the history of capitalism. Their work reveals
that accounts of globalization as a new stage of capitalism or modernization that
fail to include these histories repeat the errors of models whose Eurocentrism ultimately prevents them from being global.[16]

Consider, for example, how in *The Black Atlantic* (1993) Paul Gilroy rewrites
the history of relations between Europe, Africa, and "America" as continuously
transnational by claiming the history of slavery to be a global event. No longer
just part of the field of African-American history or the history of minority cultures, slavery becomes a central feature of Western European history, which has
often been the local point of origin (unacknowledged as such) for global narratives of "world" history. Especially in its relation to nationalism, Gilroy's project
demonstrates the critical force of an analysis that combines the local and the
global. He seeks "intermediate concepts, lodged between the local and the global,
which have wider applicability in cultural history and politics precisely because
they offer an alternative to the nationalist focus which dominates cultural criticism" (6).[17] His local focus on Black British identities as one product of the
African diaspora requires him to engage with a transnational history that includes
many regions and continents. Moreover, the transatlantic or global scope of his
discussion of slavery demonstrates the limits of racial and ethnic histories that remain confined to boundaries of the nation-state. Gilroy is critical, for example,
of U.S. Afrocentrisms that ignore the role of the Caribbean and Britain in the
Black Atlantic or that fail to account for Black British culture as one of the many
products of the African diaspora. He places the slave narrative of Frederick
Douglass in relation to Hegel's master-slave dialectic to argue that European social theory cannot be understood without an account of the history of slavery.
Rewriting the relation between the metropolis and the periphery and between
cultures that are considered global and those that are considered local, Gilroy also
renders visible new cultural formations that transcend national boundaries and
that are hybrid products of many historical traditions. In part by appropriating
the notion of the global, Gilroy articulates the exclusions and erasures that have
too often accompanied the production of global history.

Gilroy's version of the global differs from those he would criticize because his
version remains sensitive to local cultures, to the differences between, for example, Black British and U.S. African-American cultures even when they are tied to
one another across shared histories. In fact, in its focus on how an African diaspora connects Europe and America, his study has its own specificity and local
limits. He has little to say about Asia, for example, which has played an equally
important role in Britain's history of colonialism and immigration, as well as in
the construction of Black British identity, which has included those of South
Asian as well as African and Caribbean descent. Gender difference is not central

to Gilroy's understanding of Black British identity or the transatlantic dimensions of the history of slavery. His remarks about how gender and sexuality play a role in the story of the escaped slave Margaret Garner, who killed her child, and in Toni Morrison's reworking of it in *Beloved,* are provocative but open-ended. Ultimately, he admits that "it is impossible to explore these important matters here" (1993, 68). Yet these limitations do not necessarily undermine his argument if it is understood not as an exhaustive or totalizing account but as a specific intervention especially against national categories of analysis.

Although ultimately all local cultures may have significant transnational dimensions, global analysis of the kind Gilroy performs has been especially useful to characterize the diasporic cultures of exiles, migrants, and cosmopolitans. The new identities and groups created by globalization, which in Arjun Appadurai's analysis create flows of people in addition to money and objects, are themselves a new local phenomenon. The essays in the volume contribute to the project of understanding the specific circumstances under which some groups and people become "translocal" (the term itself rearticulating local/global relations) and inhabit multiple nations, regions, or locations. Rearticulations of the local and the global are central to "the theorisation of creolisation, metissage, mestizaje, and hybridity" (Gilroy 1993, 2). Specific analyses of new global and translocal identities are necessary because the circumstances under which, for example, access to travel produces cosmopolitan elites differ from the material and political necessities that produce refugees and migrant workers. Furthermore, the political and cultural significance of migration, diaspora, and dislocation cannot be presumed in advance.[18] The celebration of hybrid or translocal identities on the grounds that they disrupt stable categories of identity is a gesture that needs to be carefully scrutinized. If applied indiscriminately to describe the fate of identity under globalization, hybridity loses its analytical and political force as a concept that describes particular and local circumstances. The lure of making hybridity, along with globalization and transnationalism, into master terms with a broad theoretical reach is a temptation to be resisted. Despite this hazard, however, attention to the cultures and identities created by diaspora and migration has had the positive effect of challenging metropolitan-periphery models that construct particular locations as global or more central.

Increasingly visible in the wake of the diasporas created by forces such as colonialism and decolonization, new global or translocal cultures enable revisionist understandings of national histories. Many of the essays in the volume, for example, explore cultures and identities that are in the broadest sense "American." Yet the America or the United States they invoke is tied to many other nations and regions, including the Middle East, Africa, Mexico, Spain, Pakistan, India, Britain, France, the Caribbean, and indigenous or Native cultures. In *Cultures of United States Imperialism,* Amy Kaplan and Donald Pease suggest that studying the United States in the transnational context of the history of imperialism constitutes a very different version of American studies, one that displaces the United

States even when it is a central focus of inquiry.[19] *Articulating the Global and the Local* charts globalization as an uneven development, at once acknowledging the global power and reach of the United States—both culturally and economically—and critiquing its global position through consideration of the many other national and regional cultures that have often been excluded from analysis of U.S. national culture. The essays in Part Two demonstrate the complexity of what it means to move beyond narrowly nationalist understandings of the United States to account for the global and transnational nature of its many cultures and the cultures to which it is connected.

For instance, Charles Stivale indicates how Cajun dance preserves traditional forms of music and dance in the context of a global culture. Indeed, global culture has even disseminated Cajun dance, food, and culture through film, video, and various other forms of reproduction. Cajun dance, however, articulates the specificity of Cajun experience and needs to be contextualized within its unique matrix of production and distribution to understand fully the function and effects of this cultural form. Included in that matrix is Cajun culture's transnational history; connected to France, Canada (or Acadia), the Afro-Caribbean, and the U.S. South, Cajun culture, like Black British culture, is a highly specific hybrid product of many cultures and nations. Stivale explains how the "spaces of affect" enabled by music and dance serve as a concrete and local arena for the convergence of these global histories and as an arena within which Cajun culture negotiates its relation to other cultures, including the U.S. popular music industry.

Mia Carter's essay investigates the complexity of "cosmopolitan" identities in the wake of the diasporas produced by colonialism and decolonization. The "cosmopolitan" status of Third World intellectuals and artists has been viewed with suspicion as a sign of their lack of engagement with the more local struggles of their "home" nations and their assimilation into Western or Euro-American cultures. Challenging this position, Carter argues that there are many "cosmopolitanisms," including the hybrid identities and cultures produced by the long histories of interaction between the imperial powers and their colonies and ex-colonies.

Carter's focus on Sara Suleri, whose autobiographical work *Meatless Days* troubles simple definitions of national and cultural identity, is strategic, demonstrating that the apparently idiosyncratic or exceptional case is in fact exemplary, not least because it explodes notions of a "representative" national or regional identity. Suleri belongs to the first generation of her family to be Pakistani because the nation didn't exist as such until after Indian independence and Partition in 1947 and because her Muslim father's family relocated from what had formerly been "home" in India. The Pakistan in which Suleri was born had already changed by the time she was an adolescent when the wars of 1971 led to the separation of East Pakistan into Bangladesh. Suleri's relation to categories of colonial and postcolonial national identity is still further complicated by the fact that her mother is British—more specifically Welsh—having been courted by her father during one of his stays in England, so often an important location for elite intellectuals involved in nationalist independence movements. Suleri writes *Meatless Days* from the United States, to where she has immigrated, constructing an autobiographical account of a globally situated Pakistan from the perspective of both an insider and an outsider, which challenges that dichotomy.

In Mia Carter's analysis, the specificity and the literariness of *Meatless Days* challenge any monolithic account of cosmopolitan identity, especially constructions of cosmopolitan elites as those who betray the local context of home and nation. Carter shows how Suleri intertwines family and national histories so as to prevent the exclusion of her personal history from the national history. Suleri invokes histories of colonialism, gender, race, and nation to create a singular or local story that disrupts generalizations or global narratives about Pakistan or the Third World (itself a problematic global term that Suleri questions). In particular by reading the intricacies of Suleri's use of language and taking up the question of its debt to a modernism identified with the West, Carter is able to insist that *Meatless Days*'s value need not rest on whether or not it is representative or transgressive. Carter also emphasizes Suleri's claim for the value of family history and personal memory, as opposed to institutional history, as mechanisms for charting global processes such as the wars and partitions that have produced Pakistani and postcolonial history.

In content and style Suleri's work insists on poetry over history to refuse the demand for a "Third World" nationalist literature that provides the authentic or representative voice of local difference. This emphasis on the poetic is further elaborated in Zofia Burr's essay on Audre Lorde, which considers the global significance of a mode of writing that, at least in the United States, is often considered marginal or irrelevant to political processes. Audre Lorde's case is particularly apt for considering the relation between poetry and politics since she identified herself as both a poet and an activist and she worked in many genres besides poetry including essay and autobiographical narrative. Identifying herself as a "Black woman warrior poet," Lorde has taken on the burden of representation to redefine it and to resist processes of tokenization (1984, 43–44). She offers valuable critical reflections on the complexities of categories such as "woman of color" or "lesbian," which are the product of identity politics and U.S. discourses of multiculturalism. Not least of these contributions is her insistence that her race, gender, and sexuality be understood in relation to the way she inhabits yet another identity category—that of poet.

Burr considers whether in death Lorde will have the same power to control her reception. She warns against the danger of posthumously constructing Lorde as a writer of universal or global significance, arguing that this gesture erases her poetry's politics, which depend on its performance in a specific location. Burr thus indicates some of the hazards of globalizing analysis. Reading the dichotomy between poetry and politics in relation to divisions between the global and the local, Burr suggests that poetry has often been depoliticized through its association

with global or universal concerns that are presumed to transcend the more localized concerns of the political. One of the consequences of this construction is the
dismissal of "political poetry" on the grounds that it is too local. Burr indicates
that a refusal of the difference between poetry and politics is connected to a refusal of the distinction between the global and the local. She suggests that Lorde's
activism, including the local work of performing her poetry, transforms
local/global relations and distinctions. Lorde's poetry is significant precisely because it refuses the "global" reach; for poetry to be politically active, it must be
"located"—must connect with readers or listeners whose responses may differ depending on their locations. Considering how Lorde addresses audiences marked
by racial differences, such that the same poem can have different meanings depending on its context, Burr demonstrates how Lorde's commitment to a political poetry and to poetry as political depends on her investments in rearticulating
the local.

Central to Burr's analysis is her attention to the complex task of reading an individual poem. Burr not only scrutinizes the text of "Today Is Not the Day," a
poem Lorde wrote about her impending death, but the significance of different
instances of its publication and the reader's implication in the poem's performative dimensions. Her insistence on the density of a single poem and its multiple
locations underscores her argument that the political importance of Lorde's poetry is lost if it is collapsed into her identity as Black or lesbian. Along with
Stivale's analysis of Cajun music and Carter's reading of Suleri's stylized prose,
Burr's scrutiny of Lorde's poem demonstrates that without specific readings and
interpretations, global theories of culture and politics will remain limited in their
generalizations. These essays persuasively demonstrate the valuable contributions
of cultural studies to political and social theory.

Translocal Connections

The essays in the third section of this book extend the concerns of the previous
section not only by considering particular local contexts and their global implications but by taking up the question of how different locations are related to one
another. Exploring disjunctions and distances between locations, differences that
are a function of both geography and power, they seek new models for articulating a system of global relations that cannot be subsumed under a single explana-
tory framework. The challenge of understanding different locations from what
must, inevitably, be a located position gives rise to questions of translation.
Avoiding globalizing perspectives that presume to be able to account for all locations, these essays operate instead in terms of the translocal, providing new strategies for explaining the material and conceptual links between locations.

The notion of the translocal speaks to the challenge of providing an analysis of
a global system of social relations without overgeneralizing or establishing hierarchies in which some sites are more global or more important than others.

Translocal analysis understands the links between different locations to be un-predictable and contingent rather than representative of a single transnational condition or national identity. Without such abstract frameworks, we must con-sider anew the mechanisms by which we come to know other places, particularly as a global media network provides, often phantasmatically, a sense of global con-nection. Whether as travelers, migrants, intellectuals, or TV watchers, our expe-rience may well take translocal forms, and the specificity of each location that we experience may preclude generalizations about the existential qualities of living in a global culture. Translocal analysis finds its object not just in national politi-cal struggles or economic relations but in individual experiences of crossing the border or teaching a class—in other words, in the spaces of everyday life. It con-siders the different ways we live globally from within multiple local contexts. Like the category of the transnational, the translocal contests the usefulness of the na-tion as a category of analysis. But it goes still further and announces the need to problematize the locations, spaces, and geographies within which politics and culture intersect. It is significant, for example, that Michael Warner uses the term "translocal" in his introduction to *Fear of a Queer Planet* (1993) when consider-ing the challenges of integrating sexual politics and social theory and moreover of doing so in an international or transnational context. Accounting for sexual politics requires new ways of thinking about categories such as the nation and in-ternational relations and provides an entirely different perspective on globaliza-tion and transnationalism. The category of the translocal helps in this project of creating new schemes for articulating the relations between the local and the global.

Amitava Kumar, for example, considers the status of the postcolonial intellec-tual in the context of a South Asian diaspora and South Asia's own multiplicity of regions, communities, and languages. His own encounters with the Immi-gration and Naturalization Service (INS) become a locus for considering the dis-junctions experienced by the South Asian intellectual in diaspora who operates across multiple locations. Moreover, he chooses poetry, including his own poems, as a form through which to articulate these experiences, drawing on po-etry's powers of juxtaposition to represent the dislocated and dislocating expe-riences of the multiple identities that are only reductively described by the global term "postcolonial." Sociological data on migration, INS statistics, and other forms of quantitive information about diasporic movements are inadequate to the task of representing the experiences produced by globalization. Like Zofia Burr, Kumar proposes the value of poetry and locatedness as a means of com-municating, or translating, across differences of class, nation, and experience. He considers the problem of translation as it emerges within the structure of indi-vidual poems and as it affects the challenge of reading them in different contexts. In both his poems and his texts, as well as in the act of combining them, Kumar proposes juxtaposition as a cultural and political strategy, offering it as a model of translocal analysis. He thus questions the value of a global narrative that presumes to be able to translate all experiences and locations into a common or universal framework.

Megan Boler also takes up the issue of how global events are experienced across distance, discussing the impact of the Gulf War on her American students and her classroom teaching. Central to her argument is her concept of emotional epistemology and her insistence that intellectual and emotional processes are inseparable in the production of knowledge. By analyzing the role of emotions in cognition, Boler transforms models of the local and global, insisting that the Gulf War occurs not only in Iraq or Kuwait but in the psyches and lives of her American students. The Gulf War, enabled by global communications systems that can bridge the distance between the United States and Iraq/Kuwait while those in the United States remain numbly distanced from the carnage produced by remote-controlled missiles, poses considerable challenges to the task of analyzing relations between knowledge and power. Boler argues that the technological capacity for global communication must be considered in terms of its local impact on the psyche and emotions of individuals in many different kinds of locations. The global dimensions of the Gulf War include its "localized engineering" of the psychic lives of her students, who experience the war largely through the media. She explores why the classroom is a location that merely perpetuates her students' experiences of numbness as a response to war, and she investigates the relations of power and knowledge that construct educational institutions. Proposing critical emotional literacy as an alternative pedagogy, Boler insists on the importance of analyzing global relations at the level of local or individual experience. Furthermore, in refusing to see emotional experience as distinct from global events and in maintaining that her students' numb distance from the Gulf War is part of its violence, Boler expands the notion of the global.

Providing a coda for the volume, Lora Romero's essay sounds an important cautionary note about global analysis and the project of investigating the relations between local contexts. Romero takes the example of recent efforts to understand Chicana/o culture within the context of postcolonial studies to argue that such endeavors can problematically presume that local area studies are inadequate. She notes the negative connotations of the domestic as it applies not just to women's work but to conceptions of international politics, arguing that the privileging of the international over the domestic arena through such terminology can be dangerous. Consolidating the collection's claim that the global must not be privileged over the local, Romero cites the tense relations between Chicana/o studies and Latin American studies, which are a product of the ways that Chicana/o studies has been neglected and marginalized in constructions of Latin American cultural studies. She cautions against the assumption that international or transnational analysis is better because it is less parochial than analysis that confines itself to cultures residing within national borders or to specific area studies. She points out that historically, Chicana/o studies, with its more local or regional focus, may have intervened more forcefully than Latin American studies to challenge constructions of U.S. nationalism, despite the latter's transnational identity. Institutional histories such as Romero's provide a context within which to evaluate the presumption that inserting Chicana/o culture or U.S. cultures within a global or transnational context will automatically be progressive. If global and/or transnational contextualization intervenes against nationalist disciplinary configurations, the strategic value of local categories must be considered as well. We end the collection with this essay to suggest that translocal analysis must continue to exist in productive and critical relation to local investigations.

This volume's final sections might seem to imply that global analysis should be replaced by local stories. Indeed, we would suggest that genres such as the personal narrative, the poem, and the testimony, or forms of emotional expression that may be hard to articulate in a text, have an important role to play in discussions that are bound to generalize at a false level of abstraction if they do not account for the specificity of such stories and their locations. At the same time, the global remains an important horizon of explanation and contextualization for these personal accounts, providing a conceptual space within which links between stories can be forged. If the goal of this collection is to demonstrate that these different kinds of essays are in fact related to one another, it is because rather than settling for a relativist notion of multiple and different locations, the collection seeks new understandings of how these individual stories connect to one another, especially since their connections may also be disjunctures. This project seems all the more urgent because discourses of globalization and transnationalism, which have rapidly proliferated during the period of this book's production, promise new ways of thinking about global relations and yet, in some cases, perpetuate exactly the forms of abstract and globalized thinking against which this collection seeks to intervene. This book sets out new questions for cultural studies and for the combined analysis of culture and politics. Operating across many disciplines, locations, and genres, the essays in this volume begin that work by suggesting the many and complex relations between local situations and their global contexts.

NOTES

1. Attempts to chart the globalization of capital, decline of the nation-state, and rise of a new global culture include the essays in Featherstone 1990; King 1991; Giddens 1990; Robertson 1991; Bird, et al., 1993; Gilroy 1993; Arrighi 1994; Grewal and Kaplan 1994; Lash and Urry 1994; Held 1995; and Wilson and Dissayanake 1996. We cite and draw on these and other studies during the course of our introduction.

2. Such positions are associated with the postmodern theories of Foucault, Lyotard, and Rorty and have been taken up by a wide range of feminists, multiculturalists, and others. On postmodern theory, see the survey in Best and Kellner 1991 and Best and Kellner, forthcoming.

3. See the discussion of postmodern politics in Best and Kellner 1991 and Bertens 1995.

4. See Polyani (1957, 189) on how market liberals failed to see the importance of the nation-state and nationalism, an oversight shared by Marx. Today, it is mostly transna-

tionalist neoliberals who continue to downplay the importance of the nation and who champion transnational structures, although this was also long part of the ideology of international communism.

5. On deindustrialization, see Bluestone and Harrison 1982 and on subsequent displacing of living labor by machines and technology, see Rifkin 1995.

6. Fukuyama's "end of history" thesis more accurately describes the end of a peculiar period of cold war history; see Fukuyama 1992 and the critique in Derrida 1994.

7. See Wolfe 1972; Cohen and Rogers 1983; Bowles and Gintis 1986; and Kellner 1990.

8. See the studies in Hall and Jefferson 1976; Hebdige 1979; Grossberg, Nelson, and Treichler 1992; and During 1993.

9. See Rushdie 1994, 211.

10. For a description of this process of the fragmentation of identities and production of new simulated ones, see Baudrillard 1993 and Kellner 1995.

11. See *The Washington Post National Weekly Edition,* September 11–17, 1995: 18.

12. In Europe, Hollywood films comprise 75 to 80 percent of the box office and the explosion of new TV channels has produced a boom of U.S. television exports, bringing in revenues of more than $1 billion a year; *Time,* February 27, 1995: 36 and 40.

13. This is, of course, a normative claim as there has been a tremendous resurgence of nationalism following the collapse of communism, producing the need for renewed critiques and evaluations of nationalism as a political force.

14. See Smith and Frank 1993 and Kellner 1995 for examples of the range of issues Madonna studies can address, and Cvetkovich 1992 for discussion of Madonna's relevance to analyses of capitalism and colonialism.

15. See Stuart Hall 1991a and 1991b.

16. Many of the essays in the anthologies edited by Featherstone 1990 and King 1991 display this tendency toward a level of abstraction that leaves questions of colonialism, race and ethnicity, and gender and sexuality unmentioned. As this book goes to press, it is heartening to see the publication of *Global/Local: Cultural Production and the Transnational Imaginary* (eds. Wilson and Dissanayake 1996), a collection that successfully avoids this pitfall. Among the book's strengths is its use of the Asian/Pacific Rim as a specific geopolitical site from which to analyze global/local relations.

17. For further discussion of Gilroy's use of the local and the global, see Lott 1994 and Rothberg 1994.

18. On this issue, see Stuart Hall 1991a and 1991b, as well as Iain Chambers 1994.

19. For further discussion of American studies in a transnational context, see Gayatri Spivak's "Scattered Speculations on the Question of Culture Studies" in *Outside in the Teaching Machine,* 1995.

BIBLIOGRAPHY

Appadurai, Arjun. "Disjuncture and Difference in the Global Cultural Economy." In Featherstone, Mike, ed. *Global Culture: Nationalism, Globalization and Modernity.* London: Sage, 1990.

Arrighi, Giovanni. *The Long Twentieth Century.* London and New York: Verso, 1994.

Baudrillard, Jean. *Symbolic Exchange and Death.* London: Sage, 1993.

Bertens, Hans. *The Idea of the Postmodern.* London and New York: Routledge Press, 1995.

Best, Steven and Douglas Kellner. *Postmodern Theory: Critical Interrogations.* London and New York: MacMillan and Guilford, 1991.

Best, Steven and Douglas Kellner. *The Postmodern Adventure*. New York: Guilford Press, forthcoming.

Bird, Jon, Barry Curtis, Tim Putnam, George Robertson, and Lisa Tickner, eds. *Mapping the Futures. Local Cultures, Global Change*. London and New York: Routledge, 1993.

Bluestone, Barry and Bennett Harrison. *The Deindustrialization of America*. New York: Basic Books, 1982.

Bowles, Samuel and Herbert Gintis. *On Democracy*. New York: Basic Books, 1986.

Chambers, Iain. *Migrancy, Culture, Identity*. London and New York: Routledge, 1994.

Cohen, Joshua and Joel Rogers. *On Democracy*. New York: Penguin, 1983.

Cvetkovich, Ann. "Feminism as Cultural Capital." *Mediations* 16, No. 2 (May 1992): 57–59.

Derrida, Jacques. *Specters of Marx*. London and New York: Routledge, 1994.

During, Simon, ed. *The Cultural Studies Reader*. London and New York: Routledge, 1993.

Enloe, Cynthia. *Bananas, Beaches, and Bases: Making Feminist Sense of International Politics*. Berkeley: University of California Press, 1989.

Enloe, Cynthia. *The Morning After: Sexual Politics at the End of the Cold War*. Berkeley: University of California Press, 1993.

Featherstone, Mike, ed. *Global Culture: Nationalism, Globalization and Modernity*. London: Sage, 1990.

Frank, Lisa and Paul Smith. *Madonnarama: Essays on Sex and Popular Culture*. Pittsburgh: Cleis Press, 1993.

Fukuyama, Francis. *The End of History and the Last Man*. New York: The Free Press, 1992.

Giddens, Anthony. *Consequences of Modernity*. Cambridge and Palo Alto: Polity and Stanford University Press, 1990.

Gilroy, Paul. *The Black Atlantic: Modernity and Double Consciousness*. Cambridge: Harvard University Press, 1993.

Gottdiener, Mark. *Postmodern Semiotics*. Oxford: Blackwell, 1995.

Grewal, Inderpal and Caren Kaplan, eds. *Scattered Hegemonies: Postmodernity and Transnational Feminist Practices*. Minneapolis: University of Minnesota Press, 1994.

Grossberg, Lawrence. *We Gotta Get Out of this Place*. New York and London: Routledge, 1992.

Grossberg, Lawrence, Cary Nelson, and Paula Treichler, eds. *Cultural Studies*. London and New York: Routledge, 1992.

Hall, Stuart. "The Local and the Global: Globalization and Ethnicity." In King, Anthony D., ed. *Culture, Globalization and the World-System: Contemporary Conditions for the Representation of Identity*. Binghamton: SUNY Art Department, 1991a, 19–40.

Hall, Stuart. "Old and New Identities, Old and New Ethnicities." In King, Anthony D., ed. *Culture, Globalization and the World-System: Contemporary Conditions for the Representation of Identity*. Binghamton: SUNY Art Department, 1991b, 41–68.

Hall, Stuart and Martin Jacques, eds. *The Politics of Thatcherism*. London: Lawrence & Wishart, 1983.

Hall, Stuart and Tony Jefferson, eds. *Resistance Through Rituals: Youth Subcultures in Post-War Britain*. London: Unwin Hyman, 1976.

Hanchard. Michael. "Identity, Meaning and the African-American." *Social Text* 24 (1990): 31–42.

Harvey, David. *The Condition of Postmodernity*. Cambridge: Blackwell, 1989.

Hebdige, Dick. *Subculture: The Meaning of Style*. London and New York: Methuen, 1979.

Held, David. *Democracy and the Global Order*. Cambridge and Palo Alto: Polity Press and Stanford University Press, 1995.

Jameson, Fredric. *Postmodernism, or the Cultural Logic of Late Capitalism.* Durham, NC: Duke University Press, 1991.

Kaplan, Amy and Donald Pease. *Cultures of United States Imperialism.* Durham, NC: Duke University Press, 1993.

Kellner, Douglas. *Television and the Crisis of Democracy.* Boulder, CO: Westview Press, 1990.

Kellner, Douglas. *Media Culture.* London and New York: Routledge, 1995.

King, Anthony D., ed. *Culture, Globalization and the World System: Contemporary Conditions for the Representation of Identity.* Binghampton: SUNY Art Department, 1991.

Lash, Scott and John Urry. *Economies of Signs and Space.* London: Sage, 1994.

Lorde, Audre. "The Transformation of Silence into Language and Action." *Sister Outsider.* Trumansburg: Crossing Press, 1984.

Lott, Tommy. "Black Cultural Politics: An Interview with Paul Gilroy." *Found Object* 4 (Fall 1994): 46–81.

Marx, Karl and Friedrich Engels. *Collected Works,* Vol. 6. New York: International Publishers, 1976.

Miyoshi, Masao. "A Borderless World? From Colonialism to Transnationalism and the Decline of the Nation-State." *Critical Inquiry* 19, No. 4 (Summer 1993): 726–751.

Morley, David and Kevin Robbins. *Spaces of Identity.* London and New York: Routledge, 1995.

Polyani, Karl. *The Great Transformation.* Boston: Beacon Press, 1957 [1944].

Rifkin, Jeremy. *The End of Work.* New York: Tarcher/Putnam, 1995.

Robertson, Roland. *Globalization.* London: Sage, 1991.

Rothberg, Michael. "Small Acts, Global Acts: Paul Gilroy's Transnationalism." *Found Object* 4 (Fall 1994): 17–26.

Rushdie, Salman. *East, West.* London: Jonathan Cape, 1994.

Smith, Adam. *An Inquiry into the Nature and Causes of the Wealth of Nations,* 2 vols. London: Methuen, 1961.

Soja, Edward. *Postmodern Geographies.* London: Verso, 1989.

Spivak, Gayatri. *Outside in the Teaching Machine.* New York and London: Routledge, 1993.

Sreberney-Mohammadi, Annabelle. "The Global and the Local in International Communication." *Interaction* 11, No. 1 (1993): 106–143.

Tilly, Charles. *Big Structures, Large Processes, Huge Comparisons.* New York: Russell Sage, 1984.

Wark, McKenzie. *Virtual Geography: Living With Global Media Events.* Bloomington and Indianapolis: Indiana University Press, 1994.

Warner, Michael, ed. *Fear of a Queer Planet: Queer Politics and Social Theory.* Minneapolis: University of Minnesota Press, 1993.

Wilson, Rob and Wimal Dissanayake. *Global/Local: Cultural Production and the Transnational Imaginary.* Durham, NC: Duke University Press, 1996.

Wolfe, Alan. *The Limits of Legitimacy.* New York: Basic Books, 1972.

PART ONE

THEORIZING THE GLOBAL AND THE LOCAL

1

Collective Identity and the Democratic Nation-State in the Age of Globalization

ROLAND AXTMANN

We live in an era of ever-increasing global interconnectedness of people, places, capital, goods, and services. Although globalization is a multifaceted process manifesting itself in such forms as global tourism and the global reach of nuclear, environmental, and health risks, it has arguably been the emergence of a global economy and a global information system that has been of particular importance for the creation of a global world.

A global economy has emerged that has become institutionalized through global capital markets and globally integrated financial systems, global trade, and global production networks. In such a "global economy," the patterns of production and consumption in the world are increasingly interdependent, income and employment are determined at a global level, and national macroeconomic management is becoming increasingly anachronistic and doomed to failure. Official international bodies such as the G7, the International Monetary Fund, the World Bank, the Bank of International Settlements, GATT/World Trade Organization, and the Organization for Economic Cooperation and Development (OECD) have not amounted to a system of global political governance of the global economy, although they do advance some kind of global economic coordination and co-operation. Arguably, however, it is the cartels and joint ventures among transnational and multinational corporations and financial institutions that are the most important element of economic (self-)governance (Grant 1992).

A shorter version of this paper has been published in German in the journal *Leviathan* 23 (1995), 87–101.

The globalization of the economy is driven by the interpenetration of the advanced capitalist countries and in particular by the intensification of transfers among three economic macroregions: North America/United States, East Asia/Japan, and Europe/European Union. To the extent that capital is buzzing around the world, most of the time it finds a resting place in advanced capitalist countries. To the extent that international trade is increasing, it is an expression of the growing interdependencies of the advanced capitalist countries (Schott 1991; Dicken 1993). And despite deindustrialization in the advanced capitalist countries, most value-added manufacturing is still taking place there (Rodwin and Sazanami 1989 and 1991; Martin and Rowthorn 1986; Gordon 1988). For the three macroregions, economic globalization has resulted in a trend toward the convergence of the structures of production, finance, and technology; in the synchronization of business cycles; and in "the growing importance of trade, investment and technology flows, both inward and outward, within each domestic economy" (Eden 1991, 213). It has also resulted in increased dominance of transnational corporations. Yet it should also be noted that each of these three macroregions remains relatively closed in that cross-national investment and trade within a region is greater than between regions. To that extent, much of economic activity remains "localized."

Economic globalization thus has a pronounced geographic dimension. It has led to economic regionalization and political attempts to institutionalize regional economic cooperation. The North American Free Trade Agreement (NAFTA), the European Union, the Association of Southeast Asian Nations (ASEAN), and the Asian-Pacific Economic Co-operation (APEC), which was founded in 1989, are perhaps the better known examples. This spatial aspect to economic globalization has also been manifested in the migration flows over the last few decades. It is also underlined by the effect of the global economy on different sectors and regions within each state. Deindustrialization, for example, brings disadvantages to the manufacturing industries and specific (industrial) regions of advanced capitalist countries, while the internationalization of financial services is likely to benefit other geographical locations and socioeconomic groups within the same society: "The emerging international division of labor is therefore a divisive force in domestic society. Insofar as it encourages and accentuates domestic conflict, international integration may provoke national disintegration" (Camilleri 1990, 36–37). Hence, neither for the global system as a whole nor for its constituent units does economic globalization result in homogeneity and overall integration; rather, it is likely to accentuate heterogeneity and fragmentation. Global capitalism is still best analyzed as a system of structured inequality.

The emergence of such a global economy was premised on the development of a technological infrastructure regarding transportation and the generation and circulation of information. Although the internationalization of production and the establishment of global production networks have been particularly dependent upon faster and more cost-effective rail, sea, and air transportation and on more extensive interconnections between them, the global economy more generally has become infrastructurally dependent upon the spread of global communications networks and the systematic use of radio, television, telephone, telex, fax, computer, and satellite facilities for the generation and dissemination of information. These technological innovations and their systematic application in economic transactions have resulted in the "shrinking" of distances with faster and improved connection between places.

Whether states can benefit from global communications and information networks depends upon their access to these technologies. As in the global economy, the advanced capitalist countries dominate the development of these technologies and their deployment and control the access of other countries to them (Smith 1980). The structure of inequality and dependence of the global economic system is thus buttressed by the control over the communication media, particularly the satellite systems on which they rely for speed and global reach by the economically powerful states and capitalist institutions. Since many of these technologies were initially associated with military surveillance and have become an increasingly integral part of the global military order, they also strengthen (as well as manifest) the geopolitical dominance of the West.

By meeting the communications and information requirements of both global capitalism and modern warfare, these technologies have created the conditions for a global system of symbolic interaction and exchange (Turner 1994: 156). New communication media allow the generation and dissemination of economically valuable data; they also make possible the transfer of mental images, exposing the recipients of these images to similar, standardized ways of thinking and acting. In other words, these media and the images they transport have arguably an impact on the culture and identity of the societies exposed to them. They could be seen as foreign cultural invaders diluting indigenous cultures and being instrumental in creating a global (Western) culture (Janelle 1991; Ferguson 1993).

This view is supported by a number of considerations. According to Leslie Sklair, the technical revolution in telecommunications and information systems has made possible the worldwide spread of the "culture-ideology" of consumerism that "transforms all the public mass media and their contents into opportunities to sell ideas, values, products, in short, a consumerist worldview" (Sklair 1991, 76). Arguably, to the extent that global mass media firms and transnational advertising agencies succeed in creating globally shared consumption needs, "the consumption of the same popular material and media products, be they Schwarzenegger, *Cheers,* Pepsi, Big Macs, Disney World, clothes, cars or architectural fashions, creates a metaculture whose collective identity is based on shared patterns of consumption, be these built on choice, emulation or manipulation" (Ferguson 1992, 80). Since nascent global mass culture must speak across many languages and native cultural traditions, it is dominated "by television and by film, and by the image, imagery, and styles of mass advertising" (Hall 1991, 27). It thus operates mainly through the packaging of imageries as articulated by the visual and graphic arts and their diffusion through worldwide telecommunications networks.

The culture-ideology of consumerism and the global diffusion of particular (Western/American) images and imagery spread through worldwide telecommunications networks are not the only manifestations of this global culture. Modern Western culture finds its stable foundation, above all, in a particular cognitive style. This mode of cognition has eliminated the sacred and the magic from the world by postulating that "there are no privileged or a priori *substantive* truths. . . . All facts and all observers are equal. . . . In inquiry, all facts and all features are separable: it is *always* proper to inquire whether combinations could not be other than what had previously been supposed" (Gellner 1992, 80). The implementation of modern scientism leads to "disenchantment" with the world (Max Weber), making it a cold, morally indifferent place, but enhances the economic, military, and administrative power of the societies that embraced it. It is because of the application of this cognitive style to economic activities and political organization that the West developed the institutions of capitalism and of the bureaucratic warfare state, allowing it to impose its dominance throughout the world. Gellner argues that the practical success of this style of thought induces all of humankind to adopt this style, at least in some measure: "Scientific/industrial civilization clearly is unique . . . because it is, without any shadow of doubt, conquering, absorbing all the other cultures of the Earth. It does so because all those outside it are eager to emulate it, and if they are not, which rarely happens, their consequent weakness allows them to be easily overrun" (Gellner 1988, 200).

The "global culture argument" has a variety of facets, as Smith points out in his explication (but not endorsement) of it: "A global culture would operate at several levels simultaneously: as a cornucopia of standardized commodities, as a patchwork of denationalized ethnic or folk motifs, as a series of generalized 'human values and interests,' as a uniform 'scientific' discourse of meaning, and finally as the interdependent system of communications which forms the material base for all the other components and levels" (Smith 1990, 176). Smith is correct to point to the element of timelessness inherent in the idea of global culture as "for its purposes the past only serves to offer some decontextualized example or element for its cosmopolitan patchwork"; but he is wrong to argue that global culture is also without context, "a true melange of disparate components drawn from everywhere and nowhere" (Smith 1990, 177). Global culture remains centered in and bound to the "West" (and Japan) in its reliance and dependence on "Western technology, the concentration of capital, the concentration of techniques, the concentration of advanced labor in the Western societies, and the stories and the imagery of Western societies: these remain the driving powerhouse of this global mass culture" (Hall 1991, 28). In this perspective, cultural globalization would mean the universalization—global spread—of Western "modernity" and instrumental rationality in its institutionalized forms of scientism, capitalism, and the bureaucratic state and the popular representation of its commensurate value system in the images and imageries of "Western" mass culture (Rieff 1993; Madsen 1993).

Implicit in this argument is the assumption that cultural globalization will eventually result in global cultural homogeneity. Localisms and traditions of variance will be swept away by the forces of Western cultural imperialism. I will argue that cultural globalization, similar to economic globalization, is more likely to result in generating and upholding heterogeneity as a feature as much inherent in its logic as homogenization. Although it would be highly problematic to argue that national or cultural identities are not open to influence by mass communication media at all, this does not mean that they are necessarily shaped or constituted by them. The argument that media determines culture and cultural experience systematically denies the contextuality of culture. The social groups and collectives that are the recipients of the "global message" interpret, or bestow meaning upon, these messages on the basis of their own specific experience and memories as they grew out of their own particular histories and cultures; they creatively modify "messages" and cultural products in light of their own local needs and requirements. It is exactly the timelessness, but also the context-specific "Westernness," of the global cultural message that is undermining its capacity to create a global collective identity, "those feelings and values in respect of a sense of continuity, shared memories and a sense of common destiny of a given unit of population which has had common experiences and cultural attributes" (Smith 1990, 179). Sachs (1992) expresses extremely well the gist of this argument and the actual experience to which it relates:

> Having a memory, relating to others, participating in a larger story, calls for involvement, requires presence. This presence, naturally, is lived out in particular physical settings like piazzas or streets, mountains or seashores. And these locations are in turn imbued with experience past and present. They become places of density and depth. Therefore, certain places have a special "thickness" for certain people. It is there that the ancestors walked the earth and the relevant memories are at home. It is there that one is tied into a web of social bonds and where one is recognized by others. And it is there that people share a particular vantage point and that language, habits and outlook combine to constitute a particular style of being in the world (111).

Although Sachs evidently discusses ethnocultural identity, one should not forget there are other types of collective identities such as those formed on the basis of class, caste, gender, and religion as well as those connected with colonialism. These identities ensure the heterogeneity of local experiences and refract the past in a variety of ways and become, at least partially, constitutive of ethnonational identity. But they also ensure that cultures do not become static but remain "fields of struggle" on which they are constructed, deconstructed, and reconstructed. These collective identities thus relate to ethnonational identity in a variety of ways, constituting its "context" while at the same time preventing its "fixity." But to the extent that there does exist such an ethnonational identity, it is centered on historically and emotionally entrenched shared memories (including those of past struggles) that are sustained through a sense of continuity between generations.

The global diffusion and global acceptance in the twentieth century of the idea of the nation-state as an institutionalized global norm and ultimate symbol with regard to what a viable society should "look like" has been an important feature of globalization. It has meant the extensive global legitimation of the strong centralized state as a primary feature of the world system, thereby constraining societies to participate in the interstate system "along the 'acceptable' lines of possessing relatively homogeneous state apparatuses" (Robertson 1992, 69). In a differentiated global system with many apparently independent units, the idea and "cult" of the nation-state/society has provided "normative anchorage for all particular societies irrespective of their internal functioning," at the same time serving "as a basis for empirical integration of the system as a whole" (Lechner 1989, 17–18; Robertson 1990a, 26). In this Durkheimian perspective, globalization encourages—even requires—normative expectations of state/society formation. Historically, it was in the wake of the American and French Revolutions that nationalism aimed "to overcome local ethnocultural diversity and to produce standardized citizens whose loyalties to the nation would be unchallenged by extra-societal allegiances" (Robertson 1990b, 49). Concomitant with this political nationalism was the nationalization of culture in the pursuit of the creation of a national-societal identity to define one's own society "in relationship to the rest of the world and the global circumstance as a whole" (Robertson and Lechner 1985, 110). Hence, hand in hand with the universalization of the nation-state norm there also went the "nationalization" of culture, which found one expression in "the expectation of uniqueness of identity" and thus the norm of particularism and localism. Although the universalization of the nation-state norm contributed to the global spread of the interstate system, the idea of the cultural homogenization within the nation-state reinforced the cultural diversity of that system.

It is a key aspect of the contemporary stage of global interconnectedness that concrete societies situate themselves in the context of a world complex of societies and that they conceptualize themselves as part of a global order. As a result of this global self-reflection, the criteria for societal change and conduct tend to become "matters of inter-societal, inter-continental, inter-civilizational, and inter-doctrinal interpretation and debate" (Robertson and Chirico 1985, 237; Turner 1994). Such a situating of societies may engender strains or even discontents within societies. It heightens the significance of the problem of societal order in relation to global order and is thus likely to give rise to a large number of political-ideological and religious movements with conflicting definitions of the location of their society in relationship to the rest of the world and the global circumstance as a whole. In short, it radicalizes and politicizes the search for identity. This identity, however, is the possible result of the confrontation of a particular locality with others in the emerging world of global capitalism, global information and communication networks, global transportation technology, and global tourism. Particular-istic identity in the age of globalization is thus constructed in full awareness of the rest of the world. It is an identity that does not aim at insulation from the world but allows local units conscious, if potentially fraught, interactions with it (Robertson 1992, 69–70; Mlinar 1992, 5–12; Walker 1993, 176–179). This interac-tivity finds expression in the impact of non-Western cultures on the West or the local reception of Western culture in the form of the indigenization of Western el-ements and also in the influence that non-Western cultures exercise on one an-other (Buell 1994). Two of the main mediating mechanisms in this structure of re-flexivity are global tourism and global migration flows. Since the process of identity formation in the age of globalization is embedded in this structure of in-teractivity and reflexivity, it is always precarious and fragile.

"Particularistic" identity does not necessarily express itself in ethnonational terms. Samuel Huntington (1993) has argued controversially that the question of collective identity in a global world is likely to pose itself in civilizational terms. He contends that concomitant with the increase in interactions between peoples of different civilizations there does occur an intensification of civilization con-sciousness and awareness of differences between civilizations and commonalities within civilizations. These differences will become politically radicalized through the operation of the global system in which the West in effect "is using interna-tional institutions, military power and economic resources to run the world in ways that maintain Western predominance, protect Western interests and pro-mote Western political and economic values" (Huntington 1993, 40). A "clash of civilizations," as the title of Huntington's article puts it, is therefore by no means inevitable. Even if we took no offense at Huntington's ideological construction of an "essential" and "unified" civilizational "us" and "them," the "other," we may argue with Huntington that a "clash" is premised on a global system of inequal-ity and power differentials; that is, without Western dominance, there is no "clash of civilizations." Nevertheless, Huntington is right to argue that it is within this context of global inequality that a de-Westernization and indigenization of elites is currently occurring in many non-Western countries, counterbalancing the im-pact of Western cultures, styles, and habits that have become popular among the mass of the people (Huntington 1993, 27).

Yet these elites are still concerned with building modern institutions such as bureaucratic states and modern armies as well as technologically advanced eco-nomic structures; but by aiming to preserve indigenous values and ideas, they strive to "modernize but not to Westernize" (Huntington 1993, 41). They attempt to embrace "modernity" in its institutionalized forms of centralized bureaucratic state, capitalism, and scientism to overcome the position of powerlessness that comes with a lack of modernity. The question they have to face is whether those "modern" institutions are inextricably interlaced with Western values. Is capital-ist modernization premised on the acceptance and endorsement of individual-ism? Is the modern state necessarily a secular state? Is it possible to embrace the modern form of political organization and postulate at the same time that it should express and reflect the collective (religious) values of the moral community that constitutes it (Juergensmeyer 1993)?

As the example of Japan forcefully shows, the embrace of modernity enabled it to defend and uphold its indigenous traditions. The same appears to be true for the other "Tiger" economies in Southeast Asia (Funabashi 1993). In fact, the Confucian revival in industrial East Asia since World War II was not only a response to the previous westernization of the political and cultural elites but constituted a forceful critique of modern Western culture in its attempt to understand some the effects of industrialization, urbanization, and bureaucratization and the widespread influence of mass communication. At the same time, however, "there is strong evidence to show that the dynamic cultural forms enhancing economic productivity that industrial East Asia assumed have benefited from Confucian ethics" (Wei-ming 1991, 772).

But the various manifestations of "religious fundamentalism" across the world attest to the sociopolitical and sociocultural dislocations that the policy of modernization, even without an accompanying conscious endeavor to embrace Western values, causes in many countries. The rise of radical (fundamentalist) Islamist movements in the Middle East, beginning especially in the 1960s and gathering pace in the 1970s and 1980s, must be seen as a response to the failures of the various policies of modernization. Neither the secular nationalist regimes of a socialist and/or pan-Arabist (rather than pan-Islamist) orientation nor Kemalism in Turkey or the White Revolution in Iran was perceived as a success: "Thus, Islamic revival can be regarded at least partly as a function of the eclipse of the Arab radical nationalist movement and of other developmental experiments in the Middle East" (Ayubi 1991, 65; Sivan 1985). Culturally, the general Islamic resurgence "represents a rejection to alienation and a quest for authenticity" (Ayubi 1991: 217). But as the institutionalization of fundamentalist Islam in Iran shows, even there this "cultural nationalism" aims to allow for the existence of a militarily strong, centralized, bureaucratic state and a capitalist market economy.

How to be "modern" without becoming "Western"? The tension this dilemma creates may find expression in religious fundamentalism, civilizational consciousness, or ethnonationalism, all of which are manifestations of a politics of cultural uniqueness that is a societal response to the challenges of globalization. They can be analyzed as attempts to reconstruct traditions in permanent civilizational encounters and locally to interpret and apply universal principles. To that extent, ethnic revivalism and nationalism as much as religious fundamentalism can be understood from the point of view of the analyst as a necessary aspect of globalization. From the point of view of the participant, they may appear as an adequate response to what can be seen as the homogenizing threat of globalization and thus as a reaffirmation or reinvention of a particularistic collective identity.

In many non-Western countries, we are witnessing dialectical tensions between modernization and cultural indigenization, between the universal and the particular, and the global and the local—in short, the dialectic of homogeneity and heterogeneity. It is this tension that informs the search for an idiosyncratic collective identity and the politics of cultural uniqueness in the era of globalization. For the West, this problematic also presents itself. Religious fundamentalism, for example, is not just a phenomenon of the non-Western world, as the example of the New Christian Right in the United States attests. Beyer (1994) analyzes this movement with good reason as a reaction to processes of globalization, in this case the decline of American hegemony since about the Vietnam War and the ensuing status crisis of the United States as a nation in the world system. He argues that the repositioning of the United States in the global system created an opening for the New Christian Right as a social movement and gave some prima facie credibility to its claim that religious and moral renewal was the prerequisite for regaining world leadership. Like Islamic fundamentalism, the New Christian Right reasserts a particular (American) group-cultural exclusivity as uniquely morally and ethically valid; and it too dogmatically refuses to accept the validity of some modern values (such as science) but at the same time, holding on to other modern features such as market-based capitalism. Despite these cultural manifestations, globalization reinforces concerns with collective identity above all through its effects on the polity and politics of the democratic state. It does so by problematizing the identity-bestowing notion of citizenship in the self-determining nation-state.

In the democratic state, sovereignty has been transferred from the (monarchical or autocratic) ruler to the people, and the people have been defined as the sum of the legally equal citizens. It is the people who possess sovereignty and thus the "undisputed right to determine the framework of rules, regulations and policies within a given territory and to govern accordingly" (Held 1991, 150). Political democracy is premised on the acceptance of the notion of popular sovereignty and its institutionalization in citizenship rights. The mechanisms for inclusion into and exclusion from the polity (Who precisely constitutes the people?) are organized around social criteria (e.g., class, age, gender) and ethnic criteria (e.g., race, place of birth). Citizenship rights are thus typically built around the notion of a universalism of rights and a particularism of identity. The demos component is normally dominant though the debate over the extension of citizenship rights to nonnatives such as guest workers or immigrants/aliens manifests the dormant and easily awakened power of the ethnos component. With international migration likely to become more pronounced as a consequence of changing world labor markets, ecological devastations, and displacements caused by political-military interventions, the discourse of ethnicity and even race will also become more pronounced in debates about citizenship (Brubaker 1989).

The relative weighing of the demos and the ethnos components has always been problematic. The precise "mixture" of these components, their form and mode of institutionalization and the respective mode of legitimation are an important element of the collective identity of a political system. In the past, one political tradition saw the state as a nation unified by a common culture: The state is both a political and a cultural unity. In the French republican version of this tradition, the nation has been defined as a political community based on a constitution, laws, and citizenship. It has allowed for the possibility of admitting newcomers to the community if they adhered to the political rules and were willing to adapt to the national culture. But in this version, the required cultural assimilation of newcomers is not couched in terms of ethnic homogeneity of the state. This "ideal" of the ethnically homogeneous state is prominent in those states in which membership of the nation is defined in terms of ethnicity with a strong emphasis upon common descent, language, and culture. In such states, a policy of ethnocultural assimilation could be understood as an attempt to confront the issue of actual ethnic diversity and turn the ideal into reality. But this ideal and the related policies clash with another prominent idea that sees a culture as being a state in embryo. This idea allows cultural minorities to claim they possess a right of resistance to policies of cultural assimilation and a right to secession and independent statehood. Although the first conceptualization might lead to internal ethnic conflict possibly resulting in secession, the second is likely to lead to international conflict as a result of irredentist nationalism that expresses itself in demands that people who are members of a common "cultural nation" but who happen to be citizens of another state be allowed to join the new state. In either case, the issue at stake is not the disappearance of the state, but how ethnic, religious, and cultural diversity can be accommodated within individual states and within the international state-system.

Whatever the precise criteria for inclusion into the community of citizens, citizenship as a legal status is an important part of an individual's identity; as a set of practices it constitutes individuals as competent members of a community (Turner 1994). Democratic rule is exercised in the sovereign, territorially consolidated nation-state. In a bounded territory, people's sovereignty is the basis upon which democratic decision making takes place, and the people are the addressees, or the constituents, of the political decisions. The territorially consolidated democratic polity, which is clearly demarcated from other political communities, is seen as rightly governing itself and determining its own future through the interplay of forces operating within its boundaries. Only in a sovereign state can the people's will command without being commanded by others.

However, in a world of global interconnectedness people's sovereignty and state sovereignty have become challenged since "[t]he very process of governance can escape the reach of the nation-state. National communities by no means exclusively make and determine decisions and policies themselves, and governments by no means determine what is right or appropriate exclusively for their own citizens" (Held 1992, 21; see also Connolly 1991, 216). For example, the formation of a global economy outreaches the control of any single state; multinational and transnational corporations, stock brokers, and international money and securities dealers make production and investment decisions that affect the economic well-being of states and people without being accountable to them. Global communication and the processes of informationalization make it difficult for governments to control information and its dissemination; and with power adhering increasingly to those actors that have unconstrained access to information flows, "the nation-state—with its more traditional geopolitical concerns for policing jurisdictively its territories, populations, and markets—often comes up short with nothing near complete closure over events within its boundaries" (Luke 1993, 239). Exterritorial global forces both invade the political space of the nation-state and because of their exterritoriality operate outside the controlling reach of the nation-state. They challenge the democratic polity as space invaders and as space evaders. They affect the life of citizens by imposing constraints and limits on democratically constituted political agency without allowing the citizens substantial control over them. In this context, Connolly (1991) makes the following observation:

> This is the double bind of late-modern democracy: its present terms of territorial organization constrict its effective accountability, while any electoral campaign within its territory that acknowledged the import of this limitation would meet with a predictable rebuff at the polls. Who wants to elect representatives who concede the inefficacy of the unit they represent . . . or who compromise the principle of sovereignty through which the sense of the self-sufficiency of established institutions of accountability is secured? (217)

But has the democratic state *ever* controlled *all* that obtained within its territorial space? Has capitalism *ever* been controllable by the state? The problem posed by globalization appears to be somewhat more complex. Political legitimacy in the sovereign, democratic nation-state has typically been linked to the state's capacity to deal relatively effectively with the demands and expectations of its citizens and with the citizens' democratic rights to exercise control over the ruling elites through elections and other forms of political participation as well as through the use of law. This legitimacy is strained because policy issues increasingly require international agreement and collaboration and are therefore no longer open to the problem-solving capacity of individual nation-states. As long as it is possible for states to find acceptance among their citizens for the claim that the global policy interdependence can be confronted through international and intergovernmental arrangements that leave nation-states with a veto, this *challenge* to political legitimacy will not result in a *crisis* of legitimacy: The citizens will still maintain that their governments are democratically accountable to them for their policy decisions (Gamble 1993).

However, when and if it becomes apparent that intergovernmental collaboration is less efficient in addressing and solving global policy issues and that transnational decision-making bodies would have to be created whose decisions became binding on nation-states, the question of legitimacy would be raised again. One response to the realization of the diminished problem-solving capacity of states both as sovereign and autonomous actors and as participants in international and intergovernmental arrangements is likely to take the form of demands for, in political terms, a "splendid isolation" and, in economic terms, protectionism, thus for a policy of "exiting" from the world-system. The issue of a distinct identity of a political collectivity, which Roland Robertson (1990, 1991, 1992) discussed in the context of globalization, will resurface as a manifestation of popular disappointments with democratic regimes' abilities to meet the expectations of the citizenry and solve pressing policy issues. As the rise of right-wing extremism during the 1980s and 1990s in many of the democratic countries of the West shows, there is a distinct possibility for "xenophobic nationalism" to function as the mobilizing ideology for the establishment of authoritarian regimes in which the ethnos component of citizenship will marginalize the demos component. It is also an open question whether the countries that have established democratic regimes in "The Third Wave" (Samuel Huntington) of democratization in the last decade or so will return to more authoritarian rule once it becomes clear that the rising expectations of the population, which are part and parcel of the democratic process, cannot be met in the world of global interdependence and (still increasing) global inequality.

The argument put forward in the preceding paragraphs could be cast in a somewhat different way. The success of the nation-state in the last two hundred years or so as well as its universality and legitimacy was premised on its claim to be able to guarantee the economic well-being, the physical security, and the cultural identity of its citizens. But global capitalism, the global proliferation of nuclear weapons, and global media and culture are now undermining this claim and challenge the effectiveness of the political organizational form of the nation-state. There are thus weakening links between the citizens and the nation-state. The citizens demand political representation, physical protection, economic security, and cultural certainty. But in a global system made up of states, regions, international and supranational organizations, and transnational corporations with no clear-cut power hierarchy, the nation-state cannot accommodate these interests and mediate between its citizens and the rest of the world (Horsman and Marshall 1994).

It is within this structural configuration that nationalism can become a dominant political force for a variety of reasons. First, nationalism is structurally embedded in the changes of the interstate system. After the end of the cold war, the geostrategic interests of the superpowers could no longer be defined as necessitating the perpetuation of the freezing of international borders on the grounds of security. As a result, demands for independence within states could be voiced more persuasively along nationalist lines. Second, the formation of regional blocs (such as the European Community/Union) makes it feasible for "small" states such as the Baltic States, the Czech Republic, Slovenia, and Scotland to conceive of themselves as viable, independent states in a "greater" Europe. It thus allows for nationalist mobilization in pursuit of secession and independence.

Third, the restructuring of the global economy adds to chances of survival of at least some smaller states—with the increasing importance of high-tech, high-know-how economies, scale and space become less important in economic terms, as Hong Kong and Singapore demonstrate. Even city-states have thus a good chance of establishing themselves in the global system. Finally, globalization, particularly global capitalism, has brought in its wake regional disparities and economic dislocations. Deindustrialization and unemployment, rising prices, and declining living standards have intensified the demands by citizens for protection and security. The citizens "call on governments to act in the national interest at a time when policy tools at the disposal of the nation-state are no longer up to the task" (Horsman and Marshall 1994, 86). It is in this situation that extreme nationalism and right-wing extremism can become popular among those social classes and groups most affected by the processes of globalization. Globalization may thus lead to the reemergence of nationalism, both in its "liberal" and "extreme" variety.

Nationalism of necessity thrives on the creation of "otherness." However, otherness and difference are not only an effect of political structures; they also issue out of economic structures. Recent changes in economic production and reproduction, which aimed to establish regimes of flexible work organization, flexible technology, and flexible labor in an economy geared toward batch production and niche marketing, have radicalized questions of collective identities. In particular, flexibility of labor meant, in effect, the division of the workforce between a skilled employed core and an unskilled and partially employed periphery with a clear boundary between these segments. These economic changes caused the "[d]isorganization of broad, relatively stable, and encompassing commonalities of economic interest, associational affiliations, or cultural values and life-styles" (Offe 1987, 527). According to Offe, this disorganization led "to the virtual evaporation of classes and other self-conscious collectivities of political will, economic interest, and cultural values whose existence [is a] necessary condition for solidarity and collectivist attitudes and ideologies" (Offe 1987, 528).

The differentiation of social structure is complemented by the pluralization of lifestyles: "[C]apital has fallen in love with difference. . . . [A]dvertising thrives on selling us things that will enhance our uniqueness and individuality. It's no longer about keeping up with the Joneses, it's about being different from them. . . . [C]ultural difference sells" (Rutherford 1990, 11). This has put a premium on privileging lifestyles and consumption rather than life chances and production as means of social differentiation and distinction. It tends to privilege "status" politics over "class" politics. Together, these changes in economic production and reproduction as well as the commodification of "otherness" could be analyzed as leading not only to the destruction or undermining of the older "Fordist" bases of political and social identity and collective solidarities but also to the fragmentation of the modern "self" and the formation of multiple personal identities as

well as to the fragmentation and differentiation of culture. This process of fragmentation and multiplication can be understood as the creation of the "space"
enabling individuals to develop new loyalties and identities after the fracturing of
the old "narratives." As Stuart Hall argues, this fragmentation of self has led to an

> enormous expansion of "civil society," caused by the diversification of the different
> social worlds in which men and women can operate. . . . Of course, "civil society" is
> no ideal realm of pure freedom. Its micro-worlds include the multiplication of points
> of power and conflict. More and more of our everyday lives are caught up with these
> forms of power, and their lines of intersection. Far from there being no resistance to
> the system, there has been a proliferation of new points of antagonism, new social
> movements of resistance organized around them, and consequently, a generalization
> of "politics" to spheres which hitherto the left assumed to be apolitical (Lipschutz
> 1992, 415).

Global capitalism can thus be analyzed as creating the space for the formation
of a plurality of collectivities, such as "new social movements" that can become
the carriers of a "politics of difference" based, for example, on gender or sexual
identities. However, the effect of capitalism on identity formation goes beyond affecting the constitution of new collectivities in a "post-Fordist" economic regime.
In a recent article, Katherine Mitchell (1993) provides us with a good case study
of this problematic in the context of global capitalism. In her discussion of
Vancouver as a "global city," she analyzes how since the mid-1980s the influx of
capital from Hong Kong, particularly the residential settlement of Hong Kong
Chinese, has led to perceptions by long-term white residents of threats to their established ways of life and to fears of exclusion from business activities. These anxieties were expressed as concerns about individual and national identity as well as
concerns about urban change rather than in an explicit racist language. But these
tensions, triggered by the international spatial economic integration and that
found one expression in the search or assertion of a collective identity in local or
national terms, have to be controlled if the ongoing expansion of capitalism is to
be secured. Mitchell argues that in this context multiculturalism has been re-
worked as "an ideology of racial harmony and bridge-building" (1993, 288).
Multiculturalism appears as the ideological moment that contributes to the removal of local barriers to the spread of capitalism—barriers that could be sustained inter alia by the racialization of society. The discourse on multiculturalism, which presents racial diversity in a positive way, can thus be read as "an
attempt to gain hegemonic control over concepts of race and nation in order to
further expedite Vancouver's integration into the international network of global
capitalism" (Mitchell 1993, 265). On the one hand, it is the expression of the contradictory nature of capitalism that it generates attempts to reassert particularistic (ethnonational or racial) identities in response to its global spread and that,
on the other, it can only thrive when these sets of particularistic identities are
peacefully contained and accommodated in the ideology of multiculturalism.

Yet multiculturalism is more than an ideology. Increasingly in the era of globalization, Western societies become multicultural societies in which distinct and cohesive communities demand the recognition and institutionalization of group rights to preserve their culturally and morally distinct ways of life. States are increasingly resembling an assemblage of national, ethnic, cultural, or religious communities with distinct languages, histories, traditions, and more or less complete institutional structures. In order to ensure the full and free development of their culture, these communities demand the right to govern themselves in certain key matters, urging the transfer of power and legislative jurisdictions from central government to their own communities. This raises a series of controversial questions. It challenges liberal political philosophy in at least two ways. First, individuals as bearers of rights pursue their interests but also indulge in their passions in civil society. As bearers of rights, they also enter into political society where they associate with each other as individuals with equal rights under the law. Indeed, being a citizen is a legal status that secures the right to have rights. The abstractness of rights, their moral and ethical indeterminacy, "is a necessary condition for their universality. This universality, in turn, is based upon an ethical commitment to the equal treatment of persons, a commitment that liberalism does not view as an arbitrary or subjective preference" (Holmes 1989, 244). It is ultimately linked to the concept of "negative liberty" and the idea of individual autonomy. What issues out of these ideas is the notion of the equal dignity of all citizens, which demands a politics of universalism that aims at the equalization of rights, entitlements, and immunities among all members of the political community, in short, a politics of nondiscrimination (Taylor 1992). Multiculturalism, however, entails the claim that the ideal of a universalism of individual rights has to be complemented by the principle of discrimination in that it demands the recognition of group differences caused by the unique cultures and identities of cohesive communities.

But there is yet another challenge to liberal political thinking. Liberalism in the Kantian tradition has relegated moral questions to the "private" sphere. Because different individuals and different groups of individuals differ over the conception of the good, a reasonable way to deal with these differences is not to address them in public; we must accept a "conversational restraint" regarding these issues (Ackerman 1989). With the individual cast as the unencumbered chooser of preferences, the person is also seen as the author of the only moral meanings in existence. With the individual seen as conceptually prior to society, morality is a matter of individual choice; hence there is and can be no substantial agreement on the moral rule that ought to guide society and its individual members. However, many non-Western communities in the West do not embrace this philosophy. For many of them, moral positions are not a question of individual choice. They perceive themselves as moral communities with a widely shared and deeply held conception of the "good life." For them, the community is prior to the individual, defining, ultimately, the individual in communal terms. Multiculturalism, or rather "multicommunalism," will therefore of necessity lead to the "remoralization of politics" and potentially to cultural conflicts that will be difficult to institutionalize as they are typically based on nonnegotiable claims of authenticity.

Even within a liberal perspective, however, are we involved in confronting the concerns of "multicommunalism." Bhikhu Parekh (1994) argues that

> [t]he liberal is committed to equal respect for persons. Since human beings are culturally embedded, respect for them entails respect for their ways of life. One's sense of personal identity is closely bound up with one's language, characteristic modes of thought, customs, collective memories, and so on, in a word with one's culture. To ignore the latter is to denude the individual of what constitutes him or her as a particular kind of person and matters most to him or her, and that is hardly a way of showing respect (103).

Insofar as the respect for the dignity of the individual necessarily leads us to an acceptance of cultural pluralism, we are necessarily involved in political-moral debate over the question of the legitimacy of group rights and the institutional arrangements that go with them. Parekh points out (1994):

> Communities that are cohesive, have democratically accountable self-governing institutions, and allow their members a right of exit play a vital role in giving their members a sense of rootedness, harnessing their moral energies for common purposes, and sustaining the spirit of cultural pluralism. Rather than seek to dismantle them in the name of abstractly and narrowly defined goals of social cohesion, integration and national unity, the state should acknowledge their cultural and political value and grant them such support as they need and ask for. . . . Conducting the affairs of a society as complex as ours is too important a task to be left to the state alone. It requires partnership between the two, and encouraging cohesive communities to run their affairs themselves under the overall authority of the state is an important dimension of that partnership (107).

In terms of the political institutionalization of multicommunalism, the diversity of sociopolitical and sociocultural communities within a larger political community thus raises the question of the very nature, authority, and permanence of the larger political community of which they are part and questions assumptions of common citizenship, common identity, and social and political cohesion (Kymlicka and Norman 1994).

I have argued in this article that political, economic, and cultural aspects of globalization will result in the proliferation of cultural "particularisms," collective identities, and the political creation of "otherness." Yet we can also detect trends toward the formation of a global consciousness. There are individuals who define their identities by referring to the global world. Global capitalism has created a denationalized global business elite that shares a kind of homogenized global culture of experience, symbols, and infrastructure that supports its way of life. But what this global elite lacks is any global civic sense of responsibility—unless one accepts the pursuit of global business as a true manifestation of such civic concerns (Falk 1994). However, during the last two decades, the threats to the survival of the human race posed by nuclear, biological, and chemical warfare and by the dangers of an ecocatastrophe and concern with political and social injustice worldwide, be it with political prisoners or discrimination on the basis of race or gender, have led to the formation of movements that do not limit their activities to any one particular territory. For activists in the environmental and peace movements, in Amnesty International, and in the women's movement, the "globe" has become the reference point for political activity. They act on the basis of a global consciousness (Falk 1992; Hegedus 1989; Lipschutz 1992, 392–396; Connolly 1991, 218–219; Thränhardt 1992; Heater 1990, 229–241; Roszak 1979). These activists have been defined as "citizen-pilgrims" whose "commitment is radical and essentially religious in character, not depending on any validation by the prospect of immediate results" (Falk 1992, 74). Falk also writes:

> [Their] ethos implies a reorientation of citizenship in order to go beyond loyalty and diligent participation in the collective life of a territorially delimited society that qualifies as a sovereign state. The citizen sensitive to the claims of this emergent ethos needs to extend his or her notions of participation in dimensions of both space (beyond the territory of any particular state) and time (beyond the present, reclaiming past wisdom and safeguarding future generations) (153–154).

"Think globally, act locally" as much as "think locally, act globally" is the core of this ethos that is "necessarily deferential to the local and the diverse" (Falk 1992, 153). As Sachs (1992, 112) put it, "[t]he globe is not any longer imagined as a homogeneous space where contrasts ought to be levelled out, but as a discontinuous space where differences flourish in a multiplicity of places." Arguably, through their global orientation, the "citizen-pilgrims" are participating in the creation of a global civil society.

Such a democratic global civil society needs a public space for deliberation and the coordination of activities. Although such a space has not yet been institutionalized, it has been argued that the new information and communication technologies could possibly provide the infrastructural underpinning of a global "civil society" once their "empowering" potential has been released (Keane 1991, 116–162). James Rosenau has suggested that these technologies have already enhanced the competencies of citizens: "The advent of global television, the widening use of computers in the workplace, the growth of foreign travel and the mushrooming migrations of peoples, the spread of educational institutions at the primary, secondary, and university levels, and many other features of the post-industrial era [such as the revolution in information technology] has enhanced the analytic skills of individuals" (1992, 275). This skill revolution, he argues, increasingly enables citizens to hold their own against political authority "by knowing when, where, and how to engage in collective action" (Rosenau 1992, 291). To the extent that these technologies can become sites of resistance, they will also be the sites of struggle in the future.

The transnational social movements are manifestations of a kind of Kantian cosmopolitanism and universalism and thus of a nascent global consciousness. They demonstrate that the reinforcement of particularistic collective identities, although of the utmost significance and importance in recent years, has not been the exclusive response to the challenges posed by intersocietal, intercontinental, intercivilizational, and interdoctrinal encounters in a global world. Globalization is a contradictory process. Borne by the increase in the global reach of economic and political processes as well as the global flow of information, communication, and technology, globalization is fostering manifestations of a global consciousness that conceives of the world as one place. Despite (or rather because of) these processes, there are also strong pressures toward the assertion of regional autonomy, localism, and local identities. Homogeneity and heterogeneity and fragmentation are constitutive of processes of globalization.

The search for identity within a global world may express itself politically in the formation of a global consciousness; it may also manifest itself in religious fundamentalism, civilizational consciousness, and/or ethnonational revivalism. In Eastern Europe and elsewhere, this revivalism still focuses on the creation and protection of sovereign nation-states. The "state" and the "nation" are still concepts in which community is "imagined" (Anderson 1983). Membership in a territorially demarcated, sovereign political unit is still the relevant precondition for citizenship rights. Membership of the human race does not (yet) translate into universal human rights that incorporate political, social, economic, or ecological citizenship rights. Democratic politics is thus still channeled through the political institutions of the nation-state on the basis of a claim by the nation-state to sovereignty and the principle of citizenship. Despite the rise of global consciousness, there still exists the perception and the widespread normative acceptance of an "elective affinity" between the state and democracy (Connolly 1991, 201). Thus there does arise the tension between, on the one hand, the particularism of citizenship that, based on state sovereignty, defines the individual as a political being with freedom and duties within a territorially demarcated political unit, and on the other hand, the nascent universalizing understanding of humanity that defines the individual as a cohabitant of a fragile planet and a member of a global community of fate (Walker and Mendlovitz 1990, 5–6; Walker 1993). In the international arena, this tension translates into the complex and often conflictual relationship between the system of states and a nascent global civil society. Insofar as globalization reinforces ethnic and national identities, it contributes to the resilience of the nation-state and the state system. At the same time, while in this tension between globality and locality the nation-state as a political unit and focus of political loyalty and identity is invoked, globalization challenges the (liberal-) democratic organization of this state form.

These processes of globalization challenge us to reconceptualize the social world in which we live. Centralization and hierarchization of power within states and through states in the international system are steadily replaced by the pluralization of power among political, economic, cultural, and social actors, groups, and communities within states, between states, and across states. We move into a plurilateral world of diffused and decentralized power, into a world characterized by a variety of different loci of power and cross-cutting and intersecting power networks (Cerny 1993). Those individuals, groups, and communities partaking in the creation of these networks and affected by them will become empowered and constrained by them in ways quite different from the past when it was the nation-state that determined by and large their political "liberty" and "identity" and mediated the effects of the "outside" world. In this plurilateral world, the idea of a *summa potestas* that resides in the state as that institutional arrangement empowered to make and enforce collectively binding decisions has lost its justification if not its appeal. And so has the notion of the sovereignty of the people as a united, homogeneous body legitimating the sovereign power of "its" state through a constitution that manifests the principle of *voluntas populi suprema lex*.

In this complex and fragmented world, where is the place of "democracy"? If there is no longer a *summa potestas*, who can be held accountable by the "people"? And if we as individuals and members of groups and communities are "embedded" in a plethora of power networks bringing us into relationships of dominance and dependency with alternating sets of individuals, groups, and communities, who or what is the "constituency" that can legitimately claim the democratic right of control and participation? How do we speak of democracy in a plurilateral world, and how do we institutionalize new forms of democracy commensurate with the complexity and fragmented structure of this world? These are some of the questions we will have to confront as we move into the twenty-first century.

ACKNOWLEDGMENT

I would like to thank my colleague, Dr. Jean Houbert, University of Aberdeen, Scotland, for his critical comments on this chapter. The themes of this chapter are discussed at greater length, and with particular focus on democratic theory, in my book *Liberal Democracy into the Twenty-First Century: Globalization, Integration and the Nation-state* (Manchester: Manchester University Press, 1996).

BIBLIOGRAPHY

Ackerman, B. 1989, "Why Dialogue?" *Journal of Philosophy* 86 (January 1989), pp. 5–22.
Anderson, B. 1983, *Imagined Communities*, London: Verso.
Ayubi, N. 1991, *Political Islam. Religion and Politics in the Arab World*, London: Routledge.
Beyer, P. 1994, *Religion and Globalization*, London: Sage.

Brubaker, W. R. (ed.) 1989, *Immigration and the Politics of Citizenship in Europe and North America*, Lanham: University Press of America.

Buell, F. 1994, *National Culture and the New Global System*, Baltimore and London: The Johns Hopkins University Press.

Camilleri, J. A. 1990, "Rethinking Sovereignty in a Shrinking, Fragmented World," in: R. B. J. Walker and S. H. Mendlovitz (eds.) *Contending Sovereignties: Redefining Political Community*, London: Lynne Rienner, pp. 13–44.

Cerny, P. 1993, "Plurilateralism: Structural Differentiation and Functional Conflict in the Post-Cold War World Order," *Millennium* 22 (1993) 1, pp. 27–51.

Connolly, W. E. 1991, *Identity/Difference. Democratic Negotiations of Political Paradox*, Ithaca and London: Cornell University Press.

Dicken, P. 1993, *Global Shift. The Internationalization of Economic Activity*, 2nd ed., London: Paul Chapman.

Eden, L. 1991, "Bringing the Firm Back In: Multinationals in International Political Economy," *Millennium* 20 (1991) 2, pp. 197–224.

Ekins, P. 1992, *A New World Order. Grassroots Movements for Global Change*, London: Routledge.

Falk, R. 1992, *Explorations at the Edges of Time. The Prospects for World Order*, Philadelphia: Temple University Press.

Falk, R. 1994, "The Making of Global Citizenship," in: B. van Steenbergen (ed.) *The Condition of Citizenship*, London: Sage, pp. 127–140.

Ferguson, M. 1992, "The Mythology about Globalization," *European Journal of Communication* 7 (1992) 1, pp. 69–93.

Ferguson, M. 1993, "Invisible Divides: Communication and Identity in Canada and the U.S.," *Journal of Communication* 43 (1993) 2, pp. 42–57.

Funabashi, Y. 1993, "The Asianization of Asia," *Foreign Affairs* 72 (1993) 5, pp. 75–85.

Gamble, A. 1993, "Shaping the New World Order: Political Capacities and Policy Challenges," *Government and Opposition* 28 (1993) 3, pp. 325–338.

Gellner, E. 1988, *Plough, Sword and Book. The Structure of Human History*, London: Collins Harvill.

Gellner, E. 1992, *Postmodernism, Reason and Religion*, London: Routledge.

Gordon, D. 1988, "The Global Economy: New Edifice or Crumbling Foundations?" *New Left Review* 168 (1988), pp. 24–64.

Grant, W. 1992, *Economic Globalisation, Stateless Firms and International Governance*, Coventry: University of Warwick (PAIS paper no. 105).

Hall, S. 1991, "The Local and the Global: Globalization and Ethnicity," in: A. D. King (ed.) *Culture, Globalization and the World-System*, Houndmills, Basingstoke: Macmillan, pp. 19–39.

Hall, S. 1991a, "Brave New World," *Socialist Review* 21 (1991) 1, pp. 57–64.

Heater, D. 1990, *Citizenship. The Civic Ideal in World History, Politics and Education*, London and New York: Longman.

Hegedus, Z. 1989, "Social Movements and Social Change in Self-Creative Society: New Civil Initiatives in the International Arena," *International Sociology* 4 (1989) 1, pp. 19–36.

Held, D. 1989, "Sovereignty, National Politics and the Global System," in: D. Held *Political Theory and the Modern State*, Oxford: Polity Press, pp. 214–242.

Held, D. 1991, "Democracy, the Nation-State and the Global System," *Economy and Society* 20 (1991) 2, pp. 138–172.

Held, D. 1992, "Democracy: From City-States to a Cosmopolitan Order?" *Political Studies* 40 (1992/Special Issue), pp. 10–39.

Holmes, St. 1989, "The Permanent Structure of Antiliberal Thought," in: N. Rosenblum (ed.) *Liberalism and the Moral Life,* Cambridge, Mass.: Harvard University Press, pp. 227–253.

Horsman, M., and A. Marshall. 1994, *After the Nation-State. Citizens, Tribalism and the New World Disorder,* London: HarperCollins.

Huntington, S. 1993, "The Clash of Civilizations?" *Foreign Affairs* 72 (1993) 2, pp. 22–49.

Janelle, D. 1991, "Global Interdependence and Its Consequence," in: S. D. Brunn and T. R. Leinbach (eds.) *Collapsing Space and Time: Geographic Aspects of Communications and Information,* London: HarperCollins Academic, pp. 49–81.

Juergensmeyer, M. 1993, *The New Cold War? Religious Nationalism Confronts the Secular State,* Berkeley: University of California Press.

Keane, J. 1991, *Media and Democracy,* Oxford: Polity Press.

Kymlicka, W., and W. Norman. 1994, "Return of the Citizen: A Survey of Recent Work on Citizenship Theory," *Ethics* 104 (1994), pp. 352–381.

Lechner, F. 1989, "Cultural Aspects of the Modern World System," in: W. H. Swatos (ed.) *Religious Politics in Global and Comparative Perspective,* New York: Greenwood Press, pp. 11–27.

Lechner, F. 1991, "Religion, Law and Global Order," in: R. Robertson and W. R. Garrett (eds.) *Religion and Global Order,* New York: Paragon Press, pp. 263–280.

Lind, W. 1991, "Defending Western Culture," *Foreign Policy* 84 (1991), pp. 40–50.

Lipietz, A. 1992, *Towards a New Economic Order. Postfordism, Ecology and Democracy,* Oxford: Polity Press.

Lipschutz, R. D. 1992, "Reconstructing World Politics: The Emergence of Global Civil Society," *Millennium* 21 (1992) 3, pp. 389–420.

Luke, T. W. 1993, "Discourses of Disintegration, Texts of Transformation: Re-Reading Realism in the New World Order," *Alternatives* 18 (1993) 2, pp. 229–258.

Madsen, R. 1993, "Global Monoculture, Multiculture, and Polyculture," *Social Research* 60 (1993) 3, pp. 493–511.

Martin, R. L., and R. Rowthorn. (eds.) 1986, *The Geography of De-Industrialisation,* London: Macmillan.

Mitchell, K. 1993, "Multiculturalism, or the United Colors of Capitalism?" *Antipode* 25 (1993) 4, pp. 263–294.

Mlinar, Z. 1992, "Introduction," in: Z. Mlinar (ed.) *Globalization and Territorial Identities,* Aldershot: Avebury, pp. 1–14.

Offe, C. 1987, "Democracy Against the Welfare State?" *Political Theory* 15 (1987) 4, pp. 501–537.

Parekh, B. 1992, "The Cultural Particularity of Liberal Democracy," *Political Studies* 40 (1992/Special Issue), pp. 160–175.

Parekh, B. 1994, "Minority Rights, Majority Values," in: D. Miliband (ed.) *Reinventing the Left,* Oxford: Polity Press, pp. 101–109.

Rieff, D. 1993, "A Global Culture?" *World Policy Journal* 10 (1993/1994) 4, pp. 73–81.

Robertson, R. 1990a, "Mapping the Global Condition: Globalization as the Central Concept," in: M. Featherstone (ed.) *Global Culture. Nationalism, Globalization and Modernity,* London: Sage, pp. 15–30.

Robertson, R. 1990b, "After Nostalgia? Wilful Nostalgia and the Phases of Globalization," in: B. S. Turner (ed.) *Theories of Modernity and Postmodernity,* London: Sage, pp. 45–61.

Robertson, R. 1991, "Globalization, Modernization, and Postmodernization: The Ambiguous Position of Religion," in: R. Robertson and W. R. Garrett (eds.) *Religion and Global Order,* New York: Paragon Press, pp. 281–291.

Robertson, R. 1992, *Globalization. Social Theory and Global Culture,* London: Sage.

Robertson, R., and J. Chirico. 1985, "Humanity, Globalization and Worldwide Religious Resurgence: A Theoretical Exploration," *Sociological Analysis* 46 (1985) 3, pp. 219–242.

Robertson, R., and F. Lechner. 1985, "Modernization, Globalization and the Problem of Culture in World-Systems Theory," *Theory, Culture and Society* 2 (1985) 3, pp. 103–117.

Rodwin, L., and H. Sazanami. (eds.) 1989, *Deindustrialization and Regional Economic Transformation: The Experience of the United States,* Boston: Unwin Hyman.

Rodwin, L., and H. Sazanami. (eds.) 1991, *Industrial Change and Regional Economic Transformation: The Experience of Western Europe,* London: HarperCollins.

Rosenau, J. 1992, "Citizenship in a Changing Global Order," in: J. Rosenau and E. O. Czempiel (eds.) *Governance without Government,* Cambridge: Cambridge University Press, pp. 272–294.

Roszak, T. 1979, *Person/Planet. The Creative Disintegration of Industrial Society,* London: Victor Gollancz.

Rutherford, J. (ed) 1990, *Identity. Community, Culture, Difference,* London: Lawrence & Wishart.

Sachs, W. 1992, "One World," in: W. Sachs (ed.) *The Development Dictionary. A Guide to Knowledge as Power,* London: Zed Press, pp. 102–115.

Schott, J. 1991, "Trading Blocs and the World Trading System," *World Economy* 14 (1991) 1, pp. 1–17.

Sivan, E. 1985, *Radical Islam. Medieval Theology and Modern Politics,* New Haven/London: Yale University Press.

Sklair, L. 1991, *Sociology of the Global System,* Hemel Hempstead: Harvester Wheatsheaf.

Smith, A. 1980, *The Geopolitics of Information. How Western Culture Dominates the World,* London: Faber & Faber.

Smith, A. 1990, "Towards a Global Culture?" in: M. Featherstone (ed.) *Global Culture. Nationalism, Globalization and Modernity,* London: Sage, pp. 171–191.

Smith, A. 1991, *National Identity,* London: Penguin Books.

Taylor, C. 1992, *Multiculturalism and "The Politics of Recognition,"* Princeton: Princeton University Press.

Thränhardt, D. 1992, "Globale Probleme, globale Normen, neue globale Akteure," *Politische Vierteljahresschrift* 33 (1992) 2, pp. 219–234.

Tomlinson, J. 1991, *Cultural Imperialism. A Critical Introduction,* Baltimore: Johns Hopkins.

Turner, B. S. 1994, "Postmodern Culture/Modern Citizens," in: B. van Steenbergen (ed.) *The Condition of Citizenship,* London: Sage, pp. 153–168.

Walker, R. B. J. 1993, *Inside/Outside. International Relations as Political Theory,* Cambridge: Cambridge University Press.

Walker, R. B. J., and S. H. Mendlovitz. 1990, "Interrogating State Sovereignty," in: R. B. J. Walker and S. H. Mendlovitz (eds.) *Contending Sovereignties: Redefining Political Community,* London: Lynne Rienner.

Wei-ming, T. 1991, "The Search for Roots in Industrial East Asia: The Case of the Confucian Revival," in: M. Marty and R. S. Appleby (eds.) *Fundamentalisms Observed* (vol. 1), Chicago/London: University of Chicago Press, pp. 740–781.

2

Looking for Globality in Los Angeles

MICHAEL PETER SMITH

Almost a decade ago, in the book *The Capitalist City,* I contributed to the theoretical formation of the concept of the "global city." I characterized global cities as locations of networks of flows of capital, people, and culture that connect disparate places across the globe.[1] Since then that concept, which started out openended, has evolved into a kind of economistic description of three places: New York, London, and Tokyo, with Los Angeles sometimes thrown in for good measure. This essay will show why Los Angeles is not a "global city" or "world city" as it is now commonly referred to in the social sciences.

The focus of the global cities discourse has been on the centrality of global cities to the evolving international political economy as key "command and control" centers—as engines driving global economic growth, primarily through the capacity of their political economies to command capital flows. Global cities are depicted as dynamic magnets drawing international labor migrants as well as capital flows into their orbits. Global economic restructuring and labor migration are frequently depicted as two sides of a single dynamic—the general reorganization of capitalism orchestrated from "global cities."[2]

According to this economistic global narrative, I will argue that Los Angeles is not a global city but a "basket case"—a receiver rather than a sender of global commands and controls. I will show that its multicultural demography is the result of the spatial relocalization and temporal convergence of historically particular networks of transnational migrants and refugees rather than a result of either an overarching global "capital logic" or of the intentional agency of a local "growth machine" that has recruited an ethnically fragmented and hence tractable workforce.

Likewise Los Angeles's political economy, although benefiting from global investment by Japanese and other Asian finance capitalists (largely in a downtown real estate boom that peaked by the late 1980s), remained excessively dependent on defense spending as its central engine of growth. Its rapid economic decline since the end of the cold war renders problematic claims by some "L.A. as world city" devotees that Los Angeles is "[t]he industrial growth pole of the 20th century."[3] The articulations of the global and the local in Los Angeles are both more complex and more fascinating than those expressed within the "world cities" framework. There are global forces and processes localized in Los Angeles, to be sure, just as there are binational, national, regional, and local forces. Sorting out these forces and processes that have "come together" in Los Angeles is not easy, but it is the task at hand. The question of why L.A. has become a kind of "receiver from below," an obscure object of desire, for so many transnational migrants from so many places across the globe despite its declining economy is central to this task.

The case of Mexican migrants in Los Angeles must be dealt with first because of its complexity and because it does not fit neatly into the "globalization of Los Angeles" motif. The most obvious dimensions of the story of Mexican migration to Los Angeles are its timing and its scale. More than two-thirds of all Latinos living in Los Angeles are of Mexican origin. Many of these long-time Angelenos "born in East L.A." are Mexican-American citizens. They are the offspring of earlier generations of Mexican migrants whose migration preceded the epoch of global economic restructuring and was driven more by the ebbs and flows of U.S. agricultural policy and its permissions and constraints than by global developments. This is an old story but one that has fed the endemic local racist stereotyping of Mexican migrants as "uneducated peasants" or "low riders" by white middle-class Angelenos. These stereotypes have frequently had substantial material consequences. During the Great Depression, for example, long before California voters passed Proposition 187 but foreshadowing its racist spirit, Los Angeles initiated a voluntary deportation program that led to thousands of unwelcome Mexicans returning to their native land.[4]

A more recent dimension of Mexican migration to Los Angeles is rooted in the operation of the Immigration Reform and Control Act (IRCA) of 1986. The amnesty provisions of IRCA allowed undocumented Mexican workers who had been living in California for four years preceding the amnesty to obtain green cards. Although not envisaged in the IRCA amnesty, many of the hundreds of thousands of newly legalized male workers who had been living in binational households then chose to bring their wives and children to live with them in California, thus dramatically altering the gender composition of more recent Mexican migration.

IRCA was passed in part at the behest of California growers to ensure a large, and hence cheap, labor supply. In addition to the amnesty, other loopholes in the law allowed California growers to retain workers who had worked in California agriculture for as few as ninety days in the previous year and even to replenish their supply of legalized farm workers by replacing those newly legalized workers who chose to move from rural to urban California. The "control" portions of the law, in turn, were intended to tighten border controls against illegal immigration and to impose sanctions on employers in agriculture, manufacturing, and services who continued to hire undocumented workers.

The law had several unintended consequences. Low wages in the agricultural sector drove many male farm workers who had brought additional household members from Mexico to California to move to cities like Los Angeles in search of higher paying urban service and manufacturing jobs in the state's then still robust metropolitan economies. Both the threat of employer sanctions and the need to protect newly united family members from surveillance by employers and immigration authorities generated a virtual cottage industry in forged documents. Increasing numbers of the children of Mexican migrants entered the public schools, setting the stage for one of the most punitive, exclusionary, and unconstitutional provisions of Proposition 187.

As can be seen from these developments, the IRCA–driven expansion of recent Mexican migration is an interesting phenomenon both within California and binationally. It has changed the demographics of Los Angeles as well as many other cities and towns in California. Yet it too may be viewed as a historical extension of long-term binational relations of production, labor supply, and household formation between California and Mexico rather than as either a manifestation of economic globalization or an indicator of Los Angeles's emergence as a "world city."

A third and larger dimension of the ongoing Mexican migration to Los Angeles in the 1980s and early 1990s appears to be a by-product of global economic restructuring, but this has been part of a restructuring produced by commands and controls emanating from the International Monetary Fund (IMF) and the Mexican state apparatus rather than from any urban "growth machine" deftly articulating the local with the global. A new cohort of individuals and households migrating from Mexico to Los Angeles includes growing numbers of urban working and middle classes and even some members of the entrepreneurial strata who were prompted to move to L.A. by declining living standards and growing income polarization in Mexico produced by a combination of the austerity policies of international banks, the Mexican debt crisis, and the conscious decision of Mexico's ruling political elites to meet this crisis by export-oriented neoliberal economic policies favored by the IMF.

These developments made it difficult for many households at all but the elite level to survive on the income they could generate within Mexico's borders. This in turn led to the formation of ever more binational households capable of tapping into the income-producing possibilities of cities like Los Angeles and the remittances generated by the transnational social networks they have forged. The recent collapse of the peso on global financial markets in the wake of Mexico's current political crisis of legitimation is likely to accelerate this process, regardless of tightened border controls. By proposing dual citizenship for its transnational migrants in the wake of California's Proposition 187 initiative, the Partido

Revolutionario Institucional (PRI) dominated Mexican state apparatus appears to be preparing for precisely such an acceleration on terms that would enable the Mexican economy to continue to benefit from remittances sent to Mexican households and communities from what PRI likes to call "Mexican communities abroad" while increasing the thus far limited political influence of transnational Mexican migrants in U.S. cities.

Ironically, in the case of the Los Angeles political economy, Mexican transnational migration is not the one-way "cash drain" constructed by anti-immigrant groups in the recent racial discourse surrounding the passage of Proposition 187. Rather, the goods and services consumed by this and other segments of the Mexican-origin population in Los Angeles clearly contributes to demand-driven employment in the city and region. Yet this grassroots dimension of the Los Angeles economy is given scant attention in either the popular media or the "L.A. as global city" literature.

When we turn from the case of Mexican migration to the other leading transnational migrant groups living in Los Angeles today we discover a different sense in which L.A. might be called a global city, although not one envisioned in the global cities scenario. Much of the transnational migration to Los Angeles from the 1970s until the 1990s is a legacy of the cold war and of the global reach of U.S. foreign policy over the past forty years. If you wish to call L.A. a global city in this sense, you would have to consider the national origins of the major transnational migrant groups, especially the refugee groups that have settled there in the largest numbers, and interrogate their relationship to the failures and successes of U.S. foreign policy since the 1960s. Next to Mexicans the nationality groups comprising the largest segments of L.A.'s multiethnic population have been Korean immigrants, Southeast Asian refugees, and massive numbers of people fleeing cold war–inspired violence in Central America, particularly in El Salvador and Guatemala. L.A. is now home to the largest concentrations of Koreans, Guatemalans, and Salvadorans outside their homelands. One-tenth of all Salvadorans in the world now live in the MacArthur Park district of L.A., drawn there by the still unmet promise of sanctuary, peace, and jobs. The largest concentration of Cambodians outside Pnom Phen now lives in the metropolitan L.A. city of Long Beach.[5] As these examples make clear, the global imperialist policies of the United States over the last forty years have come home to roost in the transnational migration streams that have reconstituted L.A.'s ethnic landscape. In this respect L.A. is clearly a "globalized" city. But this does not make it a "world city" poised to command and control let alone take advantage of the new growth dynamic of the putative "Pacific Rim Century" we are about to ring in.

The Local Legacy of Global Imperialism

The term "global imperialism" is used deliberately. Now that we have come to the end of the cold war, the bipolar global empire constructed by the U.S.–led West is in disarray. The present global geopolitical condition has been aptly termed "the New World Disorder." In this new postmodern context, the "end of empire" strikes me as a good way to characterize the current state of political-economic development in Los Angeles and the "legacy of imperialism" an apt metaphor for the current state of its racial and ethnic relations. The remainder of this essay will further examine the transformation of the social structure and economic base of Los Angeles over the past decade and a half and the ways in which its major racial and ethnic groups have moved into economic niches and residential and community roles that are at the heart of much social unrest, including the urban rebellion of 1992.

The case of Korean-American small business owners in Los Angeles and their structurally antagonistic relationship to African-Americans and political refugees from Central America is an especially intriguing case in point.[6] Following the stalemate produced by the Korean War, the U.S.–allied South Korean state exhibited an authoritarian political posture and a domination of political life by its military that is only now showing signs of changing. South Korean political and economic elites also pursued an export-oriented economic development strategy that produced economic growth and rapid urbanization of its population. By the 1970s the society was producing more upwardly mobile urban professionals than its economy was capable of absorbing or its political system was willing to incorporate. Many Koreans whose social mobility was blocked in their homeland chose to immigrate to the United States throughout the 1970s and 1980s. The occupational niches open to them in the U.S. political economy were limited since they often faced anti-Asian discrimination or possessed professional credentials that were not easily transferrable to the U.S. context. Using household capital or loans borrowed from ethnic associations, many of the Korean immigrants became small business owners in large U.S. cities. This was especially true in Los Angeles, which is home to the largest concentration of Korean immigrants and Korean-Americans in the United States.

The economic niches that Korean immigrants occupied in L.A. placed them in potentially antagonistic relationships with other minorities, e.g., as convenience store and liquor store owners in mixed black and recent low-income Mexican migrant neighborhoods such as South Central L.A., as sweatshop owners employing undocumented Salvadoran and Guatemalan workers in Koreatown, as landlords for the Central American residents of MacArthur Park, Koreatown (now predominantly Latino residentially), Pico Union, and even Hollywood, a declining locale that has long since given up its global "dream machine" aspects. Not surprisingly, the landlord-tenant, employer-worker, and merchant-customer conflict in Latino-Korean relations were played out with special vehemence in the targeted destruction of Korean business property in Koreatown, Hollywood, and other neighborhoods that were part of the L.A. uprising. This dimension of the L.A. rebellion was an expression of outrage by multiply marginalized Central American refugees and recent low-income Mexican migrants, whose exclusion from mainstream economic and political institutions has been so pronounced in L.A. that these "Latinos" even have been excluded by local Mexican-American politicians who, following the uprising, were quick to downplay Latino-Korean antagonism, pointing out that no one in the long-established Mexican-American neighborhood of East L.A. had looted or rioted.

As these examples illustrate, the movement of cold war–related migrants from former U.S. "colonies" to Los Angeles and their insertion into structurally antagonistic economic, residential, and commercial roles in L.A.'s sprawling posturban landscape widened and deepened the urban unrest unleashed by the Latesha Harlins and Rodney King verdicts. The result was hardly congruent with the expectations of cold war foreign and defense policy elites—the nation's latest large-scale, interethnic urban riots. What "came together" in L.A. was not a Pacific Rim multicultural melting pot but multiethnic class warfare.

Interestingly, in the aftermath of the L.A. rebellion it has become clear that unfavorable U.S. media representations of minority Americans are both a local and a global phenomenon. Even before L.A.'s cold war–related migrants came to U.S. shores, these hostilities were fueled by the endemic racism of U.S. culture and its global transmission abroad. As a result of U.S. military interventions over the past forty years, Hollywood films along with U.S. videos and television shows distributed overseas provided racist stereotypes of black Americans in advance to (South) Koreans and migrants from other former U.S. colonies. Thus, the absorption of antiblack attitudes into their conceptual repertoires by Korean and other cold war migrants often preceded actual local experiences with African-Americans. In the Korean-American case, the global deployment of these media images played a role in the construction of a local Korean-black cultural antagonism that hardened the structurally antagonistic social roles these two groups came to occupy in the Los Angeles political economy.

It is important to realize that the sea change in the social composition of L.A. described here was in part fueled by the lure of the cultural imaginary contained in the phantasmagoric images of daily life in L.A. that form the backdrop of many films and television shows exported abroad from Southern California as popular cultural products. Such products now constitute the nation's and L.A.'s second biggest export item after aircraft. Throughout the 1980s L.A.'s global image as "world city" was further crafted by globally transmitted media extravaganzas such as the 1984 Olympics, which together with the junk bond shenanigans of Michael Milken and the speculative building frenzy unleashed by the deregulated savings and loan industry coproduced the spectacle of Los Angeles as the quintessential site of Pacific Rim nouveau riche dynamism. Stoking the illusions fostered by L.A.'s commercial and residential "real" estate boom, the prevailing media hype fostered by local real estate capitalists depicted L.A. as the world's premier multicultural melting pot, a land of opportunity where it never rained and every day ended with a sunnier tomorrow.[7] Small wonder then that not only surplus Japanese capital but also foreign petty bourgeois entrepreneurs and many of the world's economically and politically dispossessed were drawn to this place, all dreaming of a better future.

The experiences of daily life encountered by these dreamers were far different from the media images. Precisely when the global migration to Los Angeles was accelerating, its economic foundations were under siege.[8] Since the 1970s Los Angeles has had its labor market opportunities restructured in ways that do not bode well for its future in the 1990s. L.A.'s economic restructuring has in part been driven by global developments and in part by the decline of the defense industry since the end of the cold war. The 1970s saw a sharp reduction in high wage manufacturing jobs as a possible avenue for upward economic mobility for the transnational migrants and refugees who were moving into Los Angeles at that time and at an accelerated pace in the 1980s. Whereas the city of Los Angeles was once the second largest auto assembly city in the United States, the last auto plant in the Los Angles region closed its doors in 1992. General Motors and Chrysler moved to Mexico. The same was true in other previously unionized, high-wage manufacturing sectors. For example, Uniroyal went to Brazil and Turkey; Motorola and Litton joined the move to Mexico.

Thus the deindustrialization of Los Angeles and its reindustrialization in a different form into nonunionized, low wage, sweatshop labor blocked one of the avenues that earlier decades of foreign born "immigrants" had used to move up in the American economic structure. It also moved substantial numbers of working class black males into the ranks of either low-paid service work or permanent unemployment. Reliable estimates place the direct high-wage manufacturing job loss in the Los Angeles economy at two hundred thousand from 1978 to 1989. These jobs were concentrated largely in the black and Latino south central area of Los Angeles that exploded in 1992. An indirect negative multiplier effect of these job reductions and plant closures was to force the local suppliers and small businesses connected to these industrial complexes out of business adding further to the employment crisis in Los Angeles.

A second wave of plant closures is now facing Los Angeles as a result of the end of the cold war. Major defense- and aerospace-related plant and base closures since 1989 have added to the employment crisis because of the Los Angeles region's dependency on the military budget as a central engine of economic growth. This is an important consideration when reflecting upon what is meant by a "global city." What are the engines driving a regional economy? How do they change over time? How are they affected by global development patterns, as well as national patterns of public policy? To the extent that we look at the transformation of the international political economy produced by the globalization of economic relations, L.A.'s current economic plight can be viewed as an adverse impact of global capital flight. To the extent that we also look at L.A.'s most recent round of decline as a direct result of shifts in national public policy following the end of the cold war, L.A.'s plight can be seen to be driven by policies designed to reduce defense expenditures. In either case, however, Los Angeles has been on the receiving rather than the sending end of global "commands and controls." Between 1989 and 1993, 240,000 jobs disappeared in Los Angeles County. As the cold war ended, the once seemingly recession-proof aerospace and electronics (and with them the construction and real estate) industries abruptly reversed course, contracting with alarming speed. L.A.'s rapid economic decline in the 1990s suggests that far from being a central cotter pin of Pacific Rim economic vitality, Los Angeles has become a kind of declining colonial outpost of national defense and procurement policy shifts over the past forty years.

In recent years the defense-related job transformation has been precipitous. In 1993 alone, 110,000 defense related jobs were lost to the L.A. economy; L.A.'s official unemployment rate was 10.4 percent. This high-wage job decline is likely to continue as defense cuts are expected to continue throughout the 1990s despite President Bill Clinton's symbolic efforts to compensate for the cuts by a federally subsidized high-tech development initiative focused on the state he needs to get reelected. For example, a California state government commission's cost-benefit study in 1992 estimated that although California accounted for 21 percent of national defense spending before the cuts in plant and base closures were initiated, it would receive only 12 percent of the benefits of military spending cuts. The study estimated that by 1994 California would lose 240,000 defense and industry jobs. By a more recent estimate, the city of Los Angeles's free-falling economy was expected to lose an additional fifty thousand high-wage defense industry jobs by the end of 1994. This is 50,000 in addition to the 110,000 lost in the previous year.

Compare these job loss figures with the anemic results of Los Angeles's five-year-old "enterprise zone" policy, which passes for a public effort to stimulate "economic development."[9] By early 1993 the tax breaks offered to lure investment into the inner city had produced a grand total of 837 jobs with only 159 of these in Watts, 157 in Chicano East L.A., and 220 in the central city zone. Worse still, not all of this handful amounted to new jobs as many of these "enterprise zone" positions were simply existing jobs in L.A. that had been moved around by employers to take advantage of tax breaks. Thus, the city's net effect was to become worse off. Because the tax breaks added to the billion-dollar shortfall in the L.A. budget, the city had fewer tax dollars and very few new jobs.

The Social Construction of "Local Economic Development"

The "real L.A. story" is not simply a local narrative of economic dependency and decline but a tale of uneven development. As already noted, L.A.'s growing global culture industry is now one of the city's leading export sectors as well as one of the sources of its attraction to global migrants. Two other sectors of L.A.'s political economy have continued to grow. The first of these growth sectors (at least throughout the 1980s before the defense collapse) has been advanced business services, a sector whose jobs have gone to yuppies and downtown business elites. The downtown investment nexus was driven by a combination of Mayor Tom

Bradley's urban development strategy and the availability of surplus capital Japanese industrial corporations were willing to move into a secondary circuit of global real estate speculation, which they are no longer willing or able to do given the current condition of the Japanese economy, to say nothing of the political crisis in Japan.

The mythology of Los Angeles cultivated by its leading civic boosters in the late 1980s mirrored the tropes of the global cities literature. L.A. was depicted as a dynamic city poised to take advantage of the capital accumulation possibilities offered by its time-space "locational advantage" as a Pacific Rim megapole in the emergent "Pacific Rim Century." As noted earlier, the media images of L.A. as the land of opportunity for entrepreneurs, multicultural melting pot, and last U.S. frontier for the globally adventurous added further to the image of L.A. as a global city. The net result of the conjunction of global media and capital flows and local boosterism in the 1980s was a shining new downtown and L.A.'s limited (and heavily subsidized by the state) new subway system. These postmodern urban forms were consciously designed by urban planners, as Mike Davis and others have shown, to exclude most ordinary people—particularly people of color—in yet another reenactment of the nineteenth century psycho-drama of the dangerous classes being kept out of the Central Business District (CBD) by a combination of robo-cops, twenty-first century surveillance technology, high prices, limited nonbusiness or tourist hotel services, and an exclusionary street design thus making downtown L.A. a truly walled city—a closed city at the core.

As it rose from the ashes of older urban spatial uses, a messianic social imaginary dripping with modernist nostalgia was deployed by developers portraying this exclusionary business and tourist zone as a crowning achievement of the "re-centering" of Los Angeles, an achievement in which all Angelenos could rightfully take pride. It is remarkable how rapidly the dominant social construction of the "real" L.A. has changed as Los Angeles faced the decline of global real estate investment and the end of the cold war. Such hyperbole has now all but disappeared from the political discourse on urban development in Los Angeles. In the face of downtown overbuilding, falling commercial and residential real estate values, the widening employment crisis, and a sharp decline in Japanese overseas investment in real estate ventures as rates of profit among Japanese industries declined. As the economy declined, the usual civic boosterist rhetoric began to ring hollow. Even the most rampant civic boosters fell silent in the aftermath of the L.A. rebellion.

The unabated assault on jobs in the defense sector and the meager results of the "Rebuild L.A." campaign punctuated by the resignation of four successive chairpersons of the reinvestment campaign were only the tip of the iceberg of an observable loss of nerve among L.A.'s corporate and real estate elites comprising the local "growth machine." Ironically, in the face of the disappearance of 240,000 private sector jobs in Los Angeles County from 1989 to 1992, the Los Angeles Chamber of Commerce responded to the employment crisis by laying off eight of its sixty staff, including its entire economic development department. It thus had moved from unbridled civic boosterism to despair and defeatism in four short years. This is not merely ironic but symbolic. It suggests that the move from a utopian to a dystopian image of Los Angeles is being internalized even by the sectors most actively responsible for L.A.'s economic development.

It is now clear that the local growth machine poorly mediated Los Angeles's global investments in real estate. National banking deregulation, unregulated growth, commercial overbuilding in L.A., and the savings and loan (S&L) scandal were closely intertwined. In L.A. downtown office space, fueled by the availability of Japanese and S&L capital, rose from 6.3 million to 33 million square feet during the 1980s. Overbuilding produced a 19 percent vacancy rate by 1992. Developers that could not fill their buildings could not pay back their real estate loans. Foreclosures on office buildings rose from $1.1 billion to $4.1 billion between 1988 and 1991. Subsequently, the region's savings and loan industry collapsed as desperate S&Ls tried to dump foreclosed properties at deep discounts. For example, the former headquarters of the now-defunct Columbia Savings in Beverly Hills, built in 1989 at a cost of $40 million, was sold for $2.8 million in 1992.

Real estate was further depressed in greater Los Angeles as the relocation of displaced aerospace and electronics engineers shrank demand for upper-middle-income housing. Defense downsizing also had a multiplier effect on the law firms, insurers, and financial institutions servicing defense contractors whose own staff cuts produced higher vacancy rates for downtown office space and further dampened housing demand. By 1993 the L.A. real estate bubble had burst and with it the confidence of L.A.'s local growth machine.

Contested Meanings of the "Ethnic Economy"

Globalization did, however, fuel a second significant growth sector in Los Angeles in the past decade that is still actively generating jobs, largely in the ethnic communities. This is the low-wage service and manufacturing sector—the restaurant, hotel, and domestic service workers—and the light manufacturing sweatshops, whose plant openings have been in poorly paid, nonunionized, highly competitive segments such as garment manufacturing and microelectronics assembly, largely in the ethnic economy.

What sense are we to make of the global-local interplay in L.A.'s "ethnic economy"? Whether the ethnic economy is viewed as separate from the mainstream economy or as intimately tied to it through subcontracting arrangements (a raging debate among economic geographers and sociologists!), one thing is certain—it does not pay its workers very well. It also tends to be heavily dependent on a new immigrant workforce and hence has not absorbed many of the workers displaced from other sectors, such as the downwardly mobile white-collar defense and aerospace engineers portrayed so chillingly in Michael Douglas's recent film *Falling Down*. For that matter, the "ethnic economy" has not employed many blacks.

Many of the people writing about the "ethnic economy," including many social scientists, have romanticized the entrepreneurial element in this kind of economic activity and its putatively beneficent consequences for local economic development. A new study published by Paul Ong, a planner at the University of California, Los Angeles, offers a balanced discussion of the costs as well as the benefits of the ethnic economy. Ong's study demonstrates that not all is well among some segments of the new Asian immigrant and refugee populations in Los Angeles. The entrepreneurial image of the ethnic economy has fostered the belief that the new immigrants who have come to Los Angeles, particularly from Asia, are fully employed, are contributing dynamically to the local economy, and will be easily absorbed in the next generation into the mainstream economy like earlier waves of immigrants. The ethnic economy is thus envisaged as a kind of temporary stepping stone, an opportunity to learn skills and to acquire social capital and develop human potential.

Ong's study, entitled *Beyond Asian American Poverty,*[10] reveals the following facts: more than 124,000 Asian-Americans live in poverty in Los Angeles County. Although this represents only a 13 percent rate for Asian-Americans as a whole, several Asian-American nationality groups, particularly those that are part of the cold war legacy such as recently arrived Southeast Asian refugees from Cambodia and Laos, have a rate of poverty of 45 percent. Vietnamese have a 25 percent poverty rate, Pacific Islanders 24 percent. Even the touted entrepreneurial Korean population has a 16 percent poverty rate. There are people who work in the new garment industry being produced by those who happened to own and manage "ethnic enterprises;" since they pay low, marginal wages, many new Asian immigrant workers become permanently ensconced in dead-end jobs in monolingual workplaces that impede them from learning English.

Compare these figures with the usual data we look at with respect to poverty. In L.A. the poverty rate is 21 percent for African-Americans. Thus Koreans as a whole are not that much less poor than African-Americans, and Southeast Asians have twice the rate of poverty of African-Americans in Los Angeles. As a further comparison, the poverty rate in Los Angeles is 23 percent for Latinos, which is actually slightly higher than the African-American rate. In contrast, only 7 percent of non-Hispanic whites are poor. Nevertheless, with the "falling down" phenomenon alluded to earlier, this rate is climbing. Many of the poor Asians who are working in the new sweatshops in the ethnic economy are part of the "working poor." The poor southeast Asian refugee families who remain eligible for some forms of public assistance are part of what has been labeled by some commentators the "new welfare poor." Taken together these two segments of the new Asian population of Los Angeles have experienced pervasive and widespread poverty among Asian-Americans, a category that is often stereotyped in the media as a "model minority," indeed an answer to the economic development agenda of Los Angeles. In light of these stereotypes it is well to remember that Immigration and Naturalization Service (INS) data for 1983 through 1986 show that although 43 percent of legal Asian immigrants in L.A. came from managerial, technical, and professional backgrounds, 36 percent previously occupied menial, labor-intensive jobs.

Many of the latter immigrants and refugees are living a marginal existence under virtually Dickensian conditions. Consider the following qualitative findings from Ong's study: "In conducting our survey, we found low income Asian families living in horrid conditions; small deteriorating back lot units, possible illegally converted garages and apartment buildings with trash lining dimly lit hallways." In Koreatown, the study found that "attractive exterior facades often hid desolate courtyards and corridors." It also found that one in four Koreans and Chinese in inner city Los Angeles live in poverty despite media-constructed images of both group's petty bourgeois status and economic success, which in turn stereotype the groups as a whole, ignoring class, social, regional, gender, and other internal divisions within each of the "new minorities" in Los Angeles's multicultural mosaic.

Moreover in many cases, the degree of poverty is severe; it is not just that people are slightly below the poverty level. Ten percent of Vietnamese, 12 percent of Pacific Islanders, and 16 percent of all Cambodians and Laotians in Los Angeles live on an annual income of $6,307, which is less than 50 percent of the poverty threshold. The irony here is that the fiscal crisis of the state and the urban fiscal crisis of Los Angeles have reduced public spending for English as a Second Language (ESL) programs and other English language acquisition opportunities. This is beginning to trap at least one generation of new immigrants in either underfunded welfare support or dead-end low-paying work. The cutback in spending for social reproduction under Presidents Ronald Reagan and George Bush included significant reductions in federal subsidies for bilingual education programs. The State of California's own budget shortfall for 1992 included an additional $2 billion cut in the state's support for public education in general at all levels and state support for bilingual programs in particular.

Some might argue that because "ethnic enterprise" does not require the ability to speak English, language is not a "real" problem. The ethnic enclave economy is depicted as a resource that puts one generation, that lost generation I am now discussing, in a holding pattern so that the next generation can move up. The reality is much more double-edged. Such firms in the ethnic economy, although they offer paid employment, cultural continuity, and a protected internal labor market in the face of exclusion and discrimination in the mainstream economy, still give little room for self-affirmation. Instead, they tend to offer workers low wages, no benefits, and sometimes consist of self- or family exploitation by marginal entrepreneurs who themselves have been excluded from other work venues. We have seen educated Korean professionals running liquor stores, mom-and-pop grocery stores, and sweatshops and acting as rentiers. It has not played out very well, to say the least.

The phrase "the exploited of the excluded" aptly designates the workers employed by those ethnic entrepreneurs who have been blocked from entering into mainstream economic roles because they are reserved for others or because they are excluded from lending institutions and cannot get sufficient credit outside their own ethnic group to move up. Among some segments of the exploited of the excluded interesting new forms of labor organization in the L.A. ethnic economy have emerged. For instance, Latino drywallers have successfully organized against Korean and other Asian entrepreneurs in that sector to improve pay and working conditions.[11] This type of collective action suggests that when there are ethnic differences between new immigrant workers and new immigrant owners, the possibility of grassroots mobilization is increased. In hyperethnic L.A., such mobilizations tend to ethnicize class conflict.

However many of L.A.'s new immigrant businesses exclusively employ coethnics. In these instances, the appeal by immigrant entrepreneurs to "shared ethnicity" has been used as a political resource to culturally depoliticize the resistance of the workforce. The irony is that the people working in these types of "enclave" businesses are worse off because they end up being doubly marginalized, exploited in conventional economic terms, and culturally manipulated into passivity. They have no exit except to acquire English language proficiency, no easy task in the face of the fiscal crisis of the city and the state and the anti-immigrant backlash in California that currently supports a referendum that would deny basic schooling to the children of undocumented immigrants.

When It All Fell Apart:
Social Reproduction in the "Global City"

In the 1980s L.A. was characterized by both high rents and high mortgages. Every year population increased more rapidly than housing supply producing a net annual shortfall, which also included the demolition of fourteen-thousand residential housing units for the creation of the new downtown. It doesn't take an economist to figure out that this combination was a driving force in increasing rents and producing a new class of what I would call the "underhoused." There is a significant homeless problem in Los Angeles, but there is an even larger new class of underhoused people living fifteen and sixteen to a room in shared residences. Some Southeast Asian refugees are living in garages. This condition of underhousing has not been deemed sufficiently newsworthy to make the nightly news, but any attack by a deinstitutionalized "aggressive panhandler" has been deemed worthy enough. These media exclusions and inclusions have become part of the social construction of homelessness in which the victims again and again are blamed for conditions that are not of their own making. Meanwhile the contextual story of the structural disparities between population growth and housing growth that have characterized Los Angeles for fifteen years never reaches the public forum.

The foregoing analysis is linked directly to the story of the fiscal crisis of Los Angeles.[12] As a result of the latest round of cuts in defense jobs along with the

general 1990s corporate strategy of downsizing and expanding only the unbene-
fited work sector, which accounts for the rising tide of temporary work, residential real estate values in many areas of Los Angeles have become a kind of free-
falling expression of panic. Mortgage foreclosures had been rising throughout the
early 1990s; this exacerbated the fiscal crisis of Los Angeles already hard-pressed
by the downgrading of taxable property values produced by the property destroyed in the L.A. uprising. By 1993, the City of Los Angeles's municipal budget
deficit had reached $500 million, a figure reaching half the estimated property
damage in the uprising. The L.A. public school deficit in 1993 reached $400 mil-
lion. If these two figures are added together, just the general operating activities
of government in Los Angeles in terms of providing public education and other
basic services caused a revenue shortfall almost equal to the property loss produced by the L.A. rebellion. At the county level, by mid-1995 the Los Angeles
County government faced an additional $1 billion budget deficit. County ad-
ministrators' proposed solution was to "solve" the fiscal crisis by closing down the
Los Angeles County–University of Southern California Medical Center, one of the
nation's largest public hospitals. Not surprisingly, the chief loser in this contested
closure would be L.A.'s poor, who make up 40 percent of the hospital's patients.[13]

It is not surprising, in light of L.A.'s history of hypersegregation, sharp class divisions, and fragmented geography, that white middle-class Angeleno taxpayers
are simply unwilling to finance the Los Angeles Unified School District, a district
in which by 1992, 64 percent of the students were Latino, 14 percent were black,
and many of the most recent students were Southeast Asian refugees. The Los
Angeles Unified School District spends $4,187 per pupil on its public schools in
comparison to the $7,300 per pupil spent in the equally multicultural and fiscally
distressed New York City public schools. In light of the prevailing political climate
and the disproportionate voting strength of the white electorate, teachers in L.A.
public schools grudgingly took a 10 percent pay cut in 1993.

Falling property values and the fiscal crisis have only added to the white middle-class insecurity already at high levels because of all the economic restructuring and the virtual disappearance of well-paid, stable employment opportunities.
In the context of the L.A. rebellion the "falling down" phenomenon has become
racialized in the forms of "white panic" evident in record gun sales, panic real estate selling, and the media's social construction of the consequences of the L.A.
"riots." In the Los Angeles mass media, reports of declining tourism, foreign investment, and the urban fiscal crisis are often linked to if not blamed on bleak assessments of the aftermath of the "Rodney King riots." The reportage speaks as if
the urban uprising rather than long-term structural transformations and antecedent global economic crisis produced the economic decline so apparent in
Los Angeles today. Lost in this formulation is the racialized character of the declining employment opportunity structure and the chronic underfinancing of
public services because of fiscally conservative white electoral power. Controlling
for population size there are currently 1.3 police officers in Los Angeles for every

5 in New York City thus contributing to the LAPD policy of policing by terror tactics rather than by neighborhood policing. If white Angelenos, who are tax-payers, were willing to tax themselves as much as New Yorkers do, police brutal-ity suits against the City of Los Angeles would be less likely and perhaps the Rodney King episode would never have occurred. In any case, the white reactions are unfortunately predictable—more white flight, white panic, and frenzied weapons purchases. They reflect a desire to get out before "things gets worse." Following the earthquake of January 1994, this bleak mood has become almost apocalyptic. There has been an almost overreaction to the failed boosterist tropes that were prevalent in Los Angeles poised as a global city, as a world city, and as a city on the Pacific Rim on the rise and on the move. Los Angeles is now a city that is in decline and despair, on the verge of disaster, and in free-falling collapse.

A friend of mine from New York City who is a close friend of the wife of a major Hollywood director of TV situation comedies told me this story: After the last disaster—the earthquake of January 1994—this affluent Angeleno said she was moving back to her roots in the South. She said she was sick of being in Los Angeles because she thought the people there suffered from a "collective death wish." As if her rhetoric were not hyperbolic enough, some academic commenta-tors actually have been more excessive. Among them historian Kevin Starr re-cently predicted that L.A. was on its way to becoming the "Yugoslavia of American cities." I have penned this essay in the hope of preventing history from actually materializing out of the metaphors that fall from historians' lips. Unlike earth-quakes, cities and their race, class, gender, and ethnic relations are socially pro-duced, politically mediated, cognitively understandable, and historically modifi-able human creations—for better or worse.

NOTES

1. Michael Peter Smith and Joe R. Feagin, eds., *The Capitalist City: Global Restructuring and Community Politics* (Oxford: Blackwell, 1987), chapters 1 and 4; see also Michael Peter Smith, *City, State and Market* (Oxford: Blackwell, 1988), chapters 8 and 9.

2. The closest approximation to this conceptualization is to be found in the work of Saskia Sassen. See her works *The Global City* (Princeton: Princeton University Press, 1991) and *The Mobility of Labor and Capital* (Cambridge: Cambridge University Press, 1988). For a broader formulation of world cities that nonetheless includes L.A. in a list of major world cities largely in terms of its economic place in a global network of cities see the seminal essay by John Friedmann and Goetz Wolff, "World City Formation: An Agenda for Research and Action," *International Journal of Urban and Regional Research*, Vol. 6, No. 2 (1982): 309–339. The work of the self-described postmodern geographer Ed Soja has most explicitly represented L.A. as a world city, in part because of the global cultural reach of its film industry, a subject, as my subsequent discussion suggests, worthy of serious analysis in its own right. Nevertheless, for Soja it is the "progressive globalization of its political economy" and not its impact on global popular culture that makes L.A. "perhaps the epit-

omizing World City." The quotation is from p. 256 of citation 3 below. For further elaboration of this theme see Soja's major work *Postmodern Geographies* (London: Verso, 1989).

3. Ed Soja, "Taking Los Angeles Apart: Some Fragments of a Critical Human Geography," *Society and Space* Vol. 4 (1986): 259.

4. Kenneth J. Garcia, "State's History of Intolerance to Immigrants," *San Francisco Chronicle* (December 28, 1994): A13. My discussion of Mexican migration to Los Angeles has been informed by conversations with my colleague Luis Guarnizo.

5. For documentation of these trends and the class and income composition of these new migrant groups see Manuel Pastor, Jr., et al., *Latinos and the Los Angeles Uprising: The Economic Context* (Claremont, CA: Thomas Rivera Center, 1993); Paul Ong, et al., *The Widening Divide: Income Inequality and Poverty in Los Angeles* (UCLA Graduate School of Architecture and Urban Planning, 1989); Mike Davis, "Burning All Illusions in L.A.," in Don Hazen, ed., *Inside the L.A. Riots* (New York: Institute for Alternative Journalism, 1992): 97–100.

6. The subsequent discussion of this antagonism draws upon Michael Peter Smith and Joe R. Feagin, "Putting 'Race' in Its Place," in Michael Peter Smith and Joe R. Feagin, eds., *The Bubbling Cauldron: Race, Ethnicity and the Urban Crisis* (Minneapolis: University of Minnesota Press, 1995), chapter 1. See also Sumi K. Cho, "Korean Americans vs. African Americans: Conflict and Construction," in Robert Gooding-Williams, ed., *Reading Rodney King—Reading Urban Uprising* (New York and London: Routledge, 1993): 196–211; Peter Kwong, "The First Multicultural Riots," in Don Hazen, ed., *Inside the L.A. Riots* (New York: Institute for Alternative Journalism, 1992): 88–93; and Susan K. Lee, "Koreans in America," *Crossroads* (July/August, 1993): 17–18.

7. See Kenneth J. Garcia, "After Years of Boom, Los Angeles Hits Skids," *San Francisco Chronicle* (December 21, 1992): A1, A8.

8. The following discussion of the economic restructuring and defense downsizing of Los Angeles draws upon the following sources: James H. Johnson, Jr., Walter Farrell, Jr., and Melvin Oliver, "Seeds of the Los Angeles Rebellion of 1992," *International Journal of Urban and Regional Research* (1993): 115–119; James H. Johnson, Jr., Cloyzelle K. Jones, Walter C. Farrell, Jr., and Melvin Oliver, "The Los Angeles Rebellion: A Retrospective View," *Economic Development Quarterly,* Vol. 6, No. 4 (November, 1992); Paul Ong, et al., *Beyond Asian American Poverty* (LEAP Asian Pacific American Policy Institute, 1993); Vlae Kershner, "State May Suffer from Defense Cuts Throughout the 90's," *San Francisco Chronicle* (October 7, 1992).

9. My discussion of ineffectual local economic development policies, downtown overbuilding, and the subsequent S&L debacle draws upon the following sources: Eric Mann, "Los Angeles—A Year After (I): The Poverty of Corporatism," *The Nation* (March 29, 1993): 406–411; Kenneth Garcia, "After Years of Boom, Los Angeles Hits Skids," *San Francisco Chronicle* (December 21, 1992): A1, A6; Calvin Sims, "Who Said Los Angeles Could Be Rebuilt in a Day," *New York Times* (May 22, 1994): 5. For interesting historical background on this and other dimensions of the political economy and culture of Los Angeles see Mike Davis, *City of Quartz* (London: Verso, 1990).

10. The next several paragraphs rely on information contained in Ong's study. The full citation is Paul Ong, et al., *Beyond Asian American Poverty: Community Economic Development Policies and Strategies* (Asian Pacific American Public Policy Institute, 1993). Ong's cogent critique of the sociological concept of the "enclave economy" is valuable as

is his thorough documentation of the social composition of L.A. Asian-Pacific population. Another useful source is Yen Le Espiritu, "Immigration and the Peopling of Los Angeles," in Gerry Riposa and Carolyn Dersch, eds., *City of Angeles* (Dubuque: Kendall-Hunt, 1992): 67–82.

11. Mike Clements, "Drywallers' Strike Nails Down a Principle," *Los Angeles Times* (November 16, 1992): B7.

12. For elaboration of the issues raised here see the following: Seth Mydans, "Black and Hispanic Groups Battle over Schools Post in Los Angeles," *New York Times* (October 5, 1992): A12; Seth Mydans, "Separateness Grows in a Scarred Los Angeles," *New York Times* (November 15, 1992): 1, 19; Jane Gross, "Los Angeles Schools: Hobbled and Hurting," *New York Times* (February 16, 1993): C–11; Robert Reinhold, "Rebuilding Lags in Los Angeles a Year After Riots," *New York Times* (May 10, 1993): A1, A10; and Arthur M. Louis, "Mortgage Foreclosures Still Soaring," *San Francisco Chronicle* (December 9, 1993): D1.

13. Seth Mydans, "Los Angeles Official Seeks to Close Major Hospital," *New York Times* (June 20, 1995): A8.

3

The (Trans)National Basketball Association: American Commodity-Sign Culture and Global-Local Conjuncturalism

DAVID L. ANDREWS

Although somewhat unwarranted, it would nevertheless be true to say that the sociology of sport community is hardly renowned for the intellectual rigor and incisiveness of the debates engaged within its distinctly neglected domain. And yet, over the past few years, there has been an ongoing and highly sophisticated discussion within the field, focused on the relationship between sport and globalization.[1] This substantial body of work has critically and imaginatively borrowed from a variety of disciplines (e.g., sociology, economics, cultural studies, communication studies) in order to further the understanding of the complexities and influence of the global cultural economy's intrusive sporting armature. Were it not for the ghettoization of the sociology of sport as a whole, which restricts the extent to which research has been circulated within the academic community, the energetic dialogue on sport and globalization would have significantly informed wider domains of critical inquiry. Although it is not my intention to provide a critical overview of this literature, I would like to recognize it as the starting point of this discussion. More specifically, I became intrigued with the role played by globalized sporting culture in the construction of national cultural identities and experiences, a thematic that has been the focus of a number of pieces of important sociology of sport research.[2] As a consequence, within this

An earlier and much abbreviated version of this chapter was presented, in conjunction with Steven J. Jackson, at "America's World; The World's America," Fulbright American Studies Conference, University of Otago, Dunedin, New Zealand, July 1995.

chapter, it is my intention to further this problematic by developing a preliminary[3] analysis of the global structure and local influence of the National Basketball Association (NBA) as a transnational corporation whose global ubiquity inevitably contributes to the hyperreal remaking of local identities.[4]

According to some commentators, the globalizing logic currently reshaping the world economy has been engineered by developments in communications technology—specifically the triumph of instantaneous and depthless televisual networking—that have created a global marketplace in which boundaries of space and time have collapsed. The decentering of cultural spaces and places has purportedly facilitated the emergence of a standardized globally shared culture. This simulated cultural space and experience (largely, but not exclusively, driven by the machinations of American mediated popular culture) is seemingly vindicated by the universal presence of commodity-signs[5] such as the National Basketball Association, Cable News Network, Coca-Cola, Sony, *Baywatch*, Benetton, *Beverly Hills 90210*, McDonald's, the Disney Corporation, and even *Married with Children*, to name but a few. Although it would be erroneous to deny the global ubiquity of this ever-expanding economy of cultural artifacts, it would be equally fallacious to suggest that an increased circulation of commodity-signs leads to the creation of globally homogenous patterns of popular cultural existence. Rather, it is important to acknowledge the cultural dialectic at work in relation to globally intrusive texts and practices and their influence upon the production of local identities and experiences. Within contemporary culture it should not be overlooked that the consumption of global commodity-signs not only takes place within, and is therefore contingent upon, the complex specificities of localized settings, but also, at the same instance, the *local* can only be seen as a "fluid and relational space, constituted only in and through its relation to the global" (Robins 1991, 35). Given the fact that this "globally variable synaesthesia has hardly ever been noted . . . [and hence] . . . demands urgent analysis" (Appadurai 1990, 300), my aim within this chapter is to examine how the NBA has been fashioned into an explicitly American and increasingly global media(ted) institution, which inevitably contributes to the conjunctural (re)articulation of *local* identities and experiences.[6]

Reclaiming the Game

In order to decipher the NBA's contemporaneous global presence and influence (Weir, 1993), it is first necessary to provide a brief genealogy of the NBA over the past fifteen years. During this period the league was transformed from being perceived as a problematic and increasingly unpopular cultural space into becoming viewed as an integral aspect of the American popular cultural landscape, where it subsequently attained the status of a familiar feature of the global cultural economy. According to E. M. Swift, the NBA has become "an innovative, multifaceted, billion-dollar global marketing and entertainment company whose future literally knows no bounds" (Swift 1991). As remarkable as it may seem to those of us presently being asphyxiated with rampant NBA overload, in the years immediately preceding its merger with the American Basketball Association in 1977, the newly consolidated NBA was at an all-time low in terms of image and economics, according to Charles Grantham, former executive director of the NBA Player's Association (Voisin 1991, F1). The league's problems came to a head during the 1980–1981 season when only seven of the NBA's twenty-three franchises made a profit, average game attendance totaled 10,021 or about 58 percent of the capacity of the league's arenas, and the total league attendance fell over 1 million from the previous year (Swift 1991, 78). Such were the NBA's problems that the league's commissioner, David Stern, later admitted the goal at this time "was to get through the day. Then we expanded it to the week" (Heisler 1993, C10).

The NBA was severely hampered by its popular perception which invaded, and was circulated within, both public and private spaces. At the root of the league's identity crisis were the domineering presence of African-American athletes, and the racist pathologies that had historically been articulated to black masculinity that were now engaged within the context of professional basketball. African-American players, even those such as Kareem Abdul-Jabbar and Julius Erving, who dominated the league, were habitually labeled as being lazy, lacking motivation, irresponsible, flashy, selfish, and overpaid (see Blount 1979; Cady 1979; Moran 1979). However, the NBA's "image crisis" (Cady 1979) was most virulently fueled by the reactionary codes, mobilized by the popular media, that conflated racial identity with criminal deviance. As E. Kiersh graphically summarized, "As recently as the early 1980s, the sport was in disgrace. Many advertisers saw the NBA as a drug-infested, too-black league with dwarfish Nielsen ratings. Major corporations wanted no part of this game. Magic Johnson or James Worthy might sign a low five-figure sneaker deal, but that was it. Sponsors felt the NBA and its black stars had little value in pitching colas and cornflakes to Middle America" (1992, 28).

Perhaps the most influential and damaging[7] statement relating to the problems of the NBA came from Chris Cobbs's article "NBA and Cocaine: Nothing to Snort At," which appeared in the Los Angeles Times on August 19, 1980. Cobbs engaged in a shameless and none too subtle piece of reactionary scaremongering that used the much-publicized drug problems of exclusively African-American players (Bernard King, Terry Furlow, and Eddie Johnson) as irrefutable evidence of the problems of endemic drug abuse being directly related to the problem of having a league in which 70 percent of the players were African-American (Cobbs 1980, 1). In the rhetoric of the burgeoning discourse of the American New Right, an NBA embodied by threatening black masculine "enemies from within" represented a distinctly un-American, and hence unpopular, public space which seemed destined for removal from the inventory of national popular sporting institutions. Few could have predicted the rise of the NBA and the challenge it would pose to football and baseball's American sporting hegemony by the end of the 1980s.

There are many reasons for the NBA's stunning metamorphosis during the 1980s, including the implementation of measures that were seen to proactively address the league's problems. On a structural level these included the installation of an accusatory antidrug policy, the establishment of collective bargaining between owners and players, and the subsequent enforcement of a salary cap (Staudohar 1989). Added to this was the timely emergence of a new generation of outstanding players, vanguarded by Earvin "Magic" Johnson and Larry Bird, which pointed toward the possibility of renewed prosperity for the league. However, on a semiotic and perhaps even more significant level, the popular rearticulation of the NBA was engineered through the revolutionary way in which the league's administrators, guided by the NBA Commissioner David Stern,[8] creatively exploited the expanding channels of the promotional media to revitalize the game's image and popularity. Stern can be considered an innovator because he clearly possessed a tacit understanding of, and subsequently acted upon, the fact that American culture had become a "civilization of the image" (Kearney 1989, 1). Hence Stern's goal was to turn the NBA into one of the popular commodity-signs that had usurped the material economic commodity as the dynamic force and structuring principle of everyday American existence (see Baudrillard 1988a; Clarke 1991; Featherstone 1991). This was achieved by an aggressive restructuring of the NBA from an archaic professional sport industry focusing solely on the league's properties and administration, to a multifaceted marketing and entertainment conglomerate incorporating more than twenty divisions, including NBA Properties, NBA Entertainment, NBA International, and NBA Ventures. By securing prime-time television exposure on the major networks, regular billing on the expanding cable networks, and by developing in-house promotional programs, commercials, and prerecorded videocassettes, Stern immersed the NBA in the "all engulfing dynamic of [televisual] promotion" (Wernick 1991, 185) which dominated postindustrial America. Thus during the 1980s the NBA made an epic journey from the commodity to the terminal as television transformed this aberrant sporting product into an ubiquitous commodity-sign system within today's "electronically-mediated consumption communities" (Luke 1991, 1). The televisual armatures of the promotion industries reframed the meaning of the NBA to add positive meaning to this commodity-sign (Goldman 1992, 5–8). In doing so, the NBA became a hyperreal circus whose simulated, and hence self-perpetuating, popularity seduced the American masses and resulted in the league inalienably becoming a site of positive investment within the popular consciousness.

Basketball, perhaps more than any other of America's major sports, was in a position to benefit from technological and creative advances made in the television industry. This was because the game possesses a fast-paced telegenic quality that "fits into today's remote-control, MTV world, with its fast-forward, hip-hop pace. There are no lulls between pitches, no game-stopping huddles" (Weir 1993, 1A). As Russ Granik, deputy commissioner of the NBA gleefully opined, the fact that the game is fast paced makes it attractive to young people, something which also attracts advertising dollars from major corporate sponsors all vying to secure a segment of the disposable income of America's youth market, which in turn makes it a successful product for commercial television. Moreover, unlike other sports, "It's also a very accessible sport. The athlete's face—and emotions—aren't shielded by a helmet as it is in football" (Moore 1994, 1B). The high visibility of the individual players facilitated by television coverage of basketball proved a pivotal factor in the rise of the NBA. As Josh Rosenfeld (one-time NBA director of international public relations) indicated, televised basketball almost demands focusing on the "player's up-close expressions, which makes them instantaneously recognizable" to their television audience, and hence it is almost inevitable that "personally cults" will be fashioned around the NBA's "visible heads" (1994). Hence, by aggressively marketing the game, its franchises, and most importantly an economy of highly personalized commodity-signs from within its player personnel, the NBA strategically used the televisual domain to seductively engage popular consciousness (see Lee, 1993). As Gary Alan Fine noted, "What sports needs, and what the NBA has very successfully developed . . . is a coterie of players that fans can relate to. Not just Magic Johnson the player, but Magic Johnson the person. Not just Larry Bird the player, but Larry Bird the person. Even if we don't know them, we feel we know them" (Voisin 1991, F1). Like Disney before it, the NBA became a commodity-sign, an imaged commodity that created, and is in turn nurtured by, a phantasmagorical cast of simulated characters. David Stern freely admits—indeed he celebrates—the similarities between the NBA and Disney: "They have theme parks . . . and we have theme parks. Only we call them arenas. They have characters: Mickey Mouse, Goofy. Our characters are named Magic [Johnson] and Michael [Jordan]. Disney sells apparel; we sell apparel. They make home videos; we make home videos" (Swift 1991, 84).

And yet it would be negligent to overlook the fact that the NBA's strategy of creating an economy of personalized commodity-signs, which would resuscitate the popular signification of the league, was structured according to domineering logic and impulses of Reaganite racial politics.[9] Among other things, Ronald Reagan's "friendly face of fascism" (Harvey 1990, 330) was a political project that sought to deny the existence of differential racial (primarily African-American) experiences and hence racism, to justify the savaging of the welfare system. Indeed, during the early to mid-1980s, the cultural hegemony of the New Right was such that any statement of racial affiliation, identity, or experience, was deemed distinctly radical and un-American. As Reagan himself enunciated when perversely appropriating the figure of antislavery activist, Harriet Tubman, to further explicate his colorblind vision of American society, "Tubman's glory was the glory of the American experience. It was a glory which had no color or religious preference or nationality. It was simply, eloquently, the universal thirst that all people have for freedom" (1982, 575). This politics of racial ignorance removed race and racial discrimination from the political agenda and inevitably led to the exacerbation of differential racial experiences in education, employment, medicine, and housing and thus to increasing "problems of social dislocation in the inner city" (Wilson 1987, 22). In doing so, it none too subtly reinforced the aspirations, achievements, and ascendancy of America's white middle class, which was celebrated either directly or indirectly in almost every facet of American popular culture. Having emerged as nationally recognizable figures during the late 1970s, a time when the New Right was gaining mass exposure and popularity,[10] it was almost inevitable that the imaged personalities of Larry Bird and Magic Johnson should be articulated in accordance with the racial imperatives of the New Right's cultural politics.

Larry Bird's very existence—he was after all widely touted as basketball's version of the Great White Hope[11]—and Magic Johnson's endearing and nonthreatening black style and smile were both profitably massaged by the reactionary televisual domain. The material effect of the hyperreal circus that enveloped both Bird and Johnson was the remodeling of the NBA into a hyperreal popular cultural space that seemingly vindicated the simulated harmony of race relations upon which the New Right's policy of racial avoidance was founded.[12] An even more instrumental stage in the popularized racial reassamblage of the NBA into a viable commercial product centered on the production of Michael Jordan as an all-American icon—a process and phenomenon that harnessed and nurtured the racially acceptable semiotic space initiated by Bird and Johnson and ushered in an even more lucrative era of popular acceptance for the NBA.[13] In short, through the mutually reinforcing narrative strategies engaged by Nike, the NBA, and a multitude of other corporate interests, Jordan was constructed as a racially neutered (hence nonthreatening) black version of a white cultural model who projected, according to his agent David Falk, "an All-American image . . . not Norman Rockwell, but a modern American image. Norman Rockwell values, but a contemporary flair" (Castle 1991, 30). Jordan's racially transcendent image[14] was all-American precisely because, "To be an 'all-American' is, by definition, *not* to be an Asian-American, Pacific-American, American Indian, Latino, Arab-American or African-American" (Marable 1993, 113). In light of this and to an even greater degree than his immediate antecedent, Magic Johnson, Jordan became a commodity-sign devoid of racial integrity that effectively ensured the subversion of racial otherness (see Willis 1991, 108–132), but which also—because of his media ubiquity—further ensured the celebration of the NBA as a racially acceptable social and cultural space.[15]

The innovative, involved, and intertextual promotional strategy engaged by the NBA turned a racially stigmatized and struggling sports league into an energetic, expansive, and most significantly, popular American entertainment industry.[16] Such was the mass appeal of basketball that by the early 1990s it could justifiably sell itself as "a basic American pastime, as much a part of mainstream culture as baseball" (Lippert 1991, 10). Moreover, the hyperreal reconstitution of the NBA into a racially acceptable, and hence accessible, system of signification (see Lash

1990, 4–5) had profound material effects on popular consumption practices. This was evidenced by the stupendous rate of growth in the league's gross revenue as derived from ticket sales, television contracts, corporate sponsorship, and the retailing of licensed merchandise (see Helyar 1994; Swift 1991). In quantitative terms the NBA's gross revenue leapt from $110 million at the start of the 1980s to more than $1 billion by the end of the 1993–1994 season (Alms 1994, 1D).

Going Global

Although initially taking its lead from the successes, and more pertinently the failures, of both the National Football League and Major League Baseball, the NBA is now more aligned with and attuned to the corporations that dominate the entertainment marketplace. Hence David Stern admitted, "We're saying, 'What's Disney doing? What's Time-Warner doing?'" (Weir 1993, 1A). Having, in a similar fashion to both the Disney Corporation and Time-Warner, enthusiastically embraced and infused the various circuits of the promotional media that dominate contemporary existence within postindustrial America, the NBA is first and foremost an entertainment company that manufactures a phantasmagorical world of commodity-signed narratives and identities: triumphs and tragedies, successes and failures, heroes and villains. In other words, the NBA, its constituent franchises, and its ever-evolving economy superstar players have all been turned into intertextually fabricated popular icons through the increased circulation of televised game coverage, televised promotions, prerecorded videocassettes, books, magazines, CD-ROMs, and the extensive array of related sports apparel, all of which communicated the NBA's complex economy of commodity-signs to an avaricious American consuming populace. However, as well as imitating the major players in the entertainment industry in terms of flexible and diversified commodity-sign production, the late 1980s also witnessed the NBA seeking to copy the leviathans of the entertainment industry by developing a global market for its products, thus becoming a transnational corporate concern (see Robins 1991, 25–28).

To a large extent the NBA became a victim of its own success in the American market. By the early 1990s, and after almost a decade of stupendous expansion, the U.S. market had been saturated by NBA products and became relatively stagnant in terms of the all-important indicator of percentage annual growth as measured by game attendance, television audience, and retail sales figures (Helyar 1994). As Don Sperling, director of NBA Entertainment, stated in 1991, "Domestically, we're tapped. . . . Ratings have peaked. Attendance has peaked. The market here has peaked" (Voisin 1991). Soon after, David Stern warned:

> We don't want to become complacent, so we're going to fix it a little bit even if it isn't broken. In today's economy in the United States and the world, you've got to continually examine the way you do business, the audiences to whom you are trying to

appeal, the technology that affects you, the competition. . . . We certainly would like to stay where we are. But there's no way you stay some place good if all you do is try to make sure you stay entrenched. Unless you're constantly pushing forward, you're going to slide back (Moore 1992, 1B).

Having outgrown its home market, the NBA realized that sustaining its spiraling patterns of economic growth necessitated actively cultivating overseas markets, and in Stern's words, "There are 250 million potential NBA fans in the U.S., and there are 5 billion outside the U.S. . . . We like those numbers" (Comte 1993, 42). Pushing forward for the NBA meant deliberately evolving into a transnational, global corporation. As Stern forewarned, "Global development is a certainty— with or without us" (Heisler 1991, C1).

The transnational corporations that dominate the contemporary global economy represent the latest manifestation in the process of economic expansion initiated by the rise of merchant capitalism in the seventeenth century, which has seen the space of capitalism distended from the bounded confines of national, regional, and imperial structures to the unbounded global domain. In this sense, "Globalization is about the organization of production and the exploitation of markets on a world scale" (Robins 1991, 25). During each subsequent phase in this long-term capitalist project, increasingly complex corporate interests have sought to secure ever-larger economies of scale through the utilization of new productive practices and technologies involved in the creation and exploitation of expanding markets. Whereas the earliest phases in the process of commodity globalization were prompted by the economic impulses of English colonial/industrial expansion, the new commodity-sign globalization—what Stuart Hall (1991, 27) called the rise of a global mass culture—has largely, but by no means exclusively, been influenced by the interconnected technological, capital, and media flows emanating from the United States.[17] At least since the advent of the talking picture, and in a concerted fashion since the spread of television technology in the decades following the end of World War II, the various manifestations of America's media(ted) culture have increasingly made their presence felt on the world stage. The result has been the rise of an Americocentric telediscursive global vernacular advanced through the spread of post-Fordist regimes of commodity-sign production, circulation, and consumption. As Douglas Kellner indicated, America's commodity-sign culture is "exported to the entire world," and invades "cultures all over the world, producing new forms of the *global popular*" (1995, 5). The extent to which the circulation of universal American commodity-signs has resulted in the convergence of global markets, lifestyles, and identities has been the focus of contentious debate and will be discussed later in this chapter. However, it is hard to deny the fact that celebrated American commodity-signs, including the NBA and its hyperreal kingdom of franchised places and narrativized faces, have a vivid global presence. As Robert Alms commented, "U.S. sports is well positioned globally. From movies to music, American entertainment dominates the world. It's partly a matter of performers' talent, but there's also a large role for marketing savvy. It's not an accident that Mickey Mouse and Madonna are worldwide icons" (Alms 1994, 1D). Consequently, what needs to be addressed is the role played by marketing in the process that saw the NBA become "the world's hottest sports product" (Weir 1993, 1A).

The NBA triumphed in the United States because of the influence of the televisual media and explicitly that of the league's innovative promotional strategies. The NBA bombarded the American media with carefully scripted images that articulated basketball as an exhilarating, entertaining, and seemingly popular game. For example, David Stern provided strict guidelines for how games should be covered on television, which included always targeting areas where the seating was full to capacity when panning to shots of the crowd, the intention being to make it appear as if the stadium was overflowing with satisfied and enthusiastic customers, even though it may have only been two-thirds full (Swift 1991, 78). Through the use of creative television simulations, the NBA created a multitiered commodity-sign system designed to seduce the American public and stimulate popular demand for the game and its personalized effigies. In other words, David Stern "turned the NBA's Fifth Avenue headquarters into a star-making factory, creating new demand for the game and developing products and programming to satisfy it" (Helyar 1994, A1).

Despite the obvious pitfalls associated with his apocalyptic and technodeterminist conclusions, which position the individual subject as "a pure screen . . . a pure absorption and resorption of the influence networks" (Baudrillard 1988b, 27), Jean Baudrillard's implosive postmodernism makes important contributions toward the understanding of a culture in which "advertising, television, cinema, hoarding displays, crowd out the world to the extent that we related to them as the immediate context of reality" (Rojek 1990, 9). Although it is impossible, as Baudrillard would argue, to deduce whether the televisual promotion of the NBA had a conclusive influence on individual or collective action, it is equally impossible to ascertain what would have occurred without televisual promotion. Thus from a Baudrillardian viewpoint it is possible to characterize the promotional circus engaged by the NBA as an attempt to manipulate popular need and consumption by subjecting the audience to the anticipated verification of their behavior (Baudrillard 1985). Having been bombarded with television promotions, including those in which celebrity endorsers exalted the game ("I Love This Game!" "The NBA . . . It's Fan-tastic"), the NBA contributed to the formation of a world in which simulative projections of popularity have created a state of radical uncertainty with regard to individual desire, choice, opinion, and will (Baudrillard 1985). Given this, it would not seem unreasonable to assert that the NBA's shrewd manipulation of the promotional media both simulated and stimulated popular interest in the economy of commodity-signs associated with the league; a self-generating process of popular s(t)imulation that was arrestingly fueled by improved and increased game coverage, the mass circulation of an array of sign-laden ancillary merchandise, and the inauguration of a number of high-profile promotional events.

S(t)imulating the Global Market

For much of the postwar era, the celebrated spectacles of American sport had a remarkably anonymous presence in the rest of the world. Indeed, the only contact many people had with American football, baseball, or basketball was when inadvertently tuning in to the alien sounds of the American forces radio network, which brought a slice of sporting America to the U.S. military personnel stationed throughout the world. However, in recent times, the global time-space compression created by advances made in communications technology (see Harvey 1990; Lee 1993) has facilitated the rise of a global commodity-sign culture that is "dominated by the image which crosses and re-crosses linguistic frontiers much more rapidly and more easily and which speaks across languages in a much more immediate way. It is dominated by all the ways in which visual and graphic arts have entered directly into the reconstitution of popular life, of entertainment and of leisure. It is dominated by television and by film, and by the image, imagery, and styles of mass advertising" (Hall 1991, 27). Consequently, the hyperreal circus that is the NBA has taken on the structure, appearance, and influence of a global commodity-sign. This is evidenced by the fact that the NBA has been promoted as the premier dialect in the international language of sport (Weir 1993, 1A), and even the phenomenon of global compression has been illustrated through reference to the NBA, as the "world shrinks to the size of a basketball court and the global language of a thundering slam dunk" (Boeck 1990b, 1C).

Given the advent of this "age of instantaneous, global communication" (Baudrillard 1981, 177), the practice of stimulating popularity through the circulation of hyperreal televisual simulations was predictably replicated when the league's administrators sought to develop a global market for the NBA. As David Stern asserted, "Everything we do here [in the United States] . . . we can do there [in the global marketplace]" (Eskanazi 1989, 1). In true transnational fashion (Robins 1991, 27), the NBA's marketing strategies became consumer-driven (targeting particular market segments that span the globe, most notably the world's youth population) rather than geography-driven (targeting specific national or regional markets). This strategy keyed on an uncritical assumption of the lure held by American mass mediated culture over the youth populace around the world. According to David Stern's proselytizing narrative, which only partially obscured the avaricious way he eyed the potentialities of the global market, "We [the NBA] think that North American sports, properly done, can become a very interesting global export" (Alphen 1992, F3), primarily because "the NBA game is the thing. . . . It's an American original" (Whiteside 1992, 84). Such commentary betrayed the league's intention of cashing in on the millions of fans willing to buy into the excitement of American-style entertainment. . . . Sports leagues are discovering what Coca-Cola, McDonald's Corp., Disney Co. and the makers of Marlboro cigarettes figured out long ago: The trappings of America's consumer culture will sell overseas. Other countries are gaining more leisure time and higher incomes, and they represent a source of new revenues for sports teams at a time when the U.S. entertainment market is more crowded than ever and players salaries are skyrocketing (Alms 1994, 1D).

Referring back to a version of Baudrillard's argument regarding the influence of advertising, the questions of whether the global consumer is obsessed by the trappings of Americana per se or whether the global mass market is merely dominated by American commodity-signs, have largely been overlooked. Instead there exists a widespread assumption that particular cultural products, personalities, and experiences are universally popular simply because they signify America, and their consumption represents little more than a ritualistic celebration of America. Josh Rosenfeld, then NBA director of international public relations, expressed precisely this strain of Americocentric cultural conceit in his forthright assertion that "people in other countries . . . like the NBA because they want the American look and the American image. And that's what they get with the NBA . . . Americana, a piece of America" (1994).

In order to manufacture the transnational presence it coveted, the league formed an overseas division, NBA International. Peopled with specialists in business, marketing, and international relations, the NBA International's brief was to mobilize relevant media and commodity flows in order cultivate the league's visibility overseas, and thereby hopefully increase the revenue derived from the global consumption of televised games and licensed products (Boeck 1990a). NBA International is structured and organized around regional offices located in Geneva, Barcelona, Melbourne, Hong Kong, Mexico City, and Miami through which television and licensed merchandise deals are negotiated. In terms of television contracts, the majority have been signed with national networks in individual countries, such as the fifty-four-game deal recently signed with Television Azteca in Mexico. The NBA has also signed a number of strategically important regional deals with satellite and cable distributors such as Star, ESPN International, and Sky Sport. In total, by the start of the 1994–1995 season, the NBA was being broadcast in either one-hour, two-hour, or live game packages in 141 countries to an estimated audience of over 550 million households (see Hiestand 1994).

A key factor in the NBA's rapid emergence in Europe during the mid- to late 1980s was the changing structure and scope of television in the reciprocally changing European geopolitical formation. During the 1980s, many national television systems in Western Europe experienced dramatic deregulation because of the ascendance of neoconservative free market economics. The most marked manifestations of European deregulation was the severance of television from the control of national governments, and the ensuing expansion in the number of channels offered by national television systems. The number of available channels also increased as a result of technological advances made in the telecommunications industry, specifically related to cable and satellite technology, which allowed for the opportunity of almost unlimited expansion. An increased number of television channels necessitated an increase in the number of program hours to be filled. As Charles Jonscher, a London media consultant stated, "The deregulation of TV in Europe is creating an appetite for ready-made programming, some part of which is being filled by American sports" (Eskanazi 1989, 1). Thus American imports, including sport, became a staple part of Europe's new television schedule.

According to Weir, the NBA only became interested in the European television market because of interest shown by channels in Europe that sought games to include in their expanding television schedules (Weir 1993). The European interest in televising the NBA was brought to the league's attention by the interest shown by an Italian television executive, Bruno Bogarelli, who in the fall of 1982 indicated an interest in obtaining the rights to televise NBA games in Italy. He eventually bought sixteen games at a point in time when CBS broadcast only five games per season (Alms 1994). Once awakened to the interest of European television, NBA executives became keenly aware of the potential offered by the expanding television systems, for it was the league's exposure on America's expanding cable networks during the 1980s that proved a key component in popularizing the NBA. So NBA International sought to take advantage of the fragmented expansion of the European television market. As Stern announced, "Imagine owning the television rights to an exciting (basketball) program in an era where technology will be craving for such programming. . . . That's us. That's sports. So we are in pretty darn good shape going forward. We know how to market and we have extraordinary programming" (Alphen 1992, F3).

Clearly NBA International has used television as a seductive advance scout for the league by selling programming that "makes people aware of what the NBA is. . . . People aren't going to buy a Chicago Bulls hat unless they know what the Chicago Bulls is" (Rosenfeld 1994), builds familiarity with the major stars of the game, and generates a base of knowledgeable and interested consumers. However, it should not be overlooked that increasingly as the global market for the games matures, television contracts will represent an important source of revenue for the league. At an initial stage NBA International's goal with regard to national television contracts is "just to get on!" (Rosenfeld 1994), and minimal fees charged are levied for the rights to NBA coverage. Consequently, the programming is likely to be shown at a relatively unpopular hour. The aim is to spark interest within the television market and then when the time comes to renew the television contract, the league can levy a higher fee and demand a better time slot for the program. This is hoped to result in a larger audience for the program, which would once again allow the league to charge higher revenues—so the cycle continues. Consequently, in countries such as Spain, Italy, and Japan where the NBA has been on television for a number of years, the charges for NBA coverage are considerably higher than in countries such as the United Kingdom where the game has only recently gained a footing in the television schedule.

Although NBA events and games played overseas have become a fixture of the league's promotional calendar, at no point has there been any intention of setting up NBA franchises on foreign soil.[18] Thus, although Stern intimated, "We're really going to be going global. . . . We're not just in the sports business. It's media entertainment, licensing, brand names, home videos and a broad base of other businesses" (Alphen 1992, F3), Dave Checketts, president of the New York Knicks, expressed the league's global intentions more forthrightly: "I think we're just going to keep going [expanding overseas]. . . . Not for the purpose of selling teams, but to enhance licensing and TV packages" (Moore 1992, 1B). Hence, rather than colonizing the globe through franchise location, the NBA's simulated expansion was predicated on the media (in terms of images) and economic (in terms of commodities) dissolution of regional and national boundaries. This provided global citizens with ready access to the mutually reinforcing flows of globally prescient programming and products, which s(t)imulated a global demand for the NBA's economy of explicitly American commodity-signs. In other words, NBA International mobilized global channels of televisual communication and product distribution to recreate the league, its franchises, and players as being "everywhere [but nowhere] at once" (Robins 1991, 28).

Rampant Intertextuality

Up to this point it may seem that the NBA has projected itself as a transnational yet explicitly American commodity-sign solely through the global dissemination of televised game coverage. In actuality the NBA's global presence and signification, as with its rise to prominence within the American market, has been realized through the attendant circulation of an expansive economy of mutually reinforcing commodity-signs. Andrew Wernick ably captured this key concept of intertextuality in his illuminating discussion of the advertising industry: "More even than most textual constructs, ads precisely do not stand alone. It is not just that the discourse of promotion employs conventions and mobilizes values which are already embedded in the culture at large. In several respects, the meanings of ads are interdependent amongst themselves" (Wernick 1991, 92).

As Wernick intimated, the promotional dynamic of postindustrial society is prefigured on the inherent intertextuality of televisual discourse. Hence, within this promotional culture, the distinctions between programming and promotions are erased. One has only to watch NBC Sports's coverage of NBA basketball to realize this fact: "In an unprecedented move, NBC, a unit of General Electric Co., solicited advertisers first—and promised to feature them in the program about sports stars and ads if they would agree to advertise during the commercial breaks. Five took the bait, including Bristol-Myers Squibb's Nuprin and Upper Deck, as well as Coca-Cola, Hanes, and Nike" (Lipman 1991, B5).

Even in regular coverage of the NBA, the game, half-time feature, and many of the interspliced commercials are fashioned in light of, and hence designed to accentuate, the semiotic interdependence that drives contemporary culture. It is no coincidence that American corporate icons such as McDonald's, Miller Brewing, Coca-Cola, and IBM are high-profile sponsors of the league, or that Nike and Reebok habitually purchase commercial airtime during NBC's coverage during which it shows basketball-related campaigns. It should not come as a surprise to learn that as part of the recent $750 million four-year television contract signed with NBC, on an annual basis the NBA receives at least $10 million worth of strategic airtime which it uses to show its NBA Entertainment–produced *Inside Stuff* promotional vehicle, as well as the "I Love This Game" commercials, the "Stay in School" public messages, and the serial basketball campaign that featured Bill Murray (Goldman 1994).

Clearly (but perhaps somewhat preempting the discussion of global localization which follows in the concluding section) it should be recognized that the inalienable uniqueness of intertextually constructed commodity-signed cultures demands that, although increasingly constituted in and through global flows, local commodity-sign consumption and hence popular identity construction is necessarily contingent upon conjunctural specificities. In Julia Kristeva's terms, the complex sign value of the NBA as a signifier of American culture is intertextually constructed by intricate fields of transpositions of various signifying systems which are unique to their cultural location (Kristeva 1984, 59–60). Hence, not only does America signify different things in different sociocultural settings, so the precise signification and appropriation of the explicitly American NBA is equally context specific. Not only has this phenomenon been recognized by the NBA's administrators, and thus structures and directs the project of global expansion, it has also been identified as a key selling point for overseas (national, regional, and global) corporate sponsorships of the league. The television coverage sold by NBA International has been touted as offering an avenue for integrated, cross-national promotional campaigns: "Global consumer-products companies are torn between a variety of ways to reach consumers. . . . We're offering them one vehicle that does it all, that reaches a young and growing market base and that lends its own brand equity to theirs" (Grimm 1992, 20). In light of this a number of America's corporate icons have sought to enhance and refine their localized American identities in the global market by joining forces with the NBA. On a basic level such associations have been built around global, regional, and national corporate sponsorships, such as MasterCard, Coca-Cola, and Mars underwriting NBA coverage in the former Soviet Union, and "television barter deals" (Rosenfeld 1994). The latter are a result of NBA International's practice of negotiating for commercial time slots during the televising of its games when finalizing television contracts with particular networks. These commercial slots are then offered to the companies with global sponsorship deals with the NBA. This allows the NBA's corporate partners to engage in direct promotional campaigns linked to game coverage on a country-by-country basis. "If McDonald's was making a big push in Germany, then this system gives them the flexibility to do it, and the assurance that their commercials will be on at a time when their target audience is likely to be viewing. . . . For our audience is their audience" (Rosenfeld 1994).

Moreover, this practice allows both partners to benefit from the intertextual association derived from the proximity of two all-American commodity-signs. This is particularly the case when a global corporate sponsor chooses to develop advertisement campaigns that directly engage its connection with the NBA. Examples of this practice include McDonald's celebrated commercial in which Michael Jordan and Larry Bird play a game of horse for Jordan's lunch, and Coca-Cola's animated representations of NBA players "Always Jammin', Always Coca-Cola," both of which were shown around the globe.

Not only does the NBA benefit in terms of increased visibility and commodity-sign definition from the intertextual associations garnered through official sponsorship deals, its promotional strategies both in the United States and abroad are also aided and abetted by the promotional machinations of numerous basketball footwear and apparel companies, the most significant operators being Converse, Reebok, and Nike. During the latter half of the 1980s Nike developed its own economy of universal basketball personalities, as nurtured through globally circulated commercials such as the cool jazz fusion of *Jordan #23* and the harder rap edge of *Barkley #34*. Both these commercials were products of Nike Europe's creative advertisers, as was the humorous *Barkley of Seville* spot that debuted in 1992 and was designed to embellish the popular identity of this future member of the Dream Team, initially to a European but ultimately to a global audience. Charles Barkley was also the focus of another celebrated Nike commercial, the *Barkley versus Godzilla* spot, which was produced for a particular market (in this instance Japan) but which also gained universal renown. Although intertextually capitalizing upon the increased familiarity fostered by the NBA's accelerated global incursions, Nike's concerted commitment to developing a global market for its products through the televisual narration of basketball personalities proved of considerable mutual benefit to both Nike and the NBA. From Nike's viewpoint, Keith Peters, the company's director of public relations, admitted the company "almost probably" profited from the NBA's global presence (Peters 1994). In a more effusive vein Josh Rosenfeld declared, "That's the great advantage the NBA has, we have shoe companies. . . . They go out and market our players and our league for us. . . . Nike marketed Michael Jordan for us" (1994). More recently, Reebok has carried out the same function for the NBA with its aggressive global marketing of Shaquille O'Neal.

As the largest source of overseas revenue representing worldwide gross retail sales of almost $300 million during the 1993–1994 season (Anon 1994), the spread of NBA–licensed merchandise has had a significant impact upon the substantiation and reinforcement of the league's economy of popular American commodity-signs to the global popular consciousness. The NBA's is intertextually reinforced through the circulation of products such as caps, T-shirts, jackets, and a myriad of other items, all of which display one or more of the league's popular symbols, and hence act as material promotional tools for the league. "Through the ties which have developed between advertising, commercial media, and mass entertainment, the intertext of product promotion has become absorbed into an even wider promotional complex founded on the commodification, and transformation into advertising, of (produced) culture itself" (Wernick 1991, 95).

Another way through which the NBA has, in Wernick's terms, produced culture for the purpose of heightening the league's global popular presence and image was engaged by engineering promotional events such as exhibition games, tournaments, regular season games (in the case of Japan), coaching clinics, and celebrity tours that "bring everything together: the game, the players, the television, the corporate sponsors, the licensed merchandise, and the consumers" (Rosenfeld 1994).[19] The apotheosis of these intertextually manufactured and implicated spectacles came about as a result of the International Basketball Federation (FIBA) decision in April 1989 to allow professionals, most significantly NBA players, to play in international competitions organized by FIBA. This led to the appearance of what was universally labeled as the Dream Team at the 1992 Summer Olympic Games in Barcelona, a hyperreal basketball circus that proved to be the NBA's biggest overseas "marketing bonanza" (Alms 1994, 1D).

The NBA viewed the rabid media interest it had predicted would accompany the tournament as a pivotal chance to expand on the marketing strategies that the league had already put in place overseas. The selection of Dream Team players had more to do with the established global visibility of particular athletes than it was determined by fitness, desire, or playing performance. Hence an unwilling Michael Jordan and an unhealthy Larry Bird were cajoled into joining Magic Johnson as the high-profile triumvirate who would lead the NBA into a new era of global recognition (Heisler 1993). Although the increased global exposure brought about by the exploits of the Dream Team was expected, the NBA had not accounted for the scale of the phenomenon. As Rick Welts, president of NBA Properties, admitted, "I'd like to say I was smart enough to understand the real impact that the Dream Team would have, but I think it exceeded any of the most optimistic models. . . . I really think it's the single most important thing to happen to basketball. Markets that never really expressed an interest in basketball before were captivated by the Dream Team" (Moore 1992, 1B). According to Josh Rosenfeld, the Dream Team "opened up the world to the NBA" because "everybody watches the Olympics"; consequently, markets where the game had a distinctly anonymous presence became "fascinated with the NBA" (1994). As a result, this intertextually produced cultural spectacle helped realize the NBA's long-term goal of securing a popular global presence for and interest in the league, its franchises, and most significantly its players as seductive representations of American commodity-sign culture.

The Importance of (Not) Being American

As a result of its aggressive incursions into the global cultural economy, the NBA's commodified images and ancillary merchandise can be confronted with startling regularity when strolling through the commercial hyperspaces of many of the world's major cities, their habitually deindustrialized urban wastelands, or the materialistic excesses of their suburban fortresses. As Weir jingoistically enthused, "Try to imagine U.S. kids trading cards of sumo wrestlers, wearing T-shirts emblazoned with the faces of European soccer players or watching Spanish bullfighters pitch products in TV commercials. Never happen, right? But that's exactly the kind of impact Michael Jordan, Charles Barkley and their NBA colleagues are having on the rest of the world's youth" (Weir 1993, 1A).

Despite the superficial veracity of such statements, it would be a gross oversimplification to view the spread of NBA commodity-signs as being indicative of the establishment of a homogenous, primarily Americanized global culture. Continuing with this line of thought, I would argue against the irrational paranoia that has driven many critiques of global sporting popular. For instance, although providing an interesting and involved account of the disjunctive relations created by a British (sport) mediascape increasingly impacted by satellite television, Williams's pessimistic and overly deterministic understanding of popular cultural production overlooks the inherent complexities and contradictions that characterize the process and experience of globalization:

> Globalized popular culture (including the sports that are routinely taken from their localized cultural contexts and are flashed and carelessly and incongruously consumed across international global communication systems) function as a form of pervasive poetic discourse (Habermas 1987).

> This sinister discourse—a popular cultural or sporting "muzak"—creates the very least mediated universals through which peoples from the global core—and increasingly those from its periphery—communicate. The flattening out of cultural difference in postorganized capitalism seems to be a key product of the new global telecommunications economic order (Williams 1994, 377).

As Arjun Appadurai (1990) correctly pointed out, the paranoid discourse on global Americanization to which Williams alludes fails to account for the intricacies of postindustrial culture. Within the seemingly homogenizing impulses generated by the global circulation of products and images, ably exemplified by the machinations of the NBA, there lies a built-in particularity (or heterogeneity) in terms of how products and images are consumed. This is because the strangely decentered corporate multinationalism that distinguishes the postindustrial economy is founded on the flexible specialization of images as much as it is dependent on the flexible specialization of products; strategies that when combined are able to create local markets for globally circulated commodity-signs. When products, images, and services are exported to other societies from some mythical, simulated (American) homeland, to some extent they inalienably become indigenized and consumed according to the conjunctural specificities of the national culture in which the consumption is taking place.

According to Appadurai, the global cultural economy is a derivative of "the growing disjunctures between ethnoscapes, technoscapes, finanscapes, mediascapes and ideoscapes" (1990, 301). This complex and novel conceptualizing is informative for understanding the inherent tension between global homogeneity and local heterogeneity—between sameness and difference—and it would be naive to deny the significance of any of his overlapping categories. However, for the purposes of identifying the global circulation and local articulation of the NBA, I will concentrate on the notion of multifarious local/global landscapes of images (or mediascapes) centered around the NBA that are created in the conjuncturally specific disjunctures within and between ethnoscapes, ideoscapes, technoscapes, and finanscapes. These mediascapes are intertextual economies of mediated signs that offer suggestive representations of reality out of which consumers formulate the understandings and identities that substantiate their own experiences out of similarity and difference to the lives of others. In this sense, mediascapes can be seen as being both the products and producers of the shifting scapes characterizing the global configuration. Borrowing from neo-Baudrillardian discourse, Appadurai thus identifies mediascapes as providing

> large and complex repertoires of images, narrative and "ethnoscapes" to viewers throughout the world, in which the world of commodities and the world of "news" and politics are profoundly mixed. What this means is that many audiences throughout the world experience the media themselves as a complicated and interconnected repertoire of print, celluloid, electronic screens and billboards. The lines between the "realistic" and the fictional landscapes they see are blurred, so that the further away these audiences are from the direct experiences of metropolitan life, the more likely they are to construct "imagined worlds" which are chimerical, aesthetic, even fantastical objects, particularly if assessed by the criteria of some other perspective, some other "imagined world" (1990, 299).

Different contexts are necessarily structured according to the historical, cultural, political, economic, and technological specificities of the locale in question. The unique morphology of these different scapes shapes the collective consumption of the intertextual mediascape because there exist "very different sets of contextual conventions that mediate their translation" into public spaces (Appadurai 1990, 300). As a result the global consumption of products, images, and experiences is a "process of profound unevenness" (Hall 1991, 33), which can initiate a variety of responses ranging from a defensive localism that attempts to resurrect national cultural identities before they are asphyxiated by the threat of creeping otherness, to a more expansive localism which tries to "live with, and at the same moment, overcome, sublate, get hold of, and incorporate difference" (Hall 1991, 33).

Although Hall is primarily interested in the representational rediscovery of the postcolonial other within British society, as it is expressed in the flourishing "languages of the margin" (Hall 1991, 34), it is possible to view the postindustrial global formation as being a context in which localized identities are being engaged, challenged, and perhaps redefined by the increased visibility of the simulated American other; as embodied by the commodity-signs of an insurgent global mass culture, in this case the commodified and visual representations of the NBA.

Such is the intrusion of global commodity-sign culture that the NBA has reached far beyond the boundaries of what Scott Lash and John Urry labeled "the core [of contemporary global culture] . . . the heavily networked more or less global cities . . . 'a wired village of non-contiguous communities'" (1994, 28). For instance, a Chicago Bull's cap has been identified as an accessory for a number of members of Lash and Urry's nonwired global periphery, including a Greek fisherman, a Somerset grandfather, and a remote New Zealand sheep farmer.[20] Although it would be unwise to assume these peripherally located consumers (to use Lash and Urry's conceptualizing) were fully cognizant with the dominant meanings associated with the Chicago Bulls within contemporary America (successful NBA team, the team on which Michael Jordan played, etc.), it would be equally erroneous to deny that these consumers were not to some degree aware that the very style of the caps and/or the symbols stitched on to them represented an expression of cultural difference; in this particular case, they signified America. However, the mere consumption of American commodity-signs cannot be equated with the Americanization of local cultures. Whether or not the American sign-value of a Chicago Bulls cap, or any other NBA commodity-sign, is prized or wholly inconsequential to its use-value the mere tacit recognition of national cultural difference is significant to local consumers—both core and peripheral—of the global popular. Only through recognizing difference, in this case a notion of the American cultural other, does it become possible to distinguish—through varying degrees of opposition—the cultural self. In this way, it could be argued that the accelerated circulation of American commodity-signs in the postwar era has not only produced a circulation of global cultural products and practices, it has lead to the rearticulation of national and local cultural identities.

According to Lash and Urry (1994, 305), postindustrial companies often function in ways that undermine the hyperreal mediated national cultural identities formulated within the equally simulated national boundaries established by the broadcasting systems of many postwar nation-states. Evidently, the NBA does not conform to this practice. Rather than contributing to the dissolution of local and identities through the establishment of a homogenous global culture, the NBA represents a globally expansive media company that, although a product of pervasive global processes, is nonetheless responsible for energizing multiple popular and local cultures, which in Lawrence Grossberg's terms have a nonnecessary relationship to dominant but increasingly unstable national cultures (see Grossberg 1992). Global advertising and promotion is the key technology in the construction of this global mass culture that is simultaneously homogenous in terms of the commodity-signs being circulated and heterogenous in terms of the way these commodity-signs are consumed. According to Appadurai, "The globalization of culture is not the same as its homogenization, but globalization involves the use of a variety of instruments of homogenization (armaments, advertising techniques, language hegemonies, clothing styles and the like), which are absorbed into local political and cultural economies, only to be repatriated as heterogenous dialogues" (1990, 307). Unlike many other multinational corporations that engage in an operational strategy known as global localization in an attempt to blend into the local culture and effectively become a part of the indigenous ethnoscape,[21] the NBA explicitly promotes itself as a signifier of cultural difference. It is through its exaggerated American identity that the league is able to appeal to local consumers, many—but not all—of whom are explicitly looking for commodity-signs that embody difference and otherness. As Simon Barnes noted, "American-ness remains the prime selling angle for any American product: fizzy drinks, burgers, a sport, a Chicago Bulls cap to wear bill-backwards" (1994). Consequently, the NBA's inverted rendition of global localization revolves around *not* becoming an accepted armature of the local culture but remaining and retaining a sense of the cultural difference upon which much of the league's popularity is grounded. Far from downplaying the otherness of the NBA, the league consciously develops the authentic NBA experience as an authentic American experience, which is necessarily fundamentally different from the indigenous practices and experiences of the locale in question. As Rick Welts reiterated, "We are by definition an American sport. . . . We are not going to be French in France" (Alms 1994, 1D).

The NBA's global diffusion of contemporary Americana has not resulted in the fashioning and flattening of the globe "into a low-level monoculture, a gigantic KMart with no exit" (Buell 1991, 1), for the precise articulation of the NBA is as fluid and diverse as the 141 countries to which the league beams its game coverage (see Alms 1994; Hiestand 1994). Although the essential hyperreality of contemporary culture has meant that America is everywhere but nowhere at one and the same time, the popular signification of America, and hence that of American cultural products and practices, is necessarily contingent upon the unique complexities of national cultural conjunctures (Webster 1988). Put another way, America has and will continue to mean different things to different people in different cultural and historical settings. This is precisely the sentiment expressed by Lash and Urry:

> It is necessary to take into account not only the global processes of production but also the circumstances in which cultural products are received by audiences. Global programmes, even like *Dallas,* are read differently in different countries and places. Audiences possess skills in reading and using programmes, through talk in households and workplaces and through use of the VCR. At the level of audiences it is inconceivable that there could be global culture. Indeed in some respects there is an increasing contradiction between centralized production (at least in some respects) and more decentralized and fragmented reception (1994, 308).

In light of this local/global heterogeneity, it was wholly predictable that NBA administrators should have identified that the league's overseas reception is characterized by a lack of uniformity: "Every country is different, a different response from every country" (Rosenfeld 1994). Given the constraints of this chapter, which is after all intended to be an introductory overview of the global-local nexus as it pertains to the NBA, it is my intention to conclude with a brief empirical contrast that exemplifies the conjunctural localization of global commodity-sign consumption.

Beginning with the United States (which surely cannot be overlooked in discussions of the popular production and consumption of global commodity-signs) over the past fifteen years, like much of America's mediated popular culture the NBA has been transformed into a neoconservative disciplinary spectacle, which reinforces the reactionary discourses of America's *new* New Right.[22] Despite pockets of resistance in terms of how the league and its players are appropriated by members of the African-American community, to a large extent the popular media has been successful in fabricating a representational economy around the NBA, which seductively articulated a dominant, yet regressive, popular consciousness in terms of a very specific racial, class, sexual, and ultimately national cultural politics. The various NBA success stories (individual, team, league, and national) are not commonly lauded and viewed as indicators of African-American achievement, which is somewhat perplexing given the racial composition of the league.[23] Instead they are articulated as American successes. More pertinently perhaps, blame for the NBA's recent image problems has been apportioned against the assumed representatives of the very same population demonized by American neoconservatism as being responsible for the nation's widely perceived decline: the brash, aggressive, irresponsible, and unruly young urban black male (Taylor 1995). Through the seemingly contradictory strategies of racial avoidance, displacement, caricature, and stigmatization the NBA's administrators have successfully neutered the league's racial complexion and have created a racially nonthreatening product they deemed would be marketable to the all-important, mythic but incontrovertibly white, middle American. Hence the popular articulation of the league and its coterie of superstars, the phenomenon of the Dream Team, and even the "I Love This Game" campaign are as much a celebration of the racial arrogance, ignorance, and avoidance of the post-Reaganite American nation as they are promotions for the NBA itself.

In Britain the NBA has begun to be produced and consumed in a way that displays both similarities and differences to the articulation and appropriation of the league in the United States, which clearly mitigates against the existence of uniform patterns of global commodity-sign consumption. Although distinctly absent from the British media until the immediate past, the television, newspaper, and magazine coverage of the NBA has recently been elevated to a new level. After a number of years of haphazard programming, Sky Sport (a satellite channel) obtained the exclusive rights to NBA games for the 1994–1995 season and will show

seventy games mostly in the form of two-hour highlight packages. Daily newspa-
pers cover the game with increased interest, and a weekly basketball newspaper
Slam Dunk entered the market in November 1994. Added to this there are a number of NBA–related magazines that appear sporadically, plus the aggressive promotional campaigns of the NBA, as well as corporate accomplices such as Nike,
Reebok, and Converse, all of which has significantly increased the NBA's visibility in the British market. According to the ironically named John Nike, the owner
of the Thames Valley Tigers (a team in Britain's Budweiser League), "The kids in
the inner cities have caught on to the style and fashion of the National Basketball
Association and are copying everything that they see" (Liston 1994, 17). In 1990s
Britain, as in the United States, the very term "inner city" is used as a euphemism
for black, which in a British context predominantly refers to the sizable groups of
people of Afro-Caribbean and Indian or Pakistani descent that can be found in
most urban communities. Nevertheless, it would be true to say that the growing
presence and popularity of satellite television has sparked a groundswell of popular interest in the NBA, particularly among Britain's black population. As
Williams noted, "The recently retired NBA basketball player Michael Jordan is a
near-mythical sports figure in the U.S., but also in Britain. He is especially popular among inner-city black youth" (1994, 392).

   Although the NBA's popularity among the black populations of both the
United States and Britain can largely be attributed to the relative dearth of alternative representations of successful, charismatic, and exciting people of color in
the popular media as a whole, the scenarios differ when it comes to the dominant
articulations of the game.

   As previously outlined, in the United States the NBA has been strategically promoted in such a way as to downplay and overlook the vast overrepresentation of
African-Americans in terms of player personnel, so the NBA appeals also to the
white hegemony in the American marketplace. In stark contrast, within a British
context the game has been promoted as a celebration of American blackness,
which has in its various manifestations provided a significant touchstone for
British youth culture over the past forty years, through solemn adoption, ironic
appropriation, or outright rejection. In his populist account of the rise of British
"hoop fever," Sven Harding places the NBA within the latest, intertextually fabricated phase in the British importation of American blackness:

> Ask British sport fans their opinion of basketball a few months ago, and they would
> probably have told you that it was a stupid "Yank" game, played by a bunch of ridicu-
> lously lanky guys in vests, running about a school gym trying to throw a bouncy rub-
> ber ball into an old wastepaper basket nailed to a notice board. Now, thanks in no
> small part to the hip, street-cred link between rap and basketball culture, vibrant
> gangster-action-packed basketball-themed movies like *Above the Rim* and *White Men
> Can't Jump,* and the fact that in some inner cities it is (understandably) cooler to wear
> a Chicago Bulls cap than a Manchester United shirt, it looks like the blinkers are fi-
> nally coming off. And there's a new school of moneyed entrepreneurs, visionary

coaches and fiercely ambitious players poised to cash in with their souped up, music-heavy, MTV-influenced version of the game (1995, 50).

Evidently, in Britain the NBA is being promoted to appeal to a particular market segment—the ever-style-conscious youth population—as a marker of cultural and racial difference. Again this provides a glaring contrast when positioned against the racial avoidance, displacement, caricaturing, and stigmatization that distinguishes s(t)imulated popular appeal of the NBA in the United States. Through the concerted linkage of basketball with other manifestations of black American culture, and indeed with pertinent representatives of black British culture such as the reggae star Maxi Priest and the Arsenal and England football player Ian Wright—who, for a Nike endorser, displays refreshing candor when tackled on sensitive issues (see Liston 1994, 17; Williams 1994, 392)—it could be argued that, however unwittingly, the popular presence of the NBA is contributing to Stuart Hall's (1991) goal of rediscovering the postcolonial other within British society, a cultural and racial other that has for so long been silenced by the lingering racism of British imperial discourse. Although it would be foolhardy to uncritically acclaim one facet of what is after all a highly exploitive postindustrial capitalist system while condemning another, it does seem that the conjunctural articulation of the NBA in Britain provides a better chance for developing more progressive, complex, diverse, and politically appropriate popular representations of black masculinity than those that currently proliferate in the United States.

As well as representing fruitful avenues for further inquiry, the contrast between the localized articulation of the NBA in the United States and Britain exhibits the inherent variety and dynamism of (global) popular cultural production and consumption. Immersing Tony Bennett's (1986) instructive definition of popular culture within a more global context, it is thus possible to identify the global popular as representing those forms and practices that vary in content and signification from one historical period to another and from one national cultural context to another. Keeping with Bennett's theorizing, the global popular "constitute[s] the terrain on which dominant, subordinate and oppositional cultural values and ideologies meet and intermingle, in different mixes and permutations, vying with one another in their attempts to secure the spaces within which they can become influential in framing and organising popular experience and consciousness" (1986, 19). By developing an understanding of the global popular as a context that potentially provides opportunities for the establishment of both progressive and reactionary practices and regimes of signification, one can see the importance of a globally oriented cultural studies. This critical pedagogy would attempt to provide a more adequate knowledge and understanding of the global popular. It is hoped that understanding the global cultural economy and its processes would inform popular practice in such a way as to allow people to formulate their own strategies of resistance against the exclusionary practices that continue to infect contemporary societies both from global and local contingencies (see Hall 1990). Hence if the expanding domain of critical cultural studies is to be true to its political roots and is to continue to respond to "new historical articulations, new cultural events, changes in the tempo and texture of social life, new structures of social relationships and new subjectivities" (Grossberg 1989b, 415), a thorough interrogation of the global popular (something admittedly only barely initiated within this chapter) would appear somewhat overdue.

NOTES

1. See the *Sociology of Sport Journal,* 1994, vol. 11, no. 4, which is exclusively focused on the theme of sport and globalization and provides an invaluable overview and critique of the research within this area.

2. For examples of this body of research see: Harvey and Houle 1994; Houlihan 1994; Klein 1991; McKay, Lawrence, Miller, and Rowe, 1993; Maguire 1993a, 1993b, 1994; Rowe, Lawrence, Miller, and McKay 1994; and Sabo 1993.

3. This chapter represents an introductory overview (admittedly focusing primarily on the European context) of a much larger project currently being developed, which examines patterns and practices of material and interpretive consumption related to the NBA in the United Kingdom, Japan, Poland, and New Zealand.

4. Hyperreal in the sense that the effusive global circulation of images, which characterizes the postindustrial economy, has created simulated worlds—what Appadurai referred to as "mediascapes" (Appadurai 1990, 207–236). These mediascapes incorporate simulated, hyperreal, narratives against which the understandings of national/cultural/ethnic self and otherness are defined—understandings that provide the basis for negotiating identities and structuring experiences of the material world.

5. The preoccupation with the use and exchange value of a commodity, so characteristic of the modern era, has been superseded within conditions of postmodernity by the importance of a commodity's sign-value (hence commodity-sign) as it is fabricated by the domineering promotional industries. According to Robert Goldman (1992, 37), citing Debord 1977 and Lefebvre 1971:

> A commodity-sign joins together a named material entity (a good or service) as a signified with a meaningful image as a signified (e.g., Michelob beer/"good friends"). Though people have invested objects with symbolic meanings for thousands of years, the production and consumption of meanings associated with objects has become institutionally organized and specialized according to the logic of Capital in the twentieth century. Commodity relations systematically penetrate and organize cultural meanings in the interest of extending the domain of exchange values. In our "society of the spectacle" or the bureaucratic society of "controlled (sign) consumption" the linguistic unity of a signifier and signified is systematically split to fashion a commercially viable language of appearances and images.

6. This notion of (re)articulation is taken from exponents of post-Marxist cultural studies, who go beyond but do not wholeheartedly abandon Marx's dialectic historical materialism. According to this school of thought, "An articulation is thus the form of the connection that can make a unity of two different elements, under certain conditions. It is a

linkage which is not necessary, determined, absolute and essential for all time" (Hall 1986, 53). The practice of articulation develops Raymond Williams's (1981) understanding of culture as a signifying system through which the human agents make sense of their world and produce meanings through which the social order is communicated, explored, experienced, reproduced, and contested. It also accounts for the perpetual dynamism of cultural existence, for articulation implicitly involves the "production of contexts, the ongoing effort by which particular practices are removed from, and inserted into, different structures of relationships" (Grossberg 1989a, 137).

7. This article was both influential and damaging because, as well as informing subsequent pieces in the print media, it also provided the impetus and background for a cloned feature story which appeared on the CBS television's *Nightly News* of August 19, 1980. Hence, this inherently problematic argument reached and was potentially internalized and circulated by a sizeable audience.

8. David Stern has been commissioner of the NBA since February 1984 when he succeeded Larry O'Brien. Prior to this he had been the executive vice president and worked closely with O'Brien in instigating reforms.

9. Given the constraints of this paper I cannot give adequate time to a discussion of what is one of the key elements of the New Right cultural politics that continues to blight everyday existence in contemporary America. However, I can direct the reader to a number of important discussions of racial politics within post-Reaganite America, including Clarke 1991; Dent 1992; Denzin 1991; Giroux 1994; hooks 1992; Jhally and Lewis, 1992; Kellner 1995; and McCarthy and Critchlow 1993.

10. As evidenced by Ronald Reagan's successful presidential campaign in 1979, which occurred in the same year as both Bird and Johnson vied against each other for the National Collegiate Athletic Association (NCAA) Championship and were drafted into the NBA.

11. Given the popular racial imperatives mobilized by Bird's college career, it was hardly surprising that many looked to this "white superstar" as a potential savior of the NBA's debilitating racially absolutist image (see Anderson 1979; Cady 1979; and Levine 1988).

12. For discussions of the importance of Larry Bird and Magic Johnson to the rescuing of the NBA in the early 1980s see Cole and Denny, 1995; and Andrews, 1996.

13. For an extended discussion of this topic see Andrews 1994; forthcoming a; forthcoming b; Cole 1995; and Cole and Andrews, forthcoming.

14. As with many other people of color who become accepted by the popular media, the notion of Jordan as a figure who transcends race (and indeed sport) was certainly a common theme, voicing as it did the strategic evacuation of race that characterized the Reagan Revolution. For example, see Kirkpatrick 1987; and Wideman 1990.

15. Although the popular signification of Jordan as a racially neutered icon has dominated his prolonged tenure at the forefront of the media spotlight, a series of racially oriented subthemes have challenged his all-American aura. Discursive epidemics keying on Jordan's physical prowess, his predeliction for gambling, and the reasons for his father's brutal murder have periodically drawn Jordan's imaged personality into the racist diatribes that continue to dominate the popular media's depiction of African-American males. Moreover, in a Derridean sense, the very subversion of Jordan's racial identity—coupled with the attendant demonization of the stereotypical African-American other—evidence the fact that within the racist ideologies that permeate contemporary American society, race (and indeed racism) is *always already there*. For extended discussions of the com-

plexities of popular racist ideology as it pertains to the mediated construction of Michael Jordan see Andrews, 1996; and Cole and Andrews, 1996.

16. It should be noted that with the imaged persona of Jordan as its semiotic locus, the NBA has evolved into a promotional circus of diverse individualized representations of African-American masculinity (ranging from David Robinson to Dennis Rodman, via Charles Barkley) structured in true semiotic fashion "according to the relations and contrasts of both the syntagmatic and paradigmatic axes" (Gottdiener 1995, 7). This embodied economy of racial signs provides the focus for a larger project currently being developed by C. L. Cole and the author.

17. The notion of multiple flows within the global cultural economy is borrowed from Appadurai's (1990) important piece "Disjuncture and Difference in the Global Cultural Economy"; however it should be pointed out that the understanding of these flows having their primary locus of influence in the United States was borrowed from Hall.

18. The NBA seems more than willing to expand into lucrative markets within continental North America, as evidenced by the granting of franchises to Toronto and Vancouver, which entered the league in the 1995–1996 season, and also by the aggressive courting of Mexico City as a target for the next wave of expansion.

19. Such promotional events staged by the NBA include the McDonald's Open, which originated in 1987 and vies an NBA team against a European team. The first McDonald's Open was held in Madrid, with subsequent competitions staged in Paris, Rome, Barcelona, and Munich. The event is now scheduled every other year to fit in the schedule between the Olympic Games basketball competition and the FIBA Basketball World Championship Tournaments, held every four years.

20. These are just a few of the numerous examples where the author has encountered the NBA in what could be perhaps considered as unexpected locations.

21. Kevin Robins describes companies such as Sony and NBC as practicing an operational strategy of global localization, which, as an NBC vice president described it, recognizes that developing as a global corporate concern "is not just about putting factories into countries, it's being part of that culture too" (Robins 1991, 35).

22. For an interesting and insightful discussion related to the contemporary popular media's function of creating disciplinary spectacles, see Reeves and Campbell 1994.

23. According to the Center for the Study of Sport in Society's *1994 Racial Report Card* (Lapchick and Benedict 1994), African-Americans represent 79 percent of NBA player personnel.

BIBLIOGRAPHY

Alms, R. (1994, November 1). Globe trotters: NBA takes a world view of marketing. *Dallas Morning News,* p. 1D.

Alphen, T. V. (1992, January 22). NBA czar forecasts big exports for sports. *Toronto Star,* p. F3.

Anderson, D. (1979, October 25). About the all-black Knicks. *New York Times,* p. D21.

Andrews, D. L. (1994). Michael Jordan: A commodity-sign of [Post]Reaganite times. *Working Papers in Popular Cultural Studies, 2*(1), 1–50.

Andrews, D. L. (1996). The fact(s) of Michael Jordan's blackness: Excavating a floating racial signifier. *Sociology of Sport Journal, 13*(2), 125–158.

Andrews, D. L. (forthcoming b). Just what is it that makes today's lives so different, so appealing? Commodity-sign culture, Michael Jordan, and the cybernetic postmodern body. In C. L. Cole, J. W. Loy, and M. A. Messner (Eds.), *Exercising power: The making and re-making of the body.* Albany, NY: State University of New York Press.

Anon. (1994, July 11). Licenses to thrive. *Daily News Record,* p. 10.

Appadurai, A. (1990). Disjuncture and difference in the global cultural economy. *Theory, Culture & Society, 7,* 295–310.

Barnes, S. (1994, October 21). The cream on sport's American pie starts turning sour. *The Times.*

Baudrillard, J. (1981). *For a critque of the political economy of the sign.* St. Louis: Telos.

Baudrillard, J. (1985). The masses: The implosion of the social in the media. *New Literary History, 16*(3), 577–589.

Baudrillard, J. (1988a). *America.* London: Verso.

Baudrillard, J. (1988b). *The ecstasy of communication.* New York: Semiotext(e).

Bennett, T. (1986). The politics of the popular and "popular" culture. In T. Bennett, C. Mercer, and J. Woollacott (Eds.), *Popular culture and social relations,* (pp. 6–21). Milton Keynes, England: Open University.

Blount, R. (1979, February 5). Let's put life into the N.B.A. *New York Times,* p. C4.

Boeck, G. (1990a, October 10). NBA expands its horizons. *USA Today,* p. 2C.

Boeck, G. (1990b, October 10). NBA players find fortune in Europe. *USA Today,* p. 1C.

Buell, F. (1991). *National culture and the new global system.* Baltimore: Johns Hopkins University Press.

Cady, S. (1979, August 11). Basketball's image crisis. *New York Times,* p. 15.

Castle, G. (1991, January). Air to the throne. *Sport,* pp. 28–36.

Clarke, J. (1991). *New times and old enemies: essays on cultural studies and America.* London: HarperCollins.

Cobbs, C. (1980, August 19). NBA and cocaine: Nothing to snort at. *Los Angeles Times,* p. III:1.

Cole, C. L., and Andrews, D. L. (1996). "Look—Its NBA *Showtime!*": Visions of race in the popular imaginary. *Cultural Studies: A Research Annual, 1*(1) pp. 141–181.

Cole, C. L., and Denny, H. (1995). Visualizing deviance in post-Reagan America: Magic Johnson, AIDS, and the promiscuous world of professional sport. *Critical Sociology, 20*(3), 123–147.

Comte, E. (1993, June 7). How high can David Stern jump? *Forbes,* 42.

Debord, G. (1977). *Society of the spectacle.* Detroit, MI: Black & Red Press.

Dent, G. (Ed.). (1992). *Black popular culture.* Seattle: Bay Press.

Denzin, N. K. (1991). *Images of postmodern society: Social theory and contemporary cinema.* London: Sage.

Eskanazi, G. (1989, April 9). U.S. sports heading overseas: Pro leagues in America eye the globe. *New York Times,* p. 8:1.

Featherstone, M. (1991). *Consumer culture and postmodernism.* London: Sage.

Giroux, H. A. (1994). *Disturbing pleasures: Learning popular culture.* New York: Routledge.

Goldman, R. (1992). *Reading ads socially.* London: Routledge.

Goldman, K. (1994, November 17). Bill Murray "retires" to shoot for the NBA. *Wall Street Journal,* p. B10.

Gottdiener, M. (1995). *Postmodern semiotics: Material culture and the forms of postmodern life.* Oxford: Blackwell.

Grimm, M. (1992, November 16). The marketers of the year: David Stern. *Brandweek, 20.*

Grossberg, L. (1989a). The formations of cultural studies: An American in Birmingham. *Strategies*(2), 114–149.

Grossberg, L. (1989b). The circulation of cultural studies. *Critical Studies in Mass Communications, 6*(4), 413–420.

Grossberg, L. (1992). *We gotta get out of this place: Popular conservatism and postmodern culture.* London: Routledge.

Habermas, J. (1987). *The philosophical discourse of modernity.* Cambridge, England: Polity Press.

Hall, S. (1986). On postmodernism and articulation: An interview with Lawrence Grossberg. *Journal of Communication Inquiry, 10*(2), 45–60.

Hall, S. (1990). The emergence of cultural studies and the crisis of the humanities. *October, 53,* 11–23.

Hall, S. (1991). The local and the global: Globalization and ethnicity. In A. D. King (Ed.), *Culture, globalization and the world-system.* London: Macmillan.

Harding, S. (1995, February). Towers of power. *Loaded,* 50–53.

Harvey, D. (1990). *The condition of postmodernity: An enquiry into the origins of cultural change.* Oxford: Blackwell.

Harvey, J., and Houle, F. (1994). Sport, world economy, global culture, and new social movements. *Sociology of Sport Journal, 11*(4), 337–355.

Heisler, M. (1991, October 18). Uncommon marketing, *Los Angeles Times,* p. C1.

Heisler, M. (1993, June 13). The NBA. *Los Angeles Times,* p. C10.

Helyar, J. (1994, February 11). The inflated riches of the NBA are pulling at the league's seams. *Wall Street Journal,* pp. A1, A4.

Hiestand, M. (1994, December 13). NFL clears way for in-stadium highlights shows. *USA Today,* p. 3C.

hooks, b. (1992). Representing whiteness in the black imagination. In L. Grossberg, C. Nelson, and P. Treichler (Eds.), *Cultural studies,* (pp. 338–347). London: Routledge.

Houlihan, B. (1994). Homogenization, Americanization, and creolization of sport: Varieties of globalization. *Sociology of Sport Journal, 11*(4), 356–375.

Jhally, S., and Lewis, J. (1992). *Enlightened racism: The Cosby Show, audiences, and the myth of the American dream.* Boulder, CO: Westview.

Kearney, R. (1989). *The wake of imagination: Toward a postmodern culture.* Minneapolis, MN: University of Minnesota Press.

Kellner, D. (1995). *Media culture: Cultural studies, identity and politics between the modern and the postmodern.* London: Routledge.

Kiersh, E. (1992, March 22). Mr. Robinson vs. Air Jordan: The marketing battle for Olympic gold. *Los Angeles Times Magazine,* p. 28.

Kirkpatrick, C. (1987, November 9). An orbit all his own. *Sports Illustrated,* 82–86.

Klein, A. (1991). *Sugarball: The American game, the Dominican dream.* New Haven, CT: Yale University Press.

Kristeva, J. (1984). *Revolution in poetic language.* New York: Columbia University Press.

Lapchick, R. E., and Benedict, J. R. (1994). *1994 racial report card.* Boston: Northeastern University's Center for the Study of Sport in Society.

Lash, S. (1990). *Sociology of postmodernism.* London: Routledge.

Lash, S., and Urry, J. (1994). *Economies of signs and space.* London: Sage.

Lee, M. J. (1993). *Consumer culture reborn: The politics of consumption.* London: Routledge.

Lefebvre, H. (1971). *Everyday life in the modern world*. New York: Harper.

Levine, L. D. (1988). *Bird: The making of an American sports legend*. New York: McGraw-Hill.

Lipman, J. (1991, November 15). NBC blurs line between program, ads. *Wall Street Journal*, p. B5.

Lippert, B. (1991, April 8). NBA ads make game of hoops as American as. . . . *Adweek*, 10.

Liston, R. (1994, November 6). Pop go the Leopards. *The Observer*, p. 17.

Luke, T. W. (1991). Touring hyperreality: Critical theory confronts informational society. In P. Wexler (Ed.), *Critical theory now*, (pp. 1–26). London: Falmer Press.

Maguire, J. (1993a). Globalisation, sport and national identities: "The empire strikes back"? *Loisir et Societe, 16*(2), 293–322.

Maguire, J. (1993b). Globalization, sport development, and the media/sport complex. *Sport Science Review, 2*(1), 29–47.

Maguire, J. (1994). Sport, identity politics, and globalization: Diminishing contrasts and increasing varieties. *Sociology of Sport Journal, 11*(4), 398–427.

McCarthy, C., and Critchlow, W. (1993). *Race, identity, and representation in education*. New York: Routledge.

McKay, J., Lawrence, G., Miller, T., and Rowe, D. (1993). Globalization and Australian sport. *Sport Science Review, 2*(1), 10–28.

Marable, M. (1993). Beyond racial identity politics: Towards a liberal theory for multicultural democracy. *Race & Class, 35*(1), 113–130.

Moore, D. (1992, November 6). A new world for the NBA in the 90s. *Dallas Morning News*, p. 1B.

Moore, D. (1994, November 3). Transition game: League no longer flourishing, but foundation remains strong. *Dallas Morning News*, p. 1B.

Moran, M. (1979, February 5). Status of pro basketball worrying player's group. *New York Times*, p. C4.

Peters, K. (1994, December 19). Personal communication with author.

Reagan, R. (1982). *Public papers of the Presidents of the United States, 1981*. Washington, D.C.: U.S. Government Printing Office.

Reeves, J. L., and Campbell, R. (1994). *Cracked coverage: Television news, the anti-cocaine crusade, and the Reagan legacy*. Durham: Duke University Press.

Robins, K. (1991). Tradition and translation: National culture in its global context. In J. Corner and S. Harvey (Eds.), *Enterprise and heritage: Crosscurrents of national culture*, (pp. 21–44). London: Routledge.

Rojek, C. (1990). Baudrillard and leisure. *Leisure Studies, 9*, 1–20.

Rosenfeld, J. (1994, December 22). Personal communication with author.

Rowe, D., Lawrence, G., Miller, T., and McKay, J. (1994). Global sport? Core concern and peripheral vision. *Media, Culture & Society, 16*, 661–675.

Sabo, D. (1993). Sociology of sport and the new world disorder. *Sport Science Review, 2*(1), 1–9.

Staudohar, P. D. (1989). *The sports industry and collective bargaining*. Ithaca: ILR Press, Cornell University.

Swift, E. M. (1991, June 3). From corned beef to caviar. *Sports Illustrated*, 74–90.

Taylor, P. (1995, January 30). Bad actors: The growing number of selfish and spoiled players are hurting their teams and marring the NBA's image. *Sports Illustrated*, 18–23.

Voisin, A. (1991, December 3). NBA takes active role in dealing with AIDS issue. *Atlanta Constitution*, p. F1.

Webster, D. (1988). *Looka yonder! The imaginary America of populist culture*. London: Comedia.

Weir, T. (1993, June 18). Basketball's appeal is international. *U.S.A. Today*, p. 1A.

Wernick, A. (1991). *Promotional culture: Advertising, ideology and symbolic expression*. London: Sage.

Whiteside, L. (1992, December 20). Stern: The point man in NBA's team effort. *Boston Globe*, p. 84.

Wideman, J. E. (1990, November). Michael Jordan leaps the great divide. *Esquire*, 140–145, 210–216.

Williams, J. (1994). The local and the global in English soccer and the rise of satellite television. *Sociology of Sport Journal, 11*(4), 376–397.

Williams, R. (1981). *The sociology of culture*. New York: Schoken Books.

Willis, S. (1991). *A primer for daily life*. London: Routledge.

Wilson, W. J. (1987). *The truly disadvantaged: The inner city, the underclass, and public policy*. Chicago: University of Chicago Press.

4

The Politics of Corporate Ecological Restorations: Comparing Global and Local North American Contexts

ANDREW LIGHT & ERIC HIGGS

Introduction

Environmental problems were one of the first areas of social theory and policy to clearly be bound within a global problematic, challenging any hope of solving them through local solutions. The biotic systems, which are necessarily the focus of any environmental problematic, are physically global in character, which any material theory must recognize. Even a claim for environmental protection based purely on self-interest (or national interest) must eventually confront the global dimensions of the problem. But the demands of the global dimensions of such issues become ironic given the inextricably local context in which environmental issues are often theorized.

Localism and bioregionalism have become the watchwords of many environmental movements in the past couple decades, as new arguments have been advanced for the greater success of the development of human identification with nature based more on a connection with the nature that is close at hand, rather than abstractly and globally theorized. We can expect a greater affinity, for example, with the mountains of Jasper National Park in Alberta as Albertans, and consequently become better stewards of nature because of threats to that ecosystem, than through appeals to broader concepts of empathy with a global conception of "nature." But both claims of the importance of environmental questions on local and global grounds are intuitively plausible. So how do we negotiate the two? How do we create an adequate approach to environmental problems that is sensitive both to the inextricably global *and* local contexts, which are articulated in specific environmental problems?

We will attempt to contribute to the process of formulating a response to this dilemma by looking at one class of environmental issues at the heart of these questions—ecological restoration. Ecological restoration, as an activity by global and local actors, presents a unique set of problems that may, more than most environmental practices, bring out the current state of the global and local problematic in environmental issues. As a practice it reflects and is helping to shape the global and local contexts of human interaction with the nonhuman natural environment.

Ecological restoration refers to a broad set of practices directed toward the amelioration of human impact on ecosystems and has been defined by the Society for Ecological Restoration (SER) as "the process of recovering and managing altered ecosystems" (SER 1996). Rooted in traditional practices of land reclamation and motivated by the urgency of environmental degradation, ecological restoration has fused practical skills with (scientific) ecological knowledge to form a coherent environmental discipline (Jordan et al. 1987; Berger 1988).[1]

For the past half century, in earnest over the past decade, ecological restoration has proved capable of returning specific types of damaged ecosystems to a "natural" state and in some cases has created ecosystems *de novo* (e.g., wetland mitigation projects). SER, formed in 1987, has grown rapidly with several thousand members in North America and a growing number of international members. A journal, *Restoration and Management Notes,* was joined two years ago by a refereed scientific publication, *Restoration Ecology,* now the official publication of the SER. Institutionalization of restoration practice is imminent with the formation of the New Academy for Environmental Restoration, an initiative piloted by several senior members of SER. Government and corporate funding to restoration initiatives is rising rapidly, as are the number of practitioners who call themselves restorationists. For example, in an attempt to remedy damage done through extensive channelization of the Kissimmee River in Florida, various government agencies are spending hundreds of millions of dollars on returning the river closer to its earlier meandering condition (Toth 1993). As traditional approaches to ecosystem preservation reach their practical limits, ecological restoration will assume a more prominent position on the environmental policy agenda. Many environmental policy issues in the next few decades will focus on restoration. This prominence deserves careful attention from political, cultural, and environmental practitioners and theorists. Ecological restoration will redefine many of the issues of traditional concern.

A sharp debate has developed over the extent to which humanistic theoretical considerations, political worries, and cultural values are important in charting the development of ecological restoration (Higgs 1994a). Some writers (e.g., Bradshaw 1993) explicitly bolster the authority of science, while others give implicit assent to scientific restoration through their avoidance of wider concerns. On the opposite side, a number of writers have shown recently that restoration either ought to

include or necessarily does include dimensions that cannot be reduced to traditional scientific concerns (Jordan et al. 1987; Higgs 1993a). In this chapter we focus
on two types of political concerns that arise as theoretical problems involving ecological restoration: politics *in* restoration and the politics *of* restoration. By *involving* restoration, we mean questions that assume ecological restoration as a theoretical whole. That is to say, these questions assume that in some sense it is settled
what the practical referent of ecological restoration is and that ecological restoration *per se* can be considered as a sphere of activity that interacts with other
spheres of activity—cultural, political, aesthetic, and technological.[2]

Politics *in* restoration refers to questions about the possible political dimension
in ecological restoration considered as a whole, questions such as the inherent nature of the politics associated with the practice. Stemming from this area of interest are the politics *of* restoration or the political use to which restoration projects may be put. We believe that the politics in restoration is theoretically
constant—the political issues involved in restoration as a practice should remain
the same regardless of the location of the project. But the politics *of* restoration
is a different matter. From our perspective, which is grounded in a Gramscian-in-
spired critical theory, the context within which a restoration physically occurs
(the economic, political, and social spheres around it), is extraordinarily important in shaping its political role in the broader culture. For us, a locale literally
comes into being as a subject once the layers of political, economic, social, and
cultural meanings have been laid down. Restoration as the mere application of
scientific technique—or as the extension of a global paradigm—anywhere, any-
time, no longer makes sense.

The first part of this chapter argues that there is a democratic, participatory potential within the practice of ecological restoration. But since this egalitarianism is
only potentially part of each act of restoration, it is the politics of restoration that
determines whether that potential ever emerges. The second part of this chapter
makes a case for how different political contexts (here those in Canada and the
United States) condition the democratic potential for each restoration. To accomplish this we offer first corporate-sponsored restorations in the United States as an
example of how ecosystems become commodified to serve the interests of global
capital, and thus the extension of global capital's paradigmatic relationship with
nature—as a commodified object to serve the process of consumption. The cost of
this process is the abstraction away from restoration's local circumstance, which
may be the key to its positive political potential.

Canada, in contrast, has a tradition of nationalizing nature and has therefore
gained wider public assent for state interventions in ecological management including restoration, which cuts against the trend to commodify nature. Of course,
the contrast between Canada and the United States is not this sharp in practice.
Still, we will argue that neither nationalized nor commodified nature offers a political setting wherein the democratic potential of restoration can be realized fully.
The richer political context we propose values the complicated local circum-

stances that lead to effective restorations and in this way to a more participatory kind of ecological restoration. Commodified or nationalized restorations fit well within contemporary patterns of globalization, a tendency we believe will corrode the democratic potential of restoration. To the extent to which the political framework within which restoration occurs determines their participatory content, the relative democratic outcome of the practice of restoration in any given place serves as grounds for a normative critique of both the restoration and the political framework within which the restoration develops.

The Politics in Restoration

At a session on politics and restoration at the June 1993 Society for Ecological Restoration meeting, panelists and audience members spoke out about how they were not afraid to "get political" with their restoration work (Higgs 1994b; Light 1994; Perry 1994; Westfall 1994). Against the backdrop of a "scientific" atmosphere, which often frowns on the inclusion of such normative categories as politics in its research, such proclamations were very encouraging. But they were also troubling. Isn't any act of restoration inherently political in some way? To suggest that one could "get political" with restoration seemed to assume that restoration work did not include a political dimension in practice to begin with but only became political given a conscious move by the practitioner. This argument seems wrong, as wrong as saying that the act of voting itself is apolitical until one had voted for some particular party or affirmed or denied some referendum. To vote is political in itself, since doing it affirms a political commitment to the value of participation. To vote affirms the political value of voting and implicitly places one in opposition to a political argument that would deny such participation. Wasn't restoration work in itself political for similar reasons? Doesn't any act of restoration stand as a testament (at least) to the restorer's commitment to the possibility of restoration, against the position that parts of nature ought not to be restored? But such an intuition evidently needs an argument.

Preservation and Restoration

Ecological restoration as a current in the environmental mainstream is partly a reaction to preservation (Baldwin et al. 1994). Proponents of restoration may or may not want it to substitute for preservation—this controversy is unimportant here. What is important is that preservation has a clear inherent political dimension. Preservationists claim that to not preserve some thing in nature is to violate a moral and a political obligation. Under whatever description of the moral basis for preservation (biocentrist, enlightened anthropocentrist, or egoistic), there is a moral obligation to attempt to preserve some part of nature if it is deemed important to preserve by that theory. A theory demanding that some bit of nature be preserved and does not find objectionable the behavior of someone who does not preserve that bit if they can would be inconsistent if not incoherent. The political obligation is that the political sphere should be organized such that what needs to be preserved is preserved, that is, people need to be free to comply with their moral obligations to preserve that part of nature that must be preserved. A decision to preserve some part of nature that politically has been designated as an area not to be preserved is inherently political because it commits the preservationist to a view that the political system needs to be changed for that part of nature to be preserved. A decision by a preservationist not to preserve some bit of nature is also inherently political (where the existing political authorities have also decided not to preserve), since it tacitly assumes that at least in this case the political system is functioning effectively as regards that particular preservation decision.

Restoration Is Inherently Political

Ecological restoration steps into the domain of preservation and argues for an alternative to this human interaction with nature for a variety of reasons (e.g., redemption, mitigation). Restoration steps in and occupies the ground of preservation (exclusively or not) and thus inhabits the political ground of preservation. Restoration is inherently political in the same way that preservation is political. Both practices are imbued with choices—what to restore and what not to restore, what to preserve and what not to preserve—and any decision to restore or preserve is inherently political against the background of the political governance of nature. We are not claiming here that everything has such a political dimension, or every human interaction with nature has a political dimension, only that every act of restoration contains a political dimension. Sometimes this political dimension will be contentious and sometimes it will not. Sometimes it will be so trivial that it won't even be worth thinking about. But to drive a wedge between restoration and the politics *in* it is to risk serious problems with the politics *of* restoration.

What accounts for the aversion to the claim that restoration has an inherent political dimension? Why would practitioners either embrace this politics only as a separable issue or be totally repulsed by the suggestion that their work has a political dimension at all? The most straightforward answer to this question is that the general pejorative character of politics turns people off to any suggestion of a connection between politics and something important or beneficial. Politics makes things dirty. We assume that to talk about something's politics is to raise its unsavory elements. But to reduce politics to such a one-dimensional aspect of any sphere of activity seems wrong. Still, this seems to be the norm for political discussions of ecological restoration. For example, the exchange between Constance Pierce and Frederick Turner over the politics of restoration in *Beyond Preservation* is a paradigmatic example of how thinking about politics as simply a dirty issue produces insubstantial discussions of the political dimensions of and in restoration.

Pierce (1994) believes that whatever the interesting political issue is, it must be ultimately an issue of "money" politics. But this seems to be a pretty crass and unhelpful reduction. Surely the source of the funding for different projects isn't inherent to the practice of restoration. There is a clear danger in the use of restorations that are paid for by certain agents, agencies, and corporations, but to claim that this is *the* political issue in restoration obscures the significance of the politics *in* restoration. If there are no politics *in* restoration, then on what grounds can we critique the use of restorations? In other words, if there is nothing politically lost that could have been gained in every restoration, then what force does a critique of the politics of restoration have? What has been lost that should have been there? An identification of a politics in restoration would fuel a stronger critique of the politics of restoration.

Turner's reply (1994) makes a similar but more elaborate mistake. Turner sees the problem of reducing all politics to political power but never really substantively addresses the question of politics in ecological restoration. Political power is linear in Turner's account because its goal is only achievable through the acquisition of unconditioned power over some subsequent state of affairs. Turner assumes, so it seems, that political power can only be understood in terms of authoritarian one-dimensional political power. Other forms, such as democratic political power, are exercised not simply through achieving positive control over how things will be but are also defined through the free exercise of participation in a political process that may not always result in one's desired state of affairs. We do not say that people who vote for losing candidates lack any political power in a democracy since mere participation in the voting process itself is an expression of political power.[3] Politics in general (as Turner probably would agree)— and political power itself—is more complex than the manner in which it is exercised in any particular political system.[4]

Our view is that this political dimension inherent in restoration must first be explored before a substantive critique of the full politics of restoration can be achieved. If there is some positive value always potentially at work in ecological restoration, then there is a foundation upon which the improper practice of restoration can be judged as well as weighed against the background of a larger political context. But to get at this assessment, one must take a more complex look at the relationship between politics and restoration than is typically made.

The Democratic Potential in Restoration

William Jordan, one of the most influential writers on ecological restoration and the editor of one of the two main journals in the field,[5] has tried with some success to articulate a coherent restoration ecology paradigm. Included in his program are cultural, social, and of course political elements. A close look at his work reveals that Jordan would be unsatisfied with the one-dimensional views of political power at work in the analyses of Pierce and Turner. Jordan proposes that ecological restoration has an inherent political component and argues that this component is inherently democratic and therefore egalitarian. In his discussion of element five of the ecological restoration paradigm, "change and adaptation"

(1994), Jordan claims, "What is involved [in ecological restoration] is a continual dialogue rather than a program, paralleling in our dealings with the biotic community the dialogue that sustains a democratic society and makes it adaptable to change" (27). Jordan has in mind the sense in which restorations are organized around communal activities for communal concerns. In the acts themselves, people tend to participate by and large as equals, creating an egalitarian framework within which restorations are performed. Here is a possible foundation for the politics in restoration. Ecological restoration ought to connect us to each other as participants in a process that should be integrated into a close communal connection with the land.

Although Jordan's version of this claim makes the politics of restoration more complex, it may simplify the concept of democracy too much. Under his description ecological restoration could be described as inherently democratic, but only given what appears to be an overly stipulative definition of restoration—all restoration is democratic by definition. There seems to us no reason why democracy or egalitarianism inheres in the simple act of restoring a landscape unless the act necessarily must be prescribed within a certain context. But if we do that, we must be prepared to argue that certain acts are not restorations by definition, specifically those performed under undemocratic conditions. Otherwise why would we rule out restorations performed by slaves, voluntary masses blindly following an autocratic dictator, or contractors uncritically obeying the dicates of a zealous regulator? Intuitively there seems to be no reason to call into question such restorations on technical grounds unless the language of ecological restoration is such that these undemocratic restorations could automatically be ruled out. Simply stipulating democracy as a condition of restoration is unsatisfactory for achieving this sort of shift in our understanding of what counts as a good restoration or a restoration at all. Restoration is not inherently democratic, but it does have an inherent democratic potential within its inherently political domain.

To more fully explain this participatory potential, we need to quickly compare what happens in a restoration of nature as opposed to what happens in a preservation of nature from a normative standpoint. Both types of acts produce some sort of value, with each token containing its own content. But the character of the two values is generally quite different in restoration than in preservation.

No new value is produced in an act of preservation because it preserves only the values that exist antecedent to the act of preservation.[6] Since no new value is produced, no value is actively produced by the agents engaged in acts of preservation. They are doing something good, without a doubt, but they are not producing a value as a restorationist is when they restore some bit of nature that has been degraded. Restorationists are unique therefore as value makers in nature.[7] In this sense the good for nature produced by a restoration is inextricably bound with the good for the community in a way that it is not with acts of preservation.

For the preservationist of course there is value in the act of preserving and there is an existent value in nature that is preserved. But these two values are distinguishable. One can imagine a situation where a bit of value in nature is preserved without any preservationist needing to do the preserving. For example, an act of preservation could occur quite inadvertently if a bit of land changed ownership and the new owners simply had no designs on the land for whatever reason. In this case the mere change of ownership is not an act of preservation but instead a maintenance of a value based on contingent events. Compared with an intentional act of preservation, the value of nature was the same though the value of the act that produced the preservation was not.

Restoration is not the same. The value of the act of restoration and the value of the restoration are inextricably linked since as a matter of course, restorations do not accidentally occur.[8] An assessment of restorations as a practice will of necessity then assess the value to the community and the value to nature simultaneously, and part of the unique value of restoration therefore is the production of this simultaneous positive value. The value is not purely instrumental since the practice of restoration is not solely a good for the community, but it is also the production of a value in nature and is better for nature conceived as a whole. The value to the community and the value to nature can be *assessed* separately, but as a practice they are *produced* together.

Because of this unique interaction of values to nature and value to the community involved in the practice of restoration, the *character* of this value is at least marked by its participatory elements. At its core, restoration just is public participation in nature. The *content* of the values that are produced in a restoration may vary and at this time be hard to discern, but no matter what they are they will follow from this core. The character and the content of the value of restoration are tightly connected. A restoration with a poor character produces a bad content. A bad restoration characterized by a lack of community participation in the act produces a value that is marked by this loss of the egalitarian potential of restoration for the community. And this loss in value is uniquely felt at the local level where the special character of a community's relationship with the land is so intimately tied to the practice of ecological restoration. The inherent democratic potential of ecological restoration is thus, in a strong sense, a potential for local human-nature relationships.

One need not travel far in North America to find examples of local participatory restoration projects. In fact, local interest is one of the primary forces pushing the growth of restoration. Spent by years of uphill environmental battles, environmentalists and naturalists find restoration an attractive "positive" activity. Volunteer cleanups and "adopt-a-stream" programs, for example, provide a typically nonconfrontational way of bettering nature while improving community aesthetics and sometimes even property values. William Stevens has given us the most complete account of a community-based initiative in his recent book, *Miracle Under the Oaks* (1995), which describes the innovation, excitement, and community support achieved through the North Branch Prairie restoration project near Chicago (see also Jordan 1993).

The North Branch Prairie restoration began in 1977 as an attempt to revive remnant tallgrass prairies in the greater Chicago region. Tallgrass prairies were a common presettlement ecosystem that had been reduced over more than a century of urbanization and agricultural activity to a few scattered remnants. Through the initiative of the Illinois Nature Conservancy under the direction of Steve Packard, project volunteers soon discovered an ecological assembly that had ceased to exist: a mixture of oak savanna and tallgrass prairie. One of the central challenges that would prove controversial was to piece together the natural structure and function of the sites along the North Branch of the Chicago River. At one particular site, Vestal Grove, the challenge was not in simply weeding out exotics but in recreating ecological processes that had been eliminated. As Stevens reports:

> It was a dead ecosystem except for the dominant oaks and their attendant hickories; and not just dead, but lost to human ken. The classic tallgrass savannas had disappeared so quickly, before scientists could study them, that their ecological characteristics were almost unknown. Packard found the site strewn with mattresses, car seats, and milk creates that teenagers used as seats for outdoor parties. Bottles and cans were everywhere (19).

From a few sites along the North Branch of the Chicago River, activities have spread to over two hundred sites in Illinois with more than five thousand volunteers. It has become a model not only of community involvement in ecological restoration but an exemplar of how community-based restoration can operate successfully. The hard work of restoration—collecting seeds, propagating plants, planting, weeding, watering, soil conditioning, burning—requires an enormous amount of labor. Without dedicated volunteers, most restoration projects would be too expensive to compete with other environmental site options. What explains the steadfastness of such volunteer efforts? A consensus is forming in the literature (Westfall 1994; Jordan 1993) around the idea of attached localism, that is, the social and political connections that form in a particular place. There is more, however. The North Branch project would not have been successful without astute political maneuvering, constant defense of project ideals, and tenacious resistance to development pressures. The form and politics of such movements fulfills the unique democratic potential of restoration as it may be theorized to be connected primarily to its role in enhancing local nature, but more importantly the local culture of nature.

At the risk of generalizing, however, the transformation of cultural relations with nonhuman nature is most evident in projects undertaken by indigenous peoples in North America. There is more at stake in restoration for any people who view the regeneration of ecosystems as a condition of cultural strength (Deloria 1992; Rogers-Martinez 1992).[9] This is evident in the Sinkyone Intertribal Park project south of Eureka on the California coast. Decades of intensive logging in this mountainous country have produced serious erosion problems, loss of ecological diversity, and destruction of cultural sites. A 1985 legal action brought logging to a halt and since then a coalition of native groups, non-natives, and state and local governments has developed a comprehensive plan for the restoration of ecological processes and cultural practices in a 6,916-acre area. The struggle against clear-cut logging and the defense of traditional resource management practices was enormously difficult. Without popular resistance, political lobbying, planning, and alliance building, the Sinkyone region would continue to be exploited beyond any reasonable ecological and cultural scale.

The land was occupied by the To-cho-be-keah Sinkyone people for many centuries prior to Euro-American colonization. They coevolved with the ecosystems developing agroecological practices—pruning, burning, game inventory, cultivation, clearing, selective harvesting—which shaped the character of the region. The virtual elimination of the Sinkyone peoples from this area (mostly by the 1870s) affected significantly the distribution of animals and plants, movement corridors, clearings, and so on. Later intensive logging primarily for redwood created unrecognizable ecosystems:

> The Sinkyone is so choked with second-growth forest that in many areas it is difficult to walk cross-country. Douglas-fir is coming up in thickets of buckbrush (*Ceanothus* sp.) which earlier had invaded redwood groves following clear-cutting and intense slash fires. The ridges, where the people lived, are choked with manzanita (*Arctostaphylos* spp.), buckbrush and exotic and native pioneer species such as mappas grass (*Cortaderia selloana*), and coast cut-leaf fireweed (*Erechitites arguta*). Indian burial grounds and artifacts and the old Indian trails, which once linked forest openings maintained by Indians and led inland from the coast, have been obliterated by skidroads. And many of the plants once used by the Sinkyone people for food, for medicines, and for materials are either gone or rare. Native clovers were once abundant and widely used for food. At least five species are never seen now. And the native coho salmon, trout, and many species of frogs and salamanders are extinct or nearly so as a result of sediments washed down to the stream from the eroding slopes. Many Indians from the area still go to the Sinkyone to gather seaweed, mussels, surffish and abalone, but it is a pitiful harvest compared to former times (Rogers-Martinez 1992, 66).

The intent of the restoration of the Sinkyone area is much more than simply to bring back ecological diversity. Restoring ecological diversity without cultural practices would result in an ecoregion markedly different than had existed for at least eight thousand years. It is not even clear whether prior hydrological conditions, which stand in sharp contrast to the desertified landscape in certain parts of the region, are easily restored without some of the cultural practices (e.g., selective clearing). The larger challenge is the restoration of cultural practices which intertwine with ecological functions. As Rogers-Martinez inquires, "What do we want to restore? We want to restore life. We want to restore the living and sacred relationship between the people and the earth. We want to restore our spirits as we restore the land. We want to restore our culture, our songs, our myths and stories, and the Indian names for creeks and springs. We want to restore ourselves. This is what we want to restore at Sinkyone" (1992, 67).

Here we can finally begin to see how the unique characteristics of restoration as a practice, in the context of other ecological practices, eventually must be formulated within the local-global framework we sketched out at the beginning of this chapter. The material nature of restoration determines its political content, and the political content is normatively bound to the local over the global framework. Ecological restoration is as much a restoration of human relationships with nature, as it is a restoration of nature itself. But those relationships, like any other human relationships, are felt most keenly through proximity and contact rather than abstractly at a distance. A political framework for restoration that would globalize the practice should be treated with some suspect. Given the nature of the practice and its politics, the burden of proof is on those who would justify situating restoration in a global framework and thereby abstracting from the relationships between local lands and peoples. We will return to this point in more detail in the third part of this chapter.

Hegemony

We need some other way of appropriating the language of ecological restoration or at least a new strategy for securing within it a reference to democratic principles to preserve this character of the value of the act. If William Jordan's view does not give us exactly what we need to talk accurately about the politics of restoration (even though it points us in the right direction), how should we gauge the politics in the practice? One alternative that more fully acknowledges the complexities of the subject can be found in Antonio Gramsci's notion of hegemony.

Gramsci saw two ways in which political authority is formed: consent and power. Power is the straightforward rule of law enforced through state police power, and consent is formed through hegemony, or the political "normalization" of certain practices and restrictions (including the use of language) in certain ways. For example, in the United States, all things being equal, the market is allowed to govern exchange of private property, and by and large Americans find thinking of nature primarily as a resource natural and acceptable. Laws may get formed around our consent to those practices but the practices themselves are not originally juridical in nature. Even if some of us can envision a different relationship to nature, we expect most Americans to unconditionally accept this property relationship as normal. The relationship has become hegemonic.

Any thing that has a political content is open to appropriation for the purposes of forming hegemony in support of some interest. Although ecological restoration is not inherently democratic, it is inherently political and can be turned to serve the political interests we associate with democracy rather than some other political power structure. But this will happen only if we make it seem odd to people that an undemocratic restoration is a good restoration. The hegemony model asks us to fight for the political (and linguistic) associations of restoration, so that if someone finds out that a technically perfect restoration was performed by forced labor, he or she will rethink his or her judgment that the restoration itself was a good one. Linguistic is separated here from political because in the specific case of restoration the language of the practice is very much in flux at the moment. Within the Society for Ecological Restoration there has been a lot of debate in the past few years of how to (and whether to) define restorations. The attempts to define restoration so far have included a strong, contentious, normative content in the definition.[10] At stake here, for example, is whether wetlands mitigation efforts (one of the most privatized—and lucrative—forms of restoration work) will be accepted by the community of restorationists as acceptable forms of practice.[11] A view of the politics in and of restoration has to accommodate these disputes and provide a framework from within which we can understand the necessity of struggling over these issues. This approach is more realistic than simply comparing the results of these debates with our preconceived notions of what the practice inherently is at its core and then expecting our definition to make the needed argument for us.

Given such a combination of issues involved in the determination of what is a good restoration (or a restoration at all) and following our earlier comments about the relationship between the content and character of the value produced in a restoration, the approach here must distinguish carefully between the *process* of a restoration (and the judgments we could have about it) and the actual *product* of the restoration. The politics *in* restoration speaks to the process, and the politics *of* restoration is a component of the product. The key to a successful critique of the product, we contend, is careful examination of the process. If the process is thought to be apolitical, then nothing stops the product from having a positive content merely on technical grounds. Attention to hegemony links the process and the product by, for example, examining the process embraced in the language of restoration with the product.

The advantage of the hegemony view over Jordan's is that it acknowledges the fact that politics is dynamic. We have to fight for political ground, things are not automatically as we would want them to be. The hegemony model self-consciously acknowledges this ground as a contested terrain that must be fought for, so we can acknowledge the use of the politics of restoration in the service of democracy as a victory and understand that an undemocratic restoration is in some sense a loss.

The Context of the Politics of Restoration

So far we have laid out the inherent politics in restoration and argued that this politics has an inherent democratic potential. This last part is important if for no other reason than the fact that not every practice has an inherently democratic potential. In a conventional political example, this explains why we find it intuitively contradictory if some regime claims to be democratic and yet persists in engaging in practices such as political torture as a normal function of state police power. Such a practice is itself undemocratic and we believe its existence is a sign that such a regime is not really a democracy. If we failed to acknowledge the political dimension of state torture, it would be more difficult to critique it as inconsistent with larger political aims. A nonpolitical act is consistent with any political regime, it can be put to whatever political use desired without worrying about whether it is ideologically consistent to do so. This holds true for restoration. If we fail to take seriously the politics in restoration work then we will most likely find it much more difficult to critique the political use to which it is put. In this way, again we can see that the politics *in* restoration informs the politics *of* restoration. But it is the politics of restoration that sets the political context in which restorations occur and determines whether the politics in restoration ever achieves its full emancipatory potential. The development of a rich understanding of the politics involving restoration requires a commitment to local understanding and of the myriad variations in restoration practice.

The specific political context that concerns us in this section is corporate ecological restorations. In the past decade an increasing number of corporate restorations has been undertaken ostensibly to demonstrate corporate environmental concern. It takes only a light scraping of the surface to expose distressing political motivations that run against the inherent democratic potential of restoration. An overwhelming majority of these corporate restorations is located in the United States. What accounts for this phenomenon? We propose the answer lies in the distinction between commodified nature and nationalized nature. The rise and prominence of commodified nature, corporate restorations being one example, suppress the inherently democratic potential of ecological restoration. Nationalized nature, a consequence of heavy state involvement in Canada in environmental and natural resource management, produces a kind of restoration that is at once, ironically, more democratic and more easily assimilable to commodification. An alternative, which is flourishing in the divides and fissures between these two "natures," is localism. Countless volunteer community projects involving restoration manifest the democratic potential of restoration and give hope for its success. Localism of course is fragile and vulnerable to both nationalism and commodification. Without a resolute understanding of the politics of restoration, it will wither. There is then a global-local problematic that directly emerges out of the restoration literature. This tension must be resolved to protect the political practice of the politics in restoration. The increasingly global capital context of the practice threatens its local political virtues. We turn to this theme below.

Corporate Restorations

It is important to acknowledge the political context of restoration to avoid problems in evaluating the corporate appropriation of restoration which by its practice takes the open language of restoration and makes certain nondemocratic practices seem permissible and uncontroversial as part of the performance of restoration. When corporations appropriate restorations to serve only their own interests in increasing their positive image with respect to their relationship with nature, restoration is turned into a means to a corporate end and little else. To normalize these nondemocratic restorations as good restorations is to appropriate implicitly the hegemonic potential of the politics in restoration through the political use of restoration.

Jonathan Perry's work (1994a; 1994b) demonstrates this danger by examining the restoration projects of IBM and Red Wing Shoes outside of Minneapolis. These prairie restorations were undertaken, on Perry's analysis, to increase the cultural capital of the corporation as a friend of nature and a regionally grounded local enterprise. For example, IBM selectively advertises its role in restoring a prairie dreamscape without acknowledging its own role in eliminating the prairie and the healthy environment. So, Perry argues, visitors to the area receive more than a botanical education, they get an indoctrination into the relationship between IBM and nature that best serves the interests of IBM.

Perry gives a detailed reading of this landscape and the problems in it as an adequate restoration in itself (e.g., pointing out the sloppy work away from the roadside, which fewer people will actually see). Both the method of restoration (hired workers, hierarchically organized) and the purpose (publicity to increase consumption of a corporate commodity) are not necessarily democratic or egalitarian. Are these practices good restorations, for example, on Jordan's account, which requires restoration to be democratic? No. But it seems counterintuitive to say that these are not restored areas, no matter the method used to perform them or their purpose. We understand why people looking at this landscape would find it perfectly acceptable to say these were not only restorations but good ones. The landscape has been restored (even *pace* Perry, if it was a bad job). Only the most committed restorationist who followed Jordan's arguments would say otherwise. Corporations, quite unconsciously, have therefore appropriated the language of restoration by successfully completing this restoration and labeling it as such. (Perry tells us that there is a sign at the site indicating it is a restoration if the naive observer doubts it.) Absent some stipulation in the definition of restoration that requires a democratic character to the act, nothing stops this association by most people. Here we see the power of hegemony to form consent about what counts as a good restoration: A good restoration is one that merely results in a good product. Importantly, no sinister intention by corporations or individuals is needed to establish this hegemonic description of acceptable practice.

Whatever this type of corporate restoration is, it is something else than a good restoration—it is an appropriation of an image of nature for capital interests like the images of pristine nature used on television commercials for cars and beer. These images are not for nature or democratic interests or to promote better relations with nature. These projects are inherently political acts because they contain a political content: It is uncontroversial to use nature for private capital interest in this way; nature by this description is just the pleasant background to our conspicuous consumption.

But we can break this effect of the appropriation of restoration, not by just stipulating that all restorations must be democratic but by considering seriously the politics of taking advantage of the inherent democratic potential in restoration. We know from Antonio Gramsci's theory that a conscious political movement can make the argument that this sort of practice—undemocratic restorations—are not restorations, or at least they are not good restorations because they are not even attempting to live up to the democratic potential of ecological restoration. This example reinforces our earlier claim that there is more to ecological restoration than simply a good product; the process of restoration provides much of the political content. What goes into a restoration project, the processes that are historically contingent for each restoration product, is suppressed in the hegemonic assent to a technically proficient product as the sole criterion for good restorations. The process is increasingly obscured from the local community and creates disinterest in the politics of restoration at large. The way in which the restored area could have enhanced the local relationship with nature and served as a vehicle for public participation in the work of the community's relationship with nature is lost. One of the significant political challenges is to open up the process of restoration to a wider view to offer an alternative to the corporate approach to nature.

Corporate Theming

But such commodification of nature is nothing new, particularly for international capitalists (Higgs 1991b). Nowhere is the commodification of nature more evident than in the theme parks that now dot the landscape (Wilson 1991; Sorkin 1992; Fjellman 1992). Theme parks transform reality to consumable bits of information and stimulation. In doing so, they create remarkably clear commodities. Experiences that traditionally were ground in the flow of daily life are reconfigured and presented without the attendent disfigurations, complications, and agonies that beset real people in real activities (Borgmann 1992). Individuals are thereby mentally and emotionally disburdened and able to experience the themed event as pure entertainment. For this, large amounts of money are willingly given.

The Disney Corporation is the best known and most powerful of the theming corporations. Its projects and parks have spread well beyond the confines of American culture to export the new "reality" of hypermodernism to an international audience (Borgmann 1992). Just as nationalities and social activities have been rendered by Disney's "imagineers," so too is nature falling under the spell. In 1994, Disney World in Florida welcomed its newest attraction, the Wilderness Lodge. The Lodge is modeled on the opulent National Park lodges of the American west. Home to almost a thousand hotel rooms, the Lodge plays on the desire to have and maintain "wilderness." There is an eight-story fireplace that replicates the geological sequence of the Grand Canyon, log facades, a wilderness boutique, a river that is sourced in the lobby and flows over fake rocks, and a working model of Old Faithful, the venerable geyser that attracts so many tourists to Yellowstone National Park.

Jennifer Cypher traveled to Wilderness Lodge with the express purpose of finding out *how* wilderness had been configured: What was included and excluded? What were the primary signifiers? What reduction had occurred? Behind her work[12] is a desire to locate one end of the commodification of nature as regards ecological restoration. To what extent will such representations of nature further decontextualize the politics of restoration, which after all is mirrored in the corporate commodification of restoration as a practice? The answer is clear: Stripping away the background of experience, as is perforce the purpose of a themed presentation, restricts the view of the political processes that constitute the created nature. Meaning is mined with the full consent of the consumers of the created experience. The facility with such experience raises an ominous question: Will commodification of nature further restrict our ability to comprehend the democratic potential of restoration? Will it become less meaningful to suggest that the process of restoration is as important as the product of restoration?

Variations in North America

Theme parks are now consonant with the American identity. The exportation of themed experience may be the largest economic function of the United States over the next few decades, especially with the development of virtual reality technologies. That this is the case is a testament to the force of the commodification of reality and nature (Higgs 1991a). The process of commodification as we define it involves the sharp division between the product that lies in the foreground as the consumption good and the background in which resides the context of production. As mentioned earlier, it is in the background that we find the political content. The theming of experience stands as a brilliant achievement in the development of capitalist economies, and the fact that something as ineffable as "wilderness" can be recreated for entertainment is a very high achievement indeed. The cultural ease with this concept suggests that it will redefine consumption by depoliticizing its practice. The earlier discussion of corporate restoration projects indicates that this has taken place, that the worth of these sites is in their final consumption and not in their production. The democratic potential of restoration is thus obscured.

There is evidence that the commodification of restoration has not advanced as far, or at least in the same way, in Canada. There are, for example, few high-profile corporate headquarters restorations (an exception is the controversial headquarters for Ducks Unlimited in Manitoba). But such direct comparisons are complicated. Montreal is home to the Biodome, a large ecological theme park that recreates as much as possible several different ecosystems under the roof of a converted Olympic Games velodrome. Wilson addresses the difficulty of comparing Canada and the United States at the beginning of his study of "the North American landscape from Disney to the Exxon Valdez" (1991):

These are global phenomena [the commodified representations of nature], but I am
writing from this place, North America. The places I talk about are *exemplary* places:
places that reveal both the cohesions and disruptions of the past fifty years; places
redolent of the power of the land; places overlaid with another, cultural, environment—that of advertising, or tourism, or telecommunications. . . . While natural environments know no political boundaries, cultures certainly do. The border between
Canada and the United States—which used to be called "the longest undefended border in the world" until it became a joke—drops in and out of view in this discussion.
Rarely is there a specific comparison between Canadian and U.S. places, although I
have tried to draw out distinctions where they are revealing (16).

For Wilson it was insufficient to conduct a study in which the two countries were
either separated or overlaid.

Canada is a "lite" socialist democracy, having been formed of colonial aspirations of England and France and later in the twentieth century by the commercial colonialism of the United States. Canada and the United States are each
other's largest trading partners. The mercantile authority of the United States has
produced a branch plant economy in Canada. With a few exceptions, most corporations are foreign-owned and most of these are American. The entertainment
industries, Hollywood and television networks, have overshadowed Canadian
cultural production. The identity of Canadians is unclear, and this sentiment
seems to be the clearest mark of their identity.

Canada and Canadians have been active in ecological restoration, but the pattern
of involvement reflects the branch plant mentality. The late Robert Dorney, an innovator in both microscale (less than one-tenth acre) urban ecological restoration
and landscape-level restoration in Canada (Higgs 1993b), was trained at the
University of Wisconsin in the shadow of Aldo Leopold.[13] Canadians have been active in the Society for Ecological Restoration, and hosted SER's fourth annual conference in 1992 in Waterloo, Ontario. The conference drew several hundred
Canadian restorationists—or at least people who expressed interest in restoration—
but such a turnout of Canadians has not been matched at subsequent conferences.
SER is based at the University of Wisconsin, Madison, Arboretum; there is no autonomous Canadian organization.

Across Canada, restoration projects are underway on every kind of ecosystem,
and this activity appears to closely match the kinds of efforts undertaken in the
United States (where the United States is a leader in brackish semitropical wetland restoration, Canada is a leader in boreal peatland restoration). There are corporate sponsorships of restoration projects in Canada. For example, Cargill, a
multinational corporation, is funding a major wetland restoration scheme on
Frank Lake in southern Alberta to help mitigate against feedlot effluent. Although
educational institutions have not moved as aggressively in Canada to develop opportunities for restoration training, the University of Victoria is developing a
modest program and other universities are beginning to remodel their outdated
land management programs to reflect ecological sensibilities.

Comparisons beyond the anecdotal, however, are difficult. There is at present no repository of information on restoration projects in North America that would make such a study feasible. There is no easy way of determining with certainty the extent of the pattern of commodification. What we offer instead are experienced conjectures. The heavy hand of government in Canada has created an extensive network of natural areas—parks, reserves, ecologically sensitive areas, conservations areas—expressly in the public interest. Large land benefactions, nongovernmental conservation organizations such as the Nature Conservancy, have been far less prominent in Canada. Only in the last decade, with arrival of a new conservativism in the federal government, has there been extensive planning for privatizing parks, campgrounds, and developing financial incentives for private protection.

Population pressures have been modest in most regions of Canada as compared with the United States. The sense that there is always a hinterland lying beyond the edge of settlement is a profound part of the Canadian psyche. It is simplistic to admit but the end of the "frontier" never occurred in Canada. Where enormous pressures have been building for restoration of degraded landscapes in the United States as the only reasonable option for natural space in many regions, such awareness has only crept into Canada in the last two decades. The response, once again, is coming from government organizations. For example, a consortium of university researchers and staff in Jasper National Park (Canada's largest Rocky Mountain park) are proposing an ambitious research program of which one part is a comprehensive regional ecological restoration program. In Canada the public good is expressed directly, albeit cloaked in the complicated interjurisdictions of educational and governmental institutions.[14] What does such a project tell us about the democratic potential of restoration?

Nationalized nature creates a wider opening for the democratic potential of restoration to emerge. Of course, this observation disintegrates quickly if one is aware of the hegemonic consent that accompanies large-scale "public" projects. That the opening exists does not necessarily ensure democratic projects will pass through. Further, the overwhelming pressure of American commodity culture, especially in light of recent "free" trade accords, is forcing the rapid loss of distinctive Canadian approaches. Commodification is a globalizing phenomenon, and this we predict will become a determining factor in future restorations possibly including those sponsored by the state. Restoration will be valued on the corporate model, inasmuch as it appeals to the interests of consumers. We know that often public works projects end up mirroring their corporate counterparts either intentionally or unintentionally. Additionally, nothing prohibits the state from engaging in restoration for the same crass image-building interests at work in corporate projects. This is hegemony in a different guise. Projects such as the one proposed for Jasper challenges commodification by placing public interests first and taking a long-term view of participation. It is projects of this type that will keep open democratic involvement.

Equally or more important are the numerous local restoration projects organized by volunteers across the continent interested in returning loving attention
to places that have been damaged. These projects persist precisely because of a
fierce social and political will that overcomes a fixation on consumption. We see
such projects as containing the greatest potential for resistance to commodification. Even with the occasional success of nationalized projects, which may temporarily resist commodification, enough experience with the complicity of the
state in corporate interests motivates us to seek other actors to resist commodification in restoration. But local projects are often undertaken on the basis of fragile connections to the landscape and are endangered by a lack of democratic political resolve.

We are left with something of a dilemma: Given the political weakness (or
worse corruption) of many local institutions, American environmentalists may
have no other choice than to look to Canada (or other strong restoration-oriented
states) as a model of how to best preserve a participatory context of restorations
at the national level. Perhaps with a concentrated effort on the part of American
environmentalists a culture of nationalized nature in the United States separate
and distinct from commodified nature could be reinforced, thereby pushing the
profile of restorations closer to that found in Canada today. But given the current
political climate in both countries, we hesitate to rely either on the continuance
of nationalized nature in Canada or on the possibility of an environmental movement reforming around this issue in the United States *and* finding itself successful in the face of conservative challenges. Instead, at bottom, the hope for the
preservation of participation as a part of restorations is best placed in local projects. This is not to say that we favor a naive localism on all environmental questions, but only that this particular struggle for the character of restoration is best
fought on individual home fronts, before the fight can be taken to greater arenas.
Only when the contested terrain of the politics of restoration is won in the minds
of people will corporations and governments stop feeding the growth of a culture
of commodified nature.

Following that day, state institutions could be convinced to systematically differ to local communities when authorizing funds for restoration projects.
Although beyond the scope of this chapter, we would advocate policies that gave
local communities a "right of first refusal" to undertake state-financed restorations in their areas. Such a strategy would perhaps preserve the unique value produced in restorations at the local level and reverse the current trend to defer to
private corporations to implement many state-sponsored restoration initiatives.

Conclusions

Ecological restoration will be democratic only if we make it so by politically shifting the terrain of discourse about ecological restoration. We have to give reasons
why democracy and egalitarianism are wedded to restoration and therefore make

it the case that to think otherwise seems counterintuitive. To accomplish this through a change in consent seems the most democratic way to stop the bad politics of restoration. The democratic potential in ecological restoration makes a fully democratic politics of restoration and a fully democratic practice in every restoration an ideal we may never achieve. But the ideal gives us a base upon which we can critique nondemocratic restorations on grounds other than simply whether the science employed in them was the best it could possibly be and whether the product is a good one. With the argument we have made here, we can acknowledge, for example, that corporate restorations are good on some criteria (perhaps in their physical execution) but they may be lacking in other respects—their political dimensions. For practical policy questions this analysis gives us the leverage to argue that public money spent on restorations must require that they live up to their beneficial democratic potential.

From a Gramscian perspective we can see, however, that the terrain (literal and figurative) of restorations is up for grabs, which of course following Gramsci is exactly what we should expect. Subtle differences in two countries as alike as Canada and the United States are enough to engender differences in the propensity for the potential for democratic restorations to be realized in each country. But the potential for restorations to be democratic exists in each country simply because this is the politics in practice. But this potential must be recognized. If it is not then the "difference" between Canadian and U.S. restorations may become simply one on a long list of quaint, antiquated diversions on an otherwise seamless landscape—diversions such as the varying representations on our respective currencies, loons in Canada, and public monuments in the United States. But such an outcome is relatively optimistic, because at least some democratic potential would be doing some good in some Canadian restorations, even if this effect was unacknowledged.

The alternative is far worse: Corporate hegemonic control of restoration with its multinational force triumphs and restoration in both countries becomes indistinguishable even to the trained eye. In such a scenario, commodification—as a form of globalization of nature—strips away even the most general forms of difference and collapses the value of nature to a mere object relationship. If such a move is successful then any value of a local connection with nature is lost, perhaps irretrievably. Imagine the difficulty involved in attempting to reclaim the noncommodity value of an accepted commodity relation today and one sees the worry we have.

As we mentioned at the start, thinking of nature on global terms has some sort of material base. The mere existence of local relations with nature, with or without ecological restoration, is not enough to stop the global tide we have identified here. The terrain here is political not just ontological—without active vigilant defense, local relations with nature easily fall to a global onslaught. This is certainly the case in both examples of restoration we gave earlier in the chapter—the North Branch Prairie project and the Sinkyone Intertribal Park. Active political resistance, clear strategic collaboration, wide democratic participation, and a sense of the larger picture of ecological restoration are crucial elements in ensuring democratic restoration. We cannot simply theorize our way out of this problem. Because of this threat, the fight over the politics in and of ecological restoration is a struggle for the future of the very identity of nature in North America.

NOTES

1. The terms "ecological restoration" and "restoration ecology" are routinely interchanged in the literature with confusing consequences. We propose to follow the convention that the latter refers to the body of scientific research directly concerning the restoration of ecosystems. Ecological restoration is a more inclusive term incorporating the wide-ranging practices and knowledges that constitute the broad definition given above (i.e., ecological restoration subsumes restoration ecology).

2. The contrast drawn here is to theoretical problems *in* restoration ecology, the sort of thing in which philosophers such as Katz (1992) seem to be interested. Such concerns by humanities theorists (as opposed to the purely applied science questions of what techniques to use in restorations) worry us. We believe that any philosophical theory that problematizes restoration ecology is a questionable theory. We do understand however that some of the concerns of theorists like Katz are stimulated by unduly hyperbolic claims of some proponents of restoration.

3. It is of course controversial whether having a vote gives people enough political power to satisfy some democratic goals such as pluralism and equality. But certainly we would always draw the line at simple enfranchisement to distinguish between those who have some political power in a democracy and those who have none (such as women in the United States in the eighteenth century).

4. Instead of bad political power, Turner offers chaos theory as a good model for examining the dynamics of restoration. Although chaos is an interesting metaphor to explain the complexities of restoration, we need not resort to it (and subsequently to its ambiguities when applied to the humanities and social sciences) to talk about the complexities of the political or social dimensions of restoration. As a metaphor for discussions of political dynamics, we are skeptical that it alleviates the legitimate worries raised by theorists such as Althusser and Foucault who took seriously the connection between power and many forms of knowledge.

5. Jordan's journal, *Restoration and Management Notes (RMN)*, as briefly noted at the beginning of this chapter, was for some time the only journal in the field. The tacitly accepted division between *RMN* and *Restoration Ecology* is that *RMN* covers matters of primary interest to practitioners (including wider cultural, political, and social issues in restoration), whereas *Restoration Ecology* aims for a more scientific audience. It is not clear, however, that this division of labor will hold or indeed that it ought to be maintained (see Higgs 1994a).

6. This assumes of course that the value of the land is not simply reducible to the value given to it by a valuing agent. But the claim against such a reductive account would not have to be necessarily made in terms of intrinsic value. Again, the debate here need not be resolved at this time, and we believe our analysis still holds regardless of the outcome of this disagreement in the environmental ethics literature. We are assuming that most

preservationists and restorationists would admit that the value of nature is not *merely* reducible to value added by humans.

7. The specific content of the value produced in a restoration is philosophically up for grabs. But we will bracket out the question here that philosophers such as Katz (1992), mentioned previously, and Robert Elliot are interested in. Suffice it to say that *some* value is produced in a restoration, which may or may not represent the "intrinsic" value of nature.

8. Of course if we left large swaths of degraded land untouched for thousands of years, some things might come back, but absent the fall of human civilization leading to that eventuality, our point still holds.

9. Much will emerge from indigenous peoples over the next few years and the prospects are both exciting and bracing for orthodox restorationists. For example, counter to the beliefs of many ecologists concerned with natural biodiversity in restoration, Rogers-Martinez (1992) judges successful restoration by how well human livelihoods are integrated in ecosystems. Rogers-Martinez, a long-standing member of the board of the Society for Ecological Restoration, has formed the Indigenous Peoples Restoration Network to promote restoration on native lands and to shift the attitudes of white middle-class restorationists.

10. SER 1994.

11. Given the interests specifically of the U.S. federal government in such projects, the linguistic and political components of the hegemony of restoration will certainly converge. The issue here, however, is not a paper tiger; there are important restoration practitioners who resist the acceptance of wetlands mitigation for scientific as well as political reasons (Korte and Kearl 1993; Munro 1991).

12. Jennifer Cypher completed her master's thesis *The Real and the Fake; Imagineering Wilderness and Nature at Disney's Wilderness Lodge* (University of Alberta 1995) in the department of anthropology. We are grateful for her advice in this section.

13. Aldo Leopold is credited as being one of the founders of contemporary restoration practices in North America. He was the director of the University of Wisconsin, Madison, Arboretum until his tragic death in 1949 (Meine 1988).

14. The story, of course, is more complicated. A recent push for industry collaborative projects has led to lavishly funded research programs such as the "model forests" springing up across the country. Increasingly, conservation and environmental research is linked directly with industrial sponsorship.

BIBLIOGRAPHY

Baldwin, A., Judith DeLuce, and Carl Pletsch (1994) Introduction: Ecological Preservation versus Restoration and Innovation. *Beyond Preservation.* University of Minnesota Press, Minneapolis, pp. 3–16.

Berger, John (1988) *Environmental Restoration.* Bar Island Press, Bar Harbor, ME.

Borgmann, Albert (1992) *Crossing the Postmodern Divide.* University of Chicago Press, Chicago.

Bradshaw, A. D. (1993) Ecological Restoration as a Science. *Restoration Ecology.* 1:2, pp. 71–73.

Deloria, Vine (1992) Spiritual Management: Prospects for Restoration on Tribal Lands. *Restoration and Management Notes,* 10, pp. 48–50.

Fjellman, Stephen M. (1992) *Vinyl Leaves: Walt Disney World and America.* Oxford University Press, Oxford.

Gramsci, Antonio (1971) *The Prison Notebooks.* Trans. Quintin Hoare and Geffrey Smith. International Publishers, New York.

Higgs, Eric (1994a) Expanding the Scope of Ecological Restoration. *Restoration Ecology.* 2:3, pp. 137–145.

_____. (1994b) The Politics of Restoration. *Restoration and Management Notes.* 12:2, pp. 138–139.

_____. (1993a) The Ethics of Mitigation. *Restoration and Management Notes.* 9:2, pp. 138–143.

_____. (1993b) A Life in Restoration: Robert Starbird Dorney 1928–1987. *Restoration and Management Notes.* 11:2, pp. 144–147.

_____. (1991a) A Quantity of Engaging Work to Be Done: Restoration and Morality in a Technological Culture. *Restoration and Management Notes.* 9:2, pp. 97–104.

_____. (1991b) Commodification and Naturalization: The Recreation of Nature as Technology. *The Technology of Discovery and the Discovery of Technology,* Joseph Pitt, Elena Lugo (eds). Society for Philosophy and Technology, Blacksburg, VA, pp. 301–318.

Jordan III, William R. (1994) Sunflower Forest: Ecological Restoration as the Basis for a New Environmental Paradigm. *Beyond Preservation,* pp. 17–34.

_____. William R. (1993) Restoration as a Technique for Identifying and Characterizing Human Influences on Ecosystems. *Humans as Components of Ecosystems: The Ecology of Subtle Human Effects and Populated Areas,* M.J. McDonnell and S.T.A. Pickett (eds.) Springer-Verlag, New York, pp. 271–279.

Jordan III, W. R., M. E. Gilpin, and J. D. Aber (1987) *Ecological Restoration.* Cambridge University Press, Cambridge, England.

Katz, Eric (1992) The Big Lie: Human Restoration of Nature. *Research in Philosophy and Technology.* Vol. 12, pp. 231–242.

Korte, Nic, and Peter Kearl (1993) Should Western Watersheds Be Public Policy in the United States? *Environmental Management.* 17:6, pp. 729–734.

Light, Andrew (1994) Hegemony and Democracy: How the Politics in Restoration Informs the Politics of Restoration. *Restoration and Management Notes.* 12:2, pp. 140–144.

Meine, Curt (1988) *Aldo Leopold: His Life and Work.* University of Wisconsin Press, Madison, WI.

Munro, John W. (1991) Wetland Restoration in the Mitigation Context. *Restoration and Management Notes.* 9:2, pp. 80–86.

Perry, Jonathan (1994) Greening Corporate Environments: Authorship and Politics in Restoration. *Restoration and Management Notes.* 12:2, pp. 145–147.

Pierce, Constance (1994) The Poetics and Politics of Prairie Restoration. *Beyond Preservation,* pp. 226–233.

Rogers-Martinez, Dennis (1992) Northwestern Coastal Forests: The Sinkyone Intertribal Park Project. *Restoration and Management Notes,* 10, pp. 64–69.

Society for Ecological Restoration (1996) Minutes of the meeting of the Board of Directors. On file.

Sorkin, Michael (1992) *Variations on a Theme Park.* The Noonday Press, New York.

Stevens, William K. (1995) *Miracle Under the Oaks: The Revival of Nature in America.* Pocket Books, New York.

Toth, Louis A. (1993) The Ecological Basis of the Kissimmee River Restoration Plan. *Biological Sciences.* No. 1, pp. 25–51.

Turner, Frederick (1994) The Invented Landscape (Reprise). *Beyond Preservation,* pp. 251–259.

Westfall, Barbara (1994) Personal Politics: Ecological Restoration as Human-scale and Community-based. *Restoration and Management Notes.* 12:2, pp. 148–151.

Wilson, Alexander (1992) *The Culture of Nature.* Blackwell, London.

PART TWO

CULTURAL STUDIES AND THE LOCATIONS OF CULTURE

5

Of *Heccéités* and *Ritournelles:*
Movement and Affect
in the Cajun Dance Arena

CHARLES J. STIVALE

One of the most challenging areas of scholarly inquiry to emerge with and more recently in response to poststructuralist critical approaches has become known broadly as "cultural studies." That this area's time has surely come, for better or for worse depending on one's perspective, was recently confirmed with the publication of *Cultural Studies* (Grossberg, Nelson, and Treichler 1992), the edited proceedings of the 1990 international conference held at the University of Illinois, Urbana/Champaign.[1] From this ambitious volume, one can glean some understanding of the concepts that structure it, that is, the importance of the intersection between the "global" and the "local." I understand this distinction as operating in this volume in terms of particular "practices": on one hand, the focus on global (national or multinational) hegemonic "practices" and structures that overshadow and even threaten regional and specific activities and expressions; on the other hand, the focus on the local as possible modes of resistance to such global practices, i.e., local expressions that even by their very existence and transmission can offer living contradictions to the often homogenizing effect of global assimilation.

Taken conceptually, however, we can also envisage the global-local dyad in a concomitant fashion. Although the former term may point to broadly applicable theoretical tools that can engage critically the diverse facets of specific, everyday practices within local sites, the latter, pointing to "local exigencies and political demands," may tend to underestimate "the values of the lines linking the various sites of cultural studies" (Grossberg 1993, 3). In regard to the *Cultural Studies* volume, one could argue that whatever the methodological, disciplinary, and even political differences between the volume's various contributors, there exists a consistent, if usually implicit, negotiation of the global-local dyad in both senses I have suggested. Such a negotiation helps to clarify the sources of tensions inherent to the otherwise elusively defined field of cultural studies, the global taken as both totalizing danger and critical potential that intersects with local practices and circumspection in possibly enlivening and possibly threatening ways.[2] Indeed, as Lawrence Grossberg argues, "If the relation between the global and local is itself an articulated one, with each existing in and constituting the other, cultural studies needs to map the lines connecting them" (1993, 3). Reflecting on this same conjuncture, Michael Bérubé concludes that in engaging in cultural studies, "one has to negotiate a busy, Bakhtinian intersection of competing sociolects—where the lived subjectivities of ordinary people stand, ideally, in a mutually transformative relation to theories *about* the lived subjectivities of ordinary people" (1994, 166).

As a French scholar attempting to understand "cultural studies" within the context of poststructuralist theories and their relation to francophone studies, I read the *Cultural Studies* volume and related discussions with special interest. Upon consulting the volume's essays and especially its index in some detail, I confirmed a long-held suspicion regarding an apparently global assumption for undertaking the examination of local practices. With the exception of essays by Meaghan Morris and Elspeth Probyn, the exclusion from this volume of references to works by Gilles Deleuze, alone and with Félix Guattari, implicitly points to the practical limitations imposed on certain voices of poststructuralist theory for critically approaching the local. Such a limitation might well lead one to conclude, for example, that the Deleuze-Guattari critical corpus is of no utility whatsoever in cultural studies research. Without denying the possible "danger," notably the risk of totalizing effects on particular local practices posed by the complex conceptual terminology developed throughout the Deleuze-Guattari corpus, I challenge both the general limitation and this particular conclusion in terms of the global-local dyad. I employ two complementary global concepts proposed by Deleuze and Guattari in *A Thousand Plateaus* as theoretical tools for examining specific local practices: on one hand, the concepts of *heccéités* (i.e., the "thisness" of "events") and *ritournelles* (i.e., effects of differences in the event's repetition), on the other hand, the dynamic and continuous reconstitution of "spaces of affect," of forms as well as of feeling, within Louisiana Cajun dance culture.[3]

I will argue that the components of *heccéités*, affect and speed that constitute an event, provide a precise means to describe the reconfigurations in Cajun dance arenas of "spatial practices" through dialogic interaction between musicians and dancers/spectators.[4] These are "affective investments" through which "the body [understood as more than simply a semantic space and less than a unity defining our identity] is placed into an apparently immediate relation to the world" (Grossberg 1986, 185; cf. also Grossberg 1988; 1992). Furthermore, the concept of *ritournelles* serves to describe more precisely the event under scrutiny—not only the music (lyrics and rhythms) that drives the dance performance but also the physical repetition of steps and movements through which the dancers' propulsion enables them to engage in dialogue with each other as well as with the musicians. Admittedly, any written discussion is inherently hampered without the experiences of live music and dance performances and distanced necessarily from the actual physical structures within which such experiences habitually occur. However, after providing a brief historical overview of this particular area of Louisiana folklore, I hope to communicate some effects of *heccéités* and *ritournelles*, first with reference to the lyrics of one French Cajun song and then with evocations of dance/music images that must serve as a pale substitute for on-site experiences.[5] I will argue that these theoretical, global tools not only provide purchase for defining and understanding a specific set of folkloric interests and pursuits, but I also propose these terms and analyses as a way of beginning to redress what Jody Berland has identified as a limitation of discussion of cultural technologies, music "rarely conceived spatially . . . in relation to the changing production of spaces for listeners" (Grossberg, Nelson, and Treichler 1992, 39). These analyses will enable me, I hope, to envisage cultural studies as a means of straddling a zone "in-between" the local and the global by functioning as a "territorializing machine" that "attempts to map the sorts of places people can occupy and how they can occupy them" (Grossberg 1993, 15) in terms of their possibilities for investment, empowerment, and even resistance.

Cultural Origins

As background for this analysis, I wish first to present a brief account of the process of globalization at the heart of the cultural forms that I will subsequently discuss. The French founded Louisiana in 1682 (Robert Cavelier, sieur de la Salle), and the contested term *Creole* refers to descendents of the first French settlers (as distinct from French immigrants) and also to the descendents of slaves of Afro-Caribbean origin born in Louisiana. As for the Cajuns, their Acadian ancestors descend from the first European settlers in the North America: most left Europe from the area in western France between *Le Poitou* and *La Vendée* and settled in a colony founded for France in 1604, *L'Acadie* (Nova Scotia and New Brunswick). After English colonization, the descendents of these settlers refused to forswear their Catholic faith and pledge allegiance to the British king, so they were expelled in 1755 in a mass deportation that has come to be known as *le Grand Dérangement* (the Great Upheaval). After several decades and various circuitous routes, the *Acadiens* settled in southern Louisiana between 1765 and 1785. Because of class differences, these exiles remained distant from the French Creoles, settling along the bayous (south and west of New Orleans) and in the prairies and wetlands (west of the Atchafalaya Basin), interacting and intermarrying with their neighbors, including Creoles of Afro-Caribbean descent. The mostly rural *Acadiens*, whose name evolved by deformation to *Cajuns*, adapted well and prospered in their new environment throughout the nineteenth century, but because of the Civil War, their socioeconomic structures collapsed and were not rebuilt until well into the next century. The Cajuns' assimilation to American culture occurred quite slowly until after World War II, then accelerated with exposure to cultural and technological influences from outside the region.[6]

The development of Cajun music is directly related to the spaces in which social gatherings took place in the rural communities, especially the *bals de maison* (house dances) held regularly in the homes of individuals. The tradition developed that after a week of hard work, there followed a night of hard play, with local musicians providing the rhythms in the limited dance space, and a common meal and refreshments were shared by all participants. In these *bals de maison* (also known as *fais dodo* in reference to the children encouraged by parents to sleep [*fais dodo*] in the "cry room" near the dance floor), the families socialized, young men and women courted, and the musicians and dancers honed their skills. Following this tradition, the dances developed eventually in public halls. The music is a blend of German, Spanish, Scottish, Irish, Anglo-American, Afro-Caribbean, and American Indian influences with a base of French and French Acadian folk traditions, what Louisianans would call *un vrai gumbo*.[7]

In the late 1920s, the first recording of the music of Southern Louisiana was made. "Allons à Lafayette" was recorded in 1928 by Joseph and Cleoma Falcon. Over the next thirty years, the fortunes of Cajun music were linked to successive waves of musical influences that usually overwhelmed the rural form, e.g., Texas country swing in the 1930s. With the return of GIs to Louisiana following World War II, interest grew in the region's traditional music, especially thanks to the compositions and revival of the accordion by musicians such as Iry Lejeune and Nathan Abshire. Traditional Cajun music lost considerable ground in the late 1950s and especially in the 1960s with the British musical invasion, but at the same time the various national folk festivals nurtured a growing interest in ethnic musical expression. The revival of Cajun music in traditional and progressive forms is generally dated from the appearance at the 1964 Newport Folk Festival of Gladius Thibodeaux, Louis "Vinesse" Lejeune, and Dewey Balfa, who received a standing ovation. Balfa returned to Louisiana as a veritable ambassador to bring Louisiana Cajun music into greater view and to encourage younger musicians to adopt and adapt French Cajun musical forms.[8] Since then, the Cajun cultural "renaissance" has proceeded on a number of fronts, including linguistic, pedagogical, and culinary.[9] The growing interest in Cajun musical and dance expressions has provided the greatest impetus toward access to the specific cultural heritage.[10] However, this access does not exist without tensions that relate to global and local issues, particularly between fans of more "progressive" musicians (i.e., zydeco/rhythm-and-blues–oriented bands, such as Zachary Richard, Wayne Toups and ZydeCajun, Filé, Bruce Daigrepont, and Beausoleil) who record and perform nationally and internationally, and fans of more "traditional," local musicians (for example, Savoy-Doucet Band, Balfa Toujours, among many others) who tend to limit the range of their performances and recording activities.[11]

Spaces and *Heccéités*

To examine Cajun music and dance as forms of "spatial practice" and to situate these at an intersection of the global and the local, I posit a process of reconstitution of feeling I call "spaces of affect," through which Cajun musicians and fans (dancers and spectators alike) together engage in continuous dialogical exchange as responses to their reciprocal (musical and dance) performances. The formulation spaces of affect precisely constitutes a global-local intersection as a way of envisaging (global) modes of reciprocal dynamics and collective assemblages occurring in the (local) Cajun dance arena in terms of *heccéités*. Specifically, just as dancers form couples to waltz, two-step, and jitterbug in variable responses to the anticipated musical performance, the musicians prepare at each dance site to provide the musical style(s) that anticipate the physical, i.e., performative, dance demands of the particular audience. These assemblages are based therefore on traits of *heccéités*, i.e., the mutual "relations of movement and rest" and the capacities of participants on both sides of the stage front "to affect and be affected" in interactive exchange (Deleuze and Guattari 1987, 261). As Henri Lefebvre notes, music and dance rhythms "embrace both [the] cyclical and [the] linear," and it is "through the mediation of rhythms (in all three senses of 'mediation': means, medium, intermediary) [that] an animated space comes into being which is an extension of the space of bodies" (1991, 206–207). I maintain that these variable experiences of speed and affect circulating intensely between musicians and dancers/spectators contribute both to the incessant reconstitution of spaces of affect within specific performance arenas *and* to the often contradictory and usually conflicting preferences of musicians and fans alike regarding concomitant musical and dance practices, a conflict to which I will return in the final section of this chapter.[12]

Although this argument is necessarily limited by the absence of our (reader's and writer's) envelopment in the *heccéités* of a Cajun dance arena, in the dynamic process I designate as spaces of affect, I ask the reader to cast his or her memories back in time and space to those peak events when feelings and movement coalesced into indescribably, ineffably privileged experiences, occurring perhaps all too infrequently as we get older. It might have been on a playground on a warm spring night with a few friends gathered around, or in a summer camp activity with hundreds of children, or alone on a rooftop, or in a field gazing at the stars. It might have been on a sailboat, or surfing, or on dangerous white water, or on a lonely trail. It might have been with a lover or a child, in a foreign country, in the street, or the backyard over the barbecue. It might even have been in front of the classroom, or around a seminar table with students and colleagues, or alone with pencil in hand or before the computer monitor, in those fleeting moments of creation and understanding, of joy at making no apologies for what it is "we do."

If the lyrical "excess" I have just produced seems more appropriate for an article on Lamartine than on either local Cajun dance spaces or on global theoreti-

cal discourse, this affective evocation remains entirely within the problematics of
heccéités, i.e., the "in-between" zone in which local investments and resistances
engage broader issues of enunciation, articulation, and power, the very "becoming of place and space" (Grossberg forthcoming). As Deleuze and Guattari ask,
"What is the individuality of a day, a season, an event?" they respond that "a degree, an intensity, is an individual, a *Haecceity* that enters into composition with
other degrees, other intensities, to form another individual." And just as "these degrees of participation . . . imply a flutter, a vibration in the form itself that is not
reducible to the properties of a subject . . . that prevent the heat of the whole from
increasing," this is all the more reason "to effect distributions of intensity, to establish latitudes that are 'deformedly deformed,' speeds, slownesses, and degrees
of all kinds corresponding to a body or set of bodies taken as longitude: a car-
tography" (1987, 253). They muse on the variety of modes of individuations, of
heccéités, that "consist entirely of relations of movement and rest between mole-
cules and particles, capacities to affect and be affected" (1987, 261): demonology,
contes, haiku, wind in Charlotte Brontë, "five in the evening" in Lorca, meteorol-
ogy in Tournier, a walk through the crowd in Virginia Woolf, a group of girls in
Proust (1987, 261–263, 271). And were one tempted to accept "an oversimplified
conciliation, as though there were on the one hand formed subjects, of the thing
or person type, and on the other hand spatio-temporal coordinates of the haecceity type," Deleuze and Guattari insist:

> You will yield nothing to haecceities unless you realize that that is what you are, and
> that you are nothing but that. . . . You are longitude and latitude, a set of speeds and
> slownesses between formed particles, a set of nonsubjectified affects. You have the in-
> dividuality of a day, a season, a year, a *life* (regardless of its duration)—a climate, a
> wind, a fog, a swarm, a pack (regardless of its regularity). Or at least you can have it,
> you can reach it (1987, 262).

But "where are the Cajuns?" the reader (and writer) may well ask at this point.
Where do local practices (Cajun dance and music) intersect all this talk of mole-
cules and particles, this swarm of global concepts? The analysis I propose is precisely an attempt to understand the event, specifically in the Cajun music/dance
arena, from an "in-between" perspective by proposing the concept of *heccéités* as
consisting not "simply of a decor or backdrop that situates subjects, or of ap-
pendages that hold things and people to the ground" (Deleuze and Guattari 1987,
262). Rather, I wish to understand *heccéités* in the music/dance arena as "the entire assemblage in its *individuated aggregate* . . . defined by a longitude and a lat-
itude, by speeds and affects, independently of forms and subjects, which belong
to another plane" (Deleuze and Guattari 1987, 262, my emphasis). This facet of
my project, to situate the global and the local through a perhaps ineffable "in-between" of *heccéités* conceived in it-/themselves, leads to a quandary that Guattari
recognized: "As soon as one decides to quantify an affect, one loses its qualitative
dimensions and its power of singularization, of heterogenesis, in other words, its

eventful compositions, the '*heccéités*' that it promulgates" (Guattari 1990, 67).[13] Yet if *heccéités* are elusive when "quantified," it is through the concept of *ritournelles* that I hope to extend my consideration of the "individuated aggregate" within the Cajun music/dance arena.

Ritournelles and Affective Territories

I have selected a waltz performed by the group Beausoleil on their album *Bayou Boogie* because the song serves both as an exemplar for discussing the multiple connotations of the concept of *ritournelle* and as a starting point to illustrate, however approximately, the possibilities of rhythm, movement, speed, and affect that contribute to forming *heccéités* within the focal events. By providing both stanzas and the refrain, I first wish to emphasize the recurrence of similar locutions that correspond to the regular, 3/4 waltz meter:

La Valse du Malchanceux	The Unlucky [Man's] Waltz
C'est ça la valse après jouer	That's the waltz that was playing
Quand moi, j'ai fait mon idée	When I made up my mind
C'est ça la valse après jouer	That's the waltz that was playing
Chez ma belle j'ai parti	When I set out for her house
C'est ça la valse après jouer	That's the waltz that was playing
Quand à ma belle j'ai demandé	When I asked for my sweetheart's hand
C'est ça la valse après jouer	That's the waltz that was playing
Quand ses parents m'ont refusé.	When her parents refused me.
[Refrain]	
C'est ça la valse veux tu me	That's the waltz I want you to play
* joues sur le lit de ma mort*	for me on my deathbed
C'est ça la valse veux tu me	That's the waltz I want you to play
* joues le jour que je va mourir*	for me on the day that I die
C'est ça la valse veux tu me	That's the waltz I want you to play
* joues jusqu'à la porte du*	for me up to the gates of the cemetery
* cimetière*	
C'est ça la valse que moi	That's the waltz that I call
* j'appelle la valse du*	the unlucky man's waltz.
* malchanceux.*	

[II]

C'est ça la valse après siffler	That's the waltz that I was whistling
* mais dans le temps que*	at the time I was courting her
* je courtisais*	

C'est ça la valse après jouer	That's the waltz I was playing
quand je l'ai volée	when I stole her away
C'est ça la valse après jouer	That's the waltz I was playing
quand ils m'ont fait la marier	when they made me marry her
C'est ça la valse après jouer	That's the waltz that was playing
quand on s'est séparé.	when we separated.[14]

Whereas the term *ritournelle* translates as "refrain,"[15] I am interested in the way in which the lyrics of this waltz "return," properly speaking, in the stanzas as well. For the repeated lyrics, "C'est ça la valse après jouer . . . ," forms an incantation that combines the two forms of temporality of *heccéités, Aeon,* "the indefinite time of the event, the floating line that knows only speeds and continually divides that which transpires into an already-there that is at the same time not-yet-here," and *Chronos,* "the time of measure that situates things and persons, develops a form, and determines a subject" (Deleuze and Guattari 1987, 262). The verb *jouer* in each line, except at the start of stanza two, suggests this oscillation between temporalities since its use creates a "becoming-music" that permeates all thought and activity, linking the present *C'est ça la valse* to the indistinct past established in the Cajun locution *après* preceding an infinitive. Then, in the refrain itself, this "return" is modified in an explicitly dialogic manner, no longer the *après jouer* of an indefinite past but the plaintive *veux tu me joues* of an indistinct and yet inevitable future. The final verse of the refrain offers a closure of sorts through the self-referential manner of announcing the title, yet it also provides the lyrical bridge that leads the song into its instrumental phases and thus to the very moments in which the response to the dialogic plea, *veux tu me joues,* is actualized.

Thus "music exists," say Deleuze and Guattari, "because the refrain exists also, because music takes up the refrain, lays hold of it as a content in a form of expression, because it forms a block with it in order to take it somewhere else" (Deleuze and Guattari 1987, 300). This movement "somewhere else" occurs, they argue, through music's submitting the refrain to the "very special treatment of the diagonal or transversal," a treatment that consists in "uproot[ing] the refrain from its territoriality" through music's "creative, active operation . . . [of] deterritorializing the refrain" (Deleuze and Guattari 1987, 300). I will address in the next section ways in which such "deterritorializing" occurs in geopolitical terms, but for the moment, I wish to remain on the dance floor, as it were. There the dancers respond directly to the implicit dialogic "plea" of the Cajun song not so much in response to the actual lyrics as through the "creative operation," for example, of the 3/4 meter that defines the waltz.

These observations allow us to consider a second facet of the individuated aggregate within *heccéités.* A distinct trait or code of the actual waltz performance in the Cajun dance arena is the smooth walking step that assures the constant counterclockwise pattern of flows.[16] Yet, Deleuze and Guattari insist that "rhythm is not meter or cadence. . . . Meter is dogmatic, but rhythm is critical; it ties together critical moments" (1987, 313). The walking step of the Cajun waltz is linear while also determining spatial *ritournelles* that are at once territorializing, i.e., in the "becoming expressive of rhythm or melody" (1987, 316), and yet in constant movement toward deterritorialization, what Deleuze and Guattari call "territorial motifs" that form "rhythmic faces or characters" in relationship to "territorial counterpoints" that form "melodic landscapes" (1987, 317–318).

Such a constant interplay of "expressive qualities" forms appropriative "signatures that are the constituting mark of a domain, an abode" (Deleuze and Guattari 1987, 316). This interplay is evident from particular dance responses that the waltz generates in the dance arena, with several circular patterns usually contained within each other, all propelled by the rhythmic support from and dialogue with the musicians' expression. In the Cajun dance arena, each couple forms a unit with its own territorial individuation, and the very convention of the "lead" (male) and "following" (female) assures the smooth integration of this individuation into the assemblage.[17] The individuated aggregate thus responds to a rhythm "caught up in a becoming," say Deleuze and Guattari, "that sweeps up the distances between characters, making them rhythmic characters that are themselves more or less distant, more or less combinable" (1987, 320). One only needs to experience dancing with a novice partner, male or female, or even more pointedly alongside couples unable or unwilling to follow the coded "flow," to understand Deleuze and Guattari's formula, "It is a question of keeping at a distance the forces of chaos knocking at the door" (1987, 320). For such chaos and even physical damage can result on the dance floor through ineffective communication from the "lead" through hands, arms, and often cheek-to-cheek contact or as is more often the case between couples ineffectively maintaining the territorial "critical distance."

Thus to this fluid individuation of "becoming-expressive of rhythms," of the "signature" marking the domain or abode on the dance arena, corresponds a certain "decoding" or deterritorializing within the dance arena as the couples continue moving around the floor. Whatever flourishes introduced by the lead the partner "follows"—turnout combinations and even back-and-forth shuffles (the varsovienne) in uncrowded dance arenas or the simple conversational step (rocking back and forth in place) in the crowded space (Plater and Speyrer 1993, 53–56, 106)—these movements all shift the partners into different patterns within the counterclockwise flow, allowing for the "expressive qualities" at once to mark a familiar abode (e.g., the shared "style" of the coded waltz repertoire) and yet to maintain the territorial critical distance of distinct spatial differentiation. This combination of affect and speeds/slownesses thus contributes to maintaining a tension between deterritorializing, apparently "decoding," forces of movement and the simultaneously territorializing function in the dance arena.

Then at each song's end another facet of the *ritournelle* becomes evident as the couples clear the dance floor and situate themselves as spectators on the sides until the first strains of the next song call them back to the floor or leave them to participate as observers. In discussing the "event" in *Pourparlers* (1990), as well as in *The Fold* (1993, 103–112), Deleuze insists that "the event is inseparable from *temps morts* . . . [that are] in the event itself, it gives to the event its thickness [*épaisseur*]" (1990, 218; my translation). That is, the moments of alternation between songs are as constitutive of the *heccéité,* understood as "event," as are the activities in the music/dance *ritournelle.* Thus, the *temps mort* (literally, the "dead time," or suspended moment) is the complementary face of the flow continuing from one song to the next since it is in this "moment" that socializing occurs, that dancers can trade instructions on steps or simply recoup their energy. Moreover, the "signature" of this domain or abode manifests itself further at the juncture of the *temps mort,* for it is in this "pause" that the musicians prepare and the dancers anticipate the regular alternation between waltz (3/4) and two-step (4/4) meters. Indeed, any deviation from the equal alternation between these two forms, waltz to two-step/jitterbug and back to waltz, serves to "sign" or characterize the particular dance arena as more "traditional," i.e., with a dominance of waltzes, or more "progressive," i.e., with a dominance of two-step/jitterbug numbers.

Similarly, the kinds of dance steps chosen by dancers in response to songs of the faster 4/4 beat mark the particular dance arena and its possibilities for reconstitution of "spaces of affect." In certain dance halls, especially in rural Louisiana, that attract an audience of older dancers, the two-step is *de rigueur* as the dance response "appropriate" to songs of the 4/4 beat, and performers of the Cajun jitterbug are sometimes actively discouraged from practicing this step. To understand why, the participant in the Cajun dance arena immediately notes the flow and transformation of patterns therein not only in comparison to the usually regular counterclockwise flow of the waltz space but especially in terms of the possible lateral shifts occurring during a two-step number. That is, the two-step dance arena appears as a faster, fluid version of the waltz floor since both are walking steps, with the two-step requiring a regular rhythmic shift of the feet through eight beats.[18] The two-step also generates the complex deterritorializing effect that occurs with the waltz pattern of a quite literal, counterclockwise *ritournelle* around the dance floor, with variable configurations of flows and speeds held in check by the size of both the dance assemblage and space.

This effect is altered dramatically, however, when even one couple shifts from the two-step to the jitterbug. In the typical dance arena, e.g., at Randol's Restaurant in Lafayette, Louisiana, a few couples on the periphery of the dance floor may be able to maintain the fluid counterclockwise, two-step movement throughout the song but can do so only by carefully negotiating their dance pattern around and between the couples performing the more static jitterbug moves. Of course, each couple performing the latter remains constantly in motion. However, they simultaneously and necessarily stake out a specific "territory" on the dance floor by engaging in the regular push-pull, rotating parallelogram of the basic move combined with the intricate upper-body arm movements that can make the well-performed jitterbug so dazzling. Despite the dynamic impression that a jitterbug performance creates, one implicit statement that dancers make in shifting from the two-step to the jitterbug concerns their regard for the fragility of the territorial boundaries established in the fluid, counterclockwise movements of the two-step. Indeed, those dancers who maintain a steadfast allegiance to one step or the other may find their efforts thwarted, for example, by the aggregate of jitterbug couples who effectively block the possibility for counterclockwise flow or, conversely, by the two-steppers who tend to move forward against and even through the jitterbug pairs.[19]

Here we encounter the fundamental question of "distinction," the "judgement of taste" to which Pierre Bourdieu has devoted an exhaustive examination. As he points out, "explicit aesthetic choices are in fact often constituted in opposition to the choices of the groups closest in social space, with whom the competition is most direct and most immediate" (1984, 60). Deleuze and Guattari speak of this as "the disjunction noticeable between the code and the territory," the latter "aris[ing] in a free margin of the code" and formed "at the level of a certain *decoding*" (1987, 322). The implicit message communicated by the choice of steps in the dance performance, for example, may correspond for some dancers to their affirmation of cultural identity, i.e., to a certain means of determining margins and differentiating their own "becoming-expressive" in relation to such margins. Grossberg is thus correct in arguing that shared taste for some texts (and practices, I would maintain) "does not in fact guarantee that [the] common taste describes a common relationship. Taste merely describes people's different abilities to find pleasure in a particular body of texts [and practices] rather than another" (1992, 42). Still, as Bourdieu argues, "the most intolerable thing for those who regard themselves as the possessors of legitimate culture is the sacrilegious reuniting of tastes which taste dictates shall be separated" (1984, 56–57). The assertion of "taste" clearly manifests itself toward the conventions admissible in certain dance arenas, notably the predilection for less "embellished" waltz moves or for the two-step over the jitterbug. The specific territorial differences are thus marked *through* the code (i.e., conventions) evidently shared by some dancers, and despite its complexity and fluidity, this message comes across clearly to the musicians. They are likely to respond directly to the performers' and spectators' particular modes of "becoming-expressive" through their own variable musical modes of "becoming-dance," yet attendant to the fluctuations of "taste" manifested in particular dance arenas.

Text/Pretext and Dialogue

The links between music and dance performances lead us to note several other facets of *ritournelles* that occur within the Cajun music/dance arena. First, however the limited but vital repertoire of Cajun songs may be interpreted by musicians observing both differing elements of cultural tradition and manifestations of fans' tastes, it is clear that the repertoire's dissemination through recordings certainly constitutes important linguistic and cultural statements about musical self-representation and affirmation of Cajun identity. Yet the reconstitution of "spaces of affect" relies not on these recordings but on the *live performance* of the songs, usually the same songs within the Cajun repertoire. Moreover, since most dancers/spectators are now unlikely to understand these lyrics, the frequent experience of these songs is in the form of *pretext* for dancing and socializing in bars, restaurants, and (now less frequently) in *bals de maison*. This alternate and, I would argue, principal status of the songs does not necessarily preclude a linguistic communication. However, the examples of the Bruce Daigrepont Band's usual venue (Sunday evenings at the New Orleans club Tipitina's) or, until recently, Thursday night sets of the group Filé at the Maple Leaf in New Orleans are quite revealing. The vast majority of spectators and dancers at these events do not understand French, much less Cajun French; they do not even hear clearly, much less attend to the "message" contained in these lyrics.[20] Yet, dancers and musicians have no difficulty whatsoever in reconstituting the exhilarating "spaces of affect" through their mutual becoming-music/becoming-dance.

Thus the corresponding active appreciation of Cajun music by musicians and dancers/spectators alike is a sociocultural phenomenon that creates different "spaces of affect" in given Cajun dance arenas, where "music is a deterritorialization of the voice, which becomes less and less tied to language" (Deleuze and Guattari 1987, 302). This observation leads me to another component of this "affective economy" (Grossberg 1988, 285), the overall lack of uniformity in the dancers'/fans' response. This component allows us to illustrate one final facet of *ritournelles* and also to address the aforementioned geopolitical aspect of deterritorialization by comparing urban Cajun music/dance sites to rural settings. As previously noted, the reconstitution of "spaces of affect" is determined by the allegiance of dancers/spectators to particular musical sensibilities toward Cajun music, and this allegiance goes to the heart of the complex tensions existing in southern Louisiana regarding Cajun self-representation in relation to the dominant cultural formation. This is at once a question of the "frames" into which musicians and dancers/spectators may be situated vis-à-vis the cultural "event" *and* one of the dialogical relationship that develops among and between musicians and dancers/spectators.[21]

On one hand, considerations of "distinction" place couples in constant communication regarding the steps that territorialize the dance arena to greater or lesser degrees. Thus borrowing from J. Lowell Lewis (1992, 195), "inner games" may unfold on the dance floor and thus constitute "nested" subterritories therein in relation (and even resistance) to the more general flow of dance movement. However, whatever the differences and difficulties of articulations of "taste" toward the dance steps (and musical interpretations), the *heccéités*, with their variables of rest and speed and their concomitant expression and investment of affect, extend across and around the dance floor, encompassing even those not participating in the active dance movement per se. Indeed, by my use of the term "dancers/spectators" throughout this essay, I have meant to suggest this all-encompassing articulation constitutive of "spaces of affect," an expression enveloping spectators and musicians as well as dancers in the "dance flow."

On the other hand, without precluding the model of "nested frames," I prefer to envisage this dance space by drawing from M. M. Bakhtin to argue that *ritournelles* in all their forms develop in a "dialogical" relationship between musicians and dancers/spectators (cf. Bakhtin 1981, 270–275). In many rural dance halls and certain festivals of southern Louisiana, *centrifugal* relations prevail between musicians and dancers. That is, these relations are oriented outward away from the musicians with an emphasis on the performance of the dancers, in synch with the musicians' expressions but beyond them. In these centrifugal contexts not only do the musical groups most popular locally respect the fans' desire for familiar and relatively simplified musical forms, some local populations themselves (usually older fans) frown on, if not actively discourage, the responsive dance innovations, notably the Cajun jitterbug, that frequently accompany the more "progressive" musical cadences. Elsewhere such as in many urban dance arenas and especially in concert and festival settings outside Louisiana, the *centripetal* or musician-oriented relation occurs. Such circumstances (to entertain usually passive audiences and free-form, rock-nourished dancers) create demands on musicians for the "fusion" and experimental sounds that bands such as Beausoleil, Filé, and Wayne Toups and ZydeCajun bring to their music.[22]

This negotiation of centripetal/centrifugal relations between dancers/spectators and musicians allows us to address how the global and the local intersect within the elements of *heccéités* and *ritournelles*. The contrasting dance sites and modes of exchange therein certainly determine different possibilities for reconstitution of spaces of affect, possibilities that concern the global appropriation of Cajun cultural forms by apparently external American mass culture. It is clear that the creation of renewed spaces of affect through the dynamic interaction between musicians and dancers/spectators allows Cajuns (and even so-called Cajuns-by-choice) to participate literally and figuratively in the two-step of self-representation. However, this process is complicated, I maintain, by the shifting articulations of Cajun identity in relation to the ever-present "instability of frontiers" imposed from conditions of the surrounding hegemonic formation (Laclau and Mouffe 1985, 136). The joyful, affirmative strength that emerges in musical lyrics and forms (including dance steps) may strike back and at times assert its own counterinvasive mode of territoriality in the face of various forms of appropriation. Indeed, just as many lyrics in Cajun music emphasize precisely this individual integrity in the face of adversity, the attitudes of fans and musicians alike clearly support Bourdieu's contention about marking "distinction," that "the song [and, I would argue in this context, the dance], as a cultural property which (like photography) is almost universally accessible and genuinely common . . . calls for particular vigilance from those who intend to mark their difference" (1984, 60). Thus, whereas certain groups (notably, in some chapters of the Cajun French Music Association) explicitly "prohibit" members from dancing the jitterbug (aka the jig) at Association-sponsored events, other fans (particularly among the fluid uptown New Orleans dance crowd) insist on more free-form interpretations of the dance steps—waltz and jitterbug alike.

Yet in the very negotiation between seemingly conflicting articulatory practices, particularly between apparently "outside" and even global forces in relation to a locally perceived "inside" of the cultural frame, musicians often express and their fans often exhibit a deterritorializing ambivalence toward the musical and cultural identity and heritage being reinforced. For in seeking to reach ever wider audiences and thereby attain forms of popularity (and economic rewards), musicians necessarily contribute to the inherently equivocal articulations and thus to an active reterritorialization by the dominant cultural formation. In seeking an audience beyond what is frequently viewed as the *confines,* or limited market, of Cajun society in southern Louisiana, musicians and their fans often willingly participate in the appropriation of the culture's forms of expression by these same "invasive" forces. To the literal commodification of Cajun music and zydeco (e.g., in Frito-Lay and Burger King promotions), one can also add examples of such commercialized cultural representations as the film *The Big Easy* and the 1990 Dolly Parton/Louisiana ABC television special.[23]

A final example illustrates how facets of *ritournelles* in the dynamic dancer/musician dialogue can help clarify the apparent sociocultural ambivalence through strategies that arise from global/local negotiations. One dance/music segment in particular, which is available commercially, suggests the active and prevalent possibilities of communication between dancers and Cajun musicians, precisely *through* the fusion of rock, zydeco, and Cajun sounds responding to the pressures of global forces of the American music industry. The final scene from the Les Blank documentary, *"J'ai Été au Bal." The Cajun and Zydeco Music of Louisiana,* emphasizes both the centripetal, musician-oriented dialogic pole and the centrifugal, becoming-dance of this music, which consists of performances-in-dialogue that take place by featuring dancers responding to the music of Wayne Toups and his band ZydeCajun. This name alone defines the deliberate musical fusion, as Toups says, "a new wave Cajun; it's Cajun music of the future" (162).[24]

Toups's poignant introductory statement reveals his awareness of the precarious equilibrium between innovation and tradition,[25] and the filmmakers then introduce the final number, which stands in sharp contrast to the film's previous Cajun performances in terms of its setting, instrumentation, and especially Toups's distinctive musical and fashion statements. In addition to the location in a carport (a modern version of the traditional site for the *bal de maison*) and the predominantly young crowd of dancers, the instrumental break presents not the traditional fiddle but the electric piano and lead guitar, followed by Toups's own impassioned performance on electrified accordion. The instrumental finale is Toups's showcase, with the accordionist—clad in muscle shirt, headband, and garish jams—emphasizing the transformative power of the traditional lyrics of the song "Allons à Lafayette" from music to dance and back again, with electrified instrumentation and the mixture of Cajun, zydeco, and rock cadences. As for the dancers, because of the accelerated 4/4 beat, the two-step simply becomes too difficult, especially on a dance floor on which the smooth negotiating necessary for this step would be impossible. Thus the jitterbug is an entirely appropriate response to the pace set not only by the energetic beat but also by the territorializing elements in this particular "becoming-expressive of rhythm of melody" (Deleuze and Guattari 1987, 316).

This film segment brings into sharp relief the strategies deliberately pursued by bands such as Toups's ZydeCajun and Michael Doucet's Beausoleil to negotiate implicitly the global/local pressures. While surviving commercially with recording contracts and attracting listeners and dancers, new and old alike, with their "fusion" sound, these bands also seek to integrate and thereby to develop and extend their cultural heritage with and through this very sound. Live performances of these and other groups show the extent to which they remain concerned (though certainly not in the terms I adopt) with maintaining the waltz/two-step *ritournelle,* with enhancing the *heccéités,* i.e., the combined elements of speed and affect, and thus and especially with maximizing the performance dialogue between musicians and dancers/spectators in venues outside as well as within Louisiana.[26] Thus, in contrast to critics (notably Ancelet 1990 and 1992; Savoy 1988) who have addressed the global/local conflict in the apocalyptic or oppositional terms of dilution of Cajun heritage, I understand this dialectic as variations on *l'invention du quotidien* (the invention of daily life), i.e., the negotiated and shifting construction of diverse spatial practices.

It is precisely the continuing capacity to define diverse "spaces of affect" through the constitutive facets of *ritournelles* in Cajun music and dance that ensures future possibilities of innovation and renewed self-definition within the Cajun heritage. The Deleuze-Guattari methodological perspectives are productive, I believe, for understanding the expressive potentials and thresholds inherent to the local intersections of dance and musical performances. Although global concepts such as *heccéités* and *ritournelles* allow us to examine the varied forms of the dance/music dialogue in which dancers/spectators and musicians engage at each dance/music site, these concepts also help establish connections toward the ongoing sociocultural dialectic engaged in the same sites—in the dance arenas upon which the local and the global intersect and often collide. These geopolitical negotiations of "forms and feelings" are precisely the proper focus of a cultural studies understood not in a limited territorialized sense of dueling disciplines but rather as deterritorializing openings toward and negotiations between adjoining theoretical and conceptual articulations and strategies.

N O T E S

1. See Bérubé (1994, 137–160), Nelson (1991), and Pfister (1992) for discussion of this conference and/or this volume. See also Pavel's (1992) reactionary assessment of this volume and of American "cultural studies." On the conference, Bérubé remarks, in contrast to the complaint made during the Illinois conference that "these counter-hegemonic proceedings were being recorded to produce a book—and upon publication, would therefore

be forcibly inscribed into the dominant American imaginary," that "such gatherings do not sufficiently contribute to the commodification of critical discourse." He concludes that since "we do have potential readers, constituencies, and clients whom we haven't yet learned—or bothered—to address," it is incumbent upon the "Profession [to] revise thyself" (171–172).

2. See Grossberg, Nelson, and Treichler's (1992) introduction to this volume for a discussion of this elusive definition (1–16).

3. As Bogue notes, Deleuze and Guattari borrow the term "hecceities" from Duns Scotus (*haecceitas*) to designate "an 'atmosphere,' in the sense both of a particular meteorological configuration and of a given ambience or affective milieu" (1991, 134, 154). Massumi (1992) observes further that "the emphasis on the 'thisness' of things is not to draw attention to their solidity or objectness, but on the contrary to their transitoriness, the singularity of their unfolding in space-time (being as flux; metastability)" (183).

4. On "spatial practices," see de Certeau (1990, li); on the "dance arena," see Hazzard-Gordon. On dialogics, I adopt and adapt concepts suggested by Bakhtin.

5. Much rich visual documentation is available in Rhonda Case Severn's work "Discovering Acadiana" (1991).

6. This summary relies on Carl Brasseaux's oral history recounted in Severn (1992) as well as on Ancelet (1989). See also Brasseaux (1987 and 1992), Conrad (1993), and Dormon (1983).

7. Zydeco, the most recent indigenous expression of African-American Creole music in Louisiana, also developed from these same roots, but with a stronger influence of Afro-Caribbean rhythms and styles. The impact of zydeco and blues forms on Cajun music and on dance spaces is quite important, and one could further complicate these already complex questions by considering them in terms of racial tensions that have existed and continue to exist in southern Louisiana, particularly as these relate to cultural expressions such as dance and music. Although these questions are beyond the scope of this essay, which is limited to Cajun music of European origins and the dance spaces in which this music is performed, I develop in the essay's final section the relations of different musical forms, including zydeco, in terms of the global/local dyad. See Blank and Strachwitz's film *J'ai Été au Bal* (1989) that develops quite clearly the link between Cajun music and zydeco. See also the zydeco issue of *Living Blues* (1991).

8. This summary relies on Ancelet (1989), Ancelet et al. (1991), Ann Savoy (1984), and the interview with Marc Savoy in *"J'ai Été au Bal"* (1989). See also Ancelet (1984).

9. See Ancelet (1988) on teaching French in Louisiana.

10. Although it would be impossible to acknowledge all those who have contributed to the Cajun cultural "renaissance" since the mid-1960s, two spokesmen, Revon Reed and Paul C. Tate, were honored at the 1993 Mamou (Louisiana) Cajun Music Festival. See Reed, Tate, and Bihm (1969) on "voice" in Cajun music as well as Reed's renowned *Lâche Pas La Patate*.

11. A group that tends to straddle this divide is Steve Riley and the Mamou Playboys. Recording on the Rounder label, nominated for a Grammy for their 1993 album *Trace of Time*, and touring extensively, the band still maintains a strong "traditional" sound, drawing from the stock repertoire of Cajun music, while also developing new and innovative compositions enhanced by the virtuosity of Steve Riley (on accordion and fiddle) and David Greeley (on fiddle).

12. Turner (1977) discusses similar phenomena of "plural reflexivity" in terms of "liminal" or "framed spaces" (33–36). See also Turner (1982, 20–60).

13. Both Buydens (1990) and Bogue (1991) develop the possibilities of *heccéités* in the musical form; Burnett (1993) and Saper (1991) approach *heccéités,* in admittedly different ways, for the hypertext computer environment. On Deleuze-Guattari and hypertext, see Moulthrop (1994) and Rosenberg (1994).

14. Traditional: Lawrence Walker. I transcribe all lyrics exactly as printed on the record jacket except two translations that I revise: the title (from "The Unlucky Waltz") and in the second to last verse from "That's the waltz I was playing when we were married." Permission for this transcription was granted by Rounder Records.

15. See Deleuze and Guattari (1987, 310) plateau 11, "1837: Of the Refrain."

16. For a more specific analysis of "flows," see Turner (1977; 1982, 55–58).

17. On the waltz conventions, see Plater and Speyrer (1993, 35–36, 51–56).

18. Male/lead: 1) L forward 2) R together 3) L forward 4) R touches L, 1) R forward 2) L together 3) R forward 4) L touches R; female/partner: 1) R back 2) L together 3) R back 4) L touches R, 1) L back 2) R together 3) L back 4) R touches L (Plater and Speyrer 1993, 57).

19. Under the influence of recent country music dance practices, the reintroduction of line dances in the Cajun dance arena, usually to slow two-step numbers (formerly danced as the rock "freeze"), has created a new form of territorialization that can effectively block all forward, two-step flow and also impede the dynamic jitterbug movement. Acceding to these diverse and often conflicting tastes, the organizers of the 1993 Mamou Cajun Music Festival provided an open grassy space directly in front of the bandstand for line dancing, juxtaposed to but away from the wooden dance floor.

20. See Grossberg (1986, 180–182) on the "hollow or superficial" treatment of musical texts by rock-and-roll fans.

21. One might define the constitution of "spaces of affect" in terms of frames of "play" or "games" that are simply boundaries between "inside" and "outside" (Lewis 1992, 191; cf. Goffman 1986 and Bateson 1972) or that are more complex structures, e.g., embedded or "nested" frames that underlie play-forms in Western society (MacAloon 1984, 254–265; Turner 1977).

22. The "centrifugal/centripetal" dyad and the terms' necessary overlap through the mixture of both orientations in most dance arenas correspond to MacAloon's distinction that opposes the figurative "festival" (in which a joyous mood prevails) to a "spectacle" (generating a broad range of intense emotions, not necessarily joyous) (1984, 246; cf. Lewis 1992, 214). It is ironic, however, that the centripetal "spectacle" generally manifests itself quite precisely in festivals, usually those organized outside the local dance arenas of southern Louisiana. On the festival in general and its importance for Cajun self-representation, see Cantwell (1993). On the festive and ludic versus the "solemn," see also Turner (1977).

23. See the examination of these representations in Ancelet (1990).

24. See Stivale (1994) for an analysis of Les Blank's strategies of documentary representation of Cajun music and culture.

25. Toups says:

You add a little herbs and spices of rhythm and blues and a little bit of rock 'n roll—not out of line, there's a border that you can just go by, and you can't cross the border, 'cos then if you cross the border, you get away from your roots. So if you can just add little bits and pieces to it to keep the fresh feeling and the energy to give to the younger generation, but still keep that roots, tortured strong Cajun feeling in your heart, you can go a long ways (1990, 160).

26. Thus in some ways, these groups attempt to combine what Mark Slobin sees as distinct, even conflicting practices. These groups "band" with fans through an explicitly commercial relationship, but also attempt to "bond" with fans as forms of "affinity groups" that "serve as nuclei for the free-floating units of our social atmosphere, points of orientation for weary travelers looking for a cultural home" (1993, 98; see also 99–108).

BIBLIOGRAPHY

Ancelet, Barry Jean. *The Makers of Cajun Music.* Austin: University of Texas Press, 1984.
_____. "A Perspective on Teaching the 'Problem Language' in Louisiana." *The French Review* 61.3 (1988): 345–356.
_____. *Cajun Music. Its Origins and Development.* Lafayette, LA: The Center for Louisiana Studies, University of Southwestern Louisiana, 1989.
_____. "Drinking, Dancing, Brawling Gamblers Who Spend Most of Their Time in the Swamp." *The Times of Acadiana.* June 20, 1990, 12–15.
_____. "Cultural Tourism in Cajun Country: Shotgun Wedding or Marriage Made in Heaven?" *Southern Folklore* 49 (1992): 256–266.
_____, Jay Edwards, and Glen Pitre. *Cajun Country.* Jackson: The University of Mississippi Press, 1991.
Bakhtin, M. M. *The Dialogic Imagination.* Ed. Michael Holquist. Austin: University of Texas Press, 1981.
Bateson, Gregory. *Steps to an Ecology of Mind.* New York: Ballantine, 1972.
Beausoleil. *Bayou Boogie.* 1986. Cambridge, MA: Rounder Records 6015.
Berland, Jody. "Angels Dancing: Cultural Technologies and the Production of Space." In *Cultural Studies.* Ed. Lawrence Grossberg, Cary Nelson, and Paula Treichler. New York: Routledge, 1992, 38–51.
Bérubé, Michael. *Public Access. Literary Theory and American Cultural Politics.* New York: Verso, 1994.
Bogue, Ronald. *Deleuze and Guattari.* New York: Routledge, 1989.
_____. "Rhizomusicosmology." *SubStance* 66 (1991): 85–101.
Bourdieu, Pierre. *Distinction. A Social Critique of the Judgement of Taste.* Trans. Richard Nice. Cambridge: Harvard University Press, 1984 [1979].
Brasseaux, Carl. *The Founding of New Acadia: The Beginning of Acadian Life in Louisiana, 1765–1803.* Baton Rouge: Louisiana State University Press, 1987.
_____. "Oral History of Acadiana." In Rhonda Case Severn. *Discovering Acadiana,* 1991. Videocassette 2.
_____. *Acadian to Cajun. Transformation of a People, 1803–1877.* Jackson: University Press of Mississippi, 1992.
Burnett, Kathleen. "Toward a Theory of Hypertextual Design." *Postmodern Culture* 3.2 (1993): Online. January 1993.
Buydens, Mireille. *Sahara. L'esthétique de Gilles Deleuze.* Paris: Vrin, 1990.
Cantwell, Robert. *Ethnomimesis: Folklife and the Representation of Culture.* Chapel Hill: The University of North Carolina Press, 1993.

Conrad, Glenn R., ed. *The Cajuns: Essays on Their History and Culture*. Lafayette: The Center for Louisiana Studies, University of Southwestern Louisiana, 1993.

De Certeau, Michel. *L'invention du quotidien. 1. arts de faire*. Paris: Gallimard, 1990 [1980].

Deleuze, Gilles. *The Fold. Leibniz and the Baroque*. Trans. Tom Conley. Minneapolis: University of Minnesota Press, 1993 [1988].

_____. *Pourparlers*. Paris: Minuit, 1990.

_____, and Félix Guattari. *A Thousand Plateaus*. Trans. Brian Massumi. Minneapolis: University of Minnesota Press, 1987 [1980].

Dormon, James H. *The People Called Cajuns*. Lafayette: The Center for Louisiana Studies, University of Southwestern Louisiana, 1983.

Goffman, Erving. *Frame Analysis*. Boston: Northeastern University Press, 1986 [1974].

Grossberg, Lawrence. "Teaching the Popular." In *Theory in the Classroom*. Ed. Cary Nelson. Urbana and Chicago: University of Illinois Press, 1986. 177–200.

_____. "Postmodernity and Affect: All Dressed Up With No Place to Go." *Communication* 10 (1988): 271–293.

_____. *We Gotta Get Out of This Place. Popular Conservatism and Postmodern Culture*. New York: Routledge, 1992.

_____. "Cultural Studies and/in New Worlds." *Critical Studies in Mass Communications* 10 (1993): 1–22.

_____. "Space and Globalization in Cultural Studies." Forthcoming.

_____, Cary Nelson, and Paula Treichler, eds. *Cultural Studies*. New York: Routledge, 1992.

Guattari, Félix. "Ritornellos and Existential Affects." *Discourse* 12.2 (1990): 66–81.

Hazzard-Gordon, Katrina. *Jookin': The Rise of Social Dance Formations in African-American Culture*. Philadelphia: Temple University Press, 1990.

J'ai Été au Bal. I Went to the Dance. The Cajun and Zydeco Music of Louisiana. 1989. Dir. Les Blank and Chris Strachwitz. Ed. Maureen Gosling. Narr. Barry Jean Ancelet and Michael Doucet. Brazos Films.

Laclau, Ernesto, and Chantal Mouffe. *Hegemony and Socialist Strategy. Towards a Radical Democratic Politics*. New York: Verso, 1985.

Lefebvre, Henri. *The Production of Space*. Trans. Donald Nicholson-Smith. Oxford and Cambridge: Blackwell, 1991 [1974].

Lewis, J. Lowell. *Ring of Liberation. Deceptive Discourse in Brazilian Capoeira*. Chicago: University of Chicago Press, 1992.

Living Blues. 22.4 (July/August 1991).

MacAloon, John J. "Olympic Games and the Theory of Spectacle in Modern Societies." In *Rite, Drama, Festival, Spectacle. Rehearsals Toward a Theory of Cultural Performance*. Ed. John J. MacAloon. Philadelphia: ISHI, 1984. 241–280.

Massumi, Brian. *A User's Guide to Capitalism and Schizophrenia*. Cambridge: The MIT Press, 1992.

Moulthrop, Stuart. "Rhizome and Resistance: Hypertext and the Dreams of a New Culture." In *Hyper/Text/Theory*. Ed. George P. Landow. Baltimore: The Johns Hopkins University Press, 1994. 299–319.

Nelson, Cary. "Always Already Cultural Studies: Two Conferences and a Manifesto." *Journal of the Midwest Modern Language Association* 24.1 (1991): 24–38.

Pavel, Thomas. "Les études culturelles: une nouvelle discipline?" *Critique* 545 (1992): 731–742.

Pfister, Joel. "The Americanization of Cultural Studies." *The Yale Journal of Criticism* 4.2 (1992): 199–229.

Plater, Ormonde, and Cynthia and Rand Speyrer. *Cajun Dancing.* Gretna, LA: Pelican Publishing Co., 1993.

Reed, Revon. *Lâche Pas La Patate. Portrait des Acadiens de la Louisiane.* Ottawa, Canada: Editions Parti Pris, 1976.

_____, Paul Tate, and Kathy Bihm. "The Voice in the Soul of Cajun Music." *Louisiana Heritage* 1.4 (1969): 14–15.

Riley, Steve, and the Mamou Playboys. *Trace of Time.* 1993. Cambridge, MA: Rounder Records C–6053.

Rosenberg, Martin E. "Physics and Hypertext: Liberation and Complicity in Art and Pedagogy." In *Hyper/Text/Theory.* Ed. George P. Landow. Baltimore: The Johns Hopkins University Press, 1994. 268–298.

Severn, Rhonda Case. *Discovering Acadiana,* 1991. Videocassettes 1 and 2.

Saper, Craig. "Electronic Media Studies: From Video Art to Artificial Invention." *SubStance* 66 (1991): 114–134.

Savoy, Ann Allen. *Cajun Music. A Reflection of a People,* I. Eunice, LA: Bluebird Press, 1984.

Savoy, Marc. "Maintaining Traditions." *Louisiana Folk Life* 12 (1988): 9–12.

Slobin, Mark. *Subcultural Sounds. Micromusics of the West.* Hanover, NH: Wesleyan University Press/University Press of New England, 1993.

Stivale, Charles J. "'Spaces of Affect': Versions and Visions of Cajun Cultural History." *South Central Review* 11.4 (1994): 15–25.

Toups, Wayne, and Nathan Williams. "Interviews." *Caliban* 9 (1990): 160–177.

Turner, Victor. "Frame, Flow and Reflection: Ritual and Drama as Public Liminality." In *Performance in Postmodern Culture.* Eds. Michel Benamou and Charles Caramello. Madison, WI: Coda Press, 1977. 33–55.

_____. *From Ritual to Theatre. The Human Seriousness of Play.* New York: PAJ Publications, 1982.

6

Cosmopolitanism and Communion: Renegotiating Relations in Sara Suleri's *Meatless Days*

MIA CARTER

In the interplay of class and race, metropolis and periphery, "high" and "low," cosmopolitans have found a special home, because they are both capturing a new world reality that has a definite social basis in immigration and international communications, and are at the same time fulfilling the expectations of a metropolitan public. They bridge the literary world's Manichean spaces, and do so by exhibiting a political-aesthetic that is itself double. . . . They reinforce dominant tastes, but in a characteristically dual fashion—not in reluctant submission to values branded on to the skin of their cultures, but with apprenticelike devotion to a mind-boggling array of literary precursors from diverse regions and traditions . . . they are writers for whom the national affiliations that had been previously "given" as part of a common world view of the Third-World intellectual have lost their meaning.

—Timothy Brennan, "Anti-Colonial Liberalism" (1989, 38–39)

Absolute homelessness is indeed a myth, and so is cosmopolitanism in its strictly negative sense of "free[dom] from national limitations or attachments"—as in the doctrine, in George Boas's words, "that nationality is insignificant from every point of view."

—Bruce Robbins (1992, 173)

Very special thanks to Ann Cvetkovich, Doug Kellner, Barbara Harlow, Lisa Moore, Kirin Makker, Brian Doherty, Nabeel Zuberi, and the students enrolled in my graduate seminar, "Postcolonial Voices: Feminisms and Cosmopolitanisms" for their critical feedback, support, and editorial suggestions.

149

When used in regard to "Third World"[1] or minority writers, the term cosmopolitan accrues levels of signification that reveal all sorts of contradictory feelings about such writers' "worldliness"; these mixed feelings are sometimes particularly vexed when the worldly writer is a woman. In reference to colonial and postcolonial situations, the writer's vocation is assumed to involve commitment to Third World nationalist causes, fidelity to "native" cultural traditions, and continuation of the pedagogic and political functions of Third World literatures. Cosmopolitanism in this context implies affectation or treachery—rejection of one's local or native culture for the lure of "universal" Western European culture; in this view, cosmopolitan writers are represented as having forsaken the collective to enjoy instead the pleasures of individualism. Because cosmopolitanism involves issues of renunciation and/or affiliation, characterizations of cosmopolitan Third World writers have generally been dismissive or hostile; some of these depictions have been deserved. However, given the growth of diasporic Third World populations in Western and European nations and the increase of individuals' bi- or multicultural habits of identification and orientation, a reappraisal of Third World cosmopolitans/isms might be necessary. Rather than denoting betrayal or acquiescence to Western mythology and ideology, might contemporary cosmopolitanism more complicatedly denote the desire to inhabit, both metaphorically and literally, multiple locations or a singular location multiply, that is with various and sometimes conflicting types of cultural and national affiliations? If one considers the recent case of Bangladeshi writer Taslima Nasrin, one cannot help but notice that both the geographical and metaphorical connotations of cosmopolitanism have become increasingly diffuse. Nasrin's case also suggests that in many Third World nations, feminism has become synonymous with the negatively inflected definition of cosmopolitanism.

Nasrin, a feminist, medical doctor, poet, and novelist, found herself under attack in Bangladesh for what could be called her intellectual cosmopolitanism. Like Salman Rushdie's work, Nasrin's provocative novels *Lajja (Shame)* and *Shodh (Revenge)* have offended Muslim fundamentalists or absolutists[2] who consider her suggestions for the revision of Islamic laws blasphemous. Unlike Rushdie, Nasrin was writing about female autonomy and sexuality, domestic and national relations while residing at home; the result of this is that Nasrin had a *fatwa* (edict) issued against her, a price put on her head, and was eventually *forced* into cosmopolitan exile in Stockholm, Sweden, after hiding for months in a Western embassy in Dhaka, Bangladesh. Nasrin's advocation of feminist sexual and social liberation, critique of the Muslim majority's treatment of Bangladesh's minority Hindu population, and characterization of Bangladesh's xenophobia made her an enemy within.[3] Her representations of Bangladesh's national situation and insistence that gender issues be addressed in nationalist politics have positioned Nasrin as a dramatically noncompliant voice, one that is particularly disruptive because it refuses to adhere to the role in which women's voices in nationalist politics have frequently been assigned—that of choral supporter rather than critical commentator.

Taslima Nasrin's interest in feminist issues might be considered by some to be a reflection of how Western philosophies and concerns do not transfer to Third World cultures; for example, the conflicts between the imperatives of Western and Third World feminisms have been well documented.[4] However, the degree to which Taslima Nasrin's commitment to women's rights has been influenced by First World feminisms cannot be definitively ascertained. In Tahmina Ahmed's recent *Ms.* magazine article, Nasrin states that her writing and feminist sympathies were deeply affected by the injuries she observed while working in an obstetrics-gynecology unit. "I saw so many cases of assault on women," she recalls, describing young women who arrived with acid burns in their vaginas. "I wanted to use hard-hitting language to make men react" (Ahmed 1994, 18).

In an interview with Mary Anne Weaver, Nasrin also recounts observations of rape victims' ruptured vaginas and six- and seven-year-old incest victims (Weaver 1994, 59); in that interview, however, Nasrin states that her feminine rage (she does not explicitly refer to herself as a feminist[5]) began to gestate at a much earlier stage of her life:

> I think I've been angry all my life. It began as a child. From the moment I entered puberty, I couldn't leave the house. My father, who was more liberal than most, kept me locked away; my brothers escorted me to school, then came and picked me up. I was not permitted to do anything that they were permitted to do. I was, in a way, in a purdah of my own (59).

In the same interview, Nasrin admitted to having encountered the works of Virginia Woolf *(A Room of One's Own)* and Simone de Beauvoir ("a few chapters of . . . 'The Second Sex'," 60). However Western or cosmopolitan Nasrin's philosophical orientation might be, she is not at all unconcerned with the politics of home, in its national and domestic/familial configurations. In as much as one might be able to argue convincingly that Nasrin's feminism reflects the importation of "foreign" ideas, it could also be argued that her feminist concerns might represent a form of "organic intellectualism" as powerfully shaped by "local" experiences as by "imported" ideas. In other words, both the benignly protective and extremely violent[6] social realities of women's lives may lead women like Nasrin to exceed the domestic and political localities in the cultures from which they emerge. This lack of clarity in discerning original/indigenous and foreign/imported philosophies and epistemologies is one that powerfully suggests that the parameters of "home" and the world, the local and the global have shifted and continue to mutate. The result of which is the creation of increasingly complex political situations that signify variously in different cultural and geographic locations.[7]

Most recently, Nasrin has been championed by Western organizations like the Swedish PEN organization, which awarded her $20,000 after she fled Bangladesh in August 1994. The fatwa offered the equivalent of $2,500 as a reward to anyone who killed her, which, as Nasrin pointed out, is an enormous amount of money in Bangladesh (Weaver 1994, 54). Such are the strange economies associated with postcolonial or Third World cosmopolitanism; the Third World nation's exorbitant bounty perversely competes with the West's excessive and self-interested reward. Nasrin's exile is also complicated by this Western interest in her plight. However well-intentioned her commitment to social reform in Bangladesh may have been, the discursive economy of Nasrin's political expressions iterated in cosmopolitan exile take on different and disturbing resonances. She was recently quoted in Stockholm saying, "I wish to continue my fight against fundamentalism, which is spreading darkness to many parts of the world" (Associated Press 1994, A24), and has elsewhere bemoaned the demise of "enlightenment" in Bangladesh (Weaver 1994, 58). The committed feminist at home echoes imperialist Manichaeisms in exile, or appears to. Given Nasrin's literal run for her life from the growing throngs of fellow Bangladeshi citizens calling for her head, the logic of her metaphorical choice is clear; it also reveals what Gayatri Spivak has termed the "double bind" of language (1992, 770–771). Language's disruptive critical power—reflected in Nasrin's personal and political feminist articulations—and its polyvalent historical trace—the residual and current signifiers of the colonizer's/colonial discourse—illuminate the constantly circulating connections between revolutionary and hegemonic discourses. Language, its semantic violence and the actual violence it can inspire,[8] has and will be used against Nasrin in both the First and Third Worlds. In the Third, because her feminist commitments challenge her adversaries' fixed definition of Islamic culture; in the First because, whether intended or not, Nasrin's words and writings will be used to represent the "irrational anti-democracy" of Bangladesh/the Third World.

The quotations at the beginning of this chapter from Timothy Brennan's *Salman Rushdie and the Third World* and Bruce Robbins's "Comparative Cosmopolitanism" provide good points at which to begin examining the ambivalences, peculiarities, and challenges related to contemporary postcolonial cosmopolitan experience. I'll be examining the complexities of cosmopolitanism in the hybridized "literary/autobiographical" work of Sara Suleri, *Meatless Days,* in addition to some recent postcolonial scholarship that is concerned with interpreting and negotiating continuing global and cultural shifts. In the course of the article I'll be attempting to interpret *Meatless Days* with the aforementioned cross-cultural political peculiarities in mind. I'll also be attempting to mediate my own mixed feelings about Suleri's work, which ambivalently shuttle between critical assessments like Brennan's Marxist-revolutionary critical reading of postcolonial cosmopolitanism—which is influenced by the work of Antonio Gramsci and nationally engaged Third World writer-critic-activists such as Frantz Fanon, Amícal Cabral, Ngugi wa Thiong'o, Kwame Nkrumah, and others—and Robbins's less critical, pragmatic reading of cosmopolitanism and its relation to the academic enterprise. Although this may be an untenable situation, I am attempting to use the word "cosmopolitan" dialectically here, as it is measured and renegotiated in Bruce Robbins's "Comparative Cosmopolitanism," and historically contextualized, politically and economically problematized in Brennan's work. The benefit of such a reading may, perhaps, address the peculiarity of current and emerging "global and cultural economies," contemporary nationalisms, including those in and of the West, while additionally examining the mixed messages of Suleri's postcolonial cosmopolitan scholarly and artistic expressions. My desire to enact such a reading relates, *in part*, to my own biographical, literary, ideological, and academic "idiosyncrasies." These idiosyncrasies are related to my being: a "not black enough"[9] African-American raised, as were three preceding generations of my family, in an all-white community; an academic who teaches high modernist and "Third World" literatures; an "atypically different" (not that there are any *typically* different people, in the first place) person who has observed the dis-ease that my various dimensionalities have caused and can cause in social situations; and a teacher of postcolonial theory who has all too often had to face some of her students' displeasure and/or discomfort with ("too") theoretically sophisticated postcolonial critics. In short, I am interested in examining the ways in which "the personal" complicates "the political," which is itself always already complicated. My idiosyncrasies are significant here precisely because Suleri's work (and my analysis of it) has led me to consider the impact of disciplinary training, literary traditions, and epistemological influences on interpretive practices. How has my New Critical and poststructuralist training; my experiences as a social "misfit"; my romantic belief in the power of feminist sisterhood; my love of lush prose and impatience with dogmatic beliefs affected my reading of *Meatless Days?* For example, I cannot ignore the fact that my appreciation of the text is greatly influenced by its beauty and complexity, those cosmopolitanisms that I've inherited in my journey from English major to English professor. Suleri's *Meatless Days* is concerned with the troubling of cultural and national origins; it suggests that our descriptive categories and the ideological, critical, and aesthetic desires, prejudices, and expectations that influence their definition need to be further complicated. Her work points out the benefits and challenges involved with these processes of (self) examination and redefinition.

Timothy Brennan's work incisively points out the ways in which cosmopolitanism itself is cultivated and supported by the market: publishing conglomerates, the mass media, Western governmental powers. Postcolonials' aesthetic and political cosmopolitanism, he points out, enables the Western audience to continually celebrate and disseminate its humanist-internationalist-democratic mythologies. Postcolonial "literary celebrities" are specially selected and rewarded for supplying their "sceptical readings of national liberation struggles" (Brennan 1989, ix). Cosmopolitanism, he argues, enables the continuation of the West's hegemonic cultural and political power; it is, in other words, neocolonialism neatly and glamorously packaged.

Many of the Third World "celebrities" Brennan discusses powerfully support his readings of postcolonial cosmopolitans—Mario Vargas Llosa, Bharati Mukherjee, and the always available for this sort of reading classic case, V. S. Naipaul.[10] *Salman Rushdie and the Third World* continues the cogent examination of the concurrent rise of the novel and the imperial age presented in Benedict Anderson's *Imagined Communities*. However, because Brennan sustains his argument by focusing primarily on the novel form in his critique of new cosmopolitanisms, he does not specifically address the merits, ironies, or particularities of critical cosmopolitan discourses, for example, the academic publishing-consuming market that Robbins's essay addresses. His dependence on Anderson's theorization of the narrative power of nationalist discourses also presents a massified and firmly historicized depiction of "the people" and relies on a configuration of national literature that is becoming simultaneously more rare and more complex.[11] The textual stability and authoritative scriptural power of nationalist narratives Anderson's *Imagined Communities* presents has been compellingly challenged in Homi Bhabha's "Signs Taken for Wonders" and more recently in Bhabha's "DissemiNation: Time, Narrative and the Margins of the Modern Nation." "The people," Bhabha suggests, "are neither the beginning nor the end of the national narrative; they represent the cutting edge between the totalizing powers of the 'social' as homogeneous, consensual community, and the forces that signify the more specific address to contentious, unequal interests and identities within the population" (1994, 146). For example, the question of women and gender politics in either Third World or Western metropolitan nationalist movements presents one constellation of issues and subjects that troubles any certain articulation of "the people," a point to which I will return shortly.

Other contemporary instances further illuminate the ambiguities of national and international crises: communalist and tribal violence in Bangladesh, India, Pakistan, Rwanda, Bosnia, etc.; political violence in Haiti continues its cyclical patterns of revenge and retribution. How can Western representations of the Third World's "irrationality," "barbarity," or "primitivism" be effectively countered, especially when such accounts entirely overlook the history of imperialism in the countries being demonized? How does a Third World popular nationalism address the spread of global capitalism or the increase of various diasporic communities? How does one define citizenship or national affiliation near the end of the twentieth century, especially when these definitions are affected by anxieties related to expansionism (NAFTA, GATT) *and* economic decline (California's Proposition 187)? One suspects that, given the homogenizing imperatives of nationalist and fundamentalist discourses in the Third *and* First Worlds, the various perspectives of international diasporic communities might be critical in what is sure to be the tenuous definition of twenty-first-century nations and their citizenry. These contemporary situations seem to be suggesting that Third World nationalist commitment alone cannot resolve the distinct national situations. This is not at all to suggest that one just throws up the hands, shakes the head, and sighs with disappointment or disillusionment at the "tragedies" of the Third World or that one becomes a postcolonial "celebrity" spokesperson for Western culture's allegedly superior virtues. It might mean the present geopolitical moment suggests that Third World popular nationalisms will be affected by both progressive and hegemonic internal/local and internationalist/global influences, and that, for better or worse, interdependency and internationalism are part of the current situation precisely because cultural and economic currencies continue to collide and comingle. All of which suggests that even (partially) Westernized postcolonial voices might have something significant to say about the ambiguity of national feelings.

In "Comparative Cosmopolitanism," Bruce Robbins defines cosmopolitanism as a kind of "new worldliness" (1992, 170), a critical posture that addresses "planetary expansiveness of subject matter" and "unembarrassed acceptance of professional self-interest" (1992, 170). This tentatively defined and articulated critical practice, Robbins suggests, might effectively counter right-wing representations of cultural relativity, i.e., the abandonment of "culture" for multiculturalism, as well as left and right accusations of academic partiality or privilege. Characterizations of the academician's privatized or specialized discourses, local and global "special interest" agendas could be, Robbins suggests, differently appraised, represented, and reformulated as the contemporary cultural critic's cosmopolitan situation. "It is an article of our contemporary faith that . . . intellectuals and academics are not 'detached' but situated—situated, for instance, as metropolitans and/or professionals" writes Robbins. And to this he adds some crucial questions that also pertain to the following analysis of *Meatless Days:* "What precisely do we mean by the 'situatedness' we devoutly claim to believe in? What excess baggage does it carry? How tightly does it restrict access to the other places we communicate with? How far can this metaphor of locality be reconciled with the expansive awareness or worldliness that we also aspire to?" (1992, 172).

In the essay, Robbins addresses the intentionality of his use of the plural by stating, "I am primarily interested here in addressing people who, like myself, earn an uneasy living from cultural work in professions and institutions that sometimes seem aimed against the political and ethical principles which give that work such meaning as it has" (1992, 184). This statement acknowledges the Western critic's (relative) material and cultural privileges and highlights the ways in which the unwary and un-self-critical academic might find his or her politically well-intentioned voice and work coopted or contradicted by the institutional powers and traditions that support the critic. Robbins also acknowledges the plain fact that many of "us," while writing about the Third World, are writing in the West, being supported by Western institutions, being published by Western journals, and being read by a primarily Western and academic audience, and cannot, with any ease, escape the conflictual realities, uncomfortable ironies, or economic verities of this situation. By positively reappropriating cosmopolitanism, Robbins suggests, we can acknowledge its relation to capital, cultural, and national power *and* imagine a broader definition of worldliness "without," he notes, "giving up an insistence on *belonging*—an insistence that includes the possibility of presence in other places, dispersed but real forms of membership, a density of overlapping allegiances rather than the abstract emptiness of non-allegiance" (1992, 173, emphasis added).

What is now apparent is how continually cosmopolitanisms emerge, shift, and change. The first generation of cosmopolitans, primarily political theorists—Fanon, Cesaire, Cabral, Memmi, James, etc.—was followed by many of the second generation of literary cosmopolitans Brennan discusses. I'd like to suggest that we're now witnessing the second generation of cosmopolitan political theorists with people such as Gayatri Spivak, Homi Bhabha, Stuart Hall, Paul Gilroy, etc., in addition to a second and possibly third generation of literary cosmopolitans. I'd place Suleri somewhere between the second and third generations of cosmopolitans who are in many ways like, though not identical to, Rushdie and the various writers examined in Brennan's *Salman Rushdie;* however, significant concern with gender is one of the things that distinguishes the two writers and the cosmopolitan generations as well.[12] This third generation of cosmopolitan and metropolitan postcolonials would include progressives and conservatives, who in some ways reflect the binary ideological habits of cultural identification Brennan's book depicts, but who are less interested in and shaped by the traditions of high modernism and may be as disinterested in the benefits of cultural power continued identification with modernist aesthetics and neoimperial ideologies can afford. For example, I'd locate postcolonials such as Pratibha Parmar, Jessica Hagedorn, and Srinivas Krishna (director of *Masala*) in the progressive "camp" (for lack of a better description), and place Hanif Kureishi or Meena Alexander in the more Western-identified group.[13] This generational-ideological model is, of course, partial, flawed, and oversimplified. There are all sorts of contemporary writers, filmmakers, and critics who do not fall neatly into one "camp" or the other. These might include Mira Nair, whose depiction of Americanized South Asians in the mainstream-directed film *Mississippi Masala* borders on the parodic and stereotypical with its depictions of the materialistic, sexist, and desexualized middle-class South Asian men; however, the film also importantly critiques South Asian racism *and* powerfully and painfully represents the agony of decolonization in the film's flashbacks. The black Africans' rejection of their South Asian–African compatriots illuminates the traumatic ironies of decolonization.

Srinivas Krishna's *Masala* similarly represents South Asian stereotypes with its emasculated and materialistic men, but aesthetically and politically Krishna's film realizes a more "native"-oriented hybrid identity via its combination of Western filmic and Indian popular cinema images (the film's musical numbers, for example). The multigenerational characters with their various belief systems, class affiliations, and lifestyles also lend the film a kind of complexity that isn't available in *Mississippi Masala*.[14] The grandmother's television-enabled conversations with the God Krishna are evidence of this more successfully fused hybrid identity; they represent a relationship with traditional and religious culture that is, ironically, irreverent *and* sincere. In Krishna's *Masala* the processes of negotiating culture and identity are the center of the story. At the same time, however, *Masala* refuses to romanticize or glorify cultural hybridization; the character Krishna's confused alienation and displacement is especially affecting, as is the God Krishna's rejection and disappearance. The mortal Krishna's untimely death at the hand of teenage racists disallows any comforting narrative closure; one can hardly be a free-floating transnational subject when one cannot move through one's own neighborhood freely or safely. And the climactic scene in which the repudiated God, in his blue and many-armed glory, fades into thin air marks the sight of a loss not quite recognized or fully measured.

Texts like *Masala* and *Meatless Days* are disturbing because they refuse and disrupt orthodoxies without necessarily replacing them; and because their authors boldly flout communal expectations by rejecting the roles of obedient son and daughter.[15] In doing so, each documents the perplexities of difference. Cultural ambivalence, however, does not always signify stylish rootlessness or elaborately defended postures of exile; conflicted feelings may be understood as a crucial process of becoming. As we will see with the case of Suleri, becoming what or becoming in what ways are intriguing questions.

Discussions of postcolonial cosmopolitanism can be complicated with the inclusion of contemporary writers like Sara Suleri, in addition to postcolonial critics like Gayatri Spivak or Homi Bhabha, who have been concerned with gender studies (a description more appropriate to Spivak's work), poststructuralism, psychoanalytic and deconstructive theories of language and culture.[16] The significance of radical or contestory Continental thought, namely the metropolitan discourses that have not been preoccupied with continuing or celebrating the hegemony of the West, should not be overlooked. Critics such as the aforementioned present us with another generation of cosmopolitans who refuse to forget the history of imperialism and who, in their work, explore and interrogate exile and belonging rather than celebrate or romanticize it. In doing so, they investigate the fragility and/or collective power of diasporic communities and analyze the viability of national, cultural, and historical certitude.[17] Other questions arise when the imbrications of collective *and* individual national experiences are made apparent.

Traditional accounts of cosmopolitan Third World writers and intellectuals frequently overlook some of the specificities and varieties of political situations; for example, the heterogeneous elements of "the nation" or "the people" often do not figure into accounts of popular nationalisms. Because Brennan's book primarily emphasizes *heroic* depictions of Third World intellectual-resisters, the question of feminism or gender politics within Third World national movements is not central to his argument against cosmopolitanisms. *Salman Rushdie and the Third World* briefly makes mention of Rushdie's unfavorable depictions of women and the ways in which he panders to the West by representing an atavistic depiction of Islam. Brennan also acknowledges *Shame's* feminist rebels as part of the author's antinative, neocolonial agenda and its parody of the sacred; however, he also (disparagingly?) refers to feminism as "that most Western of political challenges" (1989, 126). One suspects that, given the aforementioned aside, Third

World feminism would be considered an unnatural foreign import, a Western affectation.[18]

Sara Suleri and Taslima Nasrin's respective critical and political investments
position each writer as a treacherous daughter, treacherous in progressive and
problematical ways. Nasrin's reformer outspokenness and sisterly concerns reflect
a point of view that is not concerned with national or religious-cultural borders.
Lajja (Shame), for example, represents the plight of Bangladesh's Hindu minor-
ity. However, the fact that the novel was published only three months after
Hindus destroyed the Babri Masjid mosque in India, itself a site of Hindu and
Muslim originary claims,[19] suggests that Nasrin's political passions can lead her
to make reckless and shortsighted decisions. Mary Anne Weaver reports that Lajja
(Shame), banned and confiscated in Bangladesh, became an instant hit with
Hindu fundamentalists who circulated pirated copies of the novel and "lionized
Taslima in the streets" (Weaver 1994, 55). Nasrin's illustrations of "Muslim ex-
cesses," notes Weaver, made the author the fundamentalist Bharatiya Janata
Party's (BJP) "natural ally" (1994, 55). Nasrin, she concludes, "seemed to have become both a creation of and a vehicle for religious extremists across the Indian
subcontinent" (1994, 55).

Although Meatless Days is not as inflammatory a text as Nasrin's novel, its narrator Sara represents the brave, passionate, and callous daughter who disrupts the
image of an idyllic happy household, as well as the dream of progressive postindependence nationalism. Rather than being complicitous with Western neoimpe-
rialist ideologies, these contemporary female cosmopolitans—Nasrin, Spivak,
Suleri—may be treacherous in ways that significantly complicate, and possibly
even nullify, the traditional description of postcolonial cosmopolitans' betrayals
of local politics or Third World nationalisms. Each, in different ways, engages in
battle with patriarchal and parochial belief systems; Spivak's and Suleri's works,
in particular, address the limitations of such thinking in the Third World in addition to the First.

Style and Postcolonial Situations

Sara Suleri's Meatless Days also defies generic description and confuses strictly defined First and Third World literatures' aesthetic categorization. The author's tricultural influences (Pakistan, England, and the United States) and the text's hybrid nature cause both to appear like preceding eras' cosmopolitanisms; however,
both style and voice are used subversively in Meatless Days. Suleri's book raises a
number of important questions: Although style does have ideological implications, is it necessarily synonymous with ideology? Does a Third World writer who
utilizes "high" modernist aesthetics or Western accents automatically become a
spokesperson for the West? Can Western aesthetics productively represent Third
World situations? Given "native" subjects' colonial and postcolonial cultural in-

heritances is the description "Western aesthetics" accurate, appropriate, or even fungible? How does one critically assess a literary style that represents and simultaneously deconstructs Western-European high modernist aesthetics? In a recent essay Michèle Barrett broaches these questions and the Marxist cultural critics' tendency to elide the aesthetic in readings of the cultural. Addressing the marginal position of aesthetic issues at a Marxist conference, Barrett remarks,

> It is not that Marxism has failed to develop a tradition of work on aesthetics but rather that such concerns are currently out of fashion and, indeed, are often seen as politically reprehensible.
>
> If this description is correct, the situation poses major theoretical and political problems because it has left Marxists unable to engage with bourgeois criticism, dominant educational practices, and popular sentiment. By evading the questions of aesthetic pleasure and value, Marxist criticism and radical cultural intervention place themselves in a relatively weak position (Barrett 1988, 697).

Barrett's essay identifies the strengths, limitations, and challenges involved with the insertion of aesthetics in Marxist cultural interpretations. The concurrently abstract and overdetermined nature of words like beauty, pleasure, and value are part of the rhetorical and theoretical difficulty of a Marxist aesthetic critical practice. However, she insists upon recognition that a work of art enters the social, but emerges from the ambiguous realm of the imaginary. "[T]he denial of the aesthetic," Barrett notes, "ignores the fact that the works analyzed in radical criticism are works of the imagination; they are fictional. I do not mean to suggest that this gives them any form of historical or social transcendence, but it does suggest that they do not reflect, mediate, or encode in any direct way the content and position frequently attributed to them by virtue of this social origin. This makes the conflation of author and ideology, so common in the content analysis type of radical literary criticism, particularly fraught with dangers" (1988, 702). Barrett uses to support her discussion of the elision of aesthetic analysis in Marxist criticism art critic Max Raphael's attempt to combine socially oriented and formalist analyses. While highlighting the benefits and limitations of the critic's theories,[20] Barrett insists upon the necessity for the inclusion of the aesthetic in radical readings of culture. Her primary point is that "an exclusive emphasis on ideology necessarily denies the aesthetic dimensions of the text" (1988, 699). The aesthetic remains significant precisely because of its aforementioned affiliation with bourgeois criticism, dominant educational practices, and popular sentiment (1988, 679). Finally, Barrett warns that "we should avoid the assumption that there are historically specific categories such as the aesthetic which are reactionary and bourgeois, while our new categories, such as signification and pleasure are in some way purged of these limitations" (1988, 712).

There is much about Barrett's language concerning art's relative values and democratizing effects, the issues related to the integration of explicitly formalist and political discourses and critical practices, that makes this critic slightly nervous and uncomfortable. This discomfort is, nonetheless, worthy of closer examination precisely because a work like Suleri's *Meatless Days* so completely, self-consciously, and, most importantly, so *affectively* intermingles the aesthetic and the political—or the formal and the ideological, the private and public; *Meatless Days* also explores the tensions of such unions. The book's emphasis on consumption is not accidental; the studied abstractness of *Meatless Days*, in addition to its textual open-endedness, makes the question of how the reader receives or interprets the work as central to the book as is its analysis of the parallel and contradictory aspects of family and national relations. As Linda Warley suggests in "Assembling Ingredients: Subjectivity in *Meatless Days*," "If we think of the process of reading and remembering the text of a life in terms of reading a recipe of the self, then surely some finished, consumable dish must come out of it. However, as any cook knows, a certain assembly of ingredients will not always produce the expected result; moreover, the experience of preparing the dish may be more interesting than actually consuming the final product" (Warley 1992, 107).

Suleri's gender-specific representation of Third World nationalism substantially contributes to conversations about language, culture, and power precisely because she refuses fealty to any strictly defined national literature or culture. Linda Warley examines *Meatless Days'* preoccupation with the sites of language—patriarchal, feminine, imperial, and postcolonial—and the ways in which "agency might be . . . located in the act of writing itself" (1992, 111). Her essay identifies the ways in which Suleri's book challenges generic categories and interrogates practices of nomination and definitions of subjectivity (1992, 119). Warley doesn't specifically address Third World national or cosmopolitan issues; her essay is concerned primarily with the intersections of poststructuralist and postcolonial discourses and philosophies. A close reading of Suleri's text makes explicit the connections between nationalist discourses and the frequently problematic ways in which such articulations, however utopian their first enunciation, *settle*.

Artists who self-consciously interweave the real, the political, and the historical, like Suleri, further complicate these questions about authorial intention and the artwork's ideological implications. Such inclusions certainly invite political speculations and interpretations; however, inclusions of the actual, the historical, the sociopolitical, and the autobiographical do not necessarily characterize these works as (either deeply or) superficially postmodern, *per se*. The historical specificity of colonialism and post-independence and the presence of traumatized bodies make Suleri's use of these aesthetic and formal devices supplementary to more metatextually focused postmodernist texts. However, these interminglings require rigorous and insistently speculative critical analyses; in other words, a method of interpretation that attends to the linguistic and the worldly, the imaginary and the real, and that acknowledges the always existent intersections of such binarisms—their inherent artificiality—without succumbing entirely to strictly metaphorical habits of reading the world.

Unmapping Identities:
Deconstructing History and Nation
in *Meatless Days*

I looked out in the direction of the borderlines and tried to picture their perpetual rewriting, teaching myself to think through and repeat: "Your mind is a metropolis, a legislated thing. The keener your laws the better their breakage, for civilizations will always rise and fall upon your body's steady break."

—Sara Suleri (1989, 87)

While reading *Meatless Days*, one immediately realizes, as Michèle Barrett notes, speaking of the aesthetic properties of an art work, we are in the "presence of the literary."[21] The text's serpentine sentences and prosaic rhythms quickly establish its distinctive and distinguished speaking voice. The narrator of the piece is a Sara, as is the narrator of "Karachi, 1990."[22] Sara's sophisticated cosmopolitan voice could be read as the author's own; it might additionally be understood as an elaborately and ironically *self-conscious* voice, a performed self. The cultural function of the autobiographical is examined in Suleri's works; her writing acknowledges the partially productive influences of Western European literature and culture and alters or departs from those influences. As Sidonie Smith and Julia Watson have suggested in *De/Colonizing the Subject*, postcolonial autobiographical writing is antithetical to the epistemological aims of traditional autobiographical authorship: "the postcolonial subject inhabits a politicized rather than privatized space of narrative" autobiography; therefore, the very complexity of postcolonial politics leads the colonial subject's autobiography away from what the critics refer to as "the privatized itineraries" of traditional, *self-centered* autobiographical paradigms (Smith and Watson 1992, xx).

Both *Meatless Days* and "Karachi, 1990" perform and interrogate identity in attempt to avoid representing an authorized and stabilized postcolonial subject. Sara's thoughts, feelings, and memories reveal how history is individually experienced, how it is ingested or processed, *and* how it is expressed and represented. For example, the father, who uses language authoritatively and believes that words can determine (political) meaning, is described as a cannibal, a "consumer of context" and the past (1989, 110–111). Sara is also represented as a cannibal but as an imaginary or symbolic one. In a dream, for example, her father transports the dead mother to Sara in a van and tells his daughter that they must seal the mother's body in a coffin. While the father's back is turned, Sara steals a piece of the mother's body ("a piece of her foot . . . a small bone like a knuckle") and hides it in her mouth and under her tongue. "Then," Sara recalls, "I and the dream dissolved into an extremity of tenderness" (1989, 44). Sara's act is recognized as a less than innocent one; she describes herself as "being engaged in rapid theft." What is noteworthy here is how her habits of consumption differ from the father's. The father consumes context and attempts to write it into history, while Sara consumes and remembers bodies (her mother's, her grandmother Dadi's, her sister Ifat's) and expresses them into memory. Memory is not suggested to be more truthful or reliable than history. Sara's point of view is represented as being as selective or partial as the father's, but hers is differently significant, particularly because of its feminine knowledge.

In the book's opening chapter, "Excellent Things in Women," the textual Sara's voice states, "My reference is to a place where the concept of woman was not really part of an available vocabulary: we were too busy for that, just living, and conducting precise negotiations with what it meant to be a sister or a child or a wife or a mother or a servant" (1989, 1). The impossibility of fixed definitions and the necessity of "precise negotiations" are, throughout *Meatless Days*, revealed to be the cultural consequence of having lived in a landscape containing multiple and contesting differences. The answer given to a female student who questions the underrepresentation of women writers in a "Third World" literature course illustrates the importance of insisting upon the recognition (as well as the *re*cognition) of specificities. The Western student's feminist desires do not acknowledge the dissimilarities in definitions and experiences of gender between the "Third" and "First" World. Sara ponders the equality question after surveying the varieties of female subjectivity and feminine experience familiar to her in Pakistan. Her "imperial" sister Ifat, Halima the servant, Dadi the uncanny grandmother, and her culturally displaced Welsh mother represent only *some* of the varieties of postcolonial female experience. She answers her student's query by ironically stating, "There are no women in the third world" (1989, 20).

Evaluating *Meatless Days'* ironic intonations is particularly challenging. The question of irony in postcolonial literature and discourse is an interesting one but is unfortunately beyond the scope of this study. However, this is another point at which traditional assessments of cosmopolitans' aesthetic and critical perspectives proves a useful counterpoint to Suleri's. In *Salman Rushdie and the Third World*, Brennan reminds his readers of Antonio Gramsci's discussion of irony, intellectual distance, and political action. Brennan notes that for Gramsci irony "was the attitude of 'isolated intellectuals . . . indicat[ing] the distance of the artist from the mental content of his own creation . . . a distancing related to a more or less dilettantish scepticism belonging to disillusionment, weariness, and '*superominismo* [supermanism]', whereas 'impassioned sarcasm' was the 'appropriate stylistic element for historical-political action'" (Brennan 1989, 49). Brennan's appreciation of Gramsci's aesthetic preferences is evident throughout his book; for example, his appreciation of heroic nationalists resembles Gramsci's definition of the activist intellectual. And although there is nothing that definitively genders Gramsci's activist, there is an oblique way in which, in Brennan's terms, sarcasm and revolutionary fervor are associated with the (active) masculine, whereas irony and any expression more subtle than explicitly revolutionary discourse is inscribed as feminine (passive). In relation to Suleri's work, however, the irony as intellectual distance/disengagement assessment may or may not be appropriate, depending upon the reader's point of view.

What I'm suggesting is that Suleri's use of irony is subject to interpretation because of its ambiguity *and* because one's reading of *Meatless Days* rests so heavily on the question of how, exactly, the reader responds to the book's affective, emotional level of signification. Irony is also the secret language of women in the book, *the* primary means of resisting the father's dominating and constantly demanding authoritative discourse. The text's concern with intellectual and geographical distance is always offset by its luxuriant, nearly overripe poetic passages, which are most frequently associated with memory, love, death, and the traumatic aftereffects of the loss a loved one. Distance, in other words, is also presented as a coping mechanism, a method of survival, rather than a self-comforting dilettantish posture; in *Meatless Days,* irony and affect continually intermingle.

The photograph on the book's cover further complicates one's response to the personal dimensions of *Meatless Days.* The color photo captures Ifat, the sister whose death permanently impacts Sara's life; it, like Suleri's prose, is lush and muted. It appears, upon first glance to be a painting; even the frontispiece's black and white version of the same shot appears too rich to be "natural." The photograph may be retouched or supersaturated with color and texture; or it may be a miraculously perfect image. Whatever the case, after reading the book one cannot help but read it as more than a cover decoration, recognizing its prosaic representation from Sara's point of view and discovering that the photographer was Fawzia Mustafa, who appears as long-term family friend Fawzi/Muskator(i) in the book. Suleri's prose/Sara's voice, the visual images, and the points at which the impositions of the real make their impression all reveal why *Meatless Days* is a provocative book. My mixed feelings relate to alternately feeling deeply moved by the book and put off by its aloofness, convinced by its metaphorical wisdom, and concerned about its incrementally expanding abstractions. This discomfort is, I suspect, part of the author's intention because a similar dynamic informs the central character's voice, which is both superior and self-critical, self-indulgent and self-protective. Because the focus of her gaze never extensively rests upon her self, the reader must gauge Sara's self-nonrepresentation against the alternately caustic or romantic representations of familiars. Precisely where Sara sits is difficult to locate; she represents herself in relation to others, highlighting their different habits of location. Tom's largeness and irritatingly confident architectural inventiveness reflect the father's nationalist certainties and designs and contrast Sara's former desires "to live in a house that was shaped like a mosque, basing its center on empty space" (1989, 80).[23] Mustakori's originary and existential quest exists in opposition to Sara's unfixity, her willingness to "go crashing into liquidity" (1989, 70–71). Sara sees, illustrates, and learns to live with contradiction; the reader is forced to measure the reliability of Sara's characterizations, which is, in the end, an impossible task. This seductive-repellant narrative technique appears to reflect Suleri's philosophical and political point of view. At one point in

Meatless Days, Sara describes her father as having been "first seduced by poetry, and then by history" (1989, 113); Suleri seduces her readers with literature and autobiography, then leaves the reader to measure her interest or investment in both.

In many ways, Sara Suleri fits the traditional negative characterization of the Third World cosmopolitan intellectual. Suleri lives in the West and writes and thinks in a sophisticated style. Suleri also represents the Third World critically, which given the state of affairs in the particular postcolonial situation she represents doesn't necessarily qualify as a completely disloyal act. However, Suleri herself reminds the reader that writing and representation, regardless of style, always involve treachery because of the creative impulse associated with both. Sara recalls her childish tendency to represent and disassociate:

> [A]s an infant I was absorbed with grammar before I had fully learned the names of things, which caused a single slippage in my nouns: I would call a marmalade a squirrel, and I'd call a squirrel a marmalade. Today I can understand the impulse and would very much like to call sugar an opossum; an antelope, tea. To be engulfed by grammar after all is a tricky prospect, and a voice deserves to declare its own control in any way it can, asserting in the end that it is an inventive thing (1989, 155).

Earlier, Sara recounts a conversation with her brother Shahid, in which she reminds him that fidelity, "the worst addiction of them all," is also the one "most difficult to break" (1989, 106).

Both *Meatless Days* and the story/memoir "Karachi, 1990" represent postindependence Pakistan as a confusing, chaotic place, given to frequent periods of political and communalist violence. Rather than suggesting that Pakistan's catastrophic political atmosphere is a result of an essentially backward nature, Suleri posits that the contentious sociopolitical situation is the aftermath of the totalizing and harmonious discourses of nationalism and patriarchy. *Meatless Days* examines the effects nationalist definitions and passions have on the Suleri household and the nation; the limitations of both domestic localities are identified as inherently linguistic, wholly related to the paucity of traditional cultural definitions. Sara's commitment is to family, rather than nation, and particularly to the women in the family. Home is, at one point, defined as being "where your mother is" (1989, 147). At another point Ifat explains to Sara that "men live in homes, and women live in bodies" (1989, 143); both suggest habits of location that are temporary, mobile, subject to change.

Sara's inheritance from the bi- or tricultural Suleri household is the ability to live with contradiction, to appreciate differences, variety—accents, intonations, parental habits of reading and writing, speaking or inhabiting silence; but she is only able to reclaim that legacy after escaping the literal and figurative scriptural demands of her father (Sara and her mother are chosen to attend to his writing as Pip's eyesight fails). At one point, before she leaves home, she confesses:

Sometimes, when I feel burdened by this baldest prose—I lived too long with the man of the hairless head—and tyrannized by the structure of a simple sentence, it does me good to recollect how quietly my mother measured out her dealings with impossible edges. What can I do but tell the same story again and yet again, as my acknowledgment of how dangerous it is to live in plot? (1989, 154)

Sara's coming of age involves attempting to come into language on her own terms in a manner that allows her the broadest and most flexible self-definition. *Meatless Days* presents the process of her conversion from the confines of the localized discourses of the social, the domestic and the national, to the alternatively less constricted *and ideologically uncertain* fluidity of exile, which in the book is synonymous with narrative openness.

Meatless Days attempts, in its exploration of Pakistani and Suleri family history, to enact what Suleri has described elsewhere as a rigorous critical and discursive practice that refuses to solidify or essentialize postcolonial subjectivities, histories or geographies. In "Woman Skin Deep: Feminism and the Postcolonial Condition," Suleri articulates the need for "a discursive space-clearing that allows postcolonial discourse figurative flexibility and at the same time reaffirms its radical locality within historical exigencies" (1992b, 759). She proposes that the category of postcolonialism be read as a "free-floating metaphor for cultural embattlement and as an almost obsolete signifier for the historicity of race" (1992b, 759–760). In other words, she suggests that the articulation of postcoloniality and the methodology of its critical practice emphasize the discursive and the historical, rather than privileging the experiential and the personal, thereby risking the unproblematized and unquestioned presentation of an authentic self—what Suleri refers to as a "privileged racial body" (1992b, 762).

Meatless Days achieves this kind of critically self-conscious expression; its textual praxis puts particular emphasis on the scriptural presentation of the self, one informed by deconstructive theories of language. Life and history are put into writing, then disassembled, and the fictions of family and nation are exposed in the process. For example, *Meatless Days* reveals that while the father's language is the dominant discourse in the space of the household, his is not the most significant language; and this revelation has, in the context of national and gender concerns, broader postcolonial significance.

The strategically discreet and discursively intricate presentation of the self enables Suleri to explore family and national history, public and private experience, without situating the female postcolonial subject as native informant, for Sara's stories intentionally fail to establish any epistemological certainties. Characters are presented as the embodiments of history, subjects discursively marked by geographical movements—locations, dislocations, relocations—and their cultural affiliations. The mother's love of Jane Austen, for example, reflects her appreciation of reticence as well as her awareness of the ironies of domestic life.

Ideological investments, too, leave their trace, like the father's nationalistic-historical engagement, which intensifies in the early 1940s with the forthcoming birth of Pakistan, then reiterates as a series of open questions—*Whither Pakistan?* "Wither Basic Democracy?"—when Jinnah's narrated nation fails to adhere to its original design. Suleri's text also intertwines public and collective experiences of crisis and change—partition, political coups, and assassinations—with the most devastating and private family traumas: a mother's, grandmother's, and most beloved sister's death; divorce; and the dispersal of family members. The mother's accidental death coincides with Bhutto's imprisonment and General Zulu's Islamization of Pakistan; Bhutto's execution takes place alongside grandmother Dadi's death. By juxtaposing family and nation and highlighting the ways in which one reflects *and* refracts the other, the imagined semantic borders between concepts—for example, public and private, history and memory—are destabilized. Concepts (family, nation) become fluid and the histories and memories of primary or original enunciations maintain their emotive signifying power.

Included in *Meatless Days'* exploration of family history is analysis of the sometimes mysterious and inexplicable interior landscapes of domestic life: a mother's pregnant silences, a father's demanding love, and the sometimes unbreachable distances imposed by distinct individuals and their own particular habits of being. The complicated politics of family life are examined alongside the shifting borders and severed relations of postindependence life. During the period defined by Sara as the "middle years" (Suleri 1989, 7–8)—before the demise of the two-nation theory—the dream of Pakistan that echoes across its landscape and incessantly reiterates from the father's lips and throughout the halls of the Suleri home holds some promise and provides a sense of context in changing times. The father's nation-building dreams are compared to a romance of both the relational and literary kind. He abandons poetry for politics and history and believes for a while that desire and narrative zeal—the endlessly produced tracts and outlines for nationhood—can realize and make permanent and stable the imagined community of (Quaid-i-Azam) Jinnah.

The father's sense of priorities affect the family *and* the intonations of his discourse. Insignificant words like "another" or "beginning" are rushed over, reduced to "anther" and "bigning," whereas the name of the dream-nation is savored like an exquisite morsel. "It seemed his patience could not sustain itself over the trisyllabic," Sara confesses, "tripping up his voice on most trisyllables that did not sound like 'Pakistan'—for there was a word over which he could slow down, to exude ownership as he uttered it!" (109). Sara's critique of the father aims to deauthorize the unchallenged patriarchal and magisterial reign he enjoyed in the Suleri household. Z. A. Suleri, affectionately and diminutively called Pip by his children, is presented as an egoist and idealist—a visionary and perhaps a fool, or more kindly, a visionary with a limited ken. The father is presented as a household Jinnah, a domesticated version of his glorified political hero, who lords over his children and makes them secondary to his political mission. Sara notes that a letter from Jinnah was "the one object in Pip's home that he (has) ever loved" (Suleri 1989, 115). Jinnah's letter, written in response to Pip's books—*The Road to Peace and Pakistan* (1944) and Z. A. Suleri's tribute to Jinnah, *My Leader* (1945)—thanks the author for having a "warm and affectionate corner" for him. "If this is a corner," Sara asks sister Ifat, "what on earth does the center look like?" (Suleri 1989, 115). The daughters' experience of displacement in the family home is, in part, what informs Sara's ironic intonation: "There are no women in the Third World."

Later in the book, a visit from her sister Tillat reveals to Sara the difficulty of bridging the distance from Kuwait to New Haven. As the sisters attempt to catch up with each other and close the time and space that had separated them, Sara discovers the fragility and sumptuousness of language: "Our conversations were meals, delectable, but fraught with a sense of prior copyright, because each of us was obliged to talk too much about what the other did not already know" (Suleri 1989, 21).

In the midst of fractured and precious conversation, the familiar is defamiliarized; the well-known shockingly reveals its other nature, which itself, Suleri subtly suggests, may have been a kind of reluctant prior knowledge. *Meatless Days* engenders what Gayatri Spivak has termed "transactional reading" (Spivak 1988, 3). The self-conscious style of writing, self-reflexive posture of the writer, and steadily shifting articulations enact what Spivak calls a "functional change in the sign system" (1988, 3). Words, and the original emphasis and intentionality of their utterance, slip and reveal other different meanings; the surety of knowledge is disturbed: "The site of displacement of the function of signs," Spivak suggests, "is the name of reading as active transaction between past and future" (1988, 4–5). In the text, the process of memory demands that things be more closely examined. The *kapura* believed by Sara to be sweetbreads but actually testicles are revealed *not* to be what they seem: "Something that had once sat quite simply inside its own definition was declaring independence from its name and nature, claiming a perplexity that I did not like," Sara complains (Suleri 1989, 22). And she remembers, shortly afterward, that it was her mother who had told her "that sweetbreads are sweetbreads" (1989, 23):

[M]aybe my mother knew that sweetbreads are testicles but had cunningly devised a ruse to make me consume as many parts of the world as she could before she set me loose in it. The thought appalled me. It was almost as bad as attempting to imagine what the slippage was that took me from nipple to bottle and away from the great letdown that signifies lactation. What a falling off! Gosh, I thought, to think that my mother could do that to me (1989, 23).

The *kapura*, like the stimulative madeleines in Proust's *Swann's Way*, arouse kaleidoscopic memories; but unlike Proust's cookies, the rediscovered nature of *kapura* and not the memory of their taste, provokes disassociations and uncovers more complicated realities. The mother's gifts of mystification—masquerading what might otherwise be imagined as unpalatable into something digestible—and separation, the substitutive sustenance of Ostermilk and Babyflo for breast milk, are ambiguous ones—mixed inheritances. Within the space of the Suleri household, the mother's abstracted difference—her loving distances, her Welsh posture, and abstract and profound muteness—provide respite from the flurry of words, as well as the demands to attend to his words, the father interjects into the rhythms of domestic life. The textual Sara learns to mediate between the distinct linguistic and cultural points of view embodied by her parents: between maternal absent presence and paternal active presence, between knowing silence and frequently too-sure certainty. As Sara attempts to read her family's and nation's lives, she struggles continually to come to terms with and to enunciate apparently incommensurable oppositions. Of her parents she admits, "They were rhetorically so different, the two of them, always startling each other with the difference of their speech: no wonder their children grew up with such a crazy language" (Suleri 1989, 157). Pakistan's political mutations and fluctuations also deny the significance of fixity. Bhutto's execution in 1979, Sara notes, "had the effect of making Pakistan feel unreliable, particularly to itself. . . . There was no longer any need to wait for change, because change was all there was, and we had quite forgotten the flavor of an era that stayed in place long enough to gain a name" (1989, 18).

The history and politics of the postcolonial context also intensify what Sara learns. One of her primary discoveries relates to her realization that language is slippery, that what the signifier signifies is uncertain and subject to change. This knowledge is acquired accidently and in benign moments—for example, the conversation in which the nature of the kapura is revealed; and deconstructive knowledge is also delivered in painful and traumatic moments. Ifat's death, a murder by hit and run, is one of these violent instructive instances. Ifat, the aforementioned sister whose ghostlike and luminous presence graces the cover of Meatless Days, is the sibling who attempts to bridge some of the distances in the Suleri household. And it is she too who embodies the parents' distinct differences; Ifat has the mother's unique gracefulness and the father's stubborn and dynamic intellect. "From him," Sara observes, "she learned her stance of wild inquiry, the arrogant angle at which she held her head," which Sara recognizes as a "gesture of devotion" to the father. "It made me groan aloud," she recalls, "to think that Papa could not see that Ifat was simply loving him for what he was when she handed back to him, gesture by gesture, his prickling independence of style" (1989, 139). When she marries against the wishes of the father, Ifat is banished from the household for two years, and her name becomes a forbidden word.

When Ifat's death is investigated and sensationalized, the boundary between public and private, personal and political is once again disturbingly revealed. In the course of police and journalistic investigations of the death, a letter, written to Sara by Ifat the day before her death, finally arrives in Sara's hands. "Her words to me were sweet," says Sara, "and they spoke about her life, so that—for me— their reading was almost a reprieve, suggesting endless possibility of conversation still in store for us" (1989, 125). It is Sara's brother Shahid who discounts the possibility of such a grief-stricken dream and reveals to Sara the changed nature of the correspondence: "That's not a letter to you now—it's evidence," he says (125). And Sara's most painful lesson is learned: "Ifat's letter evidence? I said a quick good-bye to the sweet assurance of those days when I could claim to know the name of things" (1989, 125–126).

Ifat is of central importance to *Meatless Days*. She is a sisterly guide to her siblings; the alternately witty, graceful, or fierce bearer of demystified knowledge. It is Ifat who deconstructs for Sara the meaning of childish nursery rhymes. Sara recounts one of these primary lessons:

> "'Who Killed Cock Robin?'—what a strange song that is, Ifat," I said to her one day. "'I, said the sparrow with my bow and arrow'—how odd that he should confess it straight away!" "You know what he's confessing, don't you?" replied Ifat with a meaningful look that always made me feel most ignorant. "It's all about sex!" . . . "You know, don't you, that all those nursery rhymes are just a way of telling children about the horrid parts of sex?" (1989, 136–137)

It is also Ifat, whose voice is described as being "overburdened with knowledge" (1989, 138), who makes Sara aware of the vulnerability of women in a dangerous and unpredictable world. When Ifat observes a car graze Sara as she crosses a road, she chases the vehicle, which is occupied by two men, and forces it off the road. "How dare you touch my sister," she challenges the men, and asks them, "Don't you understand what it is to protect the honor of your sister?" Ifat promises Sara that she will slowly kill anyone who dares to hurt her: "I'll do a Dadi," she boasts, invoking the name and invective style of the grandmother, "chop their liver into little bits and feed them to the crows" (1989, 138).

For Sara, Ifat represented the space of possibilities. She was for the siblings what the original idea of Pakistan was for the father: a balanced duality, reminiscent of the two-nation theory that once appeared the perfect solution to postindependence life—a contract between Muslims and Hindus, an attempt to make historical reparations. The embodied harmony of Ifat is like the period of grace before the war of 1971, which precedes the fracturing of East Pakistan into Bangladesh, and the disintegration of a national dream into the fragmentary politics of communalism. When the dream of Pakistan refuses to adhere to its original design and Islam is transformed into the ideology of Islamization, the father turns to religion. "The men would take it (Islam) to the streets and make it vociferate," but, Sara observes, "the great romance between religion and the populace, the embrace that engendered Pakistan, was done. So Papa prayed with the desperate ardor of a lover trying to converse life back into a finished love" (1989, 15).

When Ifat dies, the Suleri siblings accept a permanent condition of exile and displacement. Ifat's is the third and most devastating death, preceded by Dadi the grandmother's natural death, and the mother's accidental one (the Welsh woman dies in her relocated country, run down by a rickshaw). The women's deaths, notes Sara, put an end to the siblings' intimacy with Pakistan, which she describes as a land "where history is synonymous with grief and almost always at home in the attitudes of grieving" (1989, 19). "We are lost, Sara," brother Shahid says to her in a conversation that extends from England to the United States. " 'Yes, Shahid,' Sara answers firmly, 'we're lost' " (1989, 19).

The recognition of loss and the willfully (and again partially) disengaged international cosmopolitan postcoloniality Sara accepts as her historical reality is, I'd like to suggest, progressive but not without some digestive difficulties. These difficulties have very little to do with the extremely careful and precise negotiations Suleri enacts in *Meatless Days;* rather, they are related to the ways in which the text acquires additional significance as it enters the academic-literary domain. Sara's discrete postcoloniality is presented as a painfully and reluctantly accepted subjective location; however, it is also suggested to be a positionality preferable to one that does not disengage originary attachments.

Sara's friend, Mustakor, a Tanzanian Indian, is the Mowgli of *Meatless Days.* Her search for an original or recovered identity is both irritating and amusing to the members of the Suleri household. Mustakor, whose appellation shifts as the Suleri children observe her quests (she is called Mowgli, Congo Lise, Faze Mackaw, Fancy Musgrave), attempts to order and make sense of her postcolonial dislocations and relocations. She is the opposite of Sara, who accepts the impressive disorder those histories and movements have revealed to her. Mustakor, Sara notes, "came with all the tentative innocence of one who returns, seeking to understand the geographic reality of her forebears and waiting to locate in an unknown mode of speech the wraith of an intuitively familiar cadence. Those who travel curiously imagine that returning is somehow sweeter, less dangerous, than seeking out some novel history, and Mustakor evidently had such nostalgia encoded in her genes" (1989, 49). Mustakor's wandering quests are brutally parodied by the Suleri siblings, which very well may be an explicit critique of their innocently accepted dislocation; the parodies of Mustakor take place when the Suleris are alive and united, undisturbed by trauma. They are, in their position of youthful arrogance, a nation unto themselves.

Meatless Days' concluding chapter, "Saving Daylight," measures time, the approaching spring, and moves toward the recovery from trauma and the imagination of novel histories. March's seasonal renewal also represents for Sara the month which brought to her the news of her mother's and sister Ifat's deaths. It is the month's coming to life that makes prolonged mourning an impossibility. Spring brings lightness and expansiveness and reminds Sara of traumatic challenges and new possibilities. The season's contradictions trigger a chain of associations: death/life, darkness/light, destruction/production, endings/beginnings. These associations and their dynamic interrelations remind Sara of the similar structures of language, history, and memory, as well as the ways in which each of those narrative practices must be continually investigated. "Living in daylight," notes Sara, "is not so different from living between two languages; and Urdu," she continues, "opens up in my mind a passageway between the sea of possibility and what I cannot say in English" (1989, 177). However, she also cautions that "living in language is tantamount to living with other people. Both are postures in equilibrium that attend upon gravity's capacity for flotation, which is a somber way of looking out for the moment when significance can empty into habit. For significance is that which must be bailed out all the time" (1989, 177).

The characteristics that make *Meatless Days* an important and progressive text are the same things that require it to be encountered with a consumptive caveat in mind, especially in the West. Suleri's articulation of cosmopolitan postcoloniality is one that seeks to challenge what she considers the ontological and epistemological claims evident in the kinds of unproblematized identity posturings endemic to recent academic debates concerning race and difference (Suleri 1992, 760–766). Suleri's carefully negotiated articulations of identity also speak to more urgent confrontations, like the recent and bloody communalist skirmishes over India's Babri Masjid Mosque (see note 19). However, too frequently the strategic and specific implications of a book like Suleri's become oversimplified by Western critics who, despite Suleri's exemplary efforts not to position herself as an authentic speaking subject or native informant, celebrate the work as an example of a superior postcoloniality.[24] If Western critics ignore the specificities of history Suleri explores in *Meatless Days*—the transformation of idealistic nationalism into deadly communalism—it, too, is available for such a reading.

Meatless Days emits an articulation of displacement that refuses to situate itself as a localized discourse. The text disassembles national and filial relations and reveals the limitations of epistemologies and ontologies, yet still manages to maintain affective relations with the originary home. For Sara this long-distance affiliation becomes possible when she is able to appraise losses and gains and comingle memory and history, both of which are characteristically selective narrative processes. The posture is one result of Sara's maturation. "I used to think," she notes, "that our sense of place would be the first to go, after the hurly-burly of our childhood's constant movement. We would not pay much attention to our setting, I believed, but would dwell on face instead" (1989, 181). She continues,

> But now I must admit that my faces do not remain distinguishable from their contexts, that their habitation must lend feature to the structure of significance. It is hard for me to picture Nuz without seeing simultaneously Karachi's maniacal sprawl, its sandy palms and crazy traffic. Shahid looks like London now, in the curious pull with which London can remind, "I, also, was your home." Tillat in desert-land is busy, surrounding herself with oases, pools of infancy, converting in my mind a grain of sand into signs of impressive fertility. And it is still difficult to think of Ifat without remembering her particular congruence with Lahore, a place that gave her pleasure (1989, 181).

Sara's remapped relations are reflective of the kind of accumulated knowledge *Meatless Days* imparts. Her sometimes callous and willful disengagements are carefully and tentatively renegotiated and gradually fashioned into distant relations shaped by history and full of feeling.

Attempting to come to terms with familial and national histories is revealed by Sara to be an ongoing, difficult, deep—and sometimes contradictory—emotional process. Suleri's book calls to mind the speculative recollection of national/cultural identity to which Akeel Bilgrami refers in his essay, "What Is a Muslim? Fundamental Commitment and Cultural Identity." Bilgrami provides a theoretical sketch for this kind of redefined and renegotiated relationship by suggesting that a potentially reformist form of agency may be available to moderate postcolonial subjects living at home as well as metropolitan subjects living abroad, especially those who are able to remain significantly, emotionally, and politically attached to the former originary homeland. Bilgrami's immediate concern is with the definition of a negotiable Muslim identity to counter the understandable anti-imperialist although nonetheless increasingly problematic and rigidly defined Islamic absolutist (or fundamentalist) identity. What Bilgrami discovers while apartment hunting in a Hindu neighborhood in India is a fundamental commitment to Muslim identity despite having been raised in an irreligious atmosphere and despite having inhabited a self-described "aggressively secular stance . . . with communist leanings" (Bilgrami 1992, 822). Keenly aware of the neighborhood's hostile environment, Bilgrami unexpectedly hears himself articulate his identity in a surprisingly certain way when a landlord asks him about his religious background. The utterance, "I am a Muslim," dramatically reveals to him both the fluidity and psychic permanence of self- and subjective definitions. "It . . . seemed the only self-respecting thing to say in that context," Bilgrami admits. "It was clear to me that I was, without strain or artificiality, a Muslim for about *five minutes.* That is how negotiable the concept of identity can be" (Bilgrami 1992, 822, original emphasis). Bilgrami is not at all suggesting that his Muslim identity is essentially brief or fleeting; rather, he points out that there are numerous reasons and contexts for the articulation of such an identity, which are themselves complicated and contradictory.[25] Refusing to acknowledge the deep-seated political and emotional history of subjective and cultural-national relations would amount, Bilgrami suggests, to a kind of devastating self-betrayal.

Sara similarly reaches this conclusion after she reexamines her family and national relations. *Meatless Days* documents the extremely difficult processes of mediating productive *and* critical relations between public and private experiences, past and present histories, local and global realities, which precede reimagined communities. The fundamental power of affective relations is acknowledged, although the broader implications of renegotiated relations are not made explicit. Sara's relationship to her personal past is more or less resolved, whereas more immediate and present-tense political relations are undefined, revealed to be processual in nature. The power of *Meatless Days* emanates from Sara Suleri's ability to articulate the instructive yet painful forms of knowledge that loss, trauma, and political and personal disappointment impress upon the postcolonial subject.

The uncertainty of present-tense negotiations in *Meatless Days* and in Suleri's story "Karachi, 1990," is wholly related to the chaos of contemporary conflicts in India and Pakistan: communal riots; constrictive laws such as the Hudood Ordinances which, with a kind of brutal mathematics measure and limit the value and significance of women's legal testimony[26]; the general atmosphere of terror and endless cycles of reciprocal retaliations. The narrator of "Karachi, 1990," another Sara, confesses, "I'd prefer to be sea rather than city," an articulation that results from more losses: the failed promise of Benazir Bhutto's reign; the death of another sister; further distanciation from Karachi. Sara decides that her positionality must, for the time being, involve continual migrancy. Her reality resembles what Gayatri Spivak calls a state of "absolute contingency" (1992). Suleri's work leaves us theoretically in medias res, unanchored and, it is hoped, open-minded. She documents what is historically an anxious moment, and this is what makes Suleri's work both exciting and discomforting. Sara's voice reveals turbulent and awkward processes of thinking and negotiating and speaks, finally, with willfully confident bravado. What Sara recognizes and struggles to reveal is this: The space of the sea is uncertain, fraught with all sorts of unsuspected dangers, but in it also exists the space of possibilities.

However: A Postscript

Where the space of possibilities, my own (self-indulgent?) Suleri-inspired poetic abstraction leaves us in terms of the politics of location is unclear. The peculiarities of national situations, I've argued, also leave us—the worldly and revolutionary, willfully utopian and desirous; Western European, Third World, Slavic, and Eastern European—adrift. Some might argue that current global situations suggest that lyrical, poetic, or linguistically centered representations of the postcolonial and the national are especially inappropriate, especially given the distinctly grim and unlovely scenes of Rwanda, Haiti, Algeria, Bangladesh, Pakistan, Bosnia-Herzegovina, etc. Perhaps they are correct. However, language exists as one of the primary means by which we challenge and attempt to redefine the world; we do ourselves and each other a disservice when we suggest that there is but one voice in which to represent properly our various, distinct, and similar situations. Suleri's cosmopolitanism is clearly related to earlier traditions of Third World cosmopolitan writing; however, the generic and discursive challenges reflected in her writings challenge both Western and Third World national definitions and ideologies. In light of the United States' rapidly intensifying atavistic and conservative nationalism, *Meatless Days* has much to say to the U.S. audience. Suleri risks offending those who are invested in master narratives by insisting that they are at root patriarchal and limiting, in need of reassessment and continual redefinition. Like Sara, the treacherous daughter, she suggests that what postcolonial and contemporary political situations require are reimagined habits of communion.

NOTES

1. I will from here on write Third World without quotation marks, while acknowledging their usefulness in pointing out that any monolithic configuration of non-Western nations is an oversimplification, a fiction. As Sara Suleri notes in *Meatless Days*, "the third world is locatable only as a discourse of convenience. Trying to find it is like pretending that history or home is real and not located precisely where you're sitting" (Suleri 1989, 20).

2. In a recent article concerning the goals of moderate Muslims and Western representations of Islam, Akeel Bilgrami has pointed out that "Muslim fundamentalists" is an inaccurate and incorrect, if convenient, nomination. "Fundamentalist," Bilgrami suggests, "functions as an oversimplified caricature of the various groups of Muslim conservatives that oppose secular interpretations of the *Sharia*, Islamic personal and public law. Absolutist more accurately represents the minority conservative groups who oppose Quranic revision and insist that Islamic identity is nonnegotiable" (1992, 824). Bilgrami reclaims the implications of the term "fundamentalism" by recognizing fundamental commitments as those that partially correspond with *and* critique static definitions of identity; in other words, the secular Muslim realizes his or her commitment to Islam and Islamic culture by emotionally and intellectually investing in secular and religious conflicts. Geographical or critical distance, he points out, need not amount to abandonment.

3. A news service bulletin issued by the International Secretariat of Amnesty International dated July 14, 1994, published Nasrin's call to the international community for assistance: "I am in grave danger. Fundamentalists are demanding my death. They have declared prize money for my head again. Situation is dangerous now. They could kill me at any moment. Please save me." Another Internet item, written by Nadire Mater (dated July 15, 1994) detailed a number of Turkish Women's Organizations' international letter writing campaign in support of Nasrin (Women-Turkey: "Istanbul Groups Come Out in Support of Nasrin," InterPress Third World News Agency [IPS], 1994).

The *fatwa* (edict) issued against Taslima Nasrin was for the crime of blasphemy. Her novel *Lajja (Shame)*, banned by the Bangladeshi government in July 1993, supports changes in the Quran, attacks xenophobia (Bhattacharya 1994, 49), and is sympathetic toward the nation's Hindu minorities. Nasrin has been called the female Salman Rushdie in the press; she reportedly discourages the comparison. *Ms.* magazine quotes her as saying, "Both of us criticize religion, but as a women's advocate, I have to face the male chauvinists" (Ahmed 1994, 18). For more information on the Taslima Nasrin case see:

Tahmina Ahmed's "Bangladesh: A Best-selling Author Risks her Life," *Ms.* May/June 1994, vol. iv, no. 6:18.

"U.S. Support of Author Protested," News Services/*Austin American Statesman*, July 15, 1994: A13.

Hasan Saeed's "1 Killed, 150 Injured in Strike over Author in Bangladesh," Associated Press wire services/*Austin American Statesman*, July 4, 1994: A13.

"Bangladeshi's Clash on Accused Author," *New York Times*, Friday, July 1, 1994, vol. 143, p. A2, col. 4.

"Islamic Cleric Doubles Bounty for Author's Life," Associated Press wire services/*Austin American Statesman*, June 12, 1994: A19.

Pallab Bhattacharya's "A Rushdie in Bangladesh," *World Press Review*, January 1994, vol. 41, no. 1: 49.

Mary Anne Weaver's "A Fugitive from Injustice," *The New Yorker*, September 12, 1994: 48–50, 55–60.

4. See, for example, the anthology *Third World Women and the Politics of Feminism* (Indiana University Press, 1991), Chandra Talpade Mohanty, Ann Russo, and Lourdes Torres, eds.

5. For practical purposes, I will refer to Nasrin as a feminist although I aim to reveal the denotative differences involved with such a description in Third and First World localities. An acknowledged limitation of this practical decision is that the term feminist does not cover the various ways in which Nasrin became a disruptive force in Bangladesh; her advocation of the redefinition of Bangladeshi social and religious laws and strictures would more accurately describe her as a radical reformer. Although many of Nasrin's concerns are specifically gender-related, her critiques of *Shariat* laws, Muslim intolerance and xenophobia are considered by fundamentalists *and* many Bangladeshi feminists to be as provocative as her feminist articulations. Western depictions of Nasrin primarily represent her as a champion of free-speech and women's rights, which undercomplicates the reaction to her novels, journalism, and poetry in Bangladeshi while simultaneously celebrating the West's "tolerance" and "superior" cultural values.

Both the Bangladeshi description of Nasrin as a troublesome westernized woman and the Western-European representation of her as a defender of humanist and individualist tenets are, to a certain extent, fantastic projections that aim, respectively, to dislocate her as an outsider or locate Nasrin as "one of us." In either case, the particularities of Nasrin's feminist sentiments are left unexamined; the discursive assignation of "westernized" is assumed to say it all in both cultural contexts. It is uncertain, for example, if Nasrin's feminism would appear characteristically "Western" to Western feminists; additionally, some of Nasrin's Bangladeshi critics do not recognize her representation of Islam as being particularly Islamic. In Mary Anne Weaver's article, one of Nasrin's editors says of the author, "I cautioned her, from the beginning, not to write about Islam. She knows nothing about it! It was only about a year ago that she began buying books on Islam and the Koran. I don't understand what drives her. She picks up issues and goes after them like a slightly demented terrier" (Weaver 1994, 55). I am not at all suggesting that Nasrin knows nothing about feminism; my point is that her particular brand of feminism might be better understood if considered a politics influenced by situation, experience, and personal observation rather than the mimicry of foreign ideas, per se. In other words, Nasrin's beliefs are eclectic, flowering, organic. An unidentified Western diplomat in the Weaver article speaking of the origins of Nasrin's beliefs, says of the author, her statements "are like the pronouncements of *someone who has dropped in from Mars*. She's not even part of the Dhaka or the provincial élite, but comes from this little town way up in the hills. Where on earth did she get these ideas?" (1994, 49, emphasis added). The desire to pinpoint the origin from which Nasrin's beliefs emerged reflects the degree to which the process of "making up one's own mind" is recognized as disruptive. The Western diplomat, like Nasrin's more vociferous Bangladeshi critics, positions her as an alien; however, the diplomat's discomfort appears to be connected to what he (?) considers the "inappropriate" cultural and geographical source of Nasrin's ideas ("the hills," not the city, not the academy).

6. Weaver's article, for example, makes reference to two Bangladeshi women named Noorjehan who were victims of their respective village's religious passions. In January 1993, twenty-one-year-old Noorjehan Begum remarried after her first marriage was dis-

solved. "The local mullah," Weaver reports, "giving no reasons, declared that this second marriage was contrary to Islamic law. A few weeks later, just after dawn, she was led to an open field in a small village in the district of Sylhet—a stronghold of the fundamentalists—where a pit had been dug overnight. She was lowered into the pit and buried waist deep. Then, slowly and methodically, she was stoned—a hundred and one times. Her death horrified Dhaka's élites" (Weaver 1994, 50). Since Nasrin was still living in Bangladesh at this time, one can assume that such incidents only increased her outrage. A few months later the second woman named Noorjehan was tied to a stake, doused with kerosene, and burnt to death for leaving her husband for another man (54). In February of 1993, the first *fatwa* was issued against Taslima Nasrin for authorship of the novel *Lajja (Shame)*.

7. See Mary Anne Weaver's "A Fugitive from Injustice" (1994) for a discussion of the different political interpretations of Taslima Nasrin's *Lajja (Shame),* namely Indian fundamentalists' use of and response to the novel. I'd like to thank Natasha Sinutko for calling this article to my attention.

8. Since Nasrin left Bangladesh on August 10, 1994, the family members she left behind have had death threats made against them (Associated Press, August 19, 1994). Also recently, Zahirul Islam, a leader of Bangladesh's Committee to Resist Anti-Islamic Activity, reissued threats against Nasrin, imploring the diasporic Islamic community abroad to assist in capturing and returning the author to Bangladesh. At a rally in Dhaka, he reportedly addressed the crowd saying, "We want the infidel back in our country. Our Muslim *brothers* in Sweden must help us" (Associated Press, August 13, 1994, emphasis added). Given the assassinations of Salman Rushdie associates in Europe and Japan (see *Index on Censorship*, October 1993, p. 40), one cannot assume that Taslima Nasrin will be safe while in exile.

9. I have been confronted with this accusation as it is expressed in subtle and outright ways, by both black and white people, who seem disturbed by my not *being,* somehow, what or how they expected I would *be.* Often the primary cause of this discomfort is linguistic, as in "you sound white"—the evidence of inauthenticity. I make reference to this here because it partially mirrors some responses to Suleri and geographically and culturally multiply located writers like her. For example, I've heard Suleri described as not *really* Pakistani, and I've asked the speakers of such sentiments what, exactly, is meant by such a complaint. What does it mean in this increasingly diasporic age to be *really* Pakistani? Although Sara Suleri is Anglo-Indian, the ways in which she blurs distinctions are not only biologically or ethnically based. These expectations and discomforts are, it seems to me, related to assumptions that one will represent what one is, as if such things are fixed and determined. The assumption seems to be that one's aesthetic and literary cultural affiliations, linguistic and stylistic habits of expression are primarily influenced by racial or national origin. This may seem an absurd point to raise here, but I've always wondered why people of color whose habits of being transcend cultural, national, and ethnic borders are referred to in devourable terms: not black enough blacks as "Oreos," not brown enough brown people as "coconuts," not yellow enough and red enough people as "bananas" and "apples." These sorts of descriptive assignments often cause minority writers to be considered consumable and evacuatable by ethnic absolutists (to borrow Paul Gilroy's term). Or conversely to be considered entirely scrumptious by those who only see similarity to them, their tastes and values, as in, "you're just like us, we want to gobble you up." As one of *Meatless Days'* jacket blurbs says of Suleri, "She is a postcolonial Proust to Rushdie's phantasmagorical Pynchon." Palatable, consumable, canonizable. Yet another blurb states that "the voyages Suleri narrates . . . left this reader hungering for more."

10. Some of the other celebrity writers discussed in *Salman Rushdie and the Third World* include Derek Walcott, Chinua Achebe, Isabelle Allende, and Gabriel Garcia Marquez. Writers and critics who Brennan sees as continuing in the Marxist-revolutionary trajectory are Frantz Fanon, C.L.R. James, W.E.B. DuBois, Stuart Hall, and Paul Gilroy.

11. In an essay related to these Third World/First World concerns, especially as they concern different readers' political and aesthetic expectations, Rey Chow suggests that the Western critic's disparaging dismissal of Third World writers' worldliness reveals a romanticization of the Third World that satisfies Marxist interests and desires without acknowledging the privileged perch from which the Western critic pronounces "native" expression "authentic" or "compromised." Chow characterizes such critics as Maoists: "Maoism is the phoenix which arose from the ashes of the great disillusionment with Western culture in the 1960's and which found hope in the Communist Revolution" (Chow 1993, 10). Maoists, she suggests, have a "special sibling" relationship with Orientalists, whose ethnographic readings reflect their institutional and epistemological investments and highlight the critics' cultural fantasies and projections.

> Typically, the Maoist is a cultural critic who lives in capitalist society but who is fed up with capitalism—a cultural critic, in other words, who wants a social order opposed to the one that is supporting her own undertaking. The Maoist is thus a supreme example of the way desire works: What she wants is always located in the other, resulting in an identification with and valorization of that which she is not/does not have (1993, 10).

Chow provocatively argues that the Western critic's negative appraisal of Third World writers' cosmopolitanism or worldliness is a symptom of the critic's melancholia. Citing Sigmund Freud's *Mourning and Melancholia,* she identifies sinologist Stephen Owens's scathing appraisal of too Westernized Chinese world poetry as an example of the apprehension and grief the Western critic experiences when he or she cannot get over the loss of a precious, treasured object (1993, 1–4). Chow goes one step beyond Freud's analysis of the melancholic's "delusional belittling of himself when he introjects the loss of his ego" by suggesting that "postcoloniality . . . offers a use of Freud that necessitates a rethinking of his theory of the melancholic disorder" (1993, 4). Freud's construction, she notes, concentrates on subjects and objects and does not analyze how the melancholic acts in regard to other subjects. "In the case of the sinologist's relationship with his beloved object 'China,'" Chow concludes, "melancholia is complicated by the presence of a third party—the living members of Chinese culture who provide the sinologist with a means of externalizing his loss and directing his blame. What Freud sees as self-directed denigration now finds a concrete realization in the denigration of others" (1993, 4). In other words, the critic's experience of the cultural anxiety related to the disappearing past as it is embodied by the Third World writer leads him to perceive himself as an abandoned subject. Writers like Bei Dao, the subject of Owens's scorn, become not the oppressed but the oppressor, "one who agress(es) against the first world sinologist by robbing him of his love" (1993, 4).

See Rey Chow's "Introduction: Leading Questions," *Writing Diaspora: Tactics of Intervention in Contemporary Cultural Studies* (Chow 1993) for further discussion. Her essay, "Where Have All the Natives Gone," (in the same volume) is also of relevance.

12. It is noteworthy to remember that for the most part the first generation of cosmopolitan postcolonial critics were male: Memmi, Cesaire, and Fanon, in particular, primarily discuss the postcolonial subject in masculine terms.

13. Hanif Kureishi's (and Stephen Frear's) *Sammy and Rosie* and Meena Alexander's *Faultlines*, although progressive on many levels, both subtly reinscribe traditional or conservative ideologies. *Sammy and Rosie's* portrayal of lesbians and activists as hysterics is especially troubling as is the film's final image, which suggests that after the death of patriarchy (Sammy's father), the social alternative is the redisciplined by grief, heterosexual family unit, the restored marital couple—this in the face of Margaret Thatcher's return to Victorian values/normative family conservative discourse. *Faultlines*, on the other hand, embraces the West as a superior democratic culture, while deemphasizing Western forms of oppression and intolerance.

14. One of the significant differences between Nair's *Mississippi Masala* and Srinivas Krishna's *Masala* relates to each film's production history. Krishna's *Masala* is a small budget, independent film; Nair's a more affluent, and I'd argue, constrained film. *Masala* is narratively and visually quirky in a way that few mainstream films ever manage to be because of the different demands and expectations of the independent and mainstream film industries and audiences. It is these kinds of production politics that Brennan's work accentuates.

15. For two distinctly different, passionately and convincingly argued but ultimately irreconcilable responses to Krishna's *Masala*, see Yasmin Jiwani's "The Audience That Didn't Count," and Sanjay Khanna's "Cutting Your Own deals," in *Rungh: A South Asian Quarterly of Culture, Comment and Criticism*, vol. 1, no. 3 (1992): 10–16. In her article, Yasmin Jiwani accuses Krishna of having a colonialist mentality and suggests that the film is made for and directed to the white audience. She is particularly disturbed by its preoccupation with sexuality ("Western sexual liberation") and with what she considers the film's caricature of religious belief. Krishna (the director) is summed-up as an egocentric, self-hating cultural hedonist; the film, a dystopic mess:

> It was a *masala* that in the end, did to us symbolically what British colonialism did to our ancestral land—it violated us, made a mockery of our sense of being, and betrayed us to the wider society. For it was a *masala* that combined the ingredients of an internalized racism mixed with a postmodernist discourse of identity, sexuality and race, all of which were re-cast in the ahistorical plane of Krishna's vision of himself and his reality. Differences dislocated from their social, cultural and economic grounding floated in the spectacular plane of unreality taking fantastic shapes and grotesque forms (Jiwani 1992, 11).

Sanjay Khanna, on the other hand, bases his interpretation on a reading of Rita Tikko, rather than the "anti-hero Krishna" (the character Krishna, not the director). Khanna emphasizes Rita's struggle with the double burdens of race and gender. He understands Krishna's identity confusion as "the bewilderment of a young person who has been regarded as an outsider by his community, is offered little guidance, struggles to find his own way and voice, returns ready to begin a dialogue and is, in effect, told that by making his own choices, he has taken an irrevocable step and can no longer be accepted" (Jiwani 1992, 16).

I'd like to thank Stephanie White for bringing *Rungh* to me across the Canadian–U.S. border.

16. For an interesting discussion of the question of ambivalence and an overview of poststructuralist influences on postcolonial theory and discourse, see Gyan Prakash's "Postcolonial Criticism and Indian Historiography," *Social Text* 31/32 (1992): 8–18.

17. See, for example, Gayatri Spivak's "Acting Bits/Identity Talk," *Critical Inquiry* 18 (Summer 1992): 770–803. In this article, Spivak explores issues relating to cultural and national location by means of reading a number of autobiographical representations: Jamelie Hassan's installation pieces, one of which is the Canadian-Lebanese artist's translation-interpretation of Rushdie's *Midnight's Children*; Assia Djebar's *Fantasia: An Algerian Cavalcade*; with what Spivak describes as a "citation of myself engaged in identity talk" (Spivak 1991, 770). In the course of the article, she describes her experience of having felt her identity "stripped away" during an encounter with Hassan's *Midnight's Children*, which depicts photographic images of Egyptian-Palestinian children surrounded by an inscription taken from Rushdie's novel. This translation, Spivak remarks, put her own identity in parentheses and reminded her that her "context is also unsaturated and open, like all contexts" (782–783). "This is," Spivak notes, "the kind of stripping that must be undertaken together if ethnic identities in the so-called First World are to become culturally and politically productive" (785). She also suggests, via a reading of another Jamelie Hassan installation, *Meeting Nasser*, that there are important lessons to be learned from the immigrant daughter who learns to read original *and* immigrant culture selectively, "letter by letter" (790):

> If we believe that we can restore the personal, political, historical, and cross-cultural truth of art, we are silenced by the child apprentice in cultural politics as art and the performance of life: the new immigrant. The great divide between the mother and child, the mother and daughter, in the new immigrant family, is one of the most instructive things to mediate on for any student of cultural politics (790).

These sorts of discrete and willful acts of translation relate to what I am calling elsewhere in the paper the disobedient daughter or son's acts of treachery. For further discussion of the Third World artist as a treacherous interpreter see Lawrence Chua's recent interview with Gurinder Chadha (director of *Bhaji on the Beach* and *I'm British, But*) and Hanif Kureishi (Chua 1994).

18. Some examples of fairly recent scholarship that addresses the gender question and/in Third World nationalist movements can be found in *Nationalisms and Sexualities*, Andrew Parker, Mary Russo, and Patricia Yeager, eds. (London and New York: Routledge, 1992). Ketu Katrak's "Indian Nationalism, Gandhian *Satyagraha*, and Representations of Female Sexuality"; R. Radhakrishnan's "Nationalism, Gender, and the Narrative of Identity"; and Ann Rosalind Jones and Peter Stallybrass's "Dismantling Irena: The Sexualizing of Ireland in Early Modern England" all examine the perplexities of gender and nationalism.

Third World Women and the Politics of Feminism, Chandra Talpade Mohanty, Ann Russo, and Lourdes Torres, eds. (Bloomington and Indianapolis: Indiana University Press, 1991) is also of interest. Angela Gilliam's "Women's Equality and National Liberation," and Nayereh Tohidi's "Gender and Islamic Fundamentalism: Feminist Politics in Iran," have particular relevance to the subject matter of this chapter.

19. The sixteenth-century Babri Masjid mosque (or Mosque of Babar) at Ayodhya was destroyed by fundamentalist Hindus who replaced the Muslim mosque with an installation of a statue of Rama, an incarnation of the Hindu god Vishnu, whom Hindus believe was born at the site (News Services, December 3, 1992). The destruction of the mosque was supported by the Hindu nationalist BJP. The violent clashes led to the governmental

banning of five Hindu and Muslim fundamentalist organizations. The battle over the mosque resulted in the deaths of more than 1,050 (Hazarika 1992, A11), which painfully illustrates just how deadly conflicts about cultural and religious ownership, primary or original attachments can become.

For further discussion of communalist violence and the battle over the Babri Masjid/Ram Janmabhoomi Shrine see Purnima Bose's "The Global Context of Communalism: The Case of Salman Rushdie," *SAMAR: South Asian Magazine for Action and Reflection*, no. 2 (Summer 1993): 19–25.

20. While addressing Marxist criticism's marginalization of aesthetic questions, Barrett examines art critic Max Raphael's attempts to combine sociohistorical analysis with acknowledgment of the power and significance of aesthetic feeling. Raphael's critical practice, she explains, involved the intent to read visual art closely, thereby the viewer would apprehend a "conceptual reconstitution" of the work, a reading of the artwork's structural or formal *and* historical-ideological dimensions. In Raphael's terms, the critic's appraisal would involve assessment of the artwork's autonomous organic structure; "important art" would be distinguished by its ambiguity and its expressive capabilities. "Value lies, therefore, in the work that can encompass polarization and harmony, determination and playfulness, diversity and unity, tension within a logical structure," Barrett notes. Raphael's theory maintains a "scale of *relative* values" (1988, 703, original emphasis) as opposed to absolute or universal ones. However, Barrett asserts that Raphael's theory's democratic aspects are discernable via the critic's emphasis on artistic skill, versus emphasis of art's mystifactory nature of the artist's genius or inspiration—art mythologies he considered "petit-bourgeois fictions" (1988, 302).

Barrett carefully details the limitations of Raphael's artistic theory by illustrating how the critic's own artistic judgments were sometimes uneven and inconsistent. "Many of his allegedly formal readings," she notes, "were nonetheless ideological ones," his reading of Pablo Picasso's *Guernica*, for example. She also suggests that "Raphael's failure to achieve more neutral and objective positions was due to an unresolved conflict in his theoretical framework between an emphasis on artistic production (in the spirit of Walter Benjamin) and a profoundly Lukacsian subsumption of art to the category of ideology" (1988, 709).

21. Barrett is referring to Terry Eagleton's *Literary Theory* here as she discusses the currency or recognizability of aesthetic signifiers: "As Terry Eagleton puts it, if you approach me at a bus stop and murmur, "Though still unravished bride of quietness," then I am unmistakably in the presence of the literary. I know this because the texture, rhythm and resonance of your words are in excess of their abstractable meaning (1988, 698).

In the case of "Karachi, 1990," and *Meatless Days*, we know we are in the presence of the literary because of the repetitions and rhythmic intonations of the prose. In addition to the lovely prose, both works' publication by academic presses, *Raritan* and University of Chicago, respectively, also distinguishes them and further reflects their academic status and seriousness.

22. For clarity, I will refer to the author as Suleri, the character as Sara. One might best understand Sara the narrator as an elaborately studied performance of Suleri the author and professor.

23. Sara abandons this dream of a mosquelike home after witnessing the father's (melo)dramatic turn to Islam, which takes place after the partitioning (of East Pakistan into Bangladesh) and the failure of the two-nation theory. The Suleri children compare the

father's religious turn to their own posttraumatic syndrome; however, they consider his Muslimification as being as romantic and excessive as his nationalist beliefs. The children refer to their father's and their own excesses of self-sorrow as "the old *masjid* syndrome" (Suleri 1989, 80). The father grieves over the death of a nationalist dream, whereas the children, particularly the Suleri women, grieve over the losses of a mother and sister; bodies and flesh are portrayed as the Suleri women's priorities, theories and ideas, the father's.

24. One of *Meatless Days'* jacket blurbs aptly demonstrates this danger. *Los Angeles Times'* book reviewer Rone Tempest states that the text is "a jewel of insight and beauty . . . Suleri's voice has the same authority when she speaks about Pakistani politics as it does in her literary interludes." This critic completely overlooks the ways in which *Meatless Days* presents all narratives and discourses as selective, self-interested, unpredictable, and unreliable because they are influenced by desire, which Suleri suggests can blind us from other realities.

25. Bilgrami's essay does not acknowledge the possibility of there being devout *and* intellectual Muslims in the originary country; his use of "moderate" appears to imply those who are secularists rather than those who are deeply religiously inclined. One wonders if committed Islamic beliefs are necessarily noncosmopolitan. In other words, is Bilgrami's representation of Islam partial and selective? The degree to which intellectual and absolutist beliefs can correspond is difficult to measure; this appears to be a question for the present and future.

Moroccan filmmaker Farida Ben Lyazid circles around such questions in her captivating film, *A Door to the Sky* (1988?). The film, which was written and directed by Lyazid, opens with an epigraph that reads, "We belong to God and to Him shall return." Following the epigraph is a dedication to "Fatima Firha, who in the 10th century opened one of the first universities in the world." The narrative presents the story of Nadia, who returns to Morocco to see her dying father. She gets off of the plane from Paris dressed aggressively urban, in punk-inspired black leather and bicolored hair. Early in the film, Nadia voices her desire to be both Moroccan and French in answer to her completely westernized brother Driss's proclamation that he has chosen to be French. While residing in the family home among her deceased mother's paintings and family's books, Nadia begins to have visions in which God is speaking to her. Kirana, a believer and family friend, counsels Nadia and offers her Islamic prophets who she believes will appeal to Nadia's questioning and cosmopolitan nature; for example, Kirana recommends Imam Ghazu, the "soldier, politician" to Nadia and guides her though Sufi teachings. Nadia eventually rejects the West, including her French boyfriend Jean-Phillipe, whom she tells when he comes to visit her in Morocco, "I don't want to worship money any more." Central to her return to Islam and Morocco are her dreams; in one dream Nadia is thrown out of France by Monsieur Le Pen. In other dreams, Nadia receives sensual and spiritual comfort from her religious feelings. Lyazid's film powerfully represents the mystery and ecstacy of religious beliefs; this is achieved with the film's glorious palette, its use of North African music, and its highlighting of Sufi rituals. However, Lyazid's depiction of Nadia's life raises more questions than it answers; for example, Nadia's attempts to marry her two cultures are abandoned by the film's end. When she falls in love with a local man, the shelter she established to harbor and protect Muslim women and children after her father's death is abandoned. Nadia is last seen against the landscape embracing her new husband. In terms of the film's text, however, Lyazid does manage to articulate a religious-cosmopolitan point of view. Sufi mysticism is juxtaposed next to romantic mysticism, for example, Rimbaud's voice speaks to Nadia as convincingly as do the voices of the prophets. In a particularly impressive scene Nadia composes a letter to Jean-Phillipe in which she quotes Angela Davis quoting Marx and gives full voice and recontextualization to a quotation that has frequently been used to characterize Marxist intellectuals disengagement with religious questions. Nadia writes, "Comfort makes me sick. I belong here, no where else." The voice-over presents the remainder of her letter: "One part of religion is the expression of real distress, another part is the protest against real distress. Religion is the sign of the oppressed creature, the soul of a soulless world, as it is the spirit of social conditions, from which any spirit has been excluded. Religion is the opium of the masses."

26. See Sara Suleri's "Woman Skin Deep: Feminism and the Postcolonial Condition" (Suleri 1992b), pages 767–769 for further discussion.

BIBLIOGRAPHY

Ahmed, Tamina. "Bangladesh: A Best-Selling Author Risks Her Life," *Ms.*, vol. iv, no. 6 (May/June 1994):18.

Associated Press. "Author Comes Out of Hiding, Vows She Will Keep Writing," *Austin American Statesman*, Friday, August 19, 1994:A24.

"Bangladeshi's Class an Accused Author," *New York Times*, vol. 143, (July 1, 1994):A2(N), col. 4.

Barrett, Michèle. "The Place of Aesthetics in Marxist Criticism," in *Marxism and the Interpretation of Culture*. Lawrence Grossberg and Cary Nelson, eds. Indianapolis and Bloomington: Indiana University Press, 1988.

Bhabha, Homi. "Dissemination: Time, Narrative and the Margins of the Modern Nation," in *The Location of Culture*. London and New York: Routledge, 1994.

_____. "Signs Taken for Wonders: Questions of Ambivalence and Authority Under a Tree in Delhi, May 1817," in *The Location of Culture*. London and New York: Routledge, 1994.

Bhattacharya, Pallab. "A Rushdie in Bangladesh," *World Press Review*, vol. 41, no. 1 (January 1994):49.

Bilgrami, Akeel. "What Is a Muslim? Fundamental Commitment and Cultural Identity," *Critical Inquiry*, vol. 18, no. 4 (Summer 1992):821–842.

Bose, Purnima. "The Global Context of Communalism: The Case of Salman Rushdie," *SAMAR: South Asian Magazine for Action and Reflection*, no. 2 (Summer 1993):19–25.

Brennan, Tim. "Rushdie, Islam, and Postcolonial Criticism," *Social Text 31/32*, vol. 10, nos. 1 & 2 (1992):271–276.

Brennan, Timothy. *Salman Rushdie and the Third World: Myths of the Nation*. New York: St. Martin's Press, 1989.

Butler, Judith. *Gender Trouble: Feminism and the Subversion of Identity*. London and New York: Routledge, 1990.

Chua, Lawrence. "An Interview with Hanif Kureishi and Gurinder Chadha: What Does It Mean to be Black and European?" *Bomb*, vol. xxxxiii (Summer 1994):50–54.

Chow, Rey. *Writing Diaspora: Tactics of Intervention in Contemporary Cultural Studies*. Bloomington and Indianapolis: Indiana University Press, 1993.

Fanon, Frantz. "On National Culture," in *The Wretched of the Earth*. New York: Grove Press, 1963.

Gilliam, Angela. "Women's Equality and National Liberation," in Mohanty, Chandra Talpade, Ann Russo, and Lourdes Torres (eds.) *Third World Women and the Politics of Feminism.* Bloomington and Indianapolis: Indiana University Press, 1991.

Hazarika, Sanjoy. "Muslim-Hindi Violence Seems to Abate in India," New York Times News Service, *Austin American Statesman,* Saturday, December 12, 1992:A11.

Jiwani, Yasmin. "The Audience That Didn't Count," *Rungh: A South Asian Quarterly of Culture, Comment and Criticism,* vol. 1, no. 3 (1992):10–13.

Jones, Ann Rosalind, and Peter Stallybrass. "Dismantling Irena: The Sexualizing of Ireland in Early Modern England," in Parker, Andrew, Mary Russo, and Patricia Yeager (eds.) *Nationalisms and Sexualities.* London and New York: Routledge, 1992.

Katrak, Ketu H. "Indian Nationalism, Gandhian 'Satyagraha,' and Representations of Female Sexuality," in Parker, Andrew, Mary Russo, and Patricia Yeager (eds.) *Nationalisms and Sexualities.* London and New York: Routledge, 1992.

Khanna, Sanjay. "Cutting Your Own Deals," *Rungh: A South Asian Quarterly of Culture, Comment and Criticism,* vol. 1, no. 3 (1992):14–16.

Prakash, Gyan. "Postcolonial Criticism and Indian Historiography," *Social Text 31/32,* vol. 10, nos. 1 & 2 (1992):8–18.

Radhakrishnan, R. "Nationalism, Gender, and the Narrative of Identity," in Parker, Andrew, Mary Russo, and Patricia Yeager (eds.) *Nationalisms and Sexualities.* London and New York: Routledge, 1992.

Robbins, Bruce. "Comparative Cosmopolitanism," *Social Text 31/32,* vol. 10, nos. 1 & 2 (1992):169–186.

Smith, Sidonie, and Julia Watson. "Introduction," *De/Colonizing the Subject.* Sidonie Smith and Julia Watson, eds. Minneapolis: University of Minnesota Press, 1992.

Spivak, Gayatri Chakravorty. "Acting Bits/Identity Talk," *Critical Inquiry,* vol. 18, no. 4 (Summer 1992):770–803.

_____. "Subaltern Studies: Deconstructing Historiography," in *Selected Subaltern Studies.* Ranjit Guha and Gayatri Chakravorty Spivak, eds. New York and Oxford: Oxford University Press, 1988.

Suleri, Sara. "Karachi, 1990," *Raritan,* vol. xi, no. 4 (Spring 1992):50–71.

_____. (1992b) "Woman Skin Deep: Feminism and the Postcolonial Condition," 759. *Critical Inquiry,* vol. 18 (Summer 1992):756–769.

_____. *Meatless Days.* Chicago: University of Chicago Press, 1989.

Tohidi, Nayereh. "Gender and Islamic Fundamentalism: Feminist Politics in Iran," in Mohanty, Chandra Talpade, Ann Russo, and Lourdes Torres (eds.) *Third World Women and the Politics of Feminism.* Bloomington and Indianapolis: Indiana University Press, 1991.

Weaver, Mary Anne. "A Fugitive from Injustice," *The New Yorker,* September 12, 1994:48–50, 55–60.

Warley, Linda. "Assembling Ingredients: Subjectivity in Meatless Days," *Autobiography Studies: AB,* vol. 7, no. 1 (Spring 1992):107–123.

7

In the Name of Audre Lorde:
The Location of Poetry
in the United States

ZOFIA BURR

Beyond Tolerance: Bringing Poetry Home

During the "Sixth Annual Report of the Secretaries of Defense," televised December 4, 1992, moderator David Gergen noted that "Secretary Cheney and General Colin Powell regard the growing chaos in Russia as a serious national security concern for the United States," and asked of Donald Rumsfeld, Nixon's Secretary of Defense, the following question: "How would you size up what's going on in the former Soviet Union, and [the] prospects there for the future?" In his response, Rumsfeld insisted upon the fundamental alienness, for us, of the Russian outlook and of their traditions:

> [We] are behaving with respect to them and interpreting them in a context that doesn't take into account the enormous differences between the United States and Russia. I mean the fact that the government used to kill poets because they felt the need to control things so totally. In the United States I don't even think anyone in the government reads a poet [laughter] let alone cares about killing a poet. It is a fundamentally different situation (Public Broadcasting Service 1992, 3).

In order to articulate the essential bent of each society, the United States and Russia, Rumsfeld starts out by evoking a well-worn contrast between the limits set on free speech in each country. But he particularizes this contrast by pointing to each government's very different degree of tolerance toward the speech of poets rather than toward speech in general. The mania for control in the Soviet Union was such, he suggests, that *even poets* were thought worth killing. But when he goes on to underline the excessive, even lunatic, quality of such repression by stating explicitly the utterly marginal and inconsequential status of poetry in the United States, he complicates the implications of his argument. Saying that in the United States, no one in the government "even . . . reads a poet, let alone cares about killing [one]," Rumsfeld turns what started out as a complacent reiteration of the virtues of American society into humorous self-denigration of American political culture.

What started off as a canonical cold war and liberal humanist contrast between "free" or "open" and "totalitarian" or "closed" societies turns into a source of amusement. Swerving away from our initial expectations, perhaps Rumsfeld's remark now poses the alternatives of evil *or* banality, authoritarian repression or utter indifference. What started off as a straightforward self-valorizing comparison for the United States has acquired an inflection keyed to clichés about the uncultured vulgarity of American society and especially of American politics. Instead of a heroic contrast between freedom and repression, between principled liberalism and Machiavellianism run amok, American viewers of the Public Broadcasting Service special are left to chuckle at ourselves and at the spectacle of our own contempt by way of trivialization for something so powerless as poetry. Although Rumsfeld would be the last to put it this way, his formulation implies in effect that we don't censure poets because we engage instead in a practice of "repressive tolerance."[1] In this light, the "freedom" we afford the poet in the United States serves only to illuminate the impotence of the poet's word rather than to vouch for any more general or fundamental "freedom" in this society.

Although Rumsfeld's comments are meant to elucidate the profound cultural difference between "us" and "them," they depend on a mistaken assumption that poetry (and hence poets) have the *same* (inconsequential) function in both societies: The Russians' pathological difference from us is their "care" to kill so harmless a creature as a poet. Yet precisely because the Soviet Union was a society characterized by political repression and censorship, the discourse of poetry (and of literature more generally) may well have been one of the few outlets for giving voice to social and political critique, albeit by indirection or in an Aesopian language or even, paradoxically, by laying claim to a realm "outside" politics, outside the rigors of ideology. Poetry in such a society is a potent site for oppositional political formation and coded resistance to official discourses; it is emphatically a discourse of social communication and not exclusively an aesthetic discourse divorced from the functions and interests of ordinary speech.[2] In our society, where there are ostensibly few legal limits set on political critique, poetry is not unavoidably overladen with political significance. U.S. citizens can always ask, why choose poetry as a mode of political and social critique when there are so many other clearly more direct and effective channels of critique (safely) open? This perception of futility in the practice of poetry in our society is at the base of Rumsfeld's comments.[3] Far from celebrating the freedom of poetry, art, and speech in our society, Rumsfeld's comments betray a sense of loss.

A passage from Claudia Roth Pierpont's recent essay on Marina Tsvetaeva suggests how this sense of loss with respect to poetry is mystified when Western poets and writers come to handle the East-West contrast that Rumsfeld has invoked:

> "Why do you complain?" Osip Mandelstam once chided his wife. "Poetry is respected only in this country—people are killed for it." . . . By the logic of this system, it may be seen as the last indignity that Tsvetaeva was left to manage her death entirely on her own. The lack of any specifically directed state persecution—such as that which killed Mandelstam and silenced Akhmatova and finally threatened (and canonized) Pasternak—denied her even the compensation of worldly consequence, that sense of dangerous importance for which Western writers have guiltily envied Soviet suffering (1994, 98).

Here Mandelstam reportedly tells his wife Nadezdha that the murder of poets is evidence, on the part of Stalinists, of humanistic values and respect for the function of poetry. By way of its irony, however, the remark operates as a species of political critique.[4] But when this remark is taken up by "Western writers," Pierpont suggests, it is transformed into and read as a valediction on the poetic vocation. Political commentary is transformed into an autobiographical discourse about the life and fate of poets. And some U.S. writers both mourn the suffering caused by state persecution of other "poets" and long for the "sense of dangerous importance" that it gives to its victims. The lament against political injustice "there" continually transforms itself into a lament for the fate of poetry "here."[5] The relative freedom of the Western writer, purchased at the cost of the political futility of her speech, comes to seem inevitably like a pyrrhic victory. The question is, how inevitably?

Poetry may well be located on the margins of public discourse in the United States—and the figure of the margin may epitomize what it means to *be* "located," to be *merely* local. But its significance as a token of identity in discourses of geopolitical differentiation should suggest the inadequacy of a focus on the marginality of poetic discourse in our society. Because "[a] denial of poetry's relation to politics and cultural struggle is . . . itself a constitutive, structural definition of poetry" as it is predominantly conceived in the United States today, "the denial in a sense establishes a version of the very relation it would deny, turning poetry into the fixed 'other' of the political, the everyday, the contingent" (Nelson 1989, 129). We need to interrogate the kind of value we attribute to the poetic—precisely because its value as "poetry" is what is said to make it irrelevant in the political sphere. In what is still the dominant ideological perspective, poetry is taken as apolitical because it ostensibly articulates "universal truths" transcending local particularities and speaking as if to or for "everyone." With respect to poetry, then, as with respect to other things, the terms "local" and "universal" are evaluative rather than descriptive characterizations. As long as, in the context of the aesthetic, the political looks too local (or located) to register, while in the context of the global social totality, the marginalization of the poetic renders it ineffective as political discourse, choosing poetry as an avenue of politics may seem misguided. However, to the extent that the alienation caused by the reductive political discourses of our times is itself depoliticizing, there is reason to suppose that the "distance" between poetic discourse and openly, expressly political discourses can have its uses. Precisely because a poet can't assume that her audience is made up of already self-consciously politicized subjectivities, this "distance" can be read as a measure of the work to be done. Without obfuscating the place of poetry in our society, without inflating the space of poetic discourse or giving it by analogy a hollow resonance with the larger structurings of social space, I want to show how a poem can acquire a further range of motion and impact if its readers, *differently implicated* in the world the poem evokes, respond to the poem as an utterance that requires them to take account of their specific locations. Without transcending its own or its readers' specificity, poetry responded to in such a manner ceases to be easily or essentially localized.

In the rest of this chapter, I take up the poetic work of Audre Lorde and its reception since the 1970s as a particularly useful site for interrogating poetic discourse in the United States and its apparent incapacity to have an impact on the world into which it is taken. What I'm most interested in producing here is *not* a reading of Lorde, per se, or even her reception. Instead, by using the example of Lorde's work and reception, I mean to interrogate the conventions of reading that are at work in the depoliticization of poetry in general in the United States. And—without effacing the differences between poetry and other (more explicitly political) discourses—I want to point toward an approach to reading poetry that makes its political implications available. Throughout I will argue that Lorde utilizes poetic discourse with an investment in its political possibilities but that to take stock of this strategy and its effectiveness, we need to revise our understanding of political poetry in the direction of a more dynamic and readerly framework. The methodological alternative I want to pose here is one that turns away from reading practices that locate their authority with the poem and poet to reading practices that respond to particular performances of the poem as specific and strategic utterances.

The Career of Audre Lorde, Poet

Apparently ignoring or dismissing the work of the Black Arts Movement, the antiwar movement, and the women's movement of the late 1960s, most university literary education in the United States of the 1970s and 1980s taught readers of poetry to define the poetic and the political in opposition to each other. "Political poetry" was seen as too specific to its occasion (or location) to count as "poetry" in the universalizing (transhistorical) terms attributed to "great poetry." So political poetry—ostensibly limited by the location of its emergence—was seen as at best unsatisfactory and at worst no different from crude propaganda. The terms in which a reviewer of *Chosen Poems* praises Audre Lorde's work in 1982 are symptomatic of these assumptions: "Rather than a political poetry, these are the poems of a driven, politically committed woman" (1982, 1227). Here the reviewer would defend Lorde's work from the epithet "political poetry" because the notion of a "political poetry" suggests a narrow specificity of address by the poet and a reductive specificity of response by the reader; the reviewer seeks, instead, to claim for Lorde's poetry a "wider" significance and a more "universal" engagement.

In recent years, in some parts of the academy there appears to have been more room for political poetry. Explicitly oppositional political poets are certainly invited to read at universities and colleges. This has not, however, had the effect of re-empowering poetry for politics. Criticism of such poetry—often considered "oppositional" because of who seems to be speaking rather than because of what's being said—tends to be focused on the biography of the poet. Especially where the political poet is taken as a representative of a marginalized position, be she woman or nonwhite or lesbian, our attempts to care about such poetry tend to involve reference to the poet's psychic and emotional state instead of a response to the social situation the poetry addresses, a situation in which each reader is (differently) implicated.

The mainstream reception of Audre Lorde's poetry is particularly exemplary of the way in which many of our reading practices, both those that claim to be against politics in poetry and those that claim to be for politics in poetry, can diminish the political impact of literary discourse. Self-identified as black, lesbian, and poet, Lorde established her practice in the early 1970s, publishing her poetry first with explicitly political presses such as Dudley Randall's Broadside Press in Detroit. Eventually, however, Lorde published her poetry with W. W. Norton & Co. To the extent that the Norton insignia is a symbol (and vehicle) of canonization, then, Lorde's poetry is officially acknowledged and sanctioned by the keepers of the gates to the house of poetry. Lorde has always and only published her prose, however, with the women's presses Kitchen Table (Albany, New York) and Firebrand (Ithaca, New York), the former of which she was instrumental in helping to establish. This circumstance of her publication preferences has had contradictory effects. For some poetry audiences, it has tended to split her work, divorcing her poetry from a shared context with her prose, constructing it instead as an autonomous sector of aesthetic discourse to be evaluated as such. For Lorde's "activist" public, however, the tendency has been to collapse the poetry into the prose and to read both discourses as straightforward autobiography. Although each of these responses attends to a significant aspect of Lorde's work and career, I will argue that there is a more complex and significant interaction between the two gestures of artistry and activism that is central to Lorde's practice and that can help illuminate our understanding of the political function of poetry in American society.

Despite the importance of Norton as a publisher of individual poets and of poetry anthologies, the relative circulation of poetic and prose discourses in our society is such that Jan Clausen is probably right in stating that:

Her official designation as New York State Poet for 1991–93 notwithstanding, Lorde is best known for her prose works . . . for her activism on behalf of women of color; and—among feminists—for her eloquent advocacy of a flexible, non-essentialist identity politics: the "house of difference," she called it (1993, 130).

In the review in *The Nation* from which this comment is drawn, Clausen goes on to offer a reason for the relative obscurity of Lorde's poetry:

Lorde must be counted among the handful of necessary poets of her generation, yet her work has received shockingly little critical attention from any quarter: feminist writers of all colors, African-American critics or the still largely white and male American poetry establishment. The last category of indifference is easily under-stood, given not only Lorde's outsider identities but her blunt refusal to distinguish between poetry and life. Had she refused from the comfortable distance of Eastern Europe or even South Africa, she might be championed by those of the mildly left-ish literati who love to castigate American poetry for insufficient social conscience, but the case is otherwise (1993, 130).

Clausen's comment here, invoking the familiar contrast between the perceived significance of poets and poetry in East and West, seems to overstate or rather to flatten Lorde's position by describing it as a "blunt refusal to *distinguish* between poetry and life." This conflation of poetry and life, art and activism, is precisely the move that tends to relegate Lorde's poetry to the margins, even as her work has been taken up by "activist" audiences. Lorde does not champion a simple identity between (the poet's) life and art. If we are to understand and respond to the force of Lorde's poetry without either inflating it into a universalized, tran-scendent "literariness" or conflating it with the biographical particularities of her existence, we need to attend to both the intersections and the tensions between "poetry and life" in Lorde's work. Most of all we need to elaborate a critical idiom that allows us to shift the focus from the poet's life to the relationship between the poem and the *reader's* life, the poem and the reader's world.

Throughout her life, Audre Lorde's function in the role of poet was inextrica-ble from her function as a political activist. While she chose to speak by way of the identity of poet and the discourse (and conventions) of poetry, validation of the poetry as poetry was never the entire point. Recently interviewing Adrienne Rich, publisher of *The Progressive* Matthew Rothschild remembers Lorde re-sponding to applause by saying, "Applause is easy. Go out and do something." Rich adds as if to explicate the sources of that response:

Well, Audre had a strong sense of the energy that can be generated by poetry, that poetry is a source of power . . . [a]nd she resisted being turned into some kind of mascot or token—which is something that happens in the women's movement as it does anywhere else—an artist comes along and people try to capture her and take their own latent power and hand it over to someone who is viewed as stronger, braver, more powerful. She wanted people to keep their energy and keep their power, touch it through her poetry, but then go out and use it, seriously. We used to talk about this a lot—there was this phrase, I don't know if I found it or if she found it, but it was "assent without credence," where people are applauding you but they don't make what you're saying part of their life, their living. She was very, very aware of it and concerned. And she was resisting like hell being made into some token black goddess in some largely white women's gathering, as so often would be the case (Rich 1994, 34).

The difference between "assent" and "credence" as modes of response to poetry— the one having to do with "appreciation" of poetic language or of the poet as a larger-than-life figure, the other with a kind of "belief" in and action responsive to the claims of poetic utterance—might serve to distinguish a purely aesthetic and celebratory response to poetry from a response that views poetry within the worldly ensemble of ethical practice, social vision, and political action. Lorde's poetic practice, I am suggesting, self-consciously solicits the latter kind of response and seeks to prevent exclusively aestheticized engagement with her work and her person as "poet"—even as it seeks to make use of some aspects of the authority associated with that role.

The record of her reception, however, suggests that this interconnectedness of poetic and political practices in Lorde's career did not prevent the reception of her poetry, wherever she spoke or read to an audience "schooled" in poetry, from being affected by certain academic conventions for the reception of poetic discourse. Here I'm referring particularly to those literary conventions that in contemporary Anglo-American academic practice tend to erode the status of poetic discourse as activism because they approach poetry as a "performance" of communication—rather than as a kind of communication—and distinguish its ontological status from that of ordinary "speech."[6] Such conventions for the reception of poetry establish distance between the audience's appreciation of a poet's discourse and the necessity of responsive action to that discourse. Still, Lorde very much intended to employ a literary identity and some literary conventions in her own practice. Choosing to speak as a poet, Lorde underlined the extent to which her discourse was strategic and crafted rather than "natural" or "expressive." In spite of this choice, and in response to her black and lesbian identities in particular, too often her artistic performance was read by white academics as symptomatic rather than as strategic. As Michael Berube makes clear when he distinguishes between authorization and canonization, all authors of the same genre of texts are not attributed with the same "author function"[7]: "If authorization—and, finally, canonization—is . . . a different affair for writers of different races, it is precisely because American writers of different races have historically been assigned radically different author functions" (1992, 61). Throughout this chapter, it is my intention to attribute the authority associated with strategy to Lorde. Although this does not mean I uncritically accept everything Lorde has to say, it does mean that I take her public poetic speech to be addressed to her (variously positioned) readers to say something to us about ourselves-in-the-world rather than expressing something about herself. In general I advocate taking poetry—not only oppositional poetry—as strategic in order to provoke the reader's responsibility for his or her uses of it.

Lorde's political and poetical practices took place at the intersection of the conventions for the reception of the theoretically distinguishable but practically inextricable discursive modes of direct speech and poetry as verbal construct. In working this intersection, Lorde put pressure on the role, responsibility, and assumptions of the auditor in both contexts. More than understanding the "meaning" of the poem, more than evaluating the state of the poet-speaker, Lorde asked her audience to put what we came to understand by way of the poem *to use*. And more than just active engagement in a struggle, she asked us to scrutinize our situations and to acknowledge whatever privilege we have to be able to use that privilege responsibly.

The relationship between Audre Lorde's roles as poet and activist always involved a tension, I have suggested, that was crucial to both practices. This tension was perhaps most evident at Lorde's readings where she tended to address her poems to the particular audience to whom she was speaking. For instance, to alert the members of the audience to the presence or absence of others (to call attention to who was in the audience and who was not), Lorde explicitly allowed the local reading situation to inflect the poetry itself. Lorde addressed the particularities of the local audience, however, to draw her audience members' attention to our places in relation to a more global situation, and to make us aware of our responsibilities to situations that might otherwise look as if they were not about us.[8]

During Lorde's lifetime, white feminist critics like myself who argued for the importance of devoting the attention of close readings to Lorde's verse, urged this mode of response as a supplement to the activist response to Lorde's project. My interpretation of Lorde's poetry, as Katie King has said of her interpretation of Lorde's prose, "deliberately uses some of the strategies of academic close reading in order to appropriate their forms of authority . . . " (King 1988, 323). But Lorde's death on November 17, 1992, makes it harder for her readers to hang onto the productive tension that was the effect of the imbrication of her roles as activist and poet. Her poetry in particular, as what survives and as it engages the possibility of canonization, faces the danger of being monumentalized and losing its instrumental urgency. The loss of her literal presence and of her repeated demand for our response only increases the risk (that was always there) of our engagement with her poetry becoming (or remaining) merely contemplative and appreciative.[9]

In order to make these issues more concrete, I want to examine the posthumous publication of two versions of a work that has been represented as Lorde's last poem. In doing so, I aim to illustrate the pressures now that Lorde is dead toward a monumentalizing reading of her work and to demonstrate how such a reading-practice (mis)shapes and has regularly (mis)shaped our understanding of the meaning of her work, as well as the work of other oppositional poets. And by contrast, I want to show what we might get from a reading of Lorde's work that is more attuned to the issues of readerly response and responsibility and poetry as communication that I have been canvassing.

Reckoning with a Poem

The distinction between reading practices or styles of response that can neutralize the politics of Lorde's poetic practice and readings that can further that politics is exemplified in the posthumous publication of Lorde's poem that begins, "I can't just sit here/staring death in the face. . . ." The poem appears in two distinct forms under two distinct titles. In looking at each of these two versions, I take the context in which the poem is presented as limning the outlines of a mode of reading the poem that wants to have a role in shaping later readings and uses. The poem, titled "Today Could Be The Day," appeared first in the March–April 1993 issue of *Ms.* magazine soon after Lorde's death. Another version of the poem with the title, "Today Is Not The Day" appears in *The Marvelous Arithmetics of Distance*, the final collection of Lorde's poetry published by Norton in September 1993. Exploring the differences between the two versions of the poem and the contexts in which they appear, I will show that the version of the poem titled, "Today Could Be The Day" (in *Ms.* magazine), presents Lorde's poem as representing a legacy, an inheritance to be cherished by its readers, whereas the version of the poem titled, "Today Is Not The Day" (in *The Marvelous Arithmetics of Distance*), underscores the responsibilities we, as readers, each have to examine what we bring to the poems as a result of our specific locations.

There are several potentially important differences between these two versions of the poem that I leave to one side (among them the fact that the figure of Lorde's son Jonathan is left out of the version of the poem that appears in *Ms.*), but probably the most telling difference for my argument is the way the different titles play off what otherwise seems the same or similar in the two poems.

The setup for "Today Could Be The Day" in *Ms.* magazine is relentlessly elegiac. The cover of this issue announces: "Audre Lorde: In Her Own Words"; the contents page specifies: "Audre Lorde's Last Poem." This invocation of the topos of the author's last words directs us to the text of the poem, which is presented on a two-page spread, side-by-side with a full-page picture of the author and an italicized caption that reads:

> On November 17, 1992, after a 14-year battle against cancer, Audre Lorde died. To the end, she remained more than the sum of her parts—in her own words, "a Black, Lesbian, Feminist, Warrior Poet, fighting the good fight in spite of it all." This poem [referring to the poem printed on the other page of the spread]—one of the last she wrote—will appear in her posthumous collection "The Marvelous Arithmetics of Distance," forthcoming from W. W. Norton. Her presence will be sorely missed, her legacy greatly cherished (*Ms.* 1993, 58).

Reiterated both on the cover and on this page, the announcement that this is Audre Lorde "In Her Own Words"—referring indifferently to the specific poem that follows and to Lorde's habitual self-description under multiple names—collapses self-description and poetry and introduces the poem as something between autobiography and epitaph. In this context we're not encouraged to see the poem or the self-description as strategically authored discourse. Even as the caption acknowledges that the poem that follows is not literally Lorde's final work, we have been led to it as embodying "her own last words" and these are, proleptically, about her own death.

The sentence, "On November 17, 1992, after a 14-year battle against cancer, Audre Lorde died," provides a reference for the "day" in the poem's title and transforms the subjunctive possibility being handled by the poem into the irrefutable facticity of Lorde's death. How else now can we read this poem other than as about the day of Audre Lorde's death? And yet to read the poem as about the day of Lorde's death is to ignore the poem's reinscription of the whole question of death within the context of what will continue and develop beyond the dying: The "stranger" who comes to love the woman Lorde has loved, the cycle of seasons that continues beyond any individual closure, and the way that the poem describes the work that is only "half-done":

> . . . *we have water to carry*
> *honey to harvest*
> *bright seed to plant for the next fair*
> *sweet oil to exchange as we linger*
> *over each other's long ashy legs*
> *the evening light*
> *a crest on your cheekbones.*
>
> *By this rising*
> *a piece of our labor is half-done . . .*
>   (*Ms.* 1993, 59)

Regardless of this aspect of the poem's argument, at the conclusion of the introductory caption, Lorde's work is described as a "legacy to be cherished," a completed achievement, a completed story. "To the end, [Lorde] remained more than the sum of her parts," we are told, but now what remains are Lorde's poems—and they exist only as her remains.

The first two stanzas of the poem that follows the introductory caption are italicized. They read:

> *I can't just sit here*
> *staring death in the face*
> *blinking and asking for a new name*
> *by which to greet her*

> *I am not afraid to say*
> *unembellished*
> *I am dying*
> *but I do not want to do it*
> *looking the other way.*

In these stanzas the issue for the speaker is what or how to name the process she is going through—as she writes. And the strange eternity of the lyric voice underlined in these two stanzas by the repeated assertion of the "I" in the present tense is maintained throughout the rest of the poem in its repeated references to "today."

"Today is not the day," the third stanza begins in Roman type, which as a revision of the title ("Today *could* be the day") articulates the need to challenge what's already been said or suggested. But "Today is not the day," only temporarily erases the possibility the subjunctive "could" implied. It has to work against the doubt that it "could" be as it is set out by the title of this version of the poem, and reinforced by the elegiac context established by the editors of *Ms.*

Even though the poem also *ends* with the phrase "Today is not the day," ultimately the *Ms.* magazine presentation makes sure we experience the contrary. The back cover of this issue also has a picture of Lorde's face, captioned with her name and the dates 1934–1992. Whether or not "today is the day" for the speaker of the poem or for the reader, the magazine context reminds you that the day has come. The question that the poem ponders is not allowed to remain a real question, and with this closure disappears also the larger horizon onto which the question opens.

It's not only the *Ms.* magazine presentation that reads Lorde's posthumous work as epitaph. Rather *Ms.*'s presentation is indicative of a larger cultural proclivity for a form of narrative closure that turns the end of a person's life into a self-referential structure, enfolding the poet's work into this biographical narrative. As we saw with responses to the works and lives of Tsvetaeva, Mandelstam, and their peers, the poet's death comes to function as a masterplot that governs the meaning of her work and that transforms utterances in diverse registers into autobiographical discourses.

In a review of *The Marvelous Arithmetics of Distance* in *The Progressive,* the idea that the poems in this volume have the status of Audre Lorde's last words is reinforced: "Audre Lorde, the great pioneer of black feminist lesbian poetry, died last November. This is her final collection of poems, and they are personal, moving, bare, and striking. Many of the poems are poignant reckonings with her family." The review concludes:

In this sparse and commanding book, perhaps the most arresting lines are those in which she wrestles with the imminence of her own death. In "Today is not the day," she writes:

> *I am dying*
> *but I do not want to do it*
> *looking the other way.*

Audre Lorde never looked the other way ("Don't Look the Other Way," 1993, 43).

That some devoted readers will think they find in *The Marvelous Arithmetics of Distance* something like an account of Audre Lorde's last hours is not surprising given the generosity with which Lorde made the terms of her life and her death public. That the review continues in the vein of memorial or obituary is testament to the genuine loss some of Lorde's readers feel since her death. I want to suggest, however, that the retrospective or backward-looking stance of the obituary mode reflected both in the *Ms.* presentation of "Today Could Be The Day" and in the review in *The Progressive* monumentalizes the work in a way that neutralizes its politics. The closure on the poet and the poetry, although it honors the memory of the poet, elides the responsibility of the reader in the present and ignores the goal argued throughout Lorde's book that the work should go on through the reader.

Although the reviewer for *The Progressive* clearly takes "Today Is Not The Day" in the kind of epitaphic mode set up in *Ms.* magazine and other posthumous responses to Lorde's work, the poem as it appears in the context of *The Marvelous Arithmetics of Distance* presents us with an alternative that emphasizes the communicative as much as the aesthetic dimension of poetic discourse.

The front inside cover of the book's dust jacket quotes Lorde's "hopes" for *The Marvelous Arithmetics of Distance:*

Beyond the penchant for easy definitions, false exactitudes, we share a hunger for enduring value, relationship beyond hierarchy and outside reproach, a hunger for life measures, complex, direct, and flexible. . . . I want this book to be filled with shards of light thrown off from the shifting tensions between the dissimilar, for that is the real stuff of creation and growth.

"The real stuff," then, the stuff of "creation and growth," according to Lorde, is what continues from the "shifting tensions between the dissimilar" and constitutes a dynamic of interaction that extends beyond or outside of the book. In this perspective, the relationship between the reader and the poem is no less central and more consequential than that between the poet and the poem.

"Today Is Not The Day" is the penultimate poem in the collection. (I should note that the collection doesn't even pretend to follow chronological order: "Today Is Not The Day" is dated April 22, 1992, as it is in *Ms.* magazine, although the last poem in the collection, "The Electric Slide Boogie," is dated January 3, 1992.) In "Today Is Not The Day," the first two stanzas, which are the same as they are in *Ms.* magazine, seem to have a more distanciated relation to the rest of the poem: They are, quite literally, set off from the rest of the poem. The italicized stanzas seem to be quoting—as a kind of epigraph—a previous or internalized moment before the poem, whereas the third stanza, taking the title, "Today is not the day," for the first line, seems to mark the poem's proper—externalized and affirmative—beginning. The exact repetition of the title in the first line of the third stanza makes a significant contribution to the differences between the two versions of the poems that I am focusing on. In the poem as it is printed in the book, the question of the possibility that today "could" be the day is not raised until the second line of the third stanza where it is then soundly denied with the rebuttal "but it is not."

> *Today is not the day.*
> *It could be*
> *but it is not.*
> *Today is today*
> (Lorde 1993, 57)

Where the opening assertion that "Today is not the day" is a repetition of the title given in confirmation, the subsequent line, "Today is today," provides further confirmation still. The poem titled "Today Is Not The Day" much more unambiguously than the poem in *Ms.* sets aside the question of death, the rapt involvement with the inevitable, and emphasizes instead that the point is the day at hand. Ultimately the poem moves on to celebrate all that is happening that will not end with the speaker's death.

Looking at the poem "Today Is Not The Day" beside the other poems in *The Marvelous Arithmetics of Distance* and in the context of my concern with reader responsibility, it is noticeable that the speaker of that book frequently has to negotiate something like the situation that the contemporary, posthumous reader of Lorde's work has to negotiate. From this perspective the volume anticipates not so much Lorde's death as the responsibilities of the posthumous reader. In the poem titled "Legacy—Hers" the speaker addresses her dead mother, placing herself as an observer on her mother's deathbed, simultaneously figuring herself as a reader and a writer of her mother's "last hours":

> *I learn how to die*
> *from your many examples*
> *cracking the code of your living*
> *heroisms collusions invisibilities*
> *constructing my own*
> *book of your last hours* (1993, 4)

The speaker's role in *constructing her own* book of the addressee's last hours is highlighted by the last three lines of this poem:

> *your last word to me was* **wonderful**
> *and I am still seeking the rest*
> *of that terrible acrostic* (1993, 4)

The addressee's last word is transformed here into an unpredictable multiplicity of words by being figured as a puzzle for which the speaker herself must supply the rest of the pieces in order to be able to put it together. The "legacy" figured in this poem, then, challenges the heir to act.

That as a whole, *The Marvelous Arithmetics of Distance* refuses the closure, the reckoning, implied by "last words" is underlined by the last words in the book that assert "How hard it is to sleep/ in the middle of life" (1993, 60). And the "reckonings" *The Progressive*'s reviewer points to—the "poignant reckonings with her family"—are directly denied in the opening poem, which also provides the title for the volume, a poem that ends with these lines:

> *No reckoning allowed*
> *save the marvelous arithmetics*
> *of distance* (1993, 3)

Missives to the Reader

If we look back over the reception of Lorde's "political" poetry since the 1970s, we can see the dead end engendered by the disregard of the reader's relation and responsibility to the text, the neutralization of political purposes effected by reflecting them back onto the poet herself and her artistic development, as if she were writing in a hall of mirrors by herself and to herself. To "use" poems as communicative utterances that demand responsive action, as unfinished reckonings of "what we believe needs doing," requires that we resist modes of readerly response that view the author's life or work as self-contained and consummated events, modes of response that regard poems as postcards from the poet's world, rather than as missive to the reader and her world.

Both liberal and conservative critics too often end up conflating the work with the poet's revelation of herself. Although the decision to take the poet as a real person speaking her poems, rather than taking the poetic text as a script for the performance of speech, signals an attempt to read against practices that remove the poet (and thereby the politics) from the work, the gesture turns back in on itself when the speaker is read in the context of an unexamined narrative of development. For instance, for some readers the anger or struggle apparent in oppositional poetry can be read as a kind of artistic or cultural immaturity on the part of the poet or on the part of the social group the poet is taken to represent. The focus on the poet's aesthetic "maturity" serves to occlude the resistance on the part of the reader to what the poetry tells about the world both poet and reader share. For instance, Sandra Squire Fluck, writing a positive review of Lorde's *Our Dead Behind Us*, endorses "Lorde's angry poetical critique of masculinist history," a critique that "sears and threatens," but she goes on to add, "I can say yes to Lorde without being threatened or overwhelmed, yet I am grateful that she recognizes the limits of righteous anger, and will write about love, honesty, endurance, hope and joy" (1987, 14).

Fluck suggests that the issue is if a "political" poet "recognizes the limits of righteous anger," but one might ask instead what or whom those "limits" are in the service of? Surely the requirement that poetry, even oppositional political poetry, conform to the expectations and evaluations of the proper place of anger offered from the relatively privileged vantage point of many poetry readers amounts to a requirement that poetry should be affirmative rather than challenging or confrontational.

Some critics are more explicit about the requirement of conformity implicit in ostensibly aesthetic criteria of evaluation, and suggest that aesthetically mature poetry can only be made once "revolutionary ardor has subsided." An unsigned review in *Choice* in 1974 compares Lorde (in her volume *From a Land Where Other People Live*) and three other black poets (Etheridge Knight, Margaret Walker, and James Randall) to Puerto Rican poet Jose-Angel Figueroa (all Broadside Press publications). Of Lorde the reviewer says, "Lorde is a poet too little known; her style is now mature, flexible, and meticulous. Her poems revolve around her children, growing into their own myths as she once outgrew her mother's" (1974, 755). When it comes to commenting on Figueroa, the reviewer invokes the positive qualities that have been attributed to Lorde's work and to the work of the other three black poets whose individual books the review has considered, and asks, "In a decade, after Puerto Ricans have made some inroads into the economic system and their revolutionary ardor has subsided, will his poems also show reflectiveness, nostalgia, or despair, as do some of these poems by contemporary black authors? It is an interesting speculation" (1974, 755).

The virtual correlation made here between "revolutionary ardor" and thoughtlessness, not to mention the ameliorist faith that Puerto Ricans simply need to work hard and succeed and then they won't have any more need for revolutionary clamor, is intensely patronizing. But what is most relevant for my present argument is the way in which the political claims of the poetry *on the reader* are transformed into a question about the aesthetic maturity and development of the poet.

This displacement of political purpose through a criticism focused on the poet and invested in a narrative of progressive artistic development (from anger to poetry) finds its fullest development in Sandra Gilbert's "On the Edge of the Estate" (1977), a review of Audre Lorde's *New York Head Shop and Museum* and of Ruth Stone's *Cheap*. Given Gilbert's feminist stance, she is sympathetic to the function of anger as a political emotion, and she frames the review with the characteristic argument that "the dispossessed woman may discover rare treasures beyond the walls of the territory men mark out for themselves" (297). On the face of it, this is a kind of feminist reading that takes a woman's strategies for self-preservation (in the figures she creates) in a patriarchy and finds artistry there, applauding the struggle and the "art," seeing in the art a strategy for change. But comparing Lorde's position in *New York Head Shop and Museum* with Ruth Stone's position in *Cheap*, Gilbert says:

> For Ruth Stone, too, the witch-woman . . . is an emblem both of the female artist's rage and of her survival. But where Lorde's sometimes ineffectual tirades on street corners suggest that she is still learning such survival, the perfect shapeliness and icy intensity of Stone's poetry tells us that this writer has already, in a sense, achieved survival. . . . For, like Lorde's, her natural voice is lyrical, wistful, and like Lorde she is a maker of cautionary ballads and witty fairytales. . . . Just as she [Stone] noted the advantages of exclusion, though ("You can talk to yourself all you want to"), so Stone reveals the virtues of poverty: a sort of heightened consciousness associated with fasting, a ferocious clarity of perception (1977, 299).

Although Gilbert continues to speak of "the virtues of poverty" and of struggle, it is clear she distinguishes centrally between "perfect shapeliness and . . . achieved survival," on the one hand, and the "ineffectual tirades" of someone "still learning such survival," on the other hand. Good poetry, it would seem, although it can use the "ferocious clarity of perception" produced through battle, can only be written once the battle is over *and has been won.* For what is most invidious about Gilbert's comments is the implication that poetry, like history, is and ought to be the record of victors. Imbedded in sentences such as "[p]ublic pressures on her private world have made Lorde a poet of diamond-hard intensity . . ." are cultural narratives about the individual who triumphs over personal and societal circumstance. The hero's anger and frustration, we're told (and tell) over and over again, must never be too much in evidence. She must be able to rise above it. She must have the situation under control. The poet-hero, we find, must not seek to make change by way of her poetry and from the readers' responses. Instead, her poetry must reflect change and resolution already achieved.

In addressing the relationship between politics and poetry, there is a well-established tradition of focusing the issue on the (political) content of the poetry. According to this view, "political poetry" is a poetry that embodies explicit political discourse and thus a poetry that comes to seem indistinguishable from political propaganda in general. Joan Larkin, writing a review in *Ms.* magazine in 1974, comments about Lorde's *From a Land Where Other People Live:* "If I have any complaint, it is that lines sometimes tend to be prosaic, with a judgment-making adjective or adverb where there might be an implicitly forceful picture (perhaps explicit judging is always the risk in poetry of commitment)" (1974, 40). Poetry should show or be, not say; and by this criterion, all "poetry of commitment," all poetry that has something to say, runs the risk of being "prosaic." Similarly, writing in the *New York Times Book Review* in 1974, Helen Vendler cautions us regarding the political poetry project of the Broadside Press (Lorde's publisher at the time): "A nationalist press (and there have been innumerable ones) almost always fatally goes under to propaganda" (Vendler 1980, 314). Although Vendler is praising the particular poetry under review, she warns that sooner or later "nationalist" poetry will end up as simple "propaganda."

Such strictures would suggest that to be successful as poetry, a poet's work must transcend the desire to argue a point of view. In this respect, such strictures are not unlike the comments regarding the relative maturity or immaturity of the poet as an artist, a maturity that is gauged by his or her ability to transcend struggle and to look back on it reflectively. In both cases, what is being criticized is the perceived overspecificity of the poet's address: She is located too concretely within specific struggles, and more crucially she demands of the reader a similar willingness to respond from where he or she is located. What is being criticized is the failure to indulge the traditional prerogative of poetic discourse, which licenses a transcendent universality for poet, poem, *and reader.*

Our traditional notions of political poetry, whether they are focused on the content of the poetic text itself or on the biography and figure of the poet and her cause, leave us with inadequate ways of addressing the issue of politics and poetry. In order to actualize a political poetry the solution is not to try once again to divorce the idea of a person from a poetry but to shift our attention to the relationship between the poem and its audiences and their modes of response to poetic discourse. Most poetries depend on the fact that readers will hear or construct a particular speaker—however problematic that construction—in the voice of the poem. This is especially the case where a poet takes it as part of her project more fully to articulate an otherwise underrepresented or badly represented perspective. The gesture readers repeatedly make in response, however, is to assign that articulation to the realm of expression, rather than to the realm of strategic speech. In this we deny both the purposefulness of the reader and of the writer, and deflect any responsibility that might fall to the reader should she be implicated by the discourse. The oppositional writer in the United States will only have the power to effect change if we change our notions of responsibility and readership. Lorde's work, I have argued, helps us see that a political poetry is one that carries, that translates itself through its readers from the words on the page or from the poet's mouth into a provocation that relocates itself and is dispersed beyond a full reckoning in ongoing actions. But a poem can acquire such worldly resonance and range only if it is taken as specifically addressed, only if its readers, differently implicated in the world the poem evokes, respond to the poem as an utterance that requires them to take account of their specific locations.

NOTES

1. I borrow the phrase "repressive tolerance" from Herbert Marcuse's essay by that title wherein he describes the neutralizing effect of laissez-faire tolerance (toward speech in general and art in particular) as it is practiced in contemporary liberal societies: "The danger of 'destructive tolerance' (Baudelaire), of 'benevolent neutrality' toward *art* has been recognized: the market which absorbs equally well (although with often quite sudden fluctuations) art, anti-art, and non-art, all possible conflicting styles, schools, forms, provides a 'complacent receptacle, a friendly abyss' in which the radical impact of art, the protest of art against the established reality is swallowed up" (1969, 102).

2. Cary Nelson, for example, emphasizes the ways in which all poetries in a given moment do not fulfill the same political functions: "Even today, when we compare the func-

tions of poetry in different countries across the world, we will recognize that the poetry at risk of judicial or police suppression does not occupy the same cultural space as poetry welcomed or ignored by the state" (1989, 127).

3. For a more detailed discussion of the historical specificity of the notion that poetry is, by definition, politically ineffective, see Cary Nelson's *Repression and Recovery: Modern American Poetry and the Politics of Cultural Memory* (1989). Nelson describes the 1930s as a time when poetry appeared to function much more effectively (politically) in the United States than it has since. "Poetry, for a time, had the power to help people not only come to understand the material conditions of their existence but also to envision ways of changing them" (124). Nelson attributes the repression of political poetry since World War II to a number of intersecting factors and discourses: the paranoia produced by cold war politics and the rise of the New Criticism prominent among them. See also Alan Golding's *From Outlaw to Classic: Canons in American Poetry* (1995), which provides both a theory and a historical overview of American poetry canon-building practices. Golding offers a discussion of the role the New Criticism played in delegitimating poetry as a political discourse in his third chapter, "The New Criticism and American Poetry in the Academy."

4. In Nadezhda Mandelstam's memoir, *Hope Against Hope* (1970), the quotation appears in this context: "In choosing his manner of death, M. was counting on one remarkable feature of our leaders: their boundless, almost superstitious respect for poetry. 'Why do you complain?' M. used to ask. 'Poetry is respected only in this country—people are killed for it. There's no place where more people are killed for it'" (159).

5. For a version of the comparison that gives the Western writer more credit, see Seamus Heaney's "The Impact of Translation" (1988):

> In the professionalized milieu of the West, the poet is susceptible to self-deprecation and scepticism. The poet in the United States, for example, is aware that the machine of reputation-making and book distribution, whether it elevates or ignores him or her, is indifferent to the moral and ethical force of the poetry being distributed. A grant-aided pluralism of fashions and schools, a highly amplified language of praise which produces from among the most gifted a procession of ironists and dandies and reflexive talents, produces also a subliminal awareness of the alternative conditions and an anxious over-the-shoulder glance toward them.
>
> All the same, poets in the West do not regard their colleagues under pressure in the simple-minded spirit sometimes attributed to them, which is a caricature of their subtler complexes. Western poets do not assume that a tyrannical situation is mitigated because it produces heroic artists and last-ditch art. They do not envy in any way the hard fate of the artist but rather admire the faith in art itself which becomes manifest in extreme conditions (39–40).

(I am not, of course, suggesting that the East-West comparison serves, for Western writers, to "mitigate" or justify "a tyrannical situation," but precisely that it serves to redeem a faith in poetic discourse and its purposefulness.)

6. For a detailed elaboration of the academic conventions affecting the reception of literary discourse see Barbara Herrnstein Smith's *Poetic Closure: A Study of How Poems End* (1968):

> For the poem, *as an utterance,* had no initial historical occurrence. It is, was, and will always be the script for its own performance; like a play, it "occurs" only when it is

enacted. . . . The point to be emphasized . . . is that poetry is a *representational* art and that each poem is the representation of an act of speech. . . . If we are unwilling to respond to the poem as a *possible* utterance, one substantial source of its value and effect is lost to us. If, on the other hand, we respond to it as if it were a historical utterance, another substantial source of its value and effect is lost (17).

(In later work Herrnstein Smith makes it clear that only where the literary artwork is distinguished from its uses is it distinct from speech. As she points out, "the text of a literary artwork becomes, *through* a performance, a character in a natural language" [1978, 9]. This is not to say that the performed literary artwork becomes natural language or speech but that, when it functions as "a character in a natural language," speech conventions form part of its context. So the framework for its interpretation must also shift to incorporate the conventions for the reception of speech.)

For a more recent discussion that emphasizes the distinct status and functioning of literary discourse and that insists upon what is limiting or problematic about taking literature as utterance or practice, see William R. Schroeder's, "A Teachable Theory of Interpretation" (1986). Although Schroeder's work is useful in so far as it articulates current conventions of literary reception, the distinctions he makes between literary language and ordinary language are overly categorical. He asserts, for example, that "[t]he difference between interpreting texts and understanding ordinary language is that a narrative text often creates a new vocabulary, syntax, and semantics with its elements while an ordinary utterance usually relies on existing linguistic codes" (21). My own emphasis is on the literary utterance as it is performed and received—as a practice—and on its continuities with other communicative utterances.

7. "As Foucault notes, 'In a civilization like our own there are a certain number of discourses that are endowed with the "author function," while others are deprived of it' . . . but this distinction holds not only for the distinction between writers of novels and writers of laundry lists (as Foucault has it) but, in a more mundane fashion, for the distinction between canonical and noncanonical 'literary' authors as well" (Berube 1992, 57–58). "A small number of texts assigned author functions are also assigned the 'aesthetic function,' which, if I may borrow again from Murakovsky, means that they are authorized to be read 'as literature' (and not as diet books). . . . [Only] a small handful of texts so authorized are authorized for the kind of interpretation practiced by contemporary criticism" (Berube 1992, 59).

8. For a fuller account of the specificity of Lorde's use of address in a reading situation, see "Dedicated Form: Audre Lorde's Poetic Gesture For Each One of You," Chapter 4 of my dissertation, *A Poetics of Address* (1993). There I discuss, for example, Lorde's use of the ambiguous status of the pronoun "you" in her rendition of the poem "For Each of You" during a reading at Cornell in 1982. I read the emphasis she places on the pronoun as an attempt to provoke white auditors to rethink our relations to slavery and the making of Americans. Although the reading of Lorde in my dissertation tries to account for specific differences between reader's identities and responses, in this chapter I am not primarily offering a concrete analysis of any particular reading audience. I am trying, instead, to emphasize a mode of reader responsibility that requires readers to engage with poetic discourse as communicative utterance.

9. In the above quotation, King goes on to say "and to empower Lorde's texts; in short, to enable their literary canonization." My point is that while those of us educated in liter-

ary studies can appropriate the authority of academic reading practices in our public responses to Lorde's texts, we are probably mistaken in thinking that canonization is unambiguously "empowering" to the political intentions of those texts.

BIBLIOGRAPHY

Berube, Michael. *Marginal Forces/Cultural Centers: Tolson Pynchon, and the Politics of the Canon.* Ithaca: Cornell University Press, 1992.

Burr, Zofia. "A Poetics of Address: Speech and Dialogue in the Poetry of Emily Dickinson, Josephine Miles, Gwendolyn Brooks, and Audre Lorde." Dissertation, Cornell University, 1993. 154–195.

Chosen Poems, Old and New (Audre Lorde). Review in *Library Journal* 14 June 1982:1227.

Clausen, Jan. "Word Warrior." *Undersong: Chosen Poems Old and New (Revised)* (Audre Lorde). Review in *The Nation* 1 February 1993:130–133.

"Don't Look the Other Way." *The Marvelous Arithmetics of Distance* (Audre Lorde). Review in *The Progressive* November 1993:43.

Fluck, Sandra Squire. "Racist Legacy Rebuffed." *Our Dead Behind Us* (Audre Lorde). Review in *New Directions for Women* January–February 1987:14.

From a Land Where Other People Live (Audre Lorde). Review in *Choice* 11 July 1974:755.

Gilbert, Sandra M. "On the Edge of the Estate." *New York Head Shop and Museum* (Audre Lorde) and *Cheap* (Ruth Stone). Review in *Poetry* 129, February 1977:296–301.

Golding, Alan. *From Outlaw to Classic: Canons in American Poetry.* Madison: University of Wisconsin Press, 1995.

Heaney, Seamus. "The Impact of Translation." *The Government of the Tongue: Selected Prose.* New York: Noonday, 1988. 36–44.

Herrnstein Smith, Barbara. *Poetic Closure: A Study of How Poems End.* Chicago: University of Chicago Press, 1968.

———. *On the Margins of Discourse: The Relation of Literature to Language.* Chicago: University of Chicago Press, 1978.

King, Katie. "Audre Lorde's Lacquered Layerings: The Lesbian Bar as a Site of Literary Production." *Cultural Studies* 2 (1988):321–342. (Reprinted in *New Lesbian Criticism: Literary and Cultural Readings.* Ed. Sally Munt. New York: Columbia University Press 1992. 51–74.)

Larkin, Joan. "Frontiers of Language: Three Poets." *What I Want* (Kathleen Fraser), *Moscow Mansions* (Barbara Guest), and *From a Land Where Other People Live* (Audre Lorde). Reviewed in *Ms.* September 1974:38–40.

Lorde, Audre. *The Marvelous Arithmetics of Distance.* New York: Norton, 1993.

Mandelstam, Nadezdha. *Hope Against Hope: A Memoir.* Trans. Max Hayward. New York: Atheneum, 1970.

Marcuse, Herbert. "Repressive Tolerance." *A Critique of Pure Tolerance* by Robert Paul Wolff, Barrington Moore, Jr., and Herbert Marcuse. London: Jonathan Cape, 1969:93–137.

Ms. March–April 1993:58–59.

Nelson, Cary. *Repression and Recovery: Modern American Poetry and the Politics of Cultural Memory.* Madison: University of Wisconsin Press, 1989.

Pierpont, Claudia Roth. "The Rage of Aphrodite." *The New Yorker* 7 February 1994:90–98.

Public Broadcasting Service. *Sixth Annual Report of the Secretaries of Defense: U.S. Defense: Another Casualty of the Cold War.* 4 December 1992. (Page numbers from edited transcript of the television program available from The Southern Center for International Studies, Atlanta, Georgia.)

Rich, Adrienne. "I Happen to Think Poetry Makes a Huge Difference." Interview with Matthew Rothschild. *The Progressive* January 1994:31–35.

Schroeder, William R. "A Teachable Theory of Interpretation." *Theory in the Classroom.* Ed. Cary Nelson. Urbana: University of Illinois Press, 1986. 9–44.

Vendler, Helen. "Broadsides." *Part of Nature, Part of Us: Modern American Poets.* Cambridge, MA: Harvard University Press, 1980. 313–321. (Originally published as "Broadsides: Good Black Poems, One by One." *The New York Times Book Review* 29 September 1974.)

PART THREE

TRANSLOCAL CONNECTIONS

8

Translating Resistance

AMITAVA KUMAR

In an act reminiscent of George Bush's 1988 presidential campaign in which he shamelessly scapegoated an entire race by fixing it in the stereotype of a singular image of Willie Horton, in late October 1994 Susan Smith, the South Carolina mother charged with killing her two sons, lied to the police that her children had been kidnapped by a young black man in a knit cap. This Identikit image was something that the police later claimed had introduced doubt in the picture Smith had been painting. As we all know, Smith confessed to the crime after failing two lie-detector tests. But what are we to make of the suspicions aroused in the mind of Sheriff Howard Wells, in the town of Union, South Carolina, regarding the stereotyping of blacks?

Not much. It was not only the policemen but also the broader citizenry that, in California, only a week after the Smith case hit the press, fell to the ploy of seeing in the dark-faced stranger the scapegoat for their ills. In the 1994 elections, the Californians voted by a 59 percent over 41 percent margin in favor of Proposition 187, which denies public services to the undocumented workers who, it is presumed, will continue to cook, baby-sit, and provide cheap labor without having any access to health care and education for their children.

The face projected by the ominous threats of Proposition 187 is that of a stereotype. It is an anonymity that can be affixed to descriptions like "the nanny from Tijuana" or "the farm worker from Rosamorada"; it applies equally indiscriminately to "the waitress born and raised in San Diego" or "the non-English speaking, green-card holder from San Salvador." The body of the debased "other" is stigmatized even as—rather, *because*—it serves through its labor the ends of progress and the preservation of the status-quo for the affluent mainstream.

This stereotypical quotation is not limited to African-Americans or Mexican-Americans. "It is only a slight overstatement to say that Muslims and Arabs are essentially covered, discussed, apprehended, either as oil suppliers or as potential terrorists," wrote Edward Said, commenting on the media attention to the Middle East after the end of the Teheran hostage crisis (1981, 26). In Said's translation, the Western media's narrative about the Islamic world is shown to be interestedly narrow and stereotypical. As "[v]ery little of the detail, the human density, the passion of Arab-Muslim life has entered the awareness of even those people whose profession it is to report the Islamic world," Said's counternarrative demands the elaboration of other, rather particular stories in opposition to what he rightly sees as only "crude, essentialized caricatures" (1981, 26). This demand is most explicitly formulated by Said in the following passage:

> To dispel the myths and stereotypes of Orientalism, the world as a whole has to be given a opportunity, by the media and by Muslims themselves, to see Muslims and Orientals producing and, more important, diffusing a different form of history, a new kind of sociology, a new cultural awareness: in short, Muslims need to emphasize the goal of living a new form of history, investigating what Marshall Hodgson has called the Islamicate world and its many different societies with such seriousness of purpose and urgency as also to communicate the results outside the Muslim world (1981, 63).

The need to produce different histories and new writings—a demand renewed and amplified by Said after the bombing of the World Trade Center in New York in 1993—burdens cultural workers and intellectuals with the task of providing alternative readings, supplying critical contexts for the consumption of cultural texts as well as events—in short, translating what would be available as natural or incontestably plain into that which is political and with different consequences.

The construction of such an inventory is so necessary and at the same time so utterly absent that it is impossible, it seems to me, not to take a pedagogical stance toward both oneself and the surrounding culture, particularly inside the dominant ranks of understanding in the West, marked by "the sanctioned ignorance that every critic of imperialism must chart" (Spivak 1987, 29).

PRIMARY LESSONS IN POLITICAL ECONOMY

For every ten bushels of paddy she harvests
the landless laborer takes home one.

This woman, whose name is Hiria, would have to starve
for three days to buy a liter of milk

If she were to check her hunger and not eat
for a month she could buy a book of poems.

And if Hiria, who works endlessly, could starve
endlessly, in ten years she could buy that piece

> *Of land on which during short winter evenings*
> *the landlord's son plays badminton.*
>
> (Kumar 1990a, 13)

The politics of this text lies in its drawing of equations between disparate realities. But, even in drawing equations, it dispels any sense of balance or equality. More thoroughly, there is a dispelling of any sense of stability. Everything is revealed as framed by the language of ideology, and, as the following poem attempts to show, even the simplest elements of mechanics are always irreducibly political in that sense.[1]

ARITHMETIC

The road from the two-story high

Gita
mandir

to the huts of Jagjiwannagar
is three
miles
long.

The yellow building of the Police Station
faces the Gita mandir.

Now, here is the question.

How long
will it take the police
to reach
the bespectacled statue of Babasaheb Ambedkar
at the entrance of Jagjiwannagar?

That is the pure problem.

The constables are perhaps at that moment
assembled in the mandir
participating in a kirtan.
Drops of sweat
hang like pearls from their sacred threads.
The wireless message
disturbs this pleasant communion
with the gods.
It is not the re-birth of Krishna

that is announced
but a riot.

Four men today laid their hands
on a lower-caste woman
on the premises of Bharat Tannery.
The woman was raped
perhaps only by mistake.
It must have been so.
After all, how could these upper-caste
men touch an untouchable?

The strike-call by the D-S4
is perhaps an example
only of political opportunism.
And the bomb-explosion during the meeting
in Jagjiwannagar ten minutes ago
is a crude demand for attention.
Perhaps.

Given these conditions, how long
will it take the police
to reach
the bespectacled statue of Babasaheb Amedkar
at the entrance of Jagjiwannagar?

Some examples might help.
It took twenty years
after Independence
and not until Naxalbari and Srikakulam
that the rest of India woke up
to the rural reality.
It took less than thirty minutes
for the Prime Minister
to fly over his constituency
to lay the foundation-stone
of a watch factory.
It took the British
two hundred years to learn
that India was not their property.
And, in case these things interest you,
in America, it takes perhaps less than three seconds
for President Bush to sign an order
for the bombing of towns and villages

in any given country
in Central and South America.
(Kumar 1990a, 14–16)

The detours of time and the laws of arithmetic through the sites of upper-caste Hindu hegemony, a state machinery bound by customary prejudice, or the uneven and complex opposition of lower-caste Dalit populations expressed by legendary names like Babasaheb Ambedkar, Jagjiwan Ram, and D-S4—what I'm calling the detours or the disjunctive drawing into relation of disparate elements allows us to end, in my translation, with the untouchable slum dwellers facing the imperceptible, deadly sweep of the needle on President Bush's watch.

The politics of form that allows me to achieve this translation, this particular set of surprising juxtapositions, and to articulate what I believe is the global relation of late capitalism belongs very specifically to poetry. Against the linear narrative of progress, against even the coherence of objective laws either of arithmetic or of bourgeois democracy, there is produced the compounded images of social collapse, irrational rage, the extravagant spectacle of a bomb exploding in what the U.S. military-industrial complex claims as its private backyard. The various truths of the local are placed in a global configuration that mimics—thereby making visible—the performance of late capitalism. The calculus of local oppressions is presented in a global total of comparative horrors, set side by side, in opposition to the logical accounting of prosaic fictions about postcolonial independence and neocolonial success.

The Specificity of Writing

Writing is a social practice and hence irregular in its effects. As a social practice, it is performed by different agents occupying diverse positions along a variety of material grids. Its consequences are not always legible and certainly neither predictable nor symmetrical. It is a divided practice open to mediations. What, we might ask, are some of the mediations that attend a postcolonial text?

V. I. Lenin, in an article written soon after Leo Tolstoy's death and in which he presents Tolstoy's work as one of universal significance, very quickly locates the loss of the writer not so much in his death as much as in the illiteracy and pauperization of the vast populations who would be his readers:

> Tolstoy the artist is known to an infinitesimal minority even in Russia. If his great works are really to be made the possession of *all*, a struggle must be waged against the system of society which condemns millions and scores of millions to ignorance, benightedness, drudgery and poverty—a socialist revolution must be accomplished (1978, 304–305).

The "democratization of literature" apart, there was a more specific sense in which Tolstoy's writing interested Lenin. Tolstoy's writing, for Lenin, was highly problematic because it was essentially contradictory. At the same time, it was also enormously significant because these contradictions were also those afflicting the Russian peasantry in that historical period: "Tolstoy reflected the pent-up hatred, the ripening striving for a better lot, the desire to get rid of the past—and also the immature dreaming, the political inexperience, the revolutionary flabbiness" (1978, 303)

Lenin's attention to the contradictions allows the elaboration of a critical approach to literature where, according to Pierre Macherey, a literary work's "relationship to historical reality cannot be reduced to the 'spontaneous' or the 'simultaneous'" (1978, 108). In other words, the writer as well as the literary work traverses several sometimes contradictory histories. In a later article written with Etienne Balibar, Macherey extends Lenin's notion of a complex or contradictory mirroring to examine the role of literature as an ideological form and the specificity of literary production. Relying on French Marxist Louis Althusser's formulations on the nature of ideology and the role of ideological state apparatuses (ISAs), Macherey and Balibar argue that literature as an ideological form cannot be seen as separate from a complex range of determinations: the linguistic that is bound to the notion of a common language, the pedagogic, i.e., the social contradictions in the schooling apparatus, and the fictive, which is literature's role as the producer of "the real" (1981, 43–58).

Even in what I have presented here very schematically of Macherey's and Balibar's formulations, we get an idea that literary production always involves a complex and sometimes contradictory negotiation across a dispersed terrain. This notion of writing has a special significance for the postcolonial subject. Routing his own argument through Althusserian Marxism too, Homi Bhabha has argued that once one looks at literature as a "discourse or practice," it follows that one has to deal with the "the history of textual signification and ideological struggle" (1984, 106). The issue is no longer that of seizing the predetermined, correct representations; rather, it is that of intervening in and transforming the encoded effects and apparati of representation. In the case of those postcolonial intellectuals who engage in literary production even while realizing that the surrounding culture of oppression and illiteracy calls such practices into question, there remains the possibility of making writing matter by rigorously outlining its distance from the privileged center. In the context of the present volume, the notion of critique as the displacing, decentering practice employed by those who are marginalized (relying, therefore, on our acceptance of the divisions of center-margin) might be more productive than endlessly addressing the often unreal and hence fruitless opposition of global-local concerns.

I have translated and present below a long Hindi poem by a contemporary poet, Alokdhanwa, entitled "Open Fire Poster" (1988). This poem functions as an antipoem. Because his words are weak and despised the poet chooses to produce his poem as a poster inciting the taking up of arms. I should also remark that a poem that so explicitly comments on the economies of cultural reception—and dismissal—will also help us question those limits under which we have accepted often as tokens certain well-known postcolonial writers and silenced other names and other politics. This too is a part of what I have been broadly (and not only metaphorically) calling "translation."[2]

This is the twentieth April of Nineteen Seventy-Four or
a professional assassin's right
hand or the leather glove
of a detective or a spot stuck on the binoculars
of an attacker?

Whatever it be—I cannot call it just another day!

Where I am writing—this is a very old place,
here even today more than words it is tobacco
that is used.
The sky here—is only as high as
a pig.

Here the tongue gets used
the least,
here the eye gets used
the least,
here the ear gets used
the least,
here the nose gets used
the least.

Here you have only teeth and the belly,
and hands buried in mud
there is no man
only a dark hollow
that keeps begging for grain—
from one day of downpours to another day of downpours.
This woman is my mother or
a five foot iron stick—
on which hang two pieces of dry bread—

like dead birds.
Now between my daughter and my strike
there is not even a hair-breadth's difference
when the constitution is on its own terms breaking
my strike and my daughter

After these sudden elections
should I stop thinking about gunpowder?

Can I after Nineteen Seventy-Four's twentieth April
live
like a father with my children?
Like an ink-pot filled with ink, like a ball,
can I with my children
be like a green, grassy field?

If those people ever grant me entry into their poems
it is only to blindfold me
and to use me
and then leave me outside the borders
they never let me
reach the capital.
I am grabbed
by the time I begin to reach the district towns.

It is not the government—it is this country's
cheapest cigarette that has kept me company.

Growing all around my sister's feet
like yellow plants
was my childhood—
that was eaten by the police daroga's *water-buffalo.*[3]
To keep a sense of humanity alive
if there is a right to shoot a daroga
then why don't I have it?
The earth on which I sit writing
the earth on which I walk,
the earth which I plough,
the earth in which I sow seeds and
from which I gather grains and
load them in godowns—
for that earth do I have a right to shoot
or do those eunuch landlords—
who have turned this entire nation into a moneylender's dog?

This is not a poem
this is a call to open fire
that all those who use the pen
are getting from all those who work the plough.

This poem is, in a way, what it names itself, a poster calling on intellectuals to bear arms and fight with the poor and the exploited. Alokdhanwa echoes the sentiment espoused by Frantz Fanon that although poetry of different types was essential in the emergent states, the "[p]oet ought however to understand that nothing can replace the reasoned, irrevocable taking up of arms on the people's side" (1963, 226). At the same time, *contra* Fanon, there are specific ways in which this text works as a poem. For example, as a protest against the marginalization of poetry itself, the poet is allowed only as far as the peripheral district towns. The center is always kept out of poetry's reach. The poetry of protest recognizes itself as decentered. As much of Alokdhanwa's poetry attests, the poems are not offered so much as strategies to attain the center as they are to serve as testimonials or records for the damaged lives.[4] For instance, the childhood that was eaten away by the head constable's water buffalo, not to mention the loneliness in the space of the nation-state that can boast of cheap cigarettes but not a community, are the material details that make up this brand of poetry. This is clearly the poetry that is written in a language not only different from but also opposed to the prose of the constitution that is sanctimoniously destroying the poet's daughter and his strike. It is in that opposition that we find the politics of poetry.

In an essay entitled "Postcolonial Authority and Postmodern Guilt," Homi Bhabha presents fragmentary and affective writing in tension with the sentence and the sententiousness of law:

> It is one of the salutary features of postmodern theory to suggest that it is the disjunctive, fragmented, displaced agency of those who have suffered the sentence of history—subjugation, domination, diaspora, displacement—that forces one to think outside the certainty of the sententious. It is from the affective experience of social marginality that we must conceive of a political strategy of empowerment and articulation, a strategy outside the liberatory rhetoric of idealism and beyond the sovereign subject that haunts the "civil" sentence of the law (1992, 56–57).

The writing of the body, the uncivil writing of revolt, and the writing of affect and experience in Bhabha's suggestive and charged formulation operate in liminal spaces that do not ever overlap with the writing of the law and dominance. In many ways, the distinction is evocative of the difference proposed in another context by Bhabha when he wrote that "the poetry of liberation is brought up short against the leaden, deadening prose of the colonized world" (1989, 134). It can be argued that Bhabha's thinking on this question has very little to do with poetry as I've been discussing it; his attempt, after all, is to read his own discourse as "non-sententious because it speaks from a moment *in media res,* from in-between unequal and often antagonistic sites without the certainty of imagining what happens or emerges at the end" (1992, 57). But it is true that the experiments of poetry, eluding and also contesting the assuredness of prose and its sovereign voice, have much in common with the situation of provisional and mediated writing that Bhabha seems to be describing. It is important to celebrate—certainly in the postcolonial context—this writing, which is mixed, multitongued, and open-ended because it functions between divided locations and locutions, often perforce addressing dispersed constituencies. The work of translating a poem by a writer like Alokdhanwa would seem to me to be participating in that sort of a project, producing not only the "antithetical knowledge" that Said was demanding (1981, 149), the knowledge that is produced in opposition to restricting orthodoxies, but doing so in a form and style that remained alertly responsive to the ideologies of literary production and readership.

Poetry Under Global Capitalism

The British colonizers in India did not deem poetry, and certainly not the poetry written by Indians, to be of much value. In his famous tract, *The History of British India,* James Mill condemned in one dismissive stroke both poetry and Indian culture. Mill's prose unsays nothing and its contempt hurries him toward the goal of sealing the hierarchies he wants to protect. There is an unmistakable and final sense of knowingness that pervades his didactic act, a knowingness offensive precisely because it doesn't admit, in any way, as interlocutors those who are being judged. Here are some details of his discourse:

> The first literature is poetry. Poetry is the language of the passions, and men feel, before they speculate. The earliest poetry is the expression of the feelings, by which the minds of rude men are the most powerfully actuated. . . . At this first stage the literature of the Hindus has always remained. The habit of expressing every thing in verse; a habit which urgent necessity imposes upon a people unacquainted with the use of permanent signs, and which the power of custom upholds, till after a certain progress in improvement, even among those to whom permanent signs are known; we trace among the Hindus to the present day. All their compositions, with wonderfully few exceptions, are in verse. For history they have only certain narrative poems, which depart from all resemblance to truth and nature; and have evidently no further connexion with fact than the use of certain names and a few remote allusions. Their laws, like those of rude nations in general, are in verse. Their sacred books, and even their books of science. . . (1840, 48–49).

The vast undertaking of Orientalist knowledge production and the translation practices that accompanied it in India were not limited to prose, however. For example, the eighteenth-century translations of Kalidasa's *Sakuntala* by Sir William Jones went through successive reprints. As Tejaswani Niranjana informs us, these translations were a small part of "a significant technology of colonial domination," which included: "(a) the need for translation by the European, since the natives are unreliable interpreters of their own laws and culture; (b) the desire to be a lawgiver, to give the Indians their 'own' laws; and (c) the desire to 'purify' Indian culture and speak on its behalf" (1992, 16–21). The more systemic understanding of the practice of translation is the condition that helps Niranjana launch a critique of the violence of colonial discourse. As a postcolonial strategy, she promotes the deconstructionist stance against any assumption of the transparency of language and linearity of history, an assumption she finds in good measure among the colonizers. At the same time Niranjana also advocates an additional narrativizing strategy that would "translate" or rewrite history in a new way. In adopting, or at least in advancing, this double strategy Niranjana is indebted to Gayatri Spivak's earlier identification of "transactional reading"—"the name of reading as an active transaction between past and present"—as a suitable post-colonial mode of knowledge production (Spivak 1987, 202). Spivak's justified interest in making the point that the "epistemic violence" of colonialism does not leave any pure space for the writing of revolt and her alertness to the fact that gestures of rebellion might well carry within themselves the signs of complicity find in Niranjana's project a point of particular appeal. At one level, this intellectual framing leads to a special awareness of the ideological effects of the British propagation of English as the language of learning announced in Thomas Macaulay's infamous 1835 Minute on Indian education. At another level, these arguments also enable Niranjana to locate in the interface with "Western" theories such as poststructuralism, and also in concepts like "hybridity," new possibilities for radical, intellectual engagement in the postcolonial context (46 and 170).

In the context of present-day India, where highly dubious claims to nationalist purity on the part of Hindu fundamentalists are causing huge rents in the social fabric, all arguments for syncretic cultures are certainly welcome. However, it is a big mistake not to persistently ask, "Whose hybridity?" The New Delhi–based executive who can mix an Oxford accent, a Tamil meal of rice and rasam, and a high-fidelity music system from Hong Kong represents hybridity that is in a rather uncomplicated sense different from the masala-mix of a Hindi-speaking Bihar migrant rickshaw puller in Punjab who has a fondness for Bruce Lee shirts and the six or seven words of English he has picked up on the streets of what he regards as a foreign city.[5] More than that, however, the point about rewriting history has to be quickly accepted as a point of departure, and we need to pose the next question, "Whose history?" This question becomes significant when we realize that after working through the details of how Derrida or De Man derail history and how Benjamin presumably puts it back on track, all that Niranjana can lead us to is the strait gate of an argument over the translation of a brief, twelfth-century spiritual poem, an argument that is supposed to convince us of the need to problematize representation (163–186). This act seems both presumptuous and self-indulgent. It is presumptuous because it ignores the myriad ways in which what Niranjana calls "living in translation" is exemplified not necessarily by the translation of one obscure and ancient Hindu poem but by the efforts of those who reinvent communities in the midst of religious riots or the patched-up lifestyles of migrant slum dwellers in metropolises or the songs of the peasant rebellions that hijack or parody popular Hindi film songs to articulate their insurgent ideologies. And it is self-indulgent because instead of using the point about the politics of English language in India to recognize the limit of these studies,

Niranjana's conclusion appears to all the more assuredly sweep under the carpet any doubts about the language of history and the identity of its speakers.

The invocation of the postcolonial subject and the accompanying sanctioning of any and all uses of "Western" theories and languages participate primarily in the installation of a monolithic fiction that is a self-justifying function of middle-class diasporic intellectuals. A dose of self-criticism seems in order:

LORD MACAULAY'S TAIL

TheEnglishlanguage was the second name
of Lord Macaulay's pet dog.
So we became its tail.

The mistake was
that we believed this tail
actually wagged the dog.

Now the condition is such
that on that side the teeth of the dog might well be
devouring someone

but on this side
we keep wagging the tail vigorously.

(Kumar 1990a, 20)

This self-criticism takes the form of a self-questioning: What has been achieved by this alignment with "theEnglishlanguage?" When in the postcolonial psyche that conflated term becomes the broad template inscribed by associations of international capitalism and its mating with the indigenous, bourgeois ruling class, this self-questioning also translates into a critique of the celebration of commodification and U.S. cultural hegemony. It can involve, as in the front-page commentary in the Mexican newspaper, *Exelsior,* the naming of the North American Free Trade Agreement "the country's hour of shame" and the bemoaning of the Mexican submission to the U.S. heel: "The food, the clothing, the films, the advertisements, and the habits of imagination have become American. USA (yu-es-ey) runs as a cry of jubilation" (Ahlberg 1991, 18–19).

In the postcolonial space, the interrogation of the West's triumphalism ("the end of history," "the end of ideology," "the end of communism") can take the form of an insistence on an autonomous production of history. I have noted elsewhere the implication of assuming Europe as the fixed subject of history:

As a prominent left leader in India, Vinod Mishra put it: "There was a time when the specter of communism haunted Europe and now the specter of Europe is haunting communism everywhere." The question now is, does the Third World and its struggles have a future different from Europe's? It seems that Western analysts, in declaring capitalism as the chosen path for the Third World, are unprepared to grant the Third World any legitimate identity, an identity that need not be yoked to Europe's triumphs and failures (Kumar 1991, 5, 11).

This rewriting of dominant history might subsume a variety of interruptions: the disruption of the space between literature and reportage, the reinscription of a Western story in the Indian context, the appropriation of what Gilles Deleuze and Félix Guattari have called a minority discourse within the European context to amplify working-class protest in the fields of eastern India, and, last but not the least, the questioning of bourgeois-nationalist pretences to an arrivalism that claims to place the nation in a space called freedom:

> You are all perhaps familiar with the classic opening line of the Czech novelist Franz Kafka's memorable short story "Metamorphosis." Not too long ago, Kafka was turned on his head in an article written by my friend Chandrabhushan, a journalist and left-activist in Bihar, India. Chandrabhushan wrote that unlike Gregor Samsa, the vast, disenfranchised population of Bihar is turning from an insect into a human being. The large population of landless laborers and lower-caste peasants there have realized that they can no longer be "the worm trodden under the heels of history and its so-called creators" (Kumar 1991, 5 and 11).6

Opposing the privileged certainties of the triumphalist discourses are the questions about history, and these questions are sometimes the only ways we can translate the poetry of the future into texts of protest in the present. The disruptive practice of translation that Niranjana has been calling for will require a more forceful interruption of the received religious texts to produce a disturbing testament—and provocation—to the ongoing suffering and rebellion:

THE EXAMINATION OF THE BRAHMANISM OF HISTORY

The teacher conducting the exams stands outside the door smoking.
Write a short note on the Quit India Movement. (150 words)
"Aurangzab ke rule ka period kya tha . . . ?" Sounds so loud, shhh!
A wasp buzzes on the glass for all eternity, while a hundred feet

below, on the street, striking workers set fire to a State bus.
Last year's results: Pass with honors: 13, Pass: 27, Fail: 11.
Has India's non-alignment policy been successful? (500 words)
Partha rubs his balls and drops his saliva on an ant near his shoe.

The sight of a beggar, a sick man, a corpse and a sanyasi moved
the Buddha to renounce his princedom and seek the meaning of life.
If the sight of the poor and the destitute, the dead and the dying,
is all that it takes why aren't there a million Buddhas in India?

Your question-paper is a white-clad Brahman, who looks unmarked
by any memory of the martyrs of terrible struggles in the land.
List the Fundamental Rights granted in our Constitution. (200 words)
The Brahman chants the sacred words, as if to keep his enemies away.

(Kumar 1990b, 173)

The rupture that is represented by postcolonial writing is not just marked by discontinuity—the mark of colonialism, the troubled inheritance of language and mores, or an extremely problematic relationship with Western readership. It is also a site for the drawing out of affiliations, tracking ideologies of production and consumption—the inevitable striking of bargains with the offerings of history. And the writing of those in the diaspora, certainly those in the academic joints, are quite uniquely suited to draw together voices that, to borrow a phrase from Spivak, bring each other into crisis.[7] The language of poetry, like the language of politics or journalism or literary theory, is only a partial one; yet, this is the partiality that rebels against the tyrannical wholeness that masks the claims of the victorious. At its best, it presents a new "constellation" of images in a discontinuous tradition, inaugurating new configurations of history and of readers.[8] It is in that spirit I want to offer for a reading the following poem entitled "Poems for the I.N.S." It is an answer to Proposition 187, it introduces another voice in the public space, and I hope it helps in the general task of building an assemblage of informed readers and citizens. Or consider it a response to another poem, "I Love America," distributed to California Republican legislators by state assemblyman William J. Knight. That poem begins "I come for visit, get treated regal,/So I stay, who care illegal." Having made its way through the slime of a fantasy landscape of greedy swindlers and dishonest workers and of course breeding subhumans who speak in a broken syntax and (call the National Guard please!) the nightmare sound of Chevy, the heartbeat of America, being mispronounced as Chebby, the poem ends with a call that emanates like a howl from the guts of the Klan: "We think America damn good place,/Too damn good for white man's race./If they no like us, they can go,/Got lots of room in Mexico" (see Knight 1993).

POEMS FOR THE I.N.S.

I

The cigarette smoke lingered
in the blue Minnesota chill
as my friend said, "I'd like to talk
to you of other things.
Not politics again but things like
whether you are lonely."

"What could be more political

than the fact that I'm lonely,
that I am so far away
from everything I've known?"

But, the consular here has other queries.
Do you have property in India?
Land? Relatives? Anything?

"Write down, officer:
The yellow of mustard blossoms
stretching to the blue horizon.
My grandmother's tears
when she asks me what good is your learning
when it steals you from my embrace.
In our old house, with its dampness,
the music of my sister's laughter.
Four friends who bring news
of a new canal that has been dug by the villagers.
The bend in the river
near the tall trees where the spirits
of my ancestors are consecrated.
Women's voices from across the waters
that I have been hearing since my childhood.
The smell of hot pepper being roasted over a naked fire.

All of this from that one brief hour in November
during which my friend had asked her question."

II
"And how do I know
you are going to come back
—that you aren't going
to stay there in the States?"
The officer is young, wearing a tie.
He turns my passport around
till he has my picture upside down,
the loose change for my bus-ticket
rolling out of my shirt-pocket
into his lap.

III
A Marine walks around us, his attention cocked.
What does he want me to do?
"Rambo, Rambo." I shout exultantly.

But, that's too recent, let me mine
the archetypes. "Hey Charlie,
Give me a Lucky Strike. Some gum?
Want a good fuck? Very cheap. Dirty magazine?"
I do nothing, I say nothing.
In the garden outside the peacocks call.
I sip the coffee and plot my moves.
Now am I doing what he wants me to do?

IV
"Do you intend to overthrow
the government of the United States
by force or fraud?"

An old man who wants to visit
a son in New Jersey
wants me to help him
with this question on the form.
A friend tells me later of someone
who believing it was an either/or question
tried to play it safe and opted
for the overthrow of the government
by fraud.

V
"You can't trust them," one officer says.
I'm prepared to bet he is from Brooklyn.
There is no response from the other one. He is not angry,
just sad that I now work in his country.
This quiet American has pasted a sheet with Hindi alphabets
on his left, on his right there is a proverb from Punjab.
"You just can't trust them," the first one repeats,
shaking his wrist to loosen his heavy watch.
The one sitting down now raises his weary eyes.
"Did you, the first time you went there,
intend to come back?"
"Wait a minute," I say, "did you get a visa
when you first went to the moon? Fuck the moon,
tell me about Vietnam. Just how precise
were your plans there, you asshole?
And did you when you went to Panama the first time
know that you'd come back, guns blazing, a century later?
And this," I fist my cock when I say this, "and this
is what I think of your trust. Do you understand

that every time a doctor, teacher, engineer, or scholar
comes to the United States from India
you save more on bills
than what you and Charlie here
would be able to pay
till the year two thousand and four?
So that your saying that we can't be trusted
is like the owner shouting his worker's lazy
after he has stripped his skin and taken his soul.
He's sold . . . do you hear me?
Hear me
because I want this fact to be stored
like a bullet in your heart."

Maybe I did say all of this, and it was fear
that I saw in the officer's eyes
when in response to my shrug
he slowly turned the pages of my passport and stamped it.

(Kumar forthcoming)

NOTES

1. When making a statement like this I recognize the barrenness of the binary opposition "global/local." Once we take a position that views the social space as ineradicably overdetermined, the point most worthy of critical attention is that of calibrating the consequences of different forms of political interventions.

2. Alokdhanwa has been a poet writing in Hindi within the context of peasant uprisings in India that, inspired by Marxist-Leninist and Maoist currents, in the late 1960s and later shook the complacency of the bourgeois-democratic Indian state. Although unemployed and unable still to publish a book of his poems, Alokdhanwa has had significant influence on writers, poets, and activists of the left in India. I think of each of his poems as not only incisive sociocultural statements of protest but also poignant reflections on the conditions that make poetry (im)possible.

3. *Daroga* or the police head constable.

4. Once again, in the context of the present volume, I can see the need to admit poetry especially in the role I ascribe to it as a local response—against a global, somewhat abstract, imperative to organize the broad narrative of a world revolution. My small reluctance to this move lies in my preference for a reading where poetry, particularly Alokdhanwa's, is a strong response rooted in its locality but never oblivious to global preconditions and consequences.

5. The distinctions I am arguing for here are motivated by an impatience with the increasingly fashionable celebrations of "hybridity" without factoring in issues of class. Pico Iyer, the writer for *Time* magazine, has turned the selling of his travelogue of global identities into a profitable industry purposefully oblivious to the fact that his dollars purchase

him swift passage through cultural borders. "I have a wardrobe of selves from which to choose," Iyer writes, "and I savor the luxury of being able to be an Indian in Cuba or an American in Thailand; to be an Englishman in New York." When Iyer gets carried away by this charming rhetoric of a new world order and writes that "at customs we have nothing to declare but ourselves," one wants to ask him, "And your privilege?" (Iyer 1993, 15–16). To put it differently, although we might valorize "hybridity" as a way of approaching—even bridging—the global-local divide, the universalism of such claims will necessarily have to be questioned. The intercontinental wanderer's globality might be the car that runs over the dog of the migrant laborer's circumscribed locality.

6. This understanding is also alert to the fact that some differences might only mark the return of the same. For instance, the entry of Western capital into the Third World will no doubt introduce new possibilities. But for the poor in those countries these possibilities will amount to nothing more than the opportunity of working at McDonald's for wages that are even lower than what McDonald's doles out to its employees in the United States and in conditions that McDonald's employees here, however desperate they may be, would find appalling.

7. There is an implication here to which we must attend. The strict divisions between global and local collapse: To see the two terms calling each other into crisis doesn't allow us a choice of privileging one over the other. It only calls for a persistent critique of practices that would exclude either term from discussion.

8. My obvious inspiration here is Walter Benjamin. See especially his "Theses on the Philosophy of History" (1969).

BIBLIOGRAPHY

Ahlberg, Brian. "Such A Deal!" *Utne Reader.* November–December 1991. 18–19.

Alokdhanwa. "Open Fire Poster." *Samkaleen Janmat.* 25 September–1 October 1988:11–12.

Benjamin, Walter. "Theses on the Philosophy of History" in *Illuminations.* Trans. by Harry Zohn. New York: Schocken Books, 1969. 253–264.

Bhabha, Homi K. "Representation and the Colonial Text: A Critical Exploration of Some Forms of Mimeticism." *The Theory of Reading.* Frank Gloversmith. Sussex: The Harvester's Press, 1984. 93–122.

Bhabha, Homi K. "Remembering Fanon: Self, Psyche, and the Colonial Condition." *Remaking History.* Edited by Barbara Kruger and Phil Mariani. Seattle: Bay Press, 1989. 131–148.

Bhabha, Homi K. "Postcolonial Authority and Postmodern Guilt." *Cultural Studies.* Edited by Lawrence Grossberg, Cary Nelson, and Paula A. Treichler. New York and London: Routledge, 1992. 56–66.

Fanon, Frantz. *The Wretched of the Earth.* New York: Grove, 1963.

Iyer, Pico. "The Soul of an Intercontinental Wanderer." *Harper's Magazine.* April 1993:13–17.

Knight, William J. "I Love America." Reprinted in *Harper's Magazine,* November 1993:21.

Kumar, Amitava. "Four Poems." *Emergences.* Spring 1990a (2) 13–19.

_____, "*Night Raid* and Other Poetry." *Rethinking Marxism.* Fall–Winter 1990b (vol. 3, nos. 3–4) 172–177.

_____, "The Specter of Europe Is Haunting the Third World," *The Collective Voice,* November–December 1991:5–11.

_____, *Poems for the I.N.S.* (Forthcoming) *The Minnesota Review.*

Lenin, V. I. "L. N. Tolstoy," First published in *Sotsial-Demokrat,* no. 18, November 16 (29), and subsequently in Lenin's *Collected Works,* vol. 16, pp. 323–327. Reprinted in Pierre Macherey, *A Theory of Literary Production.* Trans. by Geoffrey Wall. London and New York: Routledge, 1978. See Appendix, esp. pp. 304–305.

_____, "Leo Tolstoy as the Mirror of the Russian Revolution," First published in *Proletary,* no. 35, September 11 (24), 1908, and subsequently in Lenin's *Collected Works,* vol. 15, pp. 202–209. Reprinted in Macherey, 1978. See p. 303.

Macherey, Pierre. *A Theory of Literary Production.* Trans. by Geoffrey Wall. London and New York: Routledge, 1978.

_____, and Etienne Balibar, "Literature as an Ideological Form: Some Marxist Propositions," *Praxis,* no. 5 (1981) 43–58.

Mill, James. *The History of British India.* Volume II. London: James Madden and Co., 1840.

Niranjana, Tejaswani. *Siting Translation: History, Post-Structuralism, and the Colonial Context.* Berkeley: University of California Press, 1992.

Said, Edward W. *Covering Islam.* New York: Pantheon, 1981.

Spivak, Gayatri Chakravorty. "Subaltern Studies: Deconstructing Historiography," in *In Other Worlds.* New York and London: Methuen, 1987. 197–221.

_____, "Can the Subaltern Speak?" in *Marxism and the Interpretation of Culture.* Edited by Cary Nelson and Lawrence Grossberg. Urbana and Chicago: University of Illinois Press, 1988. 271–313.

9

License to Feel:
Teaching in the Context of War(s)

MEGAN BOLER

On Tuesday, January 29, 1991, at 6:45 A.M. I read the *Sentinel* headline and front page story: Saddam Hussein threatens to attach nuclear warheads to his Scuds. In dawn's vulnerable moment, having read the news before establishing my usual media-guard censors, I am ravaged by this information and unable to focus appropriately on my role as composition and rhetoric instructor, on my agenda of thesis statements and this week's readings by Jewelle Gomez, Paula Gunn Allen, and Adrienne Rich. I enter the classroom at 8 A.M. feeling a sense of responsibility to my role in this community—or perhaps desiring a community that does not exist. I invite a discussion of the impact of the war and ask specifically how we are sustaining ourselves, where we are getting support. One after another the students tell me they have not read a paper or watched television in days or a week; they have chosen to "block it out," they say. In response to an in-class writing prompt, one student writes: "Since I'm not keeping up with the news, it's kinda nice to come in and know I'm not the only one ignoring the news because it bothers them too much ... when the war is over (hopefully very soon) I'm not sure it would have touched my life at all (except emotionally). I'm gonna forget about the war once it's over."

The examples of how this war has "emotionally touched" the students' lives perhaps won't be forgotten. One woman has a boyfriend in Saudi Arabia; laugh-

I want to give special thanks to Ann Cvetkovich, Natasha Levinson, and Roz Spafford for their responses to this essay. I am also grateful to the Center for Cultural Studies, University of California, Santa Cruz, who published an earlier version of this essay through the Cultural Studies of Science and Technology Research Group. (Levinson's response to a version of this essay presented at the 1995 Philosophy of Education Society Meetings in San Francisco can be found in the Society's Proceedings.)

ing, she had told us that when they finally spoke on the phone the first time since war broke out, he told her he was "safe" in a surveillance tower—and then he told her the tower was one of Iraq's main targets. Another woman told us that most of her friends are over there. And one young man fears the draft, as he believes his only other option would be deportation, given his immigrant status as a Korean. Yet today, not one out of sixteen speaks to the question of support or self-sustaining strategies. Their numbness reflects a profound isolation, not the least of which is our isolation from one another in this room. I am aware of a sense of hypocrisy should I remain silent about the question of the emotional impact of the Persian Gulf War on our lives. In a course dedicated to the "empowerment" of young writers, how can I not raise the haunting question about our distinctive emotional experiences at this historical moment? How can I not ask about the profound numbness, due to our veritable powerlessness, which seems to have rendered us both speechless, and further isolated from one another?

"There is a danger run by all powerless people: that we forget we are lying, or that lying becomes a weapon we carry into our relationships with people who do not have power over us" (Rich 1979, 189). Rich here speaks of women's skills of lying to men as a form of survival. We carry this weapon not only into our relationships with others but into our relationship with ourselves. This dynamic—lying in Rich's words, and numbness in mine—creates the modes of isolation I have described as crises. However, we might escape the implicit "realism" underlying these conceptions of falsehood/truth and argue that teaching is performance and that the dramatic element of teaching means a certain kind of pretense always takes place. In such a script, it appears I participate in an institutional acceptance of the war through the pretense that composition and rhetoric makes sense given a threat of nuclear disaster. What in turn does the performative element mean for students, or what might Rich's "lying" mean for them? How do the eruptions of isolation make sense either within a paradigm of performance, or in a paradigm of naive hope for community erupting through distorted representations? How do we make sense of a "real" war as it disrupts our "peace"? Or do we not make sense of it as "real," since to us it is in fact representation?

Our common experience as spectators of George Bush's war in the Persian Gulf prompted me to attempt to recognize our classroom as a community. And I know I am not alone in this attempt: Many instructors and professors I speak with use the language of "community ethos" to describe the climate they attempt to create in classrooms. At the time, another colleague told me she had asked of her class: We are a community; we are going through this together, so let's be here for each other.

The hyperdistinction of the "global" and "local" is one of the deceptive oppositions I encountered in this educational setting. If globalization refers to the web of economic, ideological, and political modes of domination and exchange whose effects include a flattening of cultures in the process of commodification and labor devaluation for the profit of few, then the common denominator of the local impact of globalization—although markedly varied—impacts communities and lives in "First" and "Third" World countries severely enough to warrant grasping this shared psychic imperialism. To privilege a discourse that builds on the distinction of global and local—economic/political versus individual/community—tends to assume that globalization doesn't require the ideological inscription of docile bodies and psyches.

To understand the effects of globalization, we must necessarily understand what gets referred to as a subset of the local: namely, the material effects of economic exploitation and ideology on the felt and thought processes of individuals and communities. No form of imperialism or colonialism has been possible without this localized engineering. As theorists producing discourses on such wrenching matters as transnational corporations and imperialist economic policies, we need attend to our own practices within equally imperialist-implicated institutions.[1]

Three features of modern life recognizably made community virtually impossible: identity politics, power relations, and fear. In this chapter, I concentrate on the latter two obstacles. All three obstacles share significant common denominators. Each is defined by negation—identification in terms of what it is not—and by predominant cultural silences. Each of these obstacles is significantly situated in a vector of the local and the global. The "local" that concerns this essay is the private, internal terrain generally segregated from the scope of education: In the instance of a war, this private domain is the site of anxieties, powerlessness, fear, and numbness, which defy language and are denied language within the educational institution. The global I examine includes the effects of media representations of the Persian Gulf War, which created our "community" or common perceptions of that war,[2] in terms of the effect of "repetitive trauma."

The identity politics of that particular classroom, in brief, communicated primarily through the placement of our bodies rather than through language and posed a significant obstacle to any utopic notion of community.[3] We were in fact a very strange community if we were one at all. The six Anglo students—four women and one man—sit together, the two African-American women sit together, the two Chinese women sit together, the Filipinos and Chicana sit together, and the Chinese and Korean men sit together. The extreme variation of our cultural values with respect to emotional expression made for further silences.[4] The students had in common their age—all about eighteen years old; generally speaking, the social class of students at the University of California, Santa Cruz, is upper middle-class; and the Filipina, Chicana, Korean, and Chinese students had in common that English was not their first language. Whatever commonalities, perhaps especially in war, the boundaries between us were not crossed, and we are shrouded in silence.

The second feature that prevents community and emotional literacies is, quite simply, the power relations that define the educator's relationship to students as an authority figure. To preserve authority, educators maintain immeasurable isolation and distance from students; for example, I generally do not reveal my social class background of growing up poor. Reciprocally, since I do have power over them, why should they make themselves emotionally vulnerable to me particularly in the public forum of the classroom?[5] In this chapter I analyze how educator/student relationships are defined by modes of pastoral power that preclude the possibility of community (Foucault 1984). Pastoral power functions as a contradictory catch-22 in which the educator, as the modern "pastor" by definition promises salvation. However, in the case of a crisis such as the Persian Gulf War, the educator cannot possibly deliver salvation. The modern educator is simultaneously positioned as globally impotent and as locally holding authoritative power. As a result, (student) resistance to this pastor is entrenched in such a way that community in relation to an outside crisis is virtually impossible. The overall effect is to isolate all involved.

The third feature that prevents community disturbs me the most. It is closely bound up with identities and with power relations but is rarely spoken of in these hallowed halls: in short, fear in its myriad forms. From the moment in 1982 when I commenced research on emotions' roles in subjectivities and knowledge production—the mutually defining relation of emotions and power—it has been patently obvious that what defines the discourses of emotion most predominantly are silences, particularly if one is examining emotional discourses within the history of the academy and higher education.[6] Within educational institutions, unacceptable/emotional behavior is defined by what it is not: namely, the prototype of the rational, curious, engaged, "balanced," well-behaved white male student. Why does a thesis of emotional epistemologies seem farfetched within the disciplined academy? Why is it so outlandish to think that, as an educational community, we might benefit from emotional literacies, from learning how to articulate the ways in which the social realm defines the private and how our passions inform our desires for knowledge? Why, in our fear and resistance, do we "lock out" the possibility of an emotional literacy regarding, for example, our vulnerabilities as well as systems of denial with respect to the pain and joy we necessarily experience in each of our globalized private and classroom lives?

Instead of saying any of this to them, I affirm that "checking out" is an invaluable survival strategy commonly used by any sort of trauma survivors to enable them to withstand the horror of repeated abuse, shock, or invasions of boundaries. I tell them also that I feel an obligation to ask them to think about the war and particularly about how it is being represented in the dominant media. I establish that for each class two persons will bring in articles—preferably foreign or alternative press—and offer a quick analysis. I change their open-ended "creative" assignment, due the following week, to a "creative" response to some representation of the war. The next week, however, when they read their poems aloud and exhibit collages in class, I am dumbfounded: In my long experience with this particular assignment in its usual form, it has been profound and productive. The result of my imposed direction to respond to the war resulted in a handful of moving poems but for the most part some of the least impressive, uninspired "creative" work I have seen.

Now, several years after the Persian Gulf War, I experience a similar moment of entering the classroom desiring community and in this instance choose a very different path. This morning, I consciously choose silence (in no small part due to the general resistances to emotional epistemologies on the part of those with more power than I in the academic communities). I enter the hall at the University of Auckland and give my lecture to the classroom of seventy students without making reference to the fact that we are at this moment a vulnerable community that in the next day or so will suffer the effects of the French nuclear detonation of a 150-pound bomb in nearby Pacific waters New Zealand has declared nuclear-free. Why I choose silence disturbs me, for it is entirely complicitous with the dominant cultural constructions of complex silences to avoid anxiety in the face of international political power games.

That the academy persistently guards against productive solidarities leads me to ask: what is it about institutionalized power relations that constructs isolation and powerlessness? In his work *Becoming Somebody: Toward a Social Psychology of School* Philip Wexler writes, "Interaction, society and self are the lacking central elements of social relations. . . . Emotion, performance, and morality are the main constitutive dimensions of action underlying the institutional processes. Gender, class, and race are ways to understand class differentiated compensatory defences against the absence of basic elements of social relations" (1992, 118). The fact that even a crisis such as a war does not allow us to reach across differences and establish community causes me to look beyond the individuals to understand the isolation. In the face of all manner of national and international horrors, we go about our business of education without consideration of the dynamics of community, identities, and emotional epistemologies that develop through the implicit values of our social interactions. Ideally, however ad hoc our community, we have a responsibility to develop emotional literacies that are part and parcel of community integrity.

What kind of community do we compose in our institutional settings? A classroom is in fact an extraordinarily "ad hoc" community. What we have in common may only be the students' shared administrative requirement for the course credit. Realistically, as an educator one is also responsible for being part of an apparatus that produces the next wave of workers and thinkers. In this minimal respect educators run the risk of dangerous hypocrisy in neglecting attention to emotional epistemologies. However, educational institutions have no commitment to community beyond the necessary behavioral requirements that enables bureaucracy.[7] Neither are educational institutions committed to an examination of the emotional epistemologies that inform social dynamics, relations, and knowledge production. Institutions are inherently committed to maintaining silences (e.g., about emotion) and/or proliferating discourses that define emotion by negation. My aim here is to outline how institutionalized power relations thwart attempts to develop emotional epistemologies.

By emotional epistemologies I mean at minimum a public recognition of the ways in which the "social" defines the "interior" realm of experience, and vice versa. Clearly a central challenge in writing about discourses of emotion is that, particularly in Western thought, emotions have tended to occupy—in philosophy, sciences, and popular discourse—the status of "naturalized entities." Viewed as biological and fixed and essential experiences or givens, we run into serious problems of reference and explanation. What is clear from this conceptual challenge is in part the power of binaries and dualisms that define our imaginative capacities, as well as our experience. I am less interested in whether or not there are in fact universally similar emotional experiences or expressions and more interested in how the dominant discourses within a given local site determine what can and cannot be felt and/or expressed. For example, we can ask how education intersects with emotional epistemologies and how a student's cultural background informs his or her sense of entitlement to speak in the classroom. More specifically, how does a sexual abuse survivor's shame and his or her required silence about this experience inform his or her license to speak with authority? Another example of emotional epistemologies can be found in teaching students how to combine passionate response with critical analysis, to define and identify how and when particular emotions inform and define knowledge.

The crisis I faced discerning my responsibility and effective teaching strategies during the Persian Gulf War extends far beyond that winter and continues to haunt me. Like the boundaries of public and private, which have become increasingly blurred in the last decades, what counts as "inside" and "outside" the appropriate focus of knowledge and education becomes increasingly complex. As an intellectual worker, what responsibility do I have to local, national, or international social and political realities in which my citizenship and institution of affiliation are implicated? Is the classroom a sanctuary from the everyday, where educators and students alike can justify abdicating any direct responsibility for "outside" political events?

The pragmatic response to my alarmist worry is, quite simply, that given the time, subject, and commodified constraints of a classroom it is not possible to do justice to an entire social agenda. Furthermore, if the class is not in a position adequately to study the political and historical events leading up to the Persian Gulf War (or Central Intelligence Agency–backed military support of dictatorships, the destruction of East Timor, the Panama Invasion, or the drug war and trade in this country), then the gesture is empty. But more disturbing to me than any particular errors made in terms of curriculum is the phenomenon I witnessed in acute form during the Persian Gulf War: What accounts for the pervasive construction of a rampant feeling of powerlessness, which none of us were able to transcend on that fateful day? To answer this, I first sketch the "twilight zone" as the psychic

terrain of emotion in the modern state of late capitalism and the students' predominant exhibitions of powerlessness and numbness. I then turn to an analysis
of the repetitive trauma effected by the media, which constructs that twilight
zone. Second, I draw on Michel Foucault's concept of pastoral power to explain
the educator's limited capacity to contradict the numbness constructed during
war. My analysis outlines the mutually interdependent ways in which feelings and
reality construct one another, with an eye toward how emotion both informs and
offers directions as well as limits possibilities.[8]

The Twilight Zone of Powerlessness:
Localized Sites of Global Shocks

Twilight: "an intermediate state that is not clearly defined." Denial is the psyche's
odd twilight zone: Sartre's "bad faith"; Rich's "lying"; Nietzsche's "forgetfulness."
Denial can only be the product of human subjectivity, a unique feature of our
species of consciousness, the space of neither knowing nor ignorance, awareness
nor misinformation. The fact that our psyches abide to varying extents in this
twilight zone arena with respect to the war, in the zone bordering powerlessness
and denial, does not mean that some of us are not engaged in effective analysis,
education, and/or resistance. An excavation of this phenomenon in relation to
emotion reveals that the twilight zone syndrome feeds on our lack of awareness
of how powerlessness functions, effects, feeds on, and drains our sense of agency
and power as active creators of self- and world-representations. By powerlessness
I mean a state that is usually silent and mutates into guilt and denial that gnaw at
us; the latter especially are forms of internalized self-hatred, "internalized oppression" in the contemporary discourse—the poisonous by-products of powerlessness. As one student wrote, "With this war, I demonstrated in an anti-war rally
for the first time in my life. I wrote writings and told everyone that this was
wrong. But despite all that the war goes on and on. The politicians do not care at
all. I have no power whatsoever to change the course of the Persian Gulf War. I
am therefore powerless. Powerless to stop an event I think is unjust."

Powerlessness, however, is a more promising feeling and concept than denial or
guilt, for beneath the numbness, which often signifies powerlessness, lies a force
that can be transformed into an immediate source of power, "immediate vigor-
ous action." Numbness is perhaps the most efficacious, postmodern survival
strategy.[9] What other could possibly work as well to get us through either a glance
or thorough reading of a newspaper—our awareness of all the occurrences and
issues not represented in that newspaper; the dailiness of our work, its pressures,
unexpected blows, and upsets; the massive contradiction of desiring peace and
driving a car. Need I go on? As I said to my students, "checking out"—numbness—is perhaps most poignantly utilized by abuse survivors. The agency involved in numbness indicates that it is an intelligent psychic survival strategy—

and no one can stop one from choosing it! But making this choice without educated consideration of our other options means that, at times, numbness may be the inadvertent effect of cultural illiteracy with respect to translating emotion into knowledge and action.[10]

What accounts for the construction of powerlessness, and how might it be interrupted within the classroom? One place to begin to understand the twilight zone of the representational psyche is an analysis of how media contributes to numbness.

The Repetitive Trauma of Media

Media can function as a repetitive trauma, successfully so in terms of the fact that one effect of monopolized ideology is isolation and powerlessness. "Repetitive trauma" is generally opposed to "acute trauma." For example, an acute trauma is a car accident, which may involve all manner of the emotional and physical pain, but observably survivors tend to remember the event quite well. Particularly in relation to memory, however, repetitive trauma has a quite different effect than acute trauma: It appears that a feature of repeated injury—to the body and/or psyche—is to forget, repress, and relegate the memory to what I call the twilight zone.[11]

In the case of an event like the Persian Gulf War, the repetition of "safe" images and rhetoric used in manufactured media has a guaranteed numbing effect. The repetition of any oft-repeated image or words might have that effect. But when the selected representation is deeply suspected as a "truth effect" rather than as a trusted source, a sense of repeated betrayal is added to the overstimulation. For example, the defusing representation of peace movements created the persistent illusion of isolation and freakishness in one's desire for peace. How do I engage with the classroom of diverse people in productive address of our distinct fears and terrors, when the language provided us consists of Pollyannish cartoon images?

Isolation in our moral existence is perpetuated through institutionalized silences as well as our own reluctances to acknowledge and discuss something so extreme as torture or war. Elaine Scarry's suggestions of the interrelations of flesh and language outline one aspect of how media functions as a repetitive trauma which becomes embodied and manifest as powerlessness. In *The Body in Pain*, she states that this reluctance increases "our vulnerability to power by ensuring that our moral intuitions and impulses which come forward so readily on behalf of human sentience, do not come forward far enough to be of any help. . . . The result of this is that the very moral intuitions that might act on behalf of the claims of sentience remain almost as interior and inarticulate as sentience itself" (1985, 60). What Scarry calls our sentient knowledge, our embodied emotion, is inextricably intertwined with the negotiation and enactment of justice.[12]

There is no doubt that the language of displaced meaning constructed to represent the Persian Gulf War as a benign event set the stage for the twilight zone I encountered in my classroom.[13] As a class, we discussed the images and language enough to share a laugh—albeit a painful one—about the irony not just of consistent understatement but point of view, for example the speaking voice maintaining fear to be the fear of crazy war resisters here in the United States rather than fear for the Iraqi casualties, or fear for Israel, or fear for U.S. soldiers.

Yet the globalized media repetitions cannot be distinguished from their severe local effect: a loss of community and hence loss of language within our classroom prevented us from transforming powerlessness we felt in the face of our government. There is a misnomer here, "our" government. The Filipina women in the classroom knew "our" government also as a presence in their own country. There was no unilateral concept of "our" government, of its concern for who counts as a citizen, or whose families had been transplanted and divided as a result of U.S. foreign military presence.

Indeed there are acute differences in the localized impact of U.S. foreign and domestic policies. During the war I visited a class conducted by Toni Cade Bambara and Buchi Emecheta,[14] and I heard two women students speak loud and clear: Those of you who chose to shut down this university haven't struggled to be allowed entrance to an education. Your peace movement is a self-serving product of privilege. And another who tells us that, as horrified as she is by this war, we didn't grow up where she grew up; she's used to bullets flying into houses from the street on favorite holidays.

These radically different meanings of signs and events explain in part how identity politics separates us even more acutely in a time of war, when the notion of "us" and "them" is put into sharp relief by national, class, and racial boundaries, and when the question, What counts as a political crisis? makes visible a multitude of crises not just overseas. The goal of challenging the psychic twilight zone is deeply threatened by the modes of administrative control available to me within the institution. An analysis of "pastoral power" helps illuminate the ways in which late-capitalist administrative power positions educators in a catch-22.

The Faces of Pastoral Power

Foucault defines pastoral power as "an old power technique which originated in Christian institutions" that "the modern Western state has integrated in a new political shape" (1984, 421). Pastoral power is most notable for the fact that "[n]ever . . . in the history of human societies . . . has there been such a tricky combination in the same political structures of individualization techniques and of totalization procedures" (421).[15] Foucault traces the originary modes of pastoral power in its earlier association of a directly religious nature and its variations in the modern, secularized form. Both historical modes of pastoral power have in common several features, which relate to the site of education. Pastoral power's objective in its modern form is salvation in this life, salvation meaning "health, well-being . . . security, protection against accidents." The "officials of pastoral power" have multiplied greatly to include for example educators and social workers.

Within the classroom, pastoral power describes the educator's impotence in the institution. Because this is the form of power available to educators in an administrative setting and because within the instance of war I cannot deliver on the implied promise of salvation, the students rightly adopt a mode of resistance to my critical attempts to situate the war. They bear a relation of resistance to me as the embodiment of an authority who demands they address the war, thereby composing their attention to this "real" event as simply another assignment not of their choice. This role sets me up as a figure of authority the students will resist—in fact, a positive sign—but ironically in a time of war their constructive resistance simultaneously prevents me from effectively intervening in the media's traumatic impact on their sensibilities.

What does this mean in the classroom? In a "normal" state of affairs, what I assure them as the telos, the state of grace, of this process are tools for self-reflection and critical analysis. But the Persian Gulf War radically shifted my functionary position as pastor. What assurances could I offer them, after all? Clearly, what I wanted on that fateful morning was some kind of vulnerable confessions (or, I prefer to think, testimonies)[16] about their internal knowledge and response to the news. But in this case, the repetitive trauma and consequence numbness that result from media images usurp my pastoral power and simultaneously castrate my power as it poses me as a pawn for the modern state.[17]

Thus we must ask, "To what degree do power relations in universities represent domination?" (Howley and Hatnett 1992, 281). If one accepts that the primary tools of power within the university have to do with prediction, control, and differentiation (more so than assimilation) as modes of constituting the normal and deviant, then we are faced with a disturbing answer: "As normalizing technologies, [these strategies] make use of differentiations that are essentially political, not intellectual. Such differentiations tend to support the transformation of power into domination by systematically limiting opportunities for recalcitrance" (282). In my classroom I witnessed increased differentiation of a political rather than intellectual character. The students' primary avenue for recalcitrance was—rightly—to resist my invocation of an intellectual and emotional discussion of the Persian Gulf War. Like it or not, as a pastor of the modern state by virtue of my position of power in the university setting, I enabled the "transformation of power into domination by systematically limiting opportunities for recalcitrance."

Pastoral power works especially effectively within institutions. For individuals to unite and express support for or opposition to the war outside of the classroom takes place in a climate less complex than the contradictory climate of a classroom. Public demonstration resists the totalizing intentions of media and Bush's unilateral offensive and resists the intention to isolate individuals from one another by bringing many bodies together in one location. It underscores the expression of individual differences as well, because in the face of a common "enemy" there can be united resistance yet extensive discussion of different strategies and intentions in resistance.

Why doesn't this mode of resistance translate to the classroom? The facile response is, first, that one must create a space for debate and analysis that calls for thoroughgoing critiques of media representations and political histories. Second, since in the classroom the teacher functions as an authority and pastor of power, there is a secondary resistance to this mode of administrative power that can stymy resistance to the wider net of power relations. It is this that caused my loneliness that fateful morning: I felt us all to be in the same boat, as it were, as a result of our shared "victimization" by the mainstream media. But the students did not share that loneliness with me, partly because we had not all read the newspaper that morning, partly because they weren't facing the same ethical dilemma as I—trying to understand my role as teacher during the war, and partly because they entered that room with compulsory footsteps.

The resistance I did witness in the classroom took the form of the student's suspicion of the media's truths. Foucault lists "suspicion" as a central form of resistance to pastoral power.

> These struggles are not exactly for or against the "individual" but rather they are struggles against the "government of individualization." They are an opposition to the effects of power which are linked with knowledge, competence, and qualification: struggles against the privileges of knowledge. But they are also an opposition against secrecy, deformation, and mystifying representations imposed on people.
>
> There is nothing "scientistic" in this (that is, a dogmatic belief in the value of scientific knowledge), but neither is it a skeptical or relativistic refusal of all verified truth. What is questioned is the way in which knowledge circulates and functions, its relations to power. In short, the regime du savoir (1984, 420).

Although the primary emotional tone I observed among my students was numbness, they also shared the more promising emotion of suspicion as evidenced by their responses to reports of a cease-fire declaration: "Well, I am so happy about this little news event. But who knows if we can believe it. They have censored everything up until now. How do we know they aren't lying? Is it really over or is this one of George Bush's schemes? The media makes it seem like they knew all along that we were going to win the war. . . ".

The suspicions posed by these eighteen-year-olds reveal a beginning critique of the *regime du savoir*. Suspicion indicates mistrust, a sense of previous betrayal, possible rational grounds for disbelief. Unlike other feelings, suspicion is linguistically active: It is also a verb, an activity. Suspicion, marking excellent progress from powerlessness, should encourage us to take emotional literacy seriously as part of the work of education.

The Challenges of Critical Emotional Literacy

For many of these students, their work in our classrooms may be one of their only forums for naming the emotions and the politics related to this war. Even if we are not willing as teachers to risk our own vulnerability, we must reevaluate what counts as knowledge for our students and whether or not emotional sensitivity and affective education represent crucial forms of epistemological awareness requisite to a transforming society. Simply stating that one does not express emotion in the classroom when in the role of authority is a culturally coded form of denial about what counts as "emotion." The classroom community, we are implicitly taught through discourses of negation, is not a place where emotional epistemology or literacy are part of the educational agenda. But in fact teachers' emotional needs are constantly attended to in the classroom: The interactions of authority, the effect of power on one's ego, the complex ways in which teachers take the last word, or use students' questions or insights to develop their own thinking cannot be separated from one's emotional needs. One can observe persistent patterns of male instructors, for example, controlling the sphere of rational discourse as an arena for their own very empassioned emotional articulation.[18]

Intervention at the level of representation does suggest a starting point for interrupting powerlessness. With respect to the repetitive trauma that helps to construct powerlessness, Walter Benjamin's straightforward direction for reading visual images is helpful on the issue of subversion. In a speech delivered in 1934, Benjamin addresses precisely how the artist/intellectual can transform or reappropriate the "means of production," as it were, rather than passively participating in the reproduction of the status quo. In his interrogation of the role of the intellectual/writer in relation to class struggle, Benjamin argues for a kind of authorship that transforms the means of production (in service to socialism) simultaneous with its production. He criticizes the New Matter-of-Fact photographers, who in one case "succeeded in transforming abject poverty, by recording it in a fashionably perfected manner, into an object of enjoyment" (1984, 304). He calls this "a flagrant example of what it means to supply a productive apparatus without changing it." Rather, he asserts, "What we require of the photographer is the ability to give his picture the caption that wrenches it from modish commerce and gives it a revolutionary useful value." By teaching skills of self-reflection and critical analysis that are available to students as they move beyond the walls of the university, we may enact Benjamin's suggestion of displacing meanings and shifting our relation to the world.

One alternative to numbness is to bridge the gap between the isolated internal life and the external visible life of "schoolwork." Elaine Scarry tells us that to articulate pain is an extraordinary challenge, for

the moment [pain] is lifted out of the ironclad privacy of the body into speech, it immediately falls back in. Nothing sustains its image in the world. . . . From the inarticulate it half emerges into speech and then quickly recedes once more. Invisible in part because of its resistance to language, it is also invisible because its own power-fulness ensures its isolation, ensures that it will not be seen in the context of other events, that it will fall back from its new arrival into language and remain devastat-ing. Its absolute claim for acknowledgment contributes to its being ultimately unac-knowledged (1985, 60–61).

In relation to the classroom, the ineffability of pain raises the challenge of dis-cussing the "reality" of war effectively. What does it mean to learn to apply lan-guage to the critical articulation of anger, rage, grief, and pain? Emotion defies language, and education discursively denies language to emotion. To leap off this precipice into uncharted discursive space is an act of courage. Scarry's redefini-tion of "work" suggests articulate embodiment as part of education:

> Work and its "work" (or work and its object, its artifact) are the names that are given to the phenomena of pain and the imagination as they begin to move from being a self-contained loop within the body to becoming the equivalent loop now projected into the external world. It is through this movement out into the world that the ex-treme privacy of the occurrence (both pain and imagining are invisible to anyone outside the boundaries of the person's body) begins to be sharable, that sentience be-comes social (1985, 170).

"Work" as process and product are certainly familiar aspects of education. However, the public expression of this sentience represents a real risk. The ex-tremely harsh prohibitions against vulnerability in academia circumscribe ex-pression within these hallowed halls. Yet we are constantly engaged in this bridg-ing and transformation of the internal and private into the public, although this process has not been fully legitimated as an educational goal.

To challenge pastoral power successfully involves an integration of structures of feeling with the work of education. The individual and collective work we en-gage in within academia is deeply etched with felt histories and meanings. We choose whether to turn away from these chasms and pulls to community or whether to learn to incorporate structures of feeling as the missing element for posttraumatic knowledges. The "controlled discomfort" Scarry describes as con-stituting some kinds of work is frequently avoided in the classroom, also attrib-utable to the discourses of danger surrounding emotion.

Three strategic lessons emerge from pondering this crisis on the intersection of the global and the local. Students and educator are not and will never be equals or peers within the institutional setting; there are more and less effective strate-gies for encouraging debate on current events; and I am not alone in my frustra-tion with the ethical crises provoked at that historical moment. Ideally, the work of developing emotional epistemologies and literacies, with an eye toward com-munity, begins to occur even at the minimum level of self-reflective questions about representation and expression within circumscribed classroom norms and scripts. In sum, I am not willing to accept that emotional literacy and the aim of challenging powerlessness are not primary goals of education. The history and norms of classroom etiquette merely represent an institutional habit and do not justify systematic strictures against community.

Despite our complicated interactions and relationships fraught with power and desire, despite the longing for impossible connections and shared visions, we can model for students a form of world transformation and resistance to globalization by showing how pain and powerlessness are constructed and can be displaced into a notion of "work." Whether this means words, essays, collective projects, understandings of our ethical obligations in chemistry and biology, or recording dreams is undetermined. However, as long as we agree that this localized site is overshadowed by the ineffability of pain, and surrender to fears inculcated by the danger-discourse surrounding expression of emotion; as long as we continue to embody with docility the norms that appear so innocent and "apolitical," we offer students no better vision of how to transform either their own pain and rage or how to enact upon the world the alternative visions each carries.

The definitions of identity, the power relations, and persistent fears defined by discourses of negation and predominant silences tell us only that we are surviving the inscriptions of the modern institution. Whereas the Persian Gulf War brought this into sharp relief because of direct and offensive U.S. military action, the myriad versions of U.S. military action both within and outside of the boundaries of this nation easily compel a sense of perpetual crisis that warrant calling educational aims into question at every historic moment. Although at times the relation between our interactions in the classroom feels hopelessly disconnected from what occurs halfway around the world, I recognize that this sense of futility intelligently is enacted through bodies, through local sites that interrupt the gloss of numb docility. In these bodies called students and teachers, within our very cells, abides an undiminishable source of energy always willing to be transformed into language, into marks upon unwilling walls.

NOTES

1. In their introduction to the collection *Colonial Discourses and Post-Colonial Theory,* editors Patrick Williams and Laura Chrisman discuss how these literatures intersect with other contemporary theories (New York: Columbia University Press, 1994). Relevant to my arguments about refusing false distinctions between discourses of the local and global, they define poststructuralism and postmodernism suggestively. The former refers to critiques of the self as conceived within bourgeois individualism; the latter challenges the notion of master narratives. While one might argue that globalization can be discussed without taking poststructuralism or postmodern theories into account, any critique of capitalism—particularly if following in Gramsci's shadow—is less than adequate without a critique of how the isolated self of pastoral power is one of the grandest master narratives of United States rhetoric.

2. For a fuller treatise of the media representations of the Persian Gulf War, see the recent anthology *Seeing Through the Media: The Persian Gulf War,* edited by Susan Jeffords

and Lauren Rabinovitz; Douglas Kellner, *The Persian Gulf TV War;* and Les Levidow "The Gulf Massacre as Paranoid Reality." I composed this essay during the Persian Gulf War and am pleased that subsequent years have yielded significant analyses of media's new "globalized" role; as Jeffords states, "the primary functions the media served during the war [were]: reconstructing history, controlling the dissemination of information, creating social consensus, and solidifying national identity" (1994, 14). See also the pioneering work of Lynn Worsham, "Emotion and Pedagogic Violence" (1990–1991).

3. In my essay "The Risks of Empathy: Interrogating Multiculturalism's Gaze" (1996), I examine the contemporary faith in empathy and social imagination as a foundation for democratic communities and challenge this faith through an interdisciplinary analysis of the complexity of power relations that define reading, identification, and any "actions" that may result from empathy. In another essay, "Emotional Quotient: The Taming of the Alien" (1996), I examine the popularized sociobiological discourses regarding "emotional intelligence" and argue that altruism may play a new role in the globalized economy. On imagination and community, see Boler, "Review Essay of Benhabib's *Situating the Self* and Bogdan's *Re-Educating the Imagination*" (1995).

4. The ethnographic work of Lutz and Abu-Lughod (1990) provides international and crosscultural research on cultural variation in emotional practices, expressions, rules, and codes. It is worth addressing the anticipated critique that a call for "emotional literacy" represents a practice most familiar through middle-class, white practices presently popular in distinct regions of the United States. It is certainly the case that "access" to the explicit discourses on emotions through the specific practices of psychotherapy are afforded by social class. Taking into account the gendered, racialized, and classed character of such popularized discourses on emotion, every one of us exists within a nexus of emotional discourses. In my larger project I have traced the dominant discourses in Western cultures to be four: the pathological (medical, scientific, social scientific, and psychological); the romantic (as is permitted in the arts, the channeling of passions, etc.); the rational (emotion channeled into debate, argument within educational practices and politics); and the more recent emergence of sociopolitical discourses of emotion through the Civil Rights and feminist movements, in which emotions such as pride and anger take on new cultural meanings.

5. The negating discourses which determine when and how vulnerability is permitted between student and teacher is a subject I address in an essay titled "Medusa's Daughters" presented at the California Association of Philosophers of Education at Stanford University, April 1993. To develop emotional literacy and epistemology raises the central question: What are the ethics of "requiring vulnerability" given the power differential of student and teacher, and given vast cultural differences potentially represented in a classroom? Similarly, the codes circumscribing the different risks of vulnerability for male and female educators in higher education pose a genuine problem: for women to maintain authority, expressions of vulnerability risk denigration of women's authority in the classroom.

6. In the introduction to the winter 1990–1991 issue of *Discourse: Journal for Theoretical Studies in Media and Culture,* Kathleen Woodward describes the work of the contributors/participants in the 1989–1990 Center for Twentieth Century Studies who took as their theme "Discourses of the Emotions." Commenting on the missing discourses of emotion she writes, "The emotions are not dead, they are simply not present in academic discourse. Discourses of the emotions (even the emotions themselves) are everywhere, omnipresent

in our everyday lives" (4). The work collected in two recent issues of *Discourse* represents excellent interdisciplinary analyses of emotion, and emotion and subjectivity, respectively: see *Discourse: Theoretical Studies in Media and Culture,* 13.1 (Fall-Winter 1990–1991); and 152 (Winter 1992–1993). It is not a coincidence that, particularly within classrooms, questions of identity politics and relations of powers are dynamics experienced and recognized but generally not directly addressed. See for example, bell hooks' essays on pedagogy and class in *Talking Back.*

7. See for example Michael Katz, *Class, Bureaucracy, and Schools* (1971) in which he traces the historical development of the bureaucratic structures of North American schools, an analysis which dovetails with Foucault's understandings of administrative, pastoral power.

8. The literature that informs my research and study of emotion is drawn from several distinct fields. For analyses that combine ethnography with social and cultural critique, see Catherine Lutz and Lila Abu-Lughod, eds., *Language and the Politics of Emotions* (1990); in sociology, see for example Arlie Hochschild, *The Managed Heart: Commercialization of Human Feeling* (1983). A few select interdisciplinary analyses relevant to thinking about such issues as war include Shoshana Felman and D. Laub, *Testimony: Crises of Witnessing in Literature, Psychoanalysis, and History* (1992); Jennifer Gore and Carmen Luke, eds., *Feminisms and Critical Pedagogy* (1992); Philip Wexler, *Becoming Somebody* (1992); Henriques et al., *Changing the Subject* (1984); Megan Boler, *Feeling Power: The Discourses of Emotion in United States Education,* Ph.D. Dissertation, University of California, Santa Cruz, 1992. In the field of literature, see Ann Cvetkovich, *Mixed Feelings* (1992). On the value of anger, see especially Peter Lyman, "The Politics of Anger: On Silence, Ressentiment, and Political Speech," in *Socialist Review* (1991); Naomi Scheman, "Anger and the Politics of Naming," in *Engendering: Constructions of Knowledge, Authority, and Privilege* (1993); in philosophy, see Elizabeth Spelman, "Anger and Insubordination," in *Women, Knowledge, and Reality;* and Lynne McFall, "What's Wrong With Bitterness," in Claudia Card, ed., *Feminist Ethics.*

9. The following student's written response to the cease-fire declaration evidences the double-edged function of numbness: "If you really want to know what I honestly think about this war being over. . . . I have no thoughts, feelings, or reactions towards it. . . . Yah I'm glad, but I really don't care at this point anymore about the war. . . . I'm happy that I know my best friend can come home safe and I don't have to worry about coming home each day and checking my machine to hear that he's dead and his body will be sent back on so and so a date. . . . Other than that I have no feeling about the war being over because I had no feeling toward the war in a very long time."

10. The phenomenon of powerlessness is experienced not only in response to an event such as war but is an everyday occurrence, bred within the walls of the university as this same student's writing continues on to say: "During my Jr. year when I was supposed to write down a classic 5-paragraph essay I did not get the format. I went through all of my notes, and listened to her when I was supposed to. Still, I could not get it together to write a better essay, no matter what I did, I felt powerless." The fact that a writing assignment engenders the same sense of powerlessness as that incurred by George Bush's military regime gives me great pause in my assumptions about liberatory education.

11. In *Desiring Identities* I examine identity as a form of repetitive trauma in order to assess the relation of silence and voice to modes of bearing witness. I analyze the relation-

ship of narrative to identity, and to catharsis in turn. In the event of repeated (rather than acute) trauma, a "storytelling" frequently does not come easily, or can occur in fixed repetition that is not transformative. Questions that emerge in this study include: how are silence and voice related to the severity and extent of trauma in terms of its repetition? How is it that repetitive trauma becomes embodied and habituated such that it is "forgotten"?

12. Raymond William's notion of "structures of feelings" permits a bridge between these puzzles of language, and emotion.

13. In 1958 Hannah Arendt, for example, addresses with great foreshadowing the loss of language as a casualty of science's language of mathematical symbols (*The Human Condition*, 4).

14. An African-American writer and a Nigerian/British writer, respectively authors of *The Salt Eaters* and *The Joys of Motherhood*.

15. In "The Subject and Power," Foucault suggests that "to understand what power relations are about . . . we should investigate the forms of resistance and attempts made to dissociate these relations [of, for example, 'administration to how people live']" (419). Foucault focuses on pastoral power's individualizing techniques that make individuals "subjects," which assists in understanding how isolation and powerlessness get constructed.

16. I explore the difference between confession and testimony as modes of reading in "The Risks of Empathy: Interrogating Multiculturalism's Gaze," forthcoming, *Cultural Studies;* an earlier version of this essay can be found in *Philosophy of Education Society Proceedings*, 1994.

17. As Howley and Hatnett write, "Pastoral power represented a transaction: the individual revealed the truth about him or herself, and the pastor guaranteed the individual's salvation. By gaining knowledge of individuals in this way, the pastor gained power over them. The pastor exercised this power only insofar as it was necessary to restore individuals to a state of grace—or, in more contemporary parlance, to the state of being normal" (1992, 273).

18. In her article "On the Regulation of Speaking and Silence," (1985) Valerie Walkerdine provides an excellent analysis of how children are introduced into the use of white, middle-class rational discourse as the channel for their emotions, particularly expressions of conflict regarding those in authority. See also Kramarae and Treichler, "Power Relationships in the Classroom," in Gabriel and Smithson, eds. *Gender in the Classroom* (1990).

BIBLIOGRAPHY

Arendt, Hannah. *The Human Condition*. Chicago: University of Chicago Press, 1958.

Benjamin, Walter. "The Author as Producer." In *Art After Modernism*. Brian Wallis (ed.). New York: New Museum of Contemporary Art, 1984. 297–310.

Boler, Megan. "Emotional Quotient: The Taming of the Alien." Paper presented at "Narrative and Metaphor Across the Disciplines." Conference held at the University of Auckland, New Zealand. July 8–10, 1996.

_____. *Feeling Power: The Discourses of Emotion in United States Education*, Ph.D. Dissertation, University of California, Santa Cruz, 1992.

_____. "Review Essay of Benhabib's *Situating the Self* and Bogdan's *Re-Educating the Imagination*." *Hypatia: A Journal of Women and Philosophy* 10, no. 4 (Fall 1995):130–142.

_____. "The Risks of Empathy: Interrogating Multiculturalism's Gaze." *Cultural Studies*, forthcoming. (An early version of this essay can be found in *Philosophy of Education Society Proceedings*, 1994.)

Card, Claudia (ed.). *Feminist Ethics*. Lawrence: University Press of Kansas, 1991.

Cvetkovich, Ann. *Mixed Feelings*. New Brunswick: Rutgers University Press, 1992.

Felman, Shoshana and Laub, D. *Testimony: Crises of Witnessing in Literature, Psychoanalysis, and History*. New York: Routledge, 1992.

Foucault, Michel. "The Subject and Power." In *Art After Modernism*. Brian Wallis (ed.). New York: New Museum of Contemporary Art, 1984. 417–434.

Gore, Jennifer and Luke, Carmen (eds.). *Feminisms and Critical Pedagogy*. New York: Routledge, 1992.

Henriques, Julian, Hollway, W., Urwin, C., Venn, C., and Walkerdine, V. *Changing the Subject*. London: Methuen, 1984.

Hochschild, Arlie. *The Managed Heart: Commercialization of Human Feeling*. Berkeley: University of California Press, 1983.

hooks, bell. *Talking Back*. Boston: South End Press, 1989.

Howley, Aimee and Richard Hatnett. "Pastoral Power and the Contemporary University." *Educational Theory* 42 (3), 1992. 271–290.

Jeffords, Susan and Rabinovitz, Lauren (eds.). *Seeing Through the Media: The Persian Gulf War*. New Brunswick: Rutgers, 1994.

Katz, Michael. *Class, Bureaucracy, and Schools*. London: Praeger, 1994.

Kellner, Douglas. *The Persian Gulf TV War*. Boulder, CO: Westview Press, 1992.

Kramarae, Chris and Treichler, Paula. "Power Relationships in the Classroom." In *Gender in the Classroom*. Susan Gabriel and Isaiah Smithson (eds.). Urbana: University of Illinois Press, 1990.

Levidow, Les. "The Gulf Massacre as Paranoid Reality." In *Culture on the Brink*. Gretchen Bender and Timothy Druckrey (eds.). Seattle: Bay Press, 1994.

Lutz, Catherine and Abu-Lughod, Lila (eds.). *Language and the Politics of Emotions*. Cambridge: Cambridge University Press, 1990.

Lyman, Peter. "The Politics of Anger: On Silence, Ressentiment, and Political Speech." *Socialist Review* 11 (3), 1991. 55–74.

Rich, Adrienne. "Women and Honor: Some Notes on Lying." *On Lies, Secrets, and Silence*. New York: Norton, 1979.

Scarry, Elaine. *The Body in Pain*. New York: Oxford University Press, 1985.

Scheman, Naomi. "Anger and the Politics of Naming." *Engenderings: Constructions of Knowledge, Authority, and Privilege*. New York: Routledge, 1993. 22–35.

Spelman, Elizabeth. "Anger and Insubordination." In *Women, Knowledge, and Reality*. Ann Garry and Marilyn Pearsall (eds.). Boston: Unwin Hyman, 1989.

Walkerdine, Valerie. "On the Regulation of Speaking and Silence." In *Language, Gender, and Childhood*. C. Steedman, C. Urwin, and V. Walkerdine (eds.). London: Routledge, 1985.

Wexler, Philip. *Becoming Somebody: Toward a Social Psychology of School*. London: Falmer Press, 1992.

Williams, Raymond. *Marxism and Literature*. New York: Oxford University Press, 1977.

Woodward, Kathleen. "Introduction." *Discourse: Journal for Theoretical Studies in Media and Culture*, Winter 1990–1991. 94–112.

Worsham, Lynn. "Emotion and Pedagogic Violence." *Discourse: Journal for Theoretical Studies in Media and Culture*, Winter 1990–1991. 119–148.

10

Nationalism and Internationalism: Domestic Differences in a Postcolonial World

LORA ROMERO

A number of recent books have used multiculturalism to shake our collective confidence in the idea of nationhood so basic to "American" literary studies. Amy Kaplan, however, in the introduction to *Cultures of United States Imperialism*, proposes an alternative strategy for scrutinizing—if not actually deactivating—the postulates of exceptionalism and unilinearity upon which scholarship in the field has depended.

Kaplan argues that despite its obvious advantages, "the critical force of multiculturalism . . . may lay itself open to [nationalist] recuperation" (1993, 15). She explains the problem in this way:

> [T]he new pluralistic model of diversity runs the risk of being bound by the old paradigm of unity if it concentrates its gaze only narrowly on the internal lineaments of American culture and leaves national borders intact instead of interrogating their formation. That is, American nationality can still be taken for granted as a monolithic and self-contained whole, no matter how diverse and conflicted, if it remains implicitly defined by its internal social relations, and not in political struggles for power with other cultures and nations, struggles which make America's conceptual and geographic borders fluid, contested, and historically changing (1993, 15).

Hence a postcolonial rather than a multicultural approach would better serve postnational studies of the United States. Such an approach would demonstrate first "how diverse [domestic] identities cohere, fragment, and change in relation to one another and to ideologies of nationhood through the crucible of international power relations" and second, "how conversely, imperialism as a political or economic process abroad is inseparable from the social relations and cultural discourses of race, gender, ethnicity, and class at home" (1993, 16).

Cultures of United States Imperialism will, I hope, encourage further efforts to coordinate the study of domestic differences and international power relations. Moreover, in an era of both immigration and affirmative action backlash, the postcolonial approach Kaplan outlines will be compelling not only because of its efficacy in addressing scholarly concern over the nationalism that helped create American literary studies but also because of its usefulness (when translated into public idioms) for intervening in debates generated by the California ballot initiatives from which a rejuvenated, post–cold war version of nationalism is now launching itself into the twenty-first century.[1]

Having paid my respects to the critical tactic theorized and enacted in *Cultures of United States Imperialism,* I'd now like to identify some challenges facing postcolonial studies conducted along the lines proposed by Kaplan. My caveats and queries are deliberately abstract. Rather than respond to current critical examples, I'd like to anticipate some of the conceptual and institutional impediments postcolonial criticism of U.S. culture might encounter as it gains (as I hope it will) practitioners and influence. What follows then is a series of interlinked reflections on the relationship between minority and postcolonial studies, prompted by the question of how best to understand the nation as an incident of historical fabrication rather than as the "common sense" from which the field of U.S. cultural studies proceeds.

Kaplan attributes much of the impetus for critics' pursuit of an international analysis of American literary studies to the influence of Chicano studies. Of the latter she writes:

> The borderlands link the study of ethnicity and immigration inextricably to the study of international relations and empire. At these borders, foreign relations do not take place outside the boundaries of America, but instead constitute American nationality.
>
> Chicano studies has brought an international perspective to American studies in part by reconceiving the concept of ethnicity (traditionally treated as a self-enclosed entity) through the theory and politics of post-coloniality (1993, 16–17).

Chicano studies has indeed often situated Chicano history within the context of Anglo-European global conquest; however, those acts of location have been marked by contestation, qualification, and self-critique.

Going back, as it were, to the future, we find one of the principle authors of the Chicano international thesis negotiating confluence with contradiction. In the

1970s historian Mario Barrera admitted that "the term 'colonialism' is applied to a very heterogeneous collection of situations, so that it is difficult to see what, if anything, they have in common" (1979, 190). Elsewhere Barrera has stated, "I think there is truly no colonial model as such" (Muñoz 1989, 153). After considering related historical phenomena such as colonialism and neocolonialism, he proposes "internal colonialism" as the term most appropriate for describing "a form of colonialism in which the dominant and subordinate populations are intermingled, so that there is no geographically distinct 'metropolis' separate from the 'colony'" (Barrera 1979, 194). Other Chicano historians and cultural critics have since argued on behalf of the descriptive and/or rhetorical advantages of "postcolonialism" over "internal colonialism."[2] The intricacies of those exchanges merit further consideration in some other forum; however, sticking to matters at hand, we (as aspiring postnationalist critics of U.S. culture) should give some thought as to why, in Chicano studies, there has been an alignment but not necessarily a containment of the study of U.S. minorities within a geopolitical history of Anglo-European colonization of the Third World.

I would argue that alignment rather than identification has seemed desirable only in part because of Chicano studies' recognition of the regionally heterogeneous nature of Anglo-European global empire. Less obviously, the contestation, qualification, and self-critique accompanying the Chicano international thesis represent a response to power differentials distinguishing the institutionalized knowledges produced by the history of Anglo-European conquest—differentials embodied in the knowledges we now practice.

Let me put this less abstractly. In the recent past, scholars doing postcolonial work under the auspices of Latin American studies have demonstrated no more interest in Chicano culture and history than those working in what is called "American (literary) studies." Latin Americanists' commitment to postcolonial investigations did not produce the field of Chicano studies; that field required the establishment of a separate and "self-enclosed" (to borrow Kaplan's phrase) discipline to bring itself into being. Even now, as Chicano studies gains recognition and prestige in American studies and American literature programs, Latin American studies programs rarely house scholars working on Chicano studies.

Any number of phenomena characteristic of contemporary higher education reenact power differentials attendant upon the regionally specific nature of Anglo-European interaction with geographically disparate peoples of color. Examples include: the disinterest of Latin Americanists in Chicano history and culture; the greater visibility (at least until recently) of postcolonial scholarship in U.S. universities; and the practice on certain campuses of representing faculty of color raised and educated outside the United States as affirmative action hires. This institutional history does not merely represent a failure on the part of postcolonial Latin American studies to recognize that the border cuts both ways.[3] Rather, it revisits the heterogeneous history of colonialism and renders it politically meaningful in the present. Just as the British and French practice of indirect rule maintained an elite native class, Spanish deployment of mestizo descendants of colonizers to govern New World territories created a class of colonial subjects for which U.S. history offers no exact equivalent.[4] The absence in the United States of an elaborate colonial administrative structure, geographically remote from the metropolis and requiring the education and professional certification of people of color for its maintenance, helps account for the evident power differentials between U.S. minorities and postcolonial populations that we now experience in the institutionalization of knowledge.

There is, of course, the additional question of power differentials between U.S. minorities and Third World people of color created by the rise of independent nation-states in former colonial territories. To take the example of the comparative histories of Chicanos and the former Spanish-American colonies, what the term postcolonial signals in the case of Latin America is some form (however complex) of political self-determination. Post-colonial would seem to imply that the fight is over and that the oppressed won.[5] Although no one in an age of international capitalism simply wins or loses in a project as complex as national liberation, it seems fair to say that U.S. ethnics do not have the power over institutions that the revolt in the colonies conferred upon Third World people of color. From this perspective, calling U.S. ethnic populations postcolonial seems, at best, premature.

But, the more that I think about it, the less I like the way the word premature inserts itself so insistently in my meditations on the relationship between U.S. ethnics and postcolonial paradigms. The word suggests the existence of a normative model in which all people of color move from a colonial to a postcolonial status. I wonder if the desire to see U.S. ethnics as postcolonials is not in fact a sign of some teleological imperative at work or is not an effort to construct a historical narrative into which the development of U.S. ethnic politics fits more neatly into the presumed global (read "universal") pattern.

The pattern, as postnationalist critics insist, is not universal but rather the historically and culturally specific phenomenon of nationalism. If postcolonial studies validates nationalism by assuming a narrative in which former colonies become modern nation-states, then how is postcolonial studies in a position to interrogate the idea of a nation? What force does it have to counteract nationalism's proven power to preempt all other forms of political collectivity (including those forms of solidarity based on gender, race, and/or class)?[6]

To bring this chapter back to where I started, I'd like to return to Kaplan's trenchant observations about the vulnerability of multiculturalism to nationalist cooptation. It seems to me that even an analysis that coordinates the ethnic and the international invites recuperations against which a postnationalist criticism would have to guard. The dominant culture dismisses minority studies as provincial, as the creation of "special interests," as an affront to the traditional intellectual's quest for universals. If there is a danger of multiculturalism's being recuperated in the interest of maintaining the concept and practices of nationalism, then there is also a danger of confirming the dominant view of minority studies by setting up postcolonialism as the "global" knowledge sanctioning the otherwise too "narrow" study of U.S. minorities.

NOTES

1. I refer, of course, to California's Proposition 187, approved by voters in November 1994 and to the more recent Proposition 209, which, if passed, would end affirmative action programs for both white women and targeted minorities at all public institutions in the state.

2. For a brief account of these debates, see Muñoz (1989, 146–149, 153–154).

3. Cf. Spillers (1991, 16).

4. Certainly, there has been complicity between official U.S. governmental institutions and the elite classes of people of color; the example of nineteenth-century land-owning Mexican-Americans in New Mexico and South Texas comes to mind. There are also compelling analogies to the colonial administrative system in, for example, the division of slave labor on the antebellum Southern plantation (domestics versus field hands). Obviously, I do not mean to suggest that there has been no class hierarchy among people of color in the United States, just that its development is distinguishable from that created and/or maintained by Anglo-European colonial governments.

5. Supporters of Proposition 209 in their public diatribes against affirmative action routinely claim that oppression of minorities in the United States no longer exists.

6. On this subject, see Radhakrishnan (1992) and Chapter 3 of Enloe (1989).

BIBLIOGRAPHY

Barrera, Mario. *Race and Class in the Southwest: A Theory of Racial Inequality.* Notre Dame: University of Notre Dame Press, 1979.

Enloe, Cynthia. *Bananas, Beaches and Bases: Making Feminist Sense of International Politics.* Berkeley and Los Angeles: University of California Press, 1989.

Kaplan, Amy. "'Left Alone with America': The Absence of Empire in the Study of American Culture." *Cultures of United States Imperialism.* Ed. Amy Kaplan and Donald E. Pease. Durham: Duke University Press, 1993:3–21.

Muñoz, Carlos Jr. *Youth, Identity, Power: The Chicano Movement.* New York: Verso, 1989.

Radhakrishnan, R. "Nationalism, Gender, and the Narrative of Identity." *Nationalisms and Sexualities.* Eds. Andrew Parker, Mary Russo, Doris Sommer, and Patricia Yaeger. New York: Routledge, 1992:77–95.

Spillers, Hortense J. "Introduction: Who Cuts the Border? Some Readings on 'America.'" *Comparative American Identities: Race, Sex, and Nationality in the Modern Text.* Ed. Hortense J. Spillers. New York: Routledge, 1991:1–25.

About the Book

This book explores how discourses of the local, the particular, the everyday, and the situated are being transformed by new discourses of globalization and transnationalism, as used both by government and business and in critical academic discourse. Unlike other studies that have focused on the politics and economics of globalization, *Articulating the Global and the Local* highlights the importance of culture and provides models for a cultural studies that addresses globalization and the dialectic of local and global forces.

Arguing for the inseparability of global and local analysis, the book demonstrates how global forces enter into local situations and how in turn global relations are articulated through local events, identities, and cultures; it includes studies of a wide range of cultural forms including sports, poetry, pedagogy, ecology, dance, cities, and democracy. *Articulating the Global and the Local* makes the ambitious claim that the category of the local transforms the debate about globalization by redefining what counts as global culture. Central to the essays are the new global and translocal cultures and identities created by the diasporic processes of colonialism and decolonization. The essays explore a variety of local, national, and transnational contexts with particular attention to race, ethnicity, gender, and sexuality as categories that force us to rethink globalization itself.

About the Editors and Contributors

David L. Andrews is assistant professor in the Department of Human Movement Sciences and Education at the University of Memphis. He has researched and published on a variety of topics related to the critical analysis of sport as an aspect of contemporary popular culture. His most recent published articles have appeared in the *Sociology of Sport Journal*, the *Australasian Journal of American Studies*, and *Cultural Studies: A Research Annual*. He is currently writing a book that critically deconstructs Michael Jordan's position and influence within contemporary American culture.

Roland Axtmann teaches political theory in the Department of Politics and International Relations at the University of Aberdeen, Scotland. He has published widely on state formation in Europe and on globalization, and has recently published a book on *Liberal Democracy into the Twenty-first Century: Globalization, Integration and the Nation-state* with Manchester University Press. He is currently completing a book on *The Civilizing Process in Austria and England, 1700–1900* (co-authored with Helmut Kuzmics).

Megan Boler holds a Ph.D. from the History of Consciousness Program at the University of California, Santa Cruz, and teaches feminist theory, media, and cultural studies as Assistant Professor of Education at the University of Auckland, New Zealand. Her work has been published in *Hypatia: Journal of Women and Philosophy* and is forthcoming in the journals *Cultural Studies* and *Educational Theory* and in the edited collection *Naming the Multiple: Poststructuralism and Education*, edited by M. Peters, Bergin, and Garvey.

Zofia Burr is assistant professor of English at George Mason University. She is the editor of *Set in Motion: Essays, Interviews, and Dialogues* by A. R. Ammons (University of Michigan Press). She is currently at work on a book titled *Poetry and Its Audiences: Address and Difference in the Works of Emily Dickinson, Josephine Miles, Gwendolyn Brooks, Audre Lorde, and Maya Angelou*.

Mia Carter is assistant professor of English at the University of Texas at Austin. She is the coeditor (with Barbara Harlow) of the forthcoming *The Imperial Archive: A Reader in Orientalism and Imperialism* (Oxford: Basil Blackwell).

Ann Cvetkovich is associate professor of English at the University of Texas at Austin. She is the author of *Mixed Feelings: Feminism, Mass Culture, and Victorian Sensationalism* and has published articles in *Film Theory Goes to the Movies* (Routledge), *Lesbian Erotics* (NYU Press), and the journals *Afterimage* and *GLQ: Journal of Lesbian and Gay Studies*.

Eric Higgs is associate professor in the Departments of Anthropology and Sociology at the University of Alberta. Author of numerous articles on ecological restoration, he is the secretary of the Society for Ecological Restoration and is currently writing a book on restoration titled *Nature by Design*.

Douglas Kellner is professor of Philosophy at the University of Texas at Austin and is author of many books on social theory, politics, history, and culture, including *Camera Politica: The Politics and Ideology of Contemporary Hollywood Film* (with Michael Ryan); *Critical Theory, Marxism, and Modernity; Jean Baudrillard: From Marxism to Postmodernism and Beyond; Postmodern Theory: Critical Interrogations* (with Steven Best); *Television and the Crisis of Democracy; The Persian Gulf TV War; Media Culture;* and *The Postmodern Adventure* (with Steven Best). He is currently working on the impact of new information and entertainment technologies on society and culture.

Amitava Kumar teaches cultural studies in the English Department at the University of Florida. He is a columnist for *Liberation* and a member of the photo co-op Impact Visuals. He has published work in a variety of publications, including *Rethinking Marxism, Modern Fiction Studies, Critical Quarterly,* and *minnesota review.*

Andrew Light is assistant professor in the Department of Philosophy at the University of Montana. He has published over a dozen articles in environmental philosophy, philosophy of technology, and political philosophy, in addition to coediting with Eric Katz *Environmental Pragmatism.* He is editor of the forthcoming volumes *The Environmental Materialism Reader* and *Anarchism, Nature, and Society: Critical Essays on Social Ecology.* He is coeditor of the journal *Philosophy and Geography* and cofounder of the Society for Philosophy and Geography. During the writing of this paper he was a postdoctoral fellow in the Environmental Health Program at the University of Alberta.

Lora Romero is assistant professor of English at Stanford University. She has published articles in *American Literature, American Literary History, Yale Journal of Criticism,* and *American Quarterly.*

Michael Peter Smith is professor of Community Studies and Development at the University of California, Davis. A cross-disciplinary urban scholar, Smith is the author of several influential books in urban studies, including *The City and Social Theory; City, State and Market; The Capitalist City: Global Restructuring and Community Politics;* and *The Bubbling Cauldron: Race, Ethnicity and the Urban Crisis.* His recent writings on transnationalism and identity formation have appeared in such journals as *Theory and Society* and *Social Text.*

Charles J. Stivale is professor of French in the Department of Romance Languages and Literatures, Wayne State University. His main research focuses on nineteenth- and twentieth-century French and francophone cultural studies. He has written books on the writers Maupassant, Stendhal, and Vallès; has guest-edited special journal issues of *SubStance* about Gilles Deleuze and Félix Guattari; and is currently writing a study of their collaborative "two-fold thought."

Index

Printed in the United Kingdom by
Lightning Source UK Ltd., Milton Keynes
139731UK00001B/92/A

9 780813 332208